Quiet Diplomacy
Memoirs of an Ambassador of Pakistan

Quiet Diplomacy

Memoirs of an Ambassador of Pakistan

JAMSHEED MARKER

Foreword by
Stanley Wolpert

OXFORD
UNIVERSITY PRESS

OXFORD
UNIVERSITY PRESS

Oxford University Press is a department of the University of Oxford.
It furthers the University's objective of excellence in research, scholarship,
and education by publishing worldwide in

Oxford New York

Auckland Cape Town Dar es Salaam Hong Kong Karachi
Kuala Lumpur Madrid Melbourne Mexico City Nairobi
New Delhi Shanghai Taipei Toronto

With offices in

Argentina Austria Brazil Chile Czech Republic France Greece
Guatemala Hungary Italy Japan Poland Portugal Singapore
South Korea Switzerland Turkey Ukraine Vietnam

Oxford is a registered trademark of Oxford University Press
in the UK and in certain other countries

Published in Pakistan by Oxford University Press

© Oxford University Press 2010

The moral rights of the author have been asserted

Database right Oxford University Press (maker)

First published 2010

This edition in Oxford Pakistan Paperbacks 2012

ISBN 978-0-19-906617-9

Typeset in Minion Pro
Printed in Pakistan by
Kagzi Printers, Karachi.
Published by
Ameena Saiyid, Oxford University Press
No. 38, Sector 15, Korangi Industrial Area, PO Box 8214,
Karachi-74900, Pakistan.

For

DIANA and FEROZA

In Memoriam

and

ARNAZ and NILOUFER

Gentle ladies all,

In eternal love and gratitude.

And Sam, now one of us.

CONTENTS

Part V: German Democratic Republic and Iceland

Part VI: Japan

Part VII: United Nations European Office, Geneva

Part VIII: Federal Republic of Germany, France, and Ireland

Part IX: The United States of America and Jamaica

Part X: The United Nations, New York

FOREWORD

❦

Quiet Diplomacy is a fascinating historic-memoir of the diplomatic life and times of one of Pakistan's wisest diplomats, whose career as its most brilliant Ambassador started in 1964, ending with the Security Council of the United Nations in 1994. Jamsheed Marker's memoir is enriched with felicitously reported details of every country in which he served, from Africa's Ghana to Romania and Bulgaria, Moscow and Finland, Canada, Germany, Ireland, Japan, France, and the United States of America. Following each report of his new diplomatic post, Marker adds a useful summary, which he calls 'Meanwhile in Pakistan', focusing on important changes back 'home' during his interlude overseas. Scholar-Diplomat that he is, Marker is always discreet in his criticism of his nation's leadership, but clearly recognizes the ineptitude and weakness of at least several of the military usurpers as well as elected civil heads of Pakistan during his tenure in its service. He also forthrightly notices its failure to establish vital educational, political, and judicial institutions early enough, to hold that nation together for more than its first-quarter century. This book should be read by everyone interested in a better understanding of Pakistan's History as well as global diplomacy.

Stanley Wolpert

ACKNOWLEDGEMENTS

To Arnaz, my wife, and Niloufer, my daughter, my love and sincerest thanks for their understanding and encouragement as I worked on this book. Their participation in most of the events described not only made this a joint adventure on which we had embarked with enthusiasm, but also helped to ensure veracity in its recall. To my brother Minoo, my thanks for reading the manuscript, suggesting corrections, and recalling facts that I had overlooked. He has always been by my side.

A special thanks to Stanley Wolpert, guide, counsel and friend, not only for the generous comments in his Foreword to the book, but for the valuable intellectual input that I have obtained from him, both through his books and in our conversations.

Finally, and most important of all, my profound gratitude to Ameena Saiyid and her able collaborators, Ghousia Gofran Ali, Rehana Khandwalla at Oxford University Press, Karachi. Their skill, competence and efficiency are of the highest professional standards. When I first encountered it, in the mid-1950s, this institution functioned out of two rooms and a cubicle on South Napier Road, and I used to drink innumerable cups of sweet tea with its Director, David Gregory, as we discussed the new books that had just emerged from the parcels on the floor. At that time OUP was little more than an outlet for books, and a very far cry from what it now is, a modern, dynamic publishing enterprise, which is the creation of Ameena Saiyid. It has brought a plethora of books on to the market, both in Pakistan and abroad, on every subject and topic that is worthwhile and of interest. And equally important, Ameena has discovered, gathered and encouraged a wide and eclectic collection of Pakistani authors. The British government, in distant London, has recognized, by one of its highest awards, Ameena's contribution to the spread of knowledge. It does not matter that a similar thought has escaped a succession of our governments situated much closer in

Islamabad. The wide variety of books published by Oxford University Press that line shelves all over Pakistan is tribute enough.

Karachi, Pakistan.   Jamsheed Marker
February 2009/July 2009.   St. Petersburg, Florida

CHAPTER ONE

Brave New World

'O brave new world
That has such people in't.'
– Shakespeare, The Tempest.

It all began in the late autumn of 1964. A telephone message, tucked in with a number of others, awaited my arrival in the office after my morning round of the wharves of Keamari Harbour in Karachi. The message read 'The Foreign Secretary called: please call back'. Presuming that it was about an invitation to a diplomatic reception, which I usually tried to avoid, I refrained from an immediate response. The next day the message reappeared, this time a trifle peremptory, 'The Foreign Secretary called again: matter important: please call back immediately'. I duly responded, and was asked to meet the Foreign Secretary, Aziz Ahmed, in his office the next morning. Aziz was a legendary figure in the Pakistan administration, and belonged to a family with a long, meritorious, and distinguished record of public service. Although we pursued very different occupations, I was privileged to enjoy a close and warm friendship with him, and with his equally distinguished brother, G. Ahmed, a friendship that went back many years, and included our wives and families as well, and which continues to this day.

In his customary fashion, Aziz went straight to the point, 'How would you like a diplomatic assignment?' He went on to say that the Pakistan government intended to expand its diplomatic representation abroad, and was looking for ex-cadre people to fill some of these appointments. Aziz named three countries in his offer, and asked if I would like to think it over. My immediate reply was that it would be a great honour to serve Pakistan in any capacity. I thought to myself that two of the posts suggested were very agreeable capitals, but seemed to me to be basically cocktail circuits with very little in terms of challenge, and I did not see any point in leaving a reasonably prosperous business and a pleasant social life in Karachi for a comfortable but a mundane embassy abroad. I told Aziz that I was prepared to go where he thought I would be most useful, but that my personal preference would be Ghana, which was the third post that he had included on his list, albeit he had offered it with a wry, cautionary grimace.

My interest was aroused by the fact that these were the early days of independence in Africa, and it could be exciting to witness events at first hand. Also, Kwame Nkrumah had emerged not only as an African leader, but was also one of the pillars of the Non-Aligned Movement, and it would be a fascinating experience to get to know and work with him. An added incentive was that Guinea and Mali were included for concurrent accreditation in the assignment, thus providing me with the opportunity to observe and to move about West Africa in the early, heady days of the transition of the continent from a colony to an independent nationhood. Additionally it would help me to experience and sense at first hand, what Harold Macmillan had at that time so vividly and famously described as 'the winds of change'. Von Bülow once defined diplomacy as 'a first class stall seat at the theatre of life', and now it seemed that I might be privileged to find one.

On leaving the Foreign Office I went immediately to the Metropole Hotel and extracted my lovely wife, Diana, from the steam and flurry of the hairdressing salon. 'He never leaves office at this time!' was her astonished comment, when informed of my presence. I told her that Aziz Ahmed had just offered me a diplomatic assignment. Her first reaction, pragmatic but a little disconcerting, was 'Why you?' But this was immediately followed by an equally characteristic and profoundly heart-warming assurance, 'If that's what you want then OK.' Diana was much too intelligent to be unaware of the full implications of our choice, however precipitate and decisive it might appear.

For me, the sacrifice in personal earnings and comforts could be compensated for by the honour and the stimulation of the new profession. For her, the immediate consequences would mean a farewell to a loving family and to deep friendships cultivated over a lifetime, and to a home and a lifestyle that had just begun to be agreeable after a series of earlier vicissitudes. It meant exchanging a known, secure, and a comfortable life for an existence that, albeit one of honour and interest, carried with it the certainty of emotional and environmental dislocation, along with the multiplicity of other inconveniences which were sure to come our way. Above all, for Diana, this meant a departure from her beloved Karachi and Pakistan, not for a short holiday abroad, but for a long and undetermined period of time. And yet this wonderful lady, clad in curlers and a hairdresser's plastic cape but still looking as lovely as ever, instantly made one of life's momentous decisions, and told me to go ahead—'I'll go anywhere in the world with you'. Diana subsequently took to her role as an ambassadress to the manner born, bringing to bear all her formidable attributes of intelligence, charm, vivacity, elegance, and a sparkling fresh honesty. Her fierce patriotism was energized into a tireless and ceaseless effort to promote the interests of Pakistan, and she evoked admiration and affection wherever she went and from everyone she met. Her stunning beauty comprised an innate dignity which, coupled with an intensely humane attitude, manifested itself in its sympathy and support for the less fortunate, regardless of race, creed, colour or nationality, and on whom she lavished material and spiritual care without reservation. In turn, they responded with deep affection and admiration, sentiments which were particularly prevalent amongst the staff members and families of the various missions in which we served.

For me, Diana's presence and influence were complete and comprehensive, and I could not imagine working without her by my side. Highly intelligent and articulate, she had an infallible ability to size up personalities and analyse events, and our constant private exchanges and discussions over our professional activities were a joyful and productive, not to mention an essential element, in my daily diplomatic life. Moreover, Diana was constantly taking her own initiatives on the diplomatic front. Her activity was never confined solely to the embassy salon or its dining room, and she always remained an intelligent and charming interlocutor. Her health had never been very robust, but whether functioning in the fetid heat and humidity of West Africa, or the frigid, snowbound and numbing winters of Russia, she maintained the same energetic pace of commitment, initiative and activities. And she carried on in this determined fashion even as she fought her own heroic battle against the cancer that tragically prevailed and finally took her life.

That day, having spoken to Diana, I crossed the road from the Metropole Hotel and entered the office of the commissioner, Karachi. The incumbent at that time was Roedad Khan, who was and still is, my closest friend. We have spent a lifetime sharing each other's joys and successes, as well as our personal tribulations and tragedies. Seeing me out of my office during working hours surprised him as much as it had done Diana, but he was thrilled at the news of Aziz Ahmed's suggestion and my response to it. 'What would you do in Karachi? Every day you will go from Bath Island to Keamari and every day you will return from Keamari to Bath Island. Is that what you want to do for the rest of your life?' This blunt assessment was typical of Roedad, and although I thought his forecast was somewhat stark, he did seem to have a point—there was more to my life than Keamari.

But all this was in the future. In the fall of 1964, we only knew that we had taken an important decision, and now awaited the turn of events. The bureaucratic procedures initiated shortly after my meeting with Aziz Ahmed were kept on hold, to be resumed in early 1965 after President Ayub Khan's re-election. I was then summoned to Rawalpindi for a short but pleasant interview with the President, who graciously informed me that he had approved my appointment as the High Commissioner to Ghana. This was my first meeting with Ayub Khan, and it evoked a respect and admiration for him that has always remained with me. In early 1965 Ayub was at the zenith of his power, with an impressive and recognized record of domestic political stability and outstanding economic development. His international standing was also of the highest repute. 'The De Gaulle of Asia' was one frequently expressed appellation. He was regarded as a modern, moderate, and progressive leader of a great Islamic state, and one whose influence extended throughout the world's councils. A widely circulated, contemporary press photograph, showing Ayub Khan, Chou En-lai, Sukarno, and Gamal Abdel Nasser standing together at the Cairo airport provided dramatic credence to this perception.

I had anticipated that my tête-à-tête with such a daunting personality might be a little intimidating, but I could not have been more mistaken. In the quiet of his neat, simple and impeccable office, devoid of all ostentation, Ayub rose from his chair as soon as his ADC announced my presence and walked over to greet me with a warm handshake. His eyes were sharp, but large and kindly, and appeared to smile at me throughout our conversation, which he deftly turned from an interview into a discussion almost as soon as we began. We talked about Pakistan and its role in international affairs, and Ayub told me of his desire to have the country recognized in the world as a moderate Muslim state—peaceful, progressive, and developing on sound economic lines, and a country that was ready to play a positive role in international affairs. He said that he would be happy to have me serve as one of Pakistan's ambassadors, adding, 'I am sure you will do a good job'. He concluded the interview with a chuckle, saying that he hoped I would not hold it against him if he preferred shooting and golf to cricket. I left the president's office with an agreeable sense of confidence and optimism.

Years later, when I was in Moscow, I had occasion to recollect this warm, friendly and civilized meeting with Ayub. My colleague, the Norwegian ambassador, told me about an incident that occurred in 1958 when he was posted to Tehran, with concurrent accreditation to Karachi and New Delhi. He had been involved in the preparations for a visit to Pakistan and India by the Norwegian minister responsible for foreign economic relations, and was suddenly faced with an awkward situation resulting from the unexpected declaration of martial law in Pakistan. This infuriated the Norwegian minister, a dedicated socialist, who wished to register his protest by cancelling his visit to Pakistan as a gesture of protest. It took all of the ambassador's powers of persuasion to convince the minister that he should keep to the original schedule, and the Norwegians duly found themselves in Karachi, where Ayub immediately received them. The meeting took place in 'a modest conference room with flapping cotton curtains and noisy air conditioners'. Ayub was in uniform, with his shirt sleeves rolled up, and with three or four advisers seated beside him at the conference table. The discussions were focused and fruitful, conducted in a friendly manner with full participation of all those present, and with Ayub never hesitant to seek and receive advice from his aides. The minister left Karachi in a pleasantly surprised mood, with most of his prejudices overcome.

In New Delhi the Norwegians were kept waiting two days before they could meet the Prime Minister. Nehru received them in 'a splendid office, with raw silk curtains and silent air conditioners, and was seated all by himself at a large, polished conference table', with about eight or ten of his aides seated behind him at a respectful distance. The meeting lasted for about an hour, about fifty minutes of which were spent by Nehru expounding on the evils of NATO and Norway's membership thereof. As they emerged from the prime minister's office into the imposing carpeted corridors, replete with guards and messengers, the bemused minister asked the ambassador, 'Can you tell me which one of these is the democracy and which the dictatorship?' The question has never really lost its relevance.

The martial law imposed by Ayub in 1958 was a turning point in Pakistan's history by setting the country on an unfortunate course that has repeatedly and stubbornly rejected attempts at correction. On the other hand, the admirable democratic traditions that have characterized the political life of independent India failed to find their way into Kashmir, which, from the start, has lived under terror and oppression. Its grim origin might perhaps be traced, to some extent, to Nehru's temperament and his emotional compulsion on the issue. The South Asian conundrum, which puzzled the Norwegian diplomats back in 1958, persists in much the same form today.

To return to my personal narrative, the formalities of my appointment came through in due course, and I was asked to report to the Foreign Ministry for a briefing that lasted about six weeks. At that time the Foreign Ministry was an organization that was truly lean, slim, and efficient. As I recall it, there was the Foreign Minister (Zulfikar Ali Bhutto), the Foreign Secretary (Aziz Ahmed), the Additional Foreign Secretary (Agha Shahi), three political Directors General (Salman Ali, Mumtaz Alvi, and Kamaluddin Ahmed), a Director General Administration (Aslam Malik), a Chief of Protocol (R.S. Chathari), and a Director General Research. The cabinets of the Foreign Minister and the Foreign Secretary were headed by directors, as were the respective desks in the political departments. I was given a heap of files to study, and since these were replenished with fearsome regularity, I was able to obtain a wide view of the sort of work that was being done in the ministry, and of the major foreign policy issues that confronted us. I noticed, with some astonishment, the extent of the Indian factor and its pervasive influence on the bureaucratic mind. Much more important and valuable were the briefings I received from the various directors. They were indeed a star-studded group. Accurate in their facts and perceptive in their analyses, each balanced presentation testified to the professional competence of this superb, enthusiastic cadre of foreign service officers. In retrospect, this is not surprising when one recalls the names of these outstanding officers who were designated as my interlocutors, but in effect were my instructors: they included, among others, Iqbal Akhund, the brothers Humayun Rashid Chowdhry and Kaiser Rashid, Najmul Saquib Khan, Aftab Ahmed Khan, Akram Zaki, Mehdi Masud, and Jamiluddin Hasan. They were an impressive team, and led me to establish an intellectual, emotional, and collegial bond with these officers of Pakistan's Foreign Service, which sustained me throughout my service, and remains as one of my proudest and most cherished personal souvenirs. Unfortunately, subsequent events have left less agreeable memories. These stem from a later period and were provoked by the depredations heaped in later years upon this one time pristine and perfectly splendid cadre of civil servants, through a series of singularly disruptive actions, including arbitrary recruitments and dismissals, perpetrated by a succession of thoughtless governments.

Before leaving for Ghana I had substantive meetings with Aziz Ahmed and Agha Shahi, both of whom had been good personal friends prior to my induction into the Foreign Ministry, and from whom I received valuable advice, counsel, and encouragement. My final call was on Z.A. Bhutto, who said he looked forward to my contribution to the work of the Foreign Ministry. I had known Bhutto in earlier times when, as 'Zulfi', he was part of our Coffee House group, meeting for noisy and rambunctious lunches during the week. His friendship with Omar Kureishi, and his love of cricket, were further links in our association, and I was quite aware of both his intellectual brilliance and his mercurial temperament. But when I joined the diplomatic service, by mutual instinct we both eschewed the previous familiarity and adopted the correct protocol of the relationship between a foreign minister and an ambassador.

I drew three broad conclusions from my brief exposure to the Foreign Ministry in Karachi in early 1965. The first was that, as mentioned earlier, it was staffed by highly competent professionals, dedicated to their craft and thoroughly enthusiastic about their duties. The second impression was that, with his assumption of office as the Foreign Minister, Zulfikar Ali Bhutto had electrified the ministry and placed his unmistakable stamp on all aspects of its workings, from broad policy issues to minute details of protocol. My third observation was that the policy orientation of the Foreign Ministry was more than a few points to the left of the centre, and that it was being pushed further in that direction by Bhutto, despite Ayub's reluctance and disinclination, and notwithstanding the undisguised suspicion of the Americans. Some months later there was a major course correction, but it took Bhutto's removal to bring this about.

I paid a courtesy call on the high commissioner of Ghana to Pakistan, who kindly hosted a dinner in my and Diana's honour. Abraham Benjamin Bah Kofi was a thorough professional, and gave me a complete and very useful briefing on the situation in Ghana, also providing me with introductions to his many friends in Accra. Abe Kofi was one of Ghana's senior diplomats, having served as ambassador in Washington and then as secretary in the Foreign Ministry in Accra. This next posting to Karachi was clearly a demotion; the result of circumstances which were essentially of the personal, palace intrigue kind. It was an early indication of the whimsical and capricious administration of Kwame Nkrumah, and one with which I was to become familiar in the months to come.

There was a final flurry of activity as I put down my business responsibilities and took up my official duties. This included, among other things, dining out in style with a host of kind friends, as well as with some of the organizations with which I had been associated including the Chamber of Commerce, Trades Unions, and the Cricket Writers Club. Diana and I were deeply touched by these gestures of affectionate hospitality, and attended them with the belief that we would be back among these friends in three years. Had we known that our departure would imply a complete change of profession and lifestyle, and not just an interregnum, our sense of poignancy would have been considerably heightened. During these moments of nostalgia, concern, and anticipation we were sustained by my cousin Eddie Dinshaw, a close and dear friend, mentor and guide, and the most generous and capable of business associates. His consideration and the knowledge that he would guide my competent staff in the future was more reassuring than anyone could have wished. Our close friendship and association continued throughout the years, undiminished by the divisions of time and space, until his tragic death, followed by that of his lovely wife Mehroo. This loss has left a void in my life which will remain forever. Eddie's sister, Khorshed, was married to Jumbo Kharas, who at the time of my induction into the Foreign Ministry was serving as Pakistan's ambassador to Spain. Jumbo had originally been an officer in the Indian Civil Service and was now a senior member of the Pakistan Foreign Service, with a record that was as impressive as it was impeccable. Upon hearing of my appointment he laced his message of congratulations with wise counsel and advice which was of inestimable value. This warm and affectionate association prevailed throughout our concurrent careers in the Foreign Service and continues to this day. The tragic death of his adorable wife Khorshed, who was his constant companion and provided the inspiration and support that made his career so distinguished, was a devastating blow and brought the deepest sorrow to all of us.

The affection and support of Diana's parents and mine, and that of my brothers Khursheed and Minoo, manifested itself in a deep but unspoken fashion during that emotional period of parting, and provided us with a support and comfort that never left us. There was one brief, nostalgic appearance in the commentary box at the National Stadium during a test match in Karachi, and then I along with Diana and our daughters Niloufer and Feroza, boarded a plane for Geneva, where we left Niloufer to attend her boarding school, whilst Diana, Feroza and I, flew on to Accra.

It may be appropriate, at this stage, to outline the track that destiny charted for the diplomatic career that forms the content of this book. I stumbled into diplomacy in the year 1965. Prior to that, following graduation from college, I had served as an officer in the Royal Indian Navy Volunteer Reserve (RINVR) in the Second World War, on convoy escort duties, minesweeping and combined operations. On leaving the navy I went into a reasonably prosperous family business until the Government of Pakistan unexpectedly sought me out, as already indicated, and proposed a diplomatic assignment. Pakistan possessed an excellent cadre of Foreign Service officers, but there were too few people, particularly in the senior grades, to cope with the increased requirements of the new missions which we were obliged to establish in the newly independent countries. The government, therefore, appointed ambassadors from other departments, and from the political and private sectors. I came under the latter category and, therefore, started my diplomatic career as an ambassador, a convenience that obviated the necessity of hacking my way to the top, as is the fate of most diplomats elsewhere. Also, I fully expected at the time when I accepted my first assignment that I would return to private life once the three-year assignment was over. The assumption proved to be erroneous—by about twenty-seven years. Naturally, I submitted my resignation whenever there was a change of government in Pakistan, but on each occasion I was asked to stay on. My contract contained a clause to the effect that the president and I could each terminate the contract at will, 'without assigning any reason whatsoever'. But I was never unmindful of the fact that he was in a rather better position to exercise this option than me.

CHIAROSCURO

THE VAGARIES OF BUREAUCRACY

Radio Pakistan had asked me to do one final commentary at a forthcoming cricket test match, an activity, which, as a private citizen, I had carried out joyfully and with enthusiasm, over several years, without seeking anybody's permission to do so. But now, as a government official, it seemed that I would need to apply, on the official form and seek permission from 'the competent authority' before I could do the broadcast. Most of the items on the questionnaire, such as artiste's name, father's name, etc., were easy to answer, but I got stumped on the one essential requirement calling for a copy of the script which, after approval 'shall not be altered at the time of broadcast'. Fortunately the 'competent authority' did not appear to be over-concerned with my inability to comply with this provision, and I found my way into the commentary box without suffering any dire consequences then or later.

PART I

AFRICA

'Ex Africa semper aliquid novi.'
('Out of Africa always something new.')
Pliny the Elder

CHAPTER TWO

Ghana

First arrivals at new places are always exciting, and this was no exception. Akbar Tyabjee, our chargé d'affaires, greeted us at the gangway as we descended from the aircraft at Accra airport and whisked us off by car to the VIP room, where we met Ghanaian officials as well as members of the diplomatic corps. The presence of the latter was a pleasant custom in Accra at that time, and is not one that is followed in most capitals. Since Pakistan and Ghana were both members of the Commonwealth, we adhered to the curious exclusivity of nomenclature by designating our envoys as high commissioners instead of ambassadors. Akbar had been our chargé d'affaires in Ghana over the past two years and was anxious to leave as soon as possible. Since I quite understood his desire, I released him without waiting for his successor. Akbar was an old friend from Karachi who had joined the Foreign Service after a stint in a business firm. Outgoing, friendly, and articulate, Akbar's subsequent career received a number of setbacks, many of them self-induced, and he went into early retirement, sadly followed by a premature death.

As I was the first resident Pakistan High Commissioner in Ghana we had to live in a hotel until suitable accommodation could be obtained. This was not easy; partly because Nkrumah's dynamic international impact had encouraged a great many countries to establish missions in Accra, so that embassy residences were at a premium, and also because of the constraints implicit in matching scarce availability with even more scarce resources. We were, therefore, very fortunate in obtaining a modest residence which had just been built by John Chinebuah, a senior and highly competent Ghana Civil Service officer, who was also the Principal Secretary to the President. He and his lovely wife Laura soon became two of our closest friends in Ghana. John was one of the superb Ghanaian civil servants who were intelligent, upright and dedicated, but of late this admirable cadre had suffered a great deal through the idiosyncrasies of the working methods of Nkrumah and his corrupt ministers. The thoroughly professional manner with which John Chinebuah and his colleagues, such as Vishnu Wasiamul, Austen Amissah and Joe Sackey, carried out their duties was wholly admirable, and diplomats found it a real pleasure working with them. By the time I arrived in Ghana the strains between the politicians and the administrators were already palpable, and these grew to explosive proportions in a very short time.

In early April 1965 I presented my credentials to President Kwame Nkrumah. The chief of protocol escorted me in an ornate old Rolls Royce from my residence to Flagstaff House, where we were met by a guard of honour and the playing of national anthems. Nkrumah welcomed me with a warm smile and a firm handshake. According to normal Ghanaian protocol, the presentation of credentials was to be a ceremonial affair, but in characteristic fashion Nkrumah dispensed with the ceremony in short order and devoted most of his time and attention to discussing substantive issues. As soon as I handed over my papers, and I conveyed the greetings from President Ayub, we got down to business. He wanted to know, as he put it, as much as possible about Pakistan from 'an accredited representative whose presence as a first time resident in Ghana he very much welcomed'. He told me that he had followed with much interest the increasingly important and effective role that Ayub Khan had played in international affairs. He questioned me closely on the developing relations between Pakistan and the People's Republic of China, our opposition to the war in Vietnam, and our increased interest in the affairs of Africa, as evidenced, inter alia, by our newly resident mission in Accra. The tenor of his conversation suggested some disillusionment with his old friend and mentor, Jawaharlal Nehru, coupled with a consideration of a tentative shift in the direction of our policies initiated by Bhutto. Nkrumah then embarked upon a tour d'horizon, with an impressive and often passionate exposition of his policies with regard to Africa. He talked of his fervent support for the Non-Aligned Movement, and in this connection expressed his concern about the deteriorating situation between Pakistan and India—'Operation Gibraltar' and the war that would follow a few months later—and all but put himself forward as a mediator. 'A war over Kashmir would benefit only the capitalists and imperialists. We must find a peaceful solution to the dispute.' Nkrumah's reactions were encouraging, and certainly more positive than the dismissive responses that we generally received when we raised the Kashmir issue with many other nations, but prudence demanded that we retain his interest whilst gently curbing his enthusiasm. Foreign Minister Kojo Botsio was at Nkrumah's side throughout the meeting but contributed nothing beyond vigorous and frequent expressions of assent to everything that Nkrumah said.

My first impression of Nkrumah was that the man was every bit as charismatic as portrayed by his skilful and elaborate propaganda machine. Of medium height, trim and fit, he moved with a lithe, smooth grace. On later occasions I observed him display the same intuitive graceful rhythm on the dance floor that seems to come so naturally to all Africans. His eyes were large, deep set, and lit up with a flash whenever he talked about anything that moved or excited him. Later, as I got to know Nkrumah better, I was able to discern the occasional flutter of duplicity in an expression that constantly exuded a ruthless determination. Whenever he laughed or smiled, which was not very often, his whole face would light up in a most infectious manner. The tone of this first meeting with Nkrumah set the tenor of my personal relationship with a bold and charismatic leader, whom I got to like more than admire as time went on. His policies, an amalgam of dynamic idealism, vainglorious self-promotion and ruthless repression, constituted a vivid enigma whose early impact continues to resonate on the African continent.

Prior to its independence, Ghana, then known as the Gold Coast, was one of the more prosperous of Britain's African colonies. Its main resources were gold and cocoa, but its real resource, as is so often the case, lay in its people, who were extremely intelligent, gentle and hospitable, and remain so to this day. The British exploitation of gold and cocoa was as thorough as it was efficient, and was supplemented by a preponderant, thriving commercial presence within the country through infrastructural institutions such as banks, insurance companies, and trading corporations. These enterprises, I later discovered, were ingeniously structured so as not to make large profits but, instead, only to break-even in the West African markets. A deliberate process of over-invoicing and under-invoicing enabled the surreptitious transfer of funds, which ensured that the major profit element remained vested with the parent corporation in the United Kingdom. This array of commercial institutions, in turn, created a strong and active expatriate community, complete with schools, colleges, hospitals, clubs, and churches. It was the classic colonial scenario, tempered in the case of the Gold Coast by a fortuitous blend of the relative benevolence of the rulers with the casual gentleness of the ruled. At the same time the British made excellent use of Ghana's other major natural resource; using the talent of its people to create a first rate civil and administrative service, a functioning judiciary with a deserved reputation for independence and impartiality, and a competent police force. The Ghanaian army, navy and the air force, though small in size, were disciplined and thoroughly professional, and were probably the most efficient units amongst the independent African nations of that time. Indeed, the Ghanaian army had just completed a successful stint with the United Nations in the Congo, and had made a significant contribution to the peacekeeping efforts there. Despite the political complications that necessitated its recall, it had emerged from the ordeal with its morale high, and its discipline intact. Thus, at the time of the independence for which Nkrumah had so assiduously and vigorously struggled, Ghana was a socially integrated and a reasonably prosperous nation.

These assets were effectively employed by Nkrumah in pursuit of his ambitious political goals. An astute, energetic and a charismatic politician, he quickly established his authority within the country and went on to reinforce it through a series of ruthless measures. Propagating his own brand of socialism, he successively diminished the institutions of parliamentary democracy and replaced them with an increasingly oppressive one-party regime. The economic corollary to this was, of course, to embark upon wholesale nationalization, and to dismantle what had been an easy-going, and reasonably prosperous free market system. The combination of these measures, and the inept and often brutal method of their imposition, built up a public resistance that gradually turned Nkrumah's popularity into the resentment that eventually led to him being ousted.

Nkrumah's impact on foreign policy was as fully dramatic as he intended it to be. His fierce drive for independence went far beyond Ghana, and he saw himself as the leader of a free Africa. One of the most-frequently chanted Ghanaian high life songs, officially sponsored at state receptions of that era, was 'Africa! Africa! Africa must be free! Africa must unite!' Nkrumah went about this in his usual flamboyant manner, organizing a series of international gatherings, which he hosted in a lavish fashion, in a monstrously expensive, newly-constructed conference centre. The edifice, even after its construction and utilization, was never quite able to shake off its bureaucratic nomenclature 'Job 600'; a stigma implicit in the squandering of public funds. A disgusted Ghanaian 'market mammy', a powerful and essential component of the prevailing unofficial market economy, once said to me, 'When we are hungry we will go and look at Job 600, and that will make our bellies full!'

Like so many autocrats, Nkrumah thrived on courtiers, and having filled the ranks with Ghanaians, extended his circle of admirers with a number of foreigners, whom he appointed as advisers or specialists, on lucrative contracts. They comprised an eclectic and colourful adornment to Nkrumah's court. There was Geoffrey Bing, an Irish MP, who later worked in Nkrumah's office as attorney general, together with his wife, a loud, pushy woman, whose strident support for African causes was only too obviously motivated by self-promotion rather than ideology. D.N. Pritt, the eminent left wing counsel, appeared from time to time to dispense inflammatory advice. From the United States came a series of celebrities, including Shirley Graham DuBois (activist and writer), and Stokely Carmichael with his wife; Miriam Makeba from South Africa, who was a regular visitor and performer at state functions; while from the Soviet Union and Eastern Europe, a number of shadowy advisers and specialists in state security, constantly weaved in and out of the country. Among other colourful personalities was Hanna Reich, one of Hitler's personal pilots, who was amongst the last to have seen the Führer in his bunker before she flew out of a besieged Berlin. The large diplomatic presence in Ghana was the corollary of Nkrumah's policy of activist neutrality during one of the more intensive periods of the Cold War, with ambassadors from the NATO and Warsaw Pact countries, the Non-Aligned, Common-wealth, Middle East, and African nations, jostling with each other for influence and information. Cocktail parties were usually lively and entertaining affairs, attended by diplomats from Egypt and Israel, East and West Germany, North Korea and North Vietnam, the US, UK, USSR, China, and Albania.

In the spring of 1965 Ghana was a political magnet of far greater consequence than its entitlement in terms of size, population and resources. This was entirely due to the personality, political skills, and sheer dynamism of Kwame Nkrumah. At the time that I arrived in Accra he was already at the apogee of his political life, recognized as a world leader, and one of the pillars of the booming Non-Aligned Movement. In preparation for my assignment I had read a few of his biographies, as well as his own magnum opus *Consciencism*. The former I found to be irritatingly hagiographic, and the latter vastly opaque. Nevertheless, there was no doubt about the fact that Nkrumah had successfully led the struggle for the independence of Ghana, which became the precursor to the decolonization process in Africa. Within his own country he was universally known and addressed by his self-ordained title of Osagyefo, whilst abroad he was recognized as one of the founding fathers of the Non-Aligned Movement, along with Nasser of Egypt, Nehru of India, Sukarno of Indonesia and Josip Broz Tito of Yugoslavia.

The West Africa that I got to know in 1965, and which cast a spell on me that will last forever, was a region caught in the throes of the consequences of an event, which had transpired on a different continent, in an earlier century. The Berlin Conference of 1884–85 was followed by the aptly named Partition Treaties. The European powers met in Berlin, gathered around a table bearing a map of Africa, and armed with pen and ruler, carved up the continent, distributing amongst themselves different slices of the colonial 'cake'. The causes of the civil wars, coups, and ethnic conflicts, that plague the continent to this day can be attributed to this single act of political chicanery, unmatched in terms of its greed, arrogance, and cynicism. Its political consequences were of course the known and accepted grim political realities of the time I got to Ghana. But there were also a number of other vestiges of colonialism that maintained their insidious presence. For example, direct communication between the countries of West Africa was quite desultory. A lone Dakota aircraft lumbered its way once a week, between Dakar and Lagos, making intermittent stops at the capitals en route. If one wished to travel in a hurry from Accra to Dakar, or even to next door Abidjan, then the quickest way to do it was via London and Paris. The same was true of other forms of communication. Telephone calls between Accra and Abidjan were routed through the former colonial capitals, London and Paris. Civil administration, jurisprudence, military discipline, and formation, all followed the colonial pattern, and so did the language and a great many cultural mores. I noted, with amusement, that when one went from Anglophone West Africa to Francophone West Africa the cuisine improved noticeably, but the plumbing tended to be déficient.

In an attempt to correct the deteriorating political situation between Ghana and the Côte d'Ivoire, the presidents of both countries decided to hold a meeting, but the results were not encouraging. I called on John Chinebuah, the Principal Secretary to Nkrumah, to find out what transpired at the talks, and was surprised to be told that he 'would have to wait until the old man told me what happened'. Nkrumah could not speak French, and Félix Houphouët-Boigny could not speak English, so I presumed that they would both communicate through interpreters, which is what happened during the formal meetings of the two delegations. But during the tête-à-tête Nkrumah and Houphouët-Boigny spoke to each other in Nzima, the dialect of a small tribe that straddled the Ghana–Côte d'Ivoire border (handiwork of the Berlin cartographers), and one which none of the members of either delegation could follow. John was not being dismissal of my enquiry; we were both coping with the consequences of that arbitrary division of borders which had been decided upon a century earlier, in Berlin.

A number of international meetings took place during my stay in Ghana, such as the bombastic Afro–Asian Peoples Solidarity Conference, but the most important was that of the Heads of State and Government of the Organization of African Unity (OAU). The venue originally chosen for this conference was Algiers, but an unknown colonel named Houari Boumédienne, had just overthrown the famous Ahmed Ben Bella in a coup d'état, much to the alarm and dissatisfaction of many African leaders, including Nkrumah, who had strong, personal and friendly ties with the fallen Algerian leader. They were in no mood to endorse the coup, and Boumédienne's legitimacy consequently, by awarding him with the OAU Summit, especially as many of them had not yet recognized the new Algerian regime. Nkrumah seized the opportunity, immediately offered Accra as an alternative venue, and after some vigorous and often acrimonious diplomacy, managed to land the prize.

Looking back on events, I feel that the OAU Summit of 1966 was probably the moment when the Nkrumah meteor burned at its brightest. As an event, however, the summit was more spectacle than substance. The galaxy of leaders who came to Accra included Nasser of Egypt; Idris I, the King of Libya (soon to be overthrown by another Afro-Arab colonel); Habib Bourguiba of Tunisia; Moktar Ould Dada of Mauretania; Ahmed Sékou Touré of Guinea; Modibo Keïta of Mali; William V.S. Tubman of Liberia; Milton Obote of Uganda; Julius Nyerere of Tanzania; Kenneth Kaunda of Zambia; and prime ministers from Morocco, Kenya, and a number of other African countries. Houphouët-Boigny of Côte d'Ivoire and Léopold Senghor of Senegal were notable absentees, whilst Boumédienne from Algeria put in an uncomfortable but surly and defiant presence. Nkrumah orchestrated the conference in its entirety, enjoying himself enormously as he did so, and his energetic leadership placed the unmistakable stamp of his authority on every aspect of the proceedings. The arrival and departure ceremonies at the airport for each of the heads of state possessed all the requisite pomp and circumstance, including honour guards, national anthems, and the line-up of cabinet ministers and resident diplomats, although the latter formation tended to wilt occasionally under the pressures of fatigue, heat, and sheer boredom. Further colour and spectacle was added to the ceremonial by groups of African drummers and dancers in traditional costumes, and a vast and conscripted crowd bellowing out the appropriate slogans under orders from the party hacks. Within the chamber, Nkrumah naturally maintained his dominance, by setting the agenda as well as the tone and tenor of the proceedings. There was the standard rhetoric of condemnation of apartheid, of the policies of the governments of South Africa and Southern Rhodesia, calls for the unity of Africa and for the liberation of countries still under colonial domination. Declarations on the Middle East were somewhat less virulent, despite the strong Arab presence, and were obvious testimony to the effectiveness of Israeli diplomacy in the countries south of the Sahara.

At my suggestion, Pakistan sent an unofficial 'observer' delegation, headed by Information Minister Khwaja Shahabuddin, which included Ambassadors Sami Dehlavi from Bern, and Khurram Khan Panni from Nairobi. We called on various African leaders in order to brief them on Kashmir, and even managed to persuade Nkrumah to include an expression of the desirability of the settlement of the Kashmir dispute in his keynote speech. The Indians, who in response to our initiative, had also sent a similar delegation, were none too pleased, but the Ghanaians, flattered by the attention that they were receiving, tolerated this activity in the corridors of their conference with smug satisfaction. Meanwhile the conference itself concluded with a diplomatic gaffe, which seems farcical in retrospect but had a dramatic impact at the time. The ornate final banquet, replete with drummers, dancers and fanfare, was delayed by two hours because the Israeli ambassador had decided, I suspect, somewhat mischievously, to respond to the grandiose neutrality policy of the Ghanaian government implicit in the invitation which he had received, by attending the ceremonial banquet. 'We sent him the invitation because we had to, but we did not expect him to attend', is what an outraged Ghanaian official told me later. The discovery of the Israeli presence in the banquet hall threw the Arab delegates into a panic, but they were able to get this information to their presidents and prime ministers just in time to stop the dignitaries' triumphal march to the high table. Nasser went into a furious sulk, and this triggered Ghanaian diplomacy into overdrive; trying on the one hand to persuade Nasser to take his seat of honour next to Nkrumah, whilst at the same time trying to persuade the obdurate Israeli ambassador to quietly exit the banquet hall. Two hours later there was a partial success. The Israeli left, but Nasser dined alone in his suite, and the seat of honour next to Nkrumah remained conspicuously vacant.

The OAU Conference in Accra brought to the fore two important elements. The first was the assertion by African nations that the continent had evolved from colonial domination to an independent status, and that they had become, in their own right, serious players on the international scene. At the same time the conference revealed the diversity and the latent animosity that would manifest itself in the tribal, ethnic, and civil wars, that were to devastate certain parts of the continent in the years to come. Apart from the obvious differences between the countries north and south of the Sahara, there was the phenomenon of the surrogate conduct of the Cold War, whose bloody and destructive nature in the Congo, Angola, Mozambique, and Ethiopia–Somalia, was in sharp contrast to the frozen NATO/Warsaw

Pact posture in the northern hemisphere. The struggles of the Cold War had become entwined with the struggles against colonialism, so that in West Africa the impact of communism on the traditional social structures was an evolving phenomenon. President Houphouët-Boigny of Côte d'Ivoire once said to me that 'If you send an African to Paris he returns a Marxist; if you send him to Moscow he returns a conservative'. Nkrumah's clarion calls for African unity failed to impress the political world largely because of his own incriminating record. It was known that he had established a number of clandestine training camps for dissidents from African countries, including Nigeria and the Côte d'Ivoire, with the object of destabilizing governments which were inimical to Nkrumah. But all this was part of the ferment of Africa at the time, and it was a fascinating diplomatic exercise to observe the manner in which the nations and peoples of the continent, moved into the post-colonial, twentieth century.

Once the excitement of the OAU Conference was over I was able to get on with my normal duties which, as every diplomat is aware, comprised a study of the political, social, and economic conditions within Ghana, and the establishment of personal relations with the people of the country in as many fields as possible. This was not at all difficult because the Ghanaians are a warm and friendly people whose hospitality and joie de vivre are a quintessential element of their many endearing qualities. Added to this was the high calibre of my colleagues in the diplomatic corps. The combination was a stimulating professional experience which I savoured to the full, and this compensated for the many frustrations and hardships imposed by the daily living conditions, which at one time had been reasonable, but slowly became extremely difficult, and continued to deteriorate even further.

As I have already noted, at the time of independence, Ghana had been a reasonably prosperous country, whose main natural resources, cocoa and gold, coupled with its ample financial reserves, had ensured a comfortable living for its people. An even more important asset was the high quality of its skilled human resources: its administrators, academics and professionals, as well as its armed forces, were amongst the best in Africa. After Nkrumah came to power he embarked upon a ruthless megalomaniacal campaign designed to recreate Ghana in his own image. Backed by the power and authority generated in the euphoria surrounding his achievements as the freedom fighter and liberator of his country, he rushed through a series of political measures that quickly concentrated power in his own hands, but at the same time started the inexorable drift to economic ruin. Basing his policies on the communist pattern, much favoured by other African leaders of early independence as well, he replaced the parliamentary system with a one-party state and eliminated all political opposition. Simultaneously, he 'roughed up' the administration and the judiciary, forcing them into the ambit of the one-party system. This had the inevitable consequence of the suppression of flight from Ghana of a large element of its ablest, professional, and skilled talent.

Nkrumah's ideological whims proved even more damaging to the economy of the country. He carried out a widespread campaign of nationalization, including the establishment of Soviet-style collective farms, with Soviet advisers in the initial stages. This was an ill-considered measure which devastated the agricultural base of the country. I had a meeting with Nkrumah shortly before I set out on a tour of the north and, at his suggestion, reported to him on my return. The state farms that I saw were in an advanced state of neglect, with tractors and other mechanized equipment, abandoned in the poorly cultivated fields. I was told that the collectivized farmers did no work all day and reported to the offices in the afternoon to collect their wages. Then they went off and did their farming on the few private plots that they owned, in order to supplement their incomes. I told Nkrumah on my return to Accra that what I had seen was a rich country with poor people, that this seemed not at all necessary, and that this superimposed system was driving the country to disaster. Nkrumah was entirely unruffled by my remarks and accepted them with an indulgent smile. He said that my 'capitalist background' had coloured my conclusions, and that I should see things 'in the wider national context'. He added, in all seriousness, 'High Commissioner, it is possible for an individual to go bankrupt, but no nation can ever become bankrupt'. Whilst I was wondering how to frame this astonishing 'obiter dictum' in my reporting telegram, Nkrumah turned to his favourite subject, his vision of Ghana's role in the leadership of Africa and the struggle against neo-colonialism. As always, I found that the moment Nkrumah talked of politics there was a spellbinding fire in his eyes and a messianic commitment to African freedom and unity. But the moment one raised any practical economic issues, a dull glaze would come over these same soulful eyes, followed by a curt dismissal—'Yes, yes, but that is not so important'.

The commander of the Ghanaian army was General Joseph Arthur Ankrah, a large, bluff and jovial extrovert, whom I got to know and like a great deal. Pakistan had commenced a minor military co-operation programme with the Ghanaian army, which included at the time the secondment of some Pakistani military doctors for specialist duties in Ghanaian military hospitals, and the provision for Ghanaian armed service officers to attend advanced courses at the famous Command and Staff College in Quetta. Since this programme was going very well on both fronts, Ankrah asked me for an increase in the quota of Ghanaian officers at the Staff College. I managed to secure this after some difficulty, as the Quetta Staff College was, and still is, a prestigious institution to which admission is sought by officers from armies all over the world. Subsequently, I noticed that the GHQ in Accra was delaying the submission of nominations, and expressed my concern to Ankrah. In response, he sent a senior officer to meet me and explain the nature of the problem that he had suddenly encountered. It seemed that, in keeping with his ambitions, Nkrumah had ordered the establishment of a Ghanaian Army Staff College, and the army top brass had been dragging its feet for the simple reason that it lacked the resources for such a venture. Nkrumah's irritated response was to cancel all foreign training assignments for Ghanaian army officers until the Staff College had been established. The senior officer who called at my office explained the situation to me quite frankly, and not without some embarrassment. I responded by saying that I fully understood the nature of the problem, and assured him that Pakistan would continue its co-operation with the Ghanaian armed forces, including the provision of admissions to the Staff College, as and when they wanted them. Thanking me profusely, and giving me a broad smile and a smart salute, he left my office. The name of the officer was Lt.-Col. E.K. Kotoka, a name which came to the fore in the coup of 1966.

Our stay in Ghana continued; our fascination combined with frustration, against the background of an increasingly lively political scene, and the sad spectacle of visibly deteriorating living conditions, with increasing shortages of food, electricity and all the other necessities of life. One of my Arab colleagues, whose previous assignment had been as deputy chief of mission in Paris, found the joy of his promotion to ambassador somewhat tempered by the living conditions that he found in Accra. 'Here, life is a struggle for existence, my brother,' was his anguished cry.

On the external front, Nkrumah's vigorous forays into international affairs in general and African affairs in particular provided a constant kaleidoscope of events and activities. Two issues primarily attracted his attention. The first, of course, was the confrontation between the Soviet Union and the West, with a perceptible intensification of the Cold War and its proxy ramifications, both in Vietnam, and in the conflicts that were increasingly erupting in Africa. Nkrumah was particularly drawn to the latter, and carried out constant overt and covert activities all over the continent, supporting liberation movements with strident public diplomacy, backed by economic, and sometimes, military assistance. More ominously, he extended covert subversive activities to those newly independent African nations that rejected his socialist approach, and embarked on an extensive campaign to destabilize these governments by financing opposition groups, and even establishing a series of clandestine training camps for saboteurs and rebels in Ghana. The primary targets were Côte d'Ivoire, Senegal, and Liberia, while relations with Nigeria, a large and near neighbour, were always tendentious.

But it was apartheid in South Africa, and the independence of Southern Rhodesia that became the two centres of gravity of Nkrumah's diplomatic posture as an African leader. His vigorous and explosive stands on these two issues not only established impressive credentials for his African leadership, but also propelled him to eminence on the international scene. As the leading African in the Non-Aligned Movement, which was itself at its zenith because of the Cold War, Nkrumah's international stature received a further boost. As so often happens, external drama was assiduously exploited to offset internal difficulties, and propaganda was intensified in an effort to distract the Ghanaian people from the deepening domestic and economic crises, which by now had assumed ominous aspects. Nkrumah's usual anti-colonial rhetoric became increasingly strident and, coupled with a growing anti-Western stance, triggered a rapid deterioration in relations with the West in general, and the United Kingdom in particular. This resulted in the rupture of diplomatic relations with London and the sullen departure of Harold Smedley, the able and competent British High Commissioner.

As a consequence of Nkrumah's pursuit of international celebrity, I found myself being summoned to Flagstaff House and the Foreign Ministry with increasing frequency. The discussions were not without disagreements, particularly with Osagyefo, but were always friendly and civilized. It was obvious that Nkrumah was yearning to project himself on the world stage, and it seemed to me that his gaze, having flitted over Kashmir, was now fixed on the big prize, Vietnam. The ambassador of the People's Republic of China was Huang Hua, who, with his erudite and beautiful wife, He Liliang, was a diplomatic tour de force. Huang Hua was a superb professional whose outstanding knowledge, skill, finesse, and patience render him an honoured place amongst the foremost diplomats of that era. It was my good fortune to develop a happy, professional, and personal friendship with him that was deep and warm, and that has lasted a lifetime. After Ghana, Huang Hua went as ambassador to a number of important countries and eventually became the first permanent representative of the People's Republic of China to the United Nations in New York, where we met again eighteen years after Ghana. In Accra, as Huang Hua and I worked closely together, we found ourselves being nudged by the president's office into Nkrumah's formulation of plans for a foray into Asia. In due course arrangements were made for a journey that would take Nkrumah for a short official visit to Pakistan, followed by a longer official visit to China, and then on to Vietnam for a formal meeting with Ho Chi Minh in Hanoi. The formalities had hardly been completed when the Ghanaian press rushed to exultant headlines in bold letters, 'KWAME! COME TO HANOI! HO'.

Nkrumah's departure at Accra airport had all the trappings and fanfare appropriate for the occasion, which was glowingly described as a journey for world peace. I sent the usual telegrams to the Ministry of Foreign Affairs in Karachi, urging rapid transmissions of reports and photographs of the Nkrumah visit for dissemination by the High Commission in Accra. As it turned out, I need not have bothered. The official Ghanaian public relations department had already, very efficiently, transmitted a graphic account of Nkrumah's stay in Karachi to the electronic and print media, and the morning papers had front page coverage of Nkrumah's visit to Karachi. These included photographs of the arrival and departure ceremonies at the airport, and the formal meetings of the two delegations headed by Ayub Khan and Nkrumah, respectively. The press reports included a lavish account of the past achievements of the two leaders, with an even more imaginative expression of the successes that would ensue with this continuing solidarity. This was the stuff that would warm the cockles of any ambassador's heart, but was denied to me by a sudden, harsh, and unexpected, reality check. Even as I picked up the morning newspapers that carried the glowing reports from Karachi, from the veranda of my residence, I could hear the sound of gunfire and the wailing of sirens all over Accra. The coup by the National Liberation Council (NLC) that led to the ousting of Nkrumah had begun, and would be successfully concluded by the end of the day, followed by widespread rejoicing by most of the residents of Accra, including, soldiers, policemen, citizens, and hordes of happy market mammies, dancing in groups all over town.

Nkrumah and his delegation were en route from Karachi to Beijing when the coup occurred, and it fell to the lot of the able Ambassador Huang Hua to break the awkward news to Nkrumah on arrival. The visit to Hanoi was cancelled, of course, and after hanging around for a few days in China, the members of the delegation made their way, in dribs and drabs, back to Accra where, apart from some public humiliation, they were not subject to incarceration or other draconian punishment. Nkrumah spent a few days in Beijing and then proceeded to Conakry, where his friend Sékou Touré, provided what must surely be the most sumptuous treatment accorded to any asylum seeker. Touré not only welcomed Nkrumah, but in due course anointed his guest as Co-President of Guinea. The gesture was touching, but not without complications in protocol, as bemused ambassadors found themselves addressing two presidents and handing over letters of credence to only one. A few years later Nkrumah died of cancer, his last years spent as Touré's guest; bitter and disconsolate in the discomfiture of his fall, and a poignant emblem of the meteoric rise and fall that attended so many of the early leaders of African independence.

Meanwhile in Ghana the leaders of the coup, designated as the National Liberation Council, availing themselves of the opportunity of their early popular support, quickly established their authority with a hefty push of the economic pendulum. At home, Nkrumah's socialist measures were reversed as rapidly as possible, whilst in foreign affairs relations with the socialist countries were pared to the bone. Many ambassadors were expelled, missions drastically reduced, and a whole host of 'advisers' from the socialist states, ranging from East Germany's Stasi intelligence officers, and experts in agriculture, mining and fishing from the USSR, Poland, Czechoslovakia, and Hungary, were sent home. On the other hand, Western presence was sought and welcomed with fervour. British interests soon re-established themselves in the administration, commerce, and the armed forces, and High Commissioner Harold Smedley (à la MacArthur) made a triumphal return to his post. The USA sent a dynamic ambassador, Franklin H. Williams, who had been a senior official in the National Association for the Advancement of Coloured People (NAACP), and in due course the World Bank also established its presence in Ghana. The Bank's mission was headed by Moeen Qureshi, a brilliant economist and decisive administrator, who went on to become the Senior Vice-President of the World Bank in Washington, D.C., and also, for a brief period, the Prime Minister of Pakistan. Moeen's incisive skill and initiatives first put a tourniquet on Ghana's economic haemorrhage, induced by Nkrumah's reckless spending, and then established a gradual but sure process of economic recovery.

The NLC chose General Ankrah, the former army commander, as president, but the effective leaders of the army–police coup were Lt.-Col. E.K. Kotoka and John Harley, the Commissioner of Police. The NLC, which set up a cabinet of army and police officers, and senior civil servants, wasted no time, as already indicated, in swinging Ghana, back, firmly into the Western camp. Nkrumah's ministers and party apparatchiks were all dismissed; some were arrested, while some jumped ship and publicly lauded the action of the NLC. The coterie of foreign advisers was sent home, most of the ambassadors from the socialist countries were recalled, and some embassies closed down entirely. Shortly after they took over, the NLC arranged a formal meeting with the diplomatic corps in Accra. As the NLC members marched in and took their seats on the dais, Colonel Kotoka looked around the hall, spotted me and gave me the thumbs up sign, accompanied by a delightful smile and wink of recognition. Since very few diplomats had any previous contacts with the NLC members, but all knew Kotoka's role and standing by now, his very friendly public gesture gained me a few brownie points among my colleagues. It also put me in a position of some advantage in terms of my diplomatic work with the new regime. Almost immediately thereafter an officer from GHQ called on me and we were able to restart the military co-operation between Pakistan and Ghana.

To my mild surprise, and considerable gratification, I found that my earlier close and known association with Nkrumah was no impediment to my relations with the new regime. This was, in my view, entirely due to the innate goodness of the Ghanaian people who always displayed goodwill and seldom carried a grudge. However, to the distress of most foreign well-wishers and against the overwhelming measure of the Ghanaian population, the optimistic tranquillity of the NLC honeymoon was shattered by a short and sharp attempted coup, rashly, and incompetently led by two junior army officers. The uprising, which was quite literally limited to the barracks and was more a mutiny than a coup, was quickly and ruthlessly suppressed, but unfortunately not before its leaders had succeeded in killing the formidable and popular Lt.-Col. Kotoka. A swift court martial of the coup leaders, followed by a gory public execution, brought the matter to a conclusion. The NLC continued to run the country in a peaceful and reasonably productive fashion until the time of my departure in the summer of 1967. But an unfortunate precedent had been set, and Ghana was destined to endure a period of turbulence, that included military coups and vengeful executions, for a number of years. I continued to follow the events in this beautiful country and its lovely people from a distance, and it is a matter of immense satisfaction that its intelligent and attractive populace have established for themselves a democratic polity and economic viability that has taken Ghana to the forefront of African nations.

CHAPTER THREE

Guinea

Shortly after we had settled down in Accra, Diana and I paid our first visit to Guinea for the presentation of credentials. The fiery president, Ahmed Sékou Touré had initiated a policy that had left Guinea even more isolated, and poorer, than the other newly-independent nations of West Africa. Getting from Accra to Conakry always presented logistical problems. There was either an ancient Dakota, or an Ilyushin IL-11, a far more noisy and precarious aircraft. On our first visit, as we lumbered in by the Dakota, we were received at Conakry airport by a lively and communicative chef de protocol, accompanied by two assistants, who drove us away in two battered Citroens. Our hotel, close to the airport, was beautifully situated on a bluff overlooking the deep blue Atlantic Ocean. We were told that it was a better hotel than the one downtown, both in terms of facilities and cuisine, and were put up in the presidential suite, which possessed the only air conditioner on the premises. Since this monster was subject to intermittent power cuts, which was most of the time, and emitted more smoke and noise than cool air when it did work, we decided to dispense with its services, and instead lived in the fresh breezes that blew in from the ocean. Room charges, we later discovered, were on a par with the Ritz in Paris. After a number of telephone calls to the ministry, the chef de protocol informed me that the credentials ceremony would take place the next afternoon and that madame was also expected to attend. Diana was pleasantly surprised by this unusual gesture, and expressed her thanks in her usual gracious fashion. To this the chef de protocol, in a flurry of Franco-African gallantry declaimed, '*Qu'est ce que la loi, Madame? C'est les homes qui fait la loi.*' ('What is law, Madame? It's men who make the law.') This cheerful, friendly, and carefree gesture, was a foretaste of the cordial reception we were accorded throughout our stay, and more than compensated for the creature discomforts that we were obliged to endure in the Conakry of that era.

In the early 1960s, when General Charles De Gaulle embarked upon his bold policy of decolonization of French possessions in West Africa, he envisioned a continuation of the association by turning bonds into limbs. From this evolved the concept of 'Francophonie', and the La Communauté Franco-Africaine (CFA), a loosely-knit affiliation, with political, economic, and cultural links, under the patronage of France. All the newly-independent francophone nations of West Africa were offered membership of the CFA, which clearly bore the stamp of De Gaulle's avuncular patronage. Léopold Senghor of Senegal and Houphouët-Boigny of Côte d'Ivoire, fully accepted and embraced this concept, and achieved a comparatively smooth transition. They derived considerable pragmatic benefits from this relationship, including automatic access to the lucrative European Common Market. Niger, Mali, Benin, and Upper Volta, responded in a less enthusiastic fashion, but Sékou Touré was the only West African leader to reject the proposal, and organized a rambunctious referendum, culminating in a thunderous '*Non!*'. For Guinea the consequences were immediate and brutal. A swift repatriation of all French personnel, including administrators, technicians, and settlers, was accompanied by an even more damaging withdrawal of all tangible assets, including heavy items like railroad freight cars, power generators and transport vehicles. And what the French could not take with them they destroyed; I saw tangled transmission lines on the highways, and smashed cranes and transit sheds in the docks. The French had ensured that Sékou Touré's defiant '*non*' came at a very heavy price.

The credentials ceremony was simple. Following a salute from a detachment of the Garde Républicain, drawn up on the steps of the presidency, formerly the residence of the colonial governor, Diana and I were shown into the reception hall, where we were presented to Sékou Touré by the chef de protocol. The former's entourage consisted of the foreign minister, the chef de cabinet, and the minister for sports and youth affairs (I never figured out the significance of his presence). Following the brief statements that accompanied the presentation and acceptance of the letters of credence, the president and I entered into a substantive discussion. A handsome man of medium height, he was impeccably dressed in a business suit, and spoke in a quiet tone of unmistakable authority. Our discussion focused on two subjects. He wanted to know about the situation in South Asia, and he wished to tell me about his policies and objectives for Guinea in particular, and Africa in general. He listened with interest to my exposition of the looming crisis over Kashmir, and though obviously concerned over the issue, merely expressed the repeated homily about the necessity for a peaceful settlement. As was expected, he was much more forceful when talking about Guinea itself, and vituperated against the French policies of neo-colonialism in West Africa. He presented me with two handsome, tourist coffee-table books on Guinea, and a surprisingly well-written tract on his own political achievements and aspirations for his country.

At the conclusion of the ceremony we were driven back to the hotel in a convoy, with sirens blaring and a motorcycle escort. As we passed through the town square in Conakry, we saw a black Citroen at the head of a main intersection where all traffic had been stopped in order to allow our motorcade to proceed. Seated in the car, and waving to us wildly like a bunch of schoolboys, was President Sékou Touré at the wheel, and the three dignitaries who had been present at the credentials ceremony. The chef de protocol said that the president had commenced his daily evening ritual of visits to a number of cafes in the city and on the beach, in order to make merry with the people late into the night, until 'Madame President sends out a messenger to bring him home'. Most of this was probably true, and there seemed little doubt that Sékou Touré enjoyed considerable popularity at that time. Even as we conducted our civilized, low-key discussions in his presidential office, I was aware that when addressing a crowd in the stadium Sékou Touré became a very different person, with thunder in his voice and fire in his speeches. It was also evident, from my observations in the country, and discussions with its local and foreign residents and diplomats, that Sékou Touré's power base was a blend of efficient party organization, coupled with a state apparatus of fairly ruthless repression. Sékou Touré guided his country for much longer than most of his contemporaries, the early leaders of the West African independence period. Indeed, making one of them his co-president, namely Nkrumah, is a quixotic gesture, unique in the annals of diplomacy. He maintained an erratic high profile on the international stage, particularly in Africa, and I met him quite frequently on these occasions. His speeches were usually predictable, in terms of content, delivery, and above all, length, and would often invoke a suppressed groan from amongst the more-experienced delegations as soon as the chairman gave him the floor. On one memorable occasion, when Indira Gandhi was presiding, she called upon Sékou Touré to deliver his statement, and then, unaware that her microphone had not been switched off, muttered wearily and sotto voce to her aide, 'Oh dear, this man is going to speak forever'. Luckily, as she spoke in Hindi and the simultaneous interpreter exercised commendable discretion, dissemination of the remark was satisfactorily contained.

Guinea's natural resources are ores, mainly bauxite, of which there is an abundance. Since there was no way in which this could be exploited in order to build a relationship with Pakistan, I searched for other alternatives and could come up with none, except for our common membership of the Organization of the Islamic Conference (OIC). Geographic distance, language, and culture, were formidable obstacles in themselves, but perhaps the most difficult was the political and economic isolation that Guinea had imposed upon itself. I made two further visits to Guinea during my tenure, but these were essentially exercises in maintaining goodwill, and contained only the usual exchange of pleasantries. The best that could be realistically done was to maintain a benign but formal level of diplomatic contact.

CHAPTER FOUR

Mali

The third country of my concurrent accreditation was Mali, a sparsely-populated, bare land, encompassing a large part of the Sahara desert, with an austere and varied beauty, much of which was reflected in the bearing and character of its proud and dignified people. A former French colony, it had, like its neighbour, chosen the socialist path, but its leader Modibo Keïta had done so without the acrimony provoked by his colleague, Sékou Touré. This meant that transition had been comparatively smooth, and that French influence continued to prevail, though not in the intrusive and high profile manner as manifested in Dakar and Abidjan. Modibo Keïta was amongst the first generation of francophone West African leaders, such as Senghor of Senegal, Houphouët-Boigny of Côte d'Ivoire, Sékou Touré of Guinea, Bongo of Cameroon, and the leaders of Togo and Haute Volta, who had been students in Paris, where they cut their political teeth in the city's écoles, cafés, boulevards, and in some cases, the Assemblée Nationale. Some, like Sékou Touré and Modibo Keïta, had chosen the socialist path and gone on to lead left-oriented parties. Others, like Senghor and Houphouët-Boigny had adopted the conservative approach, closely aligning themselves with the French ruling elite, providing generous facilities to French nationals and their commercial interests, and maintaining close personal ties with Paris, including proprietorships of chateaux, farms, and vineyards in France. For example, the Ivorian administrative service employed a large number of French nationals, whose salary scales were considerably higher than those of the Ivorians. But if the latter happened to have a French wife, he automatically moved to the more lavish French scale of pay. But whether socialist or capitalist, the francophone West Africans had an intriguing cultural affiliation, in common with all things French, particularly the language. Senghor was a renowned poet who was elevated to the famous Académie Française, one of the so-called 'immortals'. The affiliation also included, of course, cuisine, and customs, such as the three-hour déjeuner.

The credentials ceremony at Bamako, much to my satisfaction, was a simple one. A black Citroen, the ubiquitous official government vehicle in francophone West Africa, took me to the presidential palace, again the residence of the former French governor, and upon arrival, I was ushered in to meet the President. Modibo Keïta was a large man, with a gracious and friendly demeanour, and a smile that appeared to emanate from the eyes rather than the lips. I decided to chance my arm, so in my presentation speech, after reciting the customary courtesies, I launched into the Kashmir issue and made a strong presentation of Pakistan's case. Modibo Keïta's response politely overlooked this breach of diplomatic etiquette, and in measured terms urged restraint, eschewing in characteristic fashion any offers of mediation. In our subsequent conversation, he displayed a lively interest in the political factors that led to the creation of Pakistan. I later discovered that in his private life he was a devout Muslim, and linked his spiritual beliefs to the vigorous pursuit of his secular socialist credo. He talked about the poverty of his country and felt that a socialist path was the only way to achieve success. Unlike Guinea, he had not severed his ties with Paris, as he thought that the French connection could still be of benefit to his country. On the other hand, he had greatly increased his connections with the USSR, as evidenced by a large number of Soviet and East European advisers and technicians in Mali. Subsequent events would reveal that this was an error of judgment, which cost this gentle and well-intentioned leader his presidential office.

In accordance with the President's suggestion, I set off next day on a trip through the country, stopping at Mopti, then Gao, and going on to Tombouctou, a city which metaphorically conjures up a mysterious journey to nowhere. The Air Mali plane was a scary twin-engine Ilyushin IL-11, with a crew comprising a Russian pilot, a Malian co-pilot, and a hefty Malian flight attendant, aptly chosen because he was better at humping cargo than he was at serving snacks, and performed both duties with oaths either bellowed or muttered. Our route followed the Niger River, and since the aircraft was not pressurized we flew at altitudes that produced a bumpy ride as the day warmed up, but enabled me to follow the topography of the countryside with considerable fascination. My fellow passengers consisted of five French tourists, whose major objective appeared to be to get their passports stamped at the tourist office in Tombouctou as proof of their travel to nowhere, and about fifteen Malian families either heading home or to their places of work. We shared the cabin with the cargo, which was stowed in the aft part of the aircraft, and secured by some dubious looking cargo net. The identifiable items of the cargo consisted of three noisy and smelly goats, parts of a printing press consigned to the party newspaper in Tombouctou, one case of dynamite consigned to a construction project, and a number of packages—contents unknown—whose ominous appearance added considerably to my sense of unease. Our departure from Bamako was delayed by an hour and a half for 'raison technique' and 'raison de meteo', after which the battered Ilyushin shuddered its way up to its cruising altitude of 2000 metres, and we bumped our way over the Sahara desert. As soon as the plane landed at Mopti and Gao, the Russian pilot sulked off to a corner of the primitive terminal buildings, visibly nursing his grievance against a fate that had consigned him to his current duties. Meanwhile the burly Malian flight attendant had assumed his additional duties as loadmaster, and vigorously and vociferously supervised the discharging and loading of cargo from the aircraft, ensuring, to the general relief of everybody, that the dynamite was safely trundled off in a handcart at Gao. On arrival in Tombouctou I was lodged in the 'campment', a government facility at the disposal of visiting dignitaries. The accommodation and food, which were quite spartan, were supposed to be better than anything in town, and richly compensated for by the cheerful courtesy of the staff.

Tombouctou is situated at the bend of the Niger River at its most northern point, and has historically been the junction for trade from the northeast, the northwest, and the south. For centuries it was the meeting point between the caravans that crossed the Sahara carrying salt, spices, cloth, and other products, from the north, and the mighty Niger River, carrying gold and slaves from West Africa. Travellers and traders thronged to the city, which flourished as the centre of the Songhai Empire, with the University of Sankore hosting at one time over 25,000 scholars. In the late sixteenth century, Moroccan invaders defeated the Songhai rulers and destroyed their empire. The decline of Tombouctou was further accelerated by the rise of the West African sea trade, which almost completely overwhelmed the older and more difficult desert and inland river routes with their limited loads. What remains now is an almost romantic replica of an earlier phenomenon which had lasted for centuries, and so at sunset I walked from the campment to the banks of the Niger to observe the arrival of the camel caravans from across the Sahara.

The grunting camels lurched to their knees, then thumped their bellies onto the sand and waited for their attendants to remove the loads off their backs. Eased off their burden, they were led to the river to be watered and fed. Meanwhile the other men in the caravans went about preparing the evening meal, and the glow from the various campfires gradually took over from the rapidly failing light of the evening sun. I began to revel in the sensuous pleasure provided by the perfect atmosphere of the cool desert twilight, and the romantic thought that I was observing a ritual and an activity that had been going on uninterrupted and unchanged for centuries. But this foray into the idyllic reflection was soon shattered, quite literally, by the sounds of dozens of transistor radios blaring out the pop music of differing cultures, and the throaty exhortations of politicians and priests. Tombouctou was not, after all, as isolated from the world as its name implied.

The next day I paid my formal calls on the mayor, the prefect, and the commander of the gendarmerie. They told me of their problems, which were basically caused by poverty and desertification, as was very evident. Modest in character, they made no boastful party-line claims of achievements and success, but expressed with simple dignity their determination to improve the condition of their land and people. No trip to Tombouctou is complete without a visit to the famous Djinguereber Mosque, built in the fifteenth century in almost wholly African desert style, tipped by a slight but enchanting Saracenic touch. The Imam was a kind and gentle old man, who told me that much of his time was spent in settling disputes between the Tuaregs and the resident Malians, but he added with modest piety that the task was not too burdensome since both were followers of Islam and generally placed their trust in the Imam. I was shown some relics that belonged to the mosque, including its prized possession, a frayed but carefully preserved parchment copy of the Holy Quran which, the Imam claimed, was brought by the early missionaries who built the mosque. Tombouctou was reputed to still have a number of books, both religious and secular, dating from the fifteenth century, a period when it was the home of one of the world's largest libraries. Despite my enquiries I could not trace any of them, and I was told that the few that existed belonged to some private collectors.

I made two further trips to Mali during my tenure, the main purpose of which was to maintain contact and continue the token gesture of good relations. Not much was accomplished by way of adding substance to our bilateral relations, and my one satisfaction was the opportunity to get to know Modibo Keïta better, which in turn immensely increased my admiration for him both as a person and as a statesman.

CHIAROSCURO

When the missionaries first came to Africa, they had the Bible and we had the land. They said, "Let us pray!" When we opened our eyes, we had the Bible and they had the land.

– Bishop Desmond Tutu

I noticed that in West Africa Christianity was the dominant religion in the coastal regions, and Islam became more prevalent inland. This was obviously because the Christian missionaries had come by sea and the Muslim missionaries overland from North Africa. Most Ghanaians were very devout in the practice of their respective faiths, and churches and mosques were always very well attended. However, there were some who managed to so mesh their faiths with their old customs that they must have been the despair of missionaries, both Christian and Muslim. Two instances come to mind. I paid an official visit to a chief in northern Ghana, and was accordingly received by him in full regalia, seated on his stool, with his 'linguist' standing next to him, holding a totem pole. In terms of occupation, the chief worked for the Public Works Department, but since this was a ceremonial occasion, the chief received me in ceremonial garb and conversed with me only through his 'linguist', as required by custom. The chief's residence was pointed out to me and I was told that the large dome was where the chief lived and the three smaller domes housed each of his three wives.

I remarked, with the polite flattery appropriate to the occasion, that I thought that a chief of his stature would have more than three wives. The chief's answer, conveyed through his linguist, was that the high commissioner was quite right, but that the chief was a very strict Methodist.

The other incident related to a senior police officer, a devout and practicing Muslim. He recounted to me that whenever he was on the trail of a dangerous criminal he would first seek out and visit the juju man of his quarry. I complimented him on his innovative investigation technique because the juju man could obviously provide useful information on the criminal's whereabouts, habits, and techniques. 'No, no,' said my friend. 'It is to get a juju to protect myself from the criminal's spells.'

* * *

I gave a dinner at my residence in honour of the Asantehene, the senior-most and most noble of the chiefs in Ghana, the leader of the Ashantis, and an old gentleman of tremendous charm and dignity. He had been somewhat sidelined by Nkrumah, but had always maintained his poise and presence, and an impressive noble isolation. Following the departure of Nkrumah, the Asantehene had accepted my invitation and graced my home with his presence. One of the guests was my very good friend Bawa A. Yakubu, the Deputy Commissioner of Police and a senior member of the National Liberation Council. As his name and designation would indicate, he was both a Muslim and a member of the ruling cabinet. He greeted the Asantehene with the utmost respect, but turned down my offer of a chair, saying 'I can not be seated in the presence of the Asantehene'. Bawa Yakubu remained on his feet, as did most of the other Ghanaian guests, throughout the evening. I was glad that it was a buffet dinner.

* * *

At a large, open-air official dinner hosted by Nkrumah, the evening was enlivened by a superb performance of Ghanaian drumming and dancing. I was seated next to a Ghanaian lady of ample proportions, and a matching amiable disposition, who, whilst consuming mouthfuls of foufou and carrying on a lively conversation with me, also simultaneously performed the most fetching movements of her body in rhythm with the music. She asked me about dancing in Pakistan and stumped for an answer, I tried to cover my ignoble ignorance by muttering some nonsense about the intricacies of Kathakali. With incomprehension writ large on her face, she said 'But what do you do when you are happy?', and went on with her sensual gyrations.

MEANWHILE IN PAKISTAN

During the period of my stint in Africa, from April 1965 to June 1967, a great deal had happened in Pakistan, and I returned home to find the country poised for transformation. Gone was the feeling of comfort and sense of continuity generated by the political stability and economic progress of the early and middle period of the Ayub era. The results of substantial economic growth were clearly visible, but it was just as evident that this growth had increased disparities in all segments of the society. The resentment against inequality had spread from individuals to regions and finally to the state itself, with East Pakistan demanding greater access to resources. A book just published by the distinguished economist, Dr Mahbub ul Haq, which showed for the first time the concentration of national wealth among twenty families, became a war cry against an establishment that had created such inequalities in society, whilst at the same time, in the political field, the artificial fabric of Ayub's 'basic democracies' was being systematically destroyed, shred by shred. There were also the first rumbles of the populist movements that would lead, within five years, to the dismemberment of Pakistan.

Within the Foreign Office there had also been major changes. Zulfikar Ali Bhutto and Aziz Ahmed had left, one of the early consequences of the 1965 war and the subsequent Tashkent Agreement, and had been replaced by Syed Sharifuddin Pirzada and S.M. Yusuf. The ministry itself had moved from its stately edifice in Karachi to a rudimentary, temporary accommodation, pending its takeover of the Scherezade Hotel in Islamabad. I soon discovered that the changes in the ministry had gone beyond simply those of the site and the personalities. The briefings that I received made it clear that the left orientation orchestrated by Bhutto was about to undergo a substantial change, and that while the anchor to China would remain as firm as ever, Pakistan's policies would once again veer towards the West.

During the short period of time available to me at home between my transfer from Ghana to Romania, I managed to travel all over the country and found, in both East and West Pakistan, a latent but ominous and clearly discernible dissatisfaction with the country's state of affairs. Ayub had been in office for ten years, and the regime could rightly be credited with considerable achievements including, above all, a healthy and robust economy that had flourished in the atmosphere of political stability. But the 1965 war was the watershed, where, as so often happens in public life, complacency perceptively transmutes into resentment. An ill-advised and ill-conceived public campaign celebrating Ayub's 'Decade of Development' was quite rightly regarded as a monument to sycophancy, and predictably backfired. In general, the atmosphere was of a society that was ready for change, and the two astute politicians who sensed this mood had just begun to mobilize their resources. In West Pakistan, the discarded Zulfikar Ali Bhutto, had formed the Pakistan People's Party and given it a new populist socio-economic programme; meanwhile in East Pakistan Sheikh Mujibur Rehman had assumed control of the Awami League and was in the process of directing the passive acceptance of the prevailing political order into a militant, radical spearhead, that was clearly headed towards secession. This is a political oxymoron that I have never been able to work out. How can the exit of the majority party in a political union be called 'secession'? But in the politics of Pakistan all kinds of things can happen.

I left Pakistan for my new assignment in Eastern Europe with the conviction that the foundations of the old order that we had known over the past decade had received a major jolt, and that things were about to change.

PART II

ROMANIA AND BULGARIA

CHAPTER FIVE

Romania

'From each according to his ability, to each according to his needs.'
– Karl Marx, *Critique of the Gotha Programme*, 1875

In August 1967 we landed at Baneasa airport, Bucharest, and I commenced an assignment in communist Eastern Europe which would eventually amount to a period of ten years. Prior to my arrival I attempted a quick re-perusal of *Das Kapital* and *The Communist Manifesto*, two volumes with which I had a passing acquaintance during my college days, and which I regarded as the New and Old Testaments of communism, but their contents seemed as turgid as ever and I abandoned them, knowing that I would shortly be able to observe the system in real life. The decision to establish the embassy in Bucharest was another of Bhutto's typically farsighted acts, taken in recognition of the intriguing new foreign policy initiatives of the Romanian government under the emerging leadership of Nicolae Ceausescu. In essence this involved an ostensible independence from the Moscow diktat, whilst retaining a rigid, doctrinaire adherence to communism in internal affairs. Accordingly, Romania established diplomatic relations with countries all over the world, including Israel and the Franco regime in Spain. More importantly, when Sino–Soviet differences were at their greatest and creating a veritable schism in international communist ideology, Bucharest assumed an assertive attitude of neutrality. Although both Moscow and Beijing regarded this as a puny irritant and took it in their stride, for the Romanian regime this was an achievement of considerable domestic propaganda value. With such a scenario in the background, the Romania of 1967 promised to be an interesting field for diplomatic activity. But as so often happens, the realities of difficult living conditions coupled with harshly enforced official restrictions, impose a formidable corrective to this attitude.

This was certainly true in the case of my predecessor and good friend, Ambassador Ahsan-ul-Haq. Belonging to a noble Bengali family, Ahsan had built a successful business career, and had been inducted into the Foreign Office for much the same reasons as myself. He was posted to Indonesia where he had done an outstanding job, and established an excellent personal relationship with President Sukarno, the famous and charismatic leader who played such an important role in founding of the Non-Aligned Movement, hosting its inaugural conference in Bandung. At the conclusion of his highly successful tenure in Jakarta, Ahsan was invited to open our resident embassy in Bucharest. But unfortunately a combination of ill health and adverse living conditions compelled Ahsan to resign from the service and return to his previous activities in the private sector. When we arrived in Bucharest in August 1967 and were received at the airport by the protocol officers and our extremely competent First Secretary, Waliullah Khan Khaishgi, I found that that the Pakistan embassy was a bit like an aircraft stuck halfway down the runway after an aborted take-off. We had reasonable premises for a chancery, which was occupied, apart from Khaishgi and myself, by a personal assistant/cipher assistant and an accountant/administrative assistant from Pakistan, two Romanian ladies who acted as secretary/interpreters, one Romanian driver and one Romanian messenger. As there was no residence for the ambassador, we were lodged in the Hotel Athenee Plaza, an old classical building in the Central Europe baroque style, agreeable to behold from the outside but extremely disagreeable to live in, since even the basic necessities were either not available or under constant breakdown and repair. Prices were on a par with five-star hotels in London and Paris, and the first week's stay provided a complete understanding of Ahsan's decision to leave the place. After some months of acrimonious and frustrating discussions with the Romanian authorities—my first exposure to a society where everything exists in the public sector and nothing in the private sector—we were able to secure, a large and lovely old building which had managed to retain much of its original charm and graciousness on Strada Paris.

Bucharest was a beautiful city laid out in imitation of Paris, complete with its Arc de Triomphe and the broad, tree-lined boulevards of Hausmann's design; the linden, chestnut, and lilac foliage presenting an aspect of freshness and beauty that was always pleasing. For the diplomatic corps the Foreign Ministry had provided and maintained a splendid club at its own cost, complete with forests, lakes and a nine-hole golf course. This had originally belonged to the king, and it was obvious that the golf course had been designed to flatter his majesty's handicap, the bunkers being neatly placed in the most unobtrusive fashion, so that even I began to consider myself a reasonably good golfer. Since contact between the Romanians and the foreigners was practically forbidden by a ban that was enforced by the Securitate with ruthless ferocity, the club became a centre of diplomatic life and activity, and the focal point for the exchange of information as well as a fertile environment for gossip, salacious scandal, and adultery. The clubhouse was bugged of course, but one could always talk freely on the fairways. For many diplomats, the Romanian language with its Roman script provided comparatively easy access to the people and the media, but this useful facility was considerably depleted by the draconian curbs placed on any contact between Romanian citizens and foreigners, and by the dull, deadly, and predictable propaganda churned out by the state's information media. Nevertheless the Romanians liked to think of themselves as a Latin island in a Slavic sea, and proclaimed it ad nauseam. Whilst acquiring a rudimentary proficiency in the language, my attention was attracted by the commonality of words between Urdu and Romanian, the obvious link being the Turkish language. Apart from culinary items like *pilaf* and *kebab*, there were a number of words—*dushman, maidan, sundook, chishma*—which were common in Urdu and Romanian. Others were close; *musafir*, which means 'traveller' in Urdu, is the Romanian word for 'guest'. I recollect having put together my private little glossary of about sixty such words.

Romania possessed a stunning variety of natural beauty, from the majestic crescent of the Carpathian Mountains to the rich wheat fields, the Danube delta with its fascinating flora and fauna, and the golden sands of the Black Sea shores. Added to that were the ancient castles and fortresses, including Brandt castle, the residence of the gruesome Count Dracula, and the superb painted monasteries of Moldova, where we once spent a memorable night in the bedroom of the former Bishop of Iaşj. Taking advantage of the fact that diplomats were allowed to travel freely all over the country, except significantly in the regions that were on the border with the USSR, we gathered an idea of the immense natural wealth of Romania. At the same time we could observe the extent of the poverty of the people and the nature of the political repression that governed their lives, confirming the assertion that Romania was a rich country populated by poor people.

Shortly after my arrival in Bucharest I had the professional good fortune to observe a development that had a considerable bearing on Romania's relations with the communist bloc, following three important conferences in Eastern Europe: at Budapest, Sofia, and Dresden. Romania walked out of the first, in exaggerated dramatic fashion, she refused to be a signatory to the only operative resolution that emerged from the second conference at Sofia, and was somewhat ominously omitted from the list of invitees to the Dresden Conference.

On 29 February 1968 at Budapest, the Romanians established a noisy presence and deluged the participants with material that emphasized the Romanian attitude towards international communism, including safeguards for the independence and equality of each participating communist party delegation. This included the statement that there would be no criticism of the internal or external policies of any communist party, whether or not that party was represented at Budapest, and that the conference decisions or directives would not be binding on all the participants. Since the Budapest Conference, which had been organized under the patronage of Moscow, took place when the schism in the communist world was at its most intense, it put the Romanian position of neutrality to the acid test, and I thought that their delegation did very well. They pointed out, quite correctly, that out of the eighty-eight extant communist parties, twenty-two were absent from the Budapest meeting, and of these six were actually the ruling communist parties within their countries. The Romanians made the very valid point that the absence of communist parties from China, North Vietnam, North Korea, Cuba, Albania, and Yugoslavia was deplorable because 'The conference on the struggle against imperialism is not attended by the representatives of the very people directly engaged in the sharpest struggle, in a fierce war against imperialist aggression'. This obviously infuriated the Soviets, who persuaded one of their puppets, the Syrian delegation, to launch a fierce attack against the Romanians. The Romanian delegation accordingly withdrew from the Budapest Conference, late at night and in a dramatic fashion. Meanwhile, at three in the morning of a bitter Bucharest winter, President Nicolae Ceausescu first telephoned Leonid Brezhnev in Moscow that the Romanian delegation was being recalled from Budapest, and then hauled all the ambassadors of the socialist countries in Bucharest out of bed, summoned them to the Council of State, and read them a statement to the same effect. The outspoken Polish ambassador, who later recounted to me the event in a state of still unabated fury, said that he informed Ceausescu that since this was essentially a party affair, the Romanian decision should have been conveyed to the Polish delegation at Budapest, and that he, a diplomatic officer, saw no justification in being summoned under such precipitate and uncomfortable circumstances.

The meeting of the Political Consultative Committee of the Warsaw Pact member countries at Sofia, on the 6 and 7 March 1968, took place soon after the Budapest Conference, and despite some earlier speculation about attendance, the Romanians participated fully. The day before the conference opened the Soviet delegation, which included Leonid Brezhnev and Aleksei Kosygin, passed through Romania by train and held discussions with the Romanian leaders during a three-hour stopover at the Bucharest railway station. The Sofia Conference achieved its major objectives, and unlike Budapest, the Romanians returned with their principles as well as their dignity intact.

The Dresden Conference was hastily convened on 25 March 1968, to discuss the events in Czechoslovakia and was attended by the heads of party/government of the USSR, Czechoslovakia, Hungary, Poland, East Germany, and Bulgaria. The Romanians had been deliberately excluded, and I was initially told by some senior members of the Foreign Ministry that Romania was not really interested in Dresden, since they had no desire to interfere in what was essentially an internal matter for Czechoslovakia. Subsequently, the line adopted by the Romanians was less lofty, and they behaved like an aggrieved party expressing resentment at being excluded from Dresden.

It was clear that the preponderance of the USSR, through its size and contiguity, exerted a political gravitational field of overwhelming magnitude upon Romania. This was a fact of life, of which both the countries were aware, and whilst Romania as a satellite was able to vary its angle of rotation on its own axis, its place in the overall political firmament of the world was quite definitely fixed in an orbit of the Soviet Union.

Nevertheless, in establishing a rapport with China, in opening diplomatic relations with West Germany, in their grudging and meagre participation in the Warsaw Pact military exercises, and in their opposition to the USSR position in both the Middle East crisis as well as the Nuclear Disarmament Treaty, the Romanians managed to conduct a remarkable exercise in defiance of the law of political gravity. They knew also that in this tightrope act they were very much on their own. A NATO ambassador, somewhat cold-bloodedly, explained to me the facts of the situation, 'When things are beginning to get so promising in our détente with Russia, who is going to stick his neck out for little Romania and support their stupidity against the Russians?'

In April 1968 Ceausescu significantly increased his grip on the party and his control of the country. At a plenary meeting of the Central Committee of the Romanian Communist Party he dismissed Alexandru Draghici, a powerful Moscow-oriented Vice-President and Minister of the Interior. Furthermore, in his speech, reminiscent of Nikita Khrushchev's 1956 secret speech to the Twentieth Congress of the USSR in denunciation of Stalin, Ceausescu made an equally strong and astonishing denunciation of Gheorghe Gheorghiu-Dej, the legendary founder figure of the Romanian Communist Party, accusing the latter of 'abuses and grave violations of socialist legality'. With this there came the usual purge of the old guard of the party and their replacement by Ceausescu's hand-picked loyalists, so that by the end of the year, at the conference of the Romanian Communist Party, Ceausescu was able to make himself President of the Council of State, whilst still retaining the post of Secretary General of the Romanian Communist Party. Having thus secured absolute power, both in form and in substance, Ceausescu carried out a further reshuffle of posts, filling them with appointees of his choice. More importantly, he engineered an ideological realignment, whereby Romanian communism would maintain a rigid, doctrinaire posture in internal affairs, with the proviso that the gospel of Marxism–Leninism would be preached according to Ceausescu, and not according to either Brezhnev or Mao Tse-tung.

President Ayub Khan made a state visit to Romania from 20 to 26 October 1967, and brought with him a substantial delegation which included his daughter, the charming, beautiful, and gracious Nasim Aurangzeb, who did a splendid job as the first lady of the delegation. The official party also included Foreign Minister Sharifuddin Pirzada and his wife; Fida Hasan, the Principal Secretary to the President; and my good friend, the dynamic Altaf Gauhar, who at that time was reputed to exercise an influence considerably greater than his designation as the Information Secretary. This state visit was one of the main reasons for my somewhat precipitate move to Bucharest. Since it was to be for a duration of six days it involved a plethora of preliminary plans and arrangements. This was not easy to do, working out of a hotel infamous for its dilapidated facilities, but I soon discovered that there were compensations for the fact that one worked with the machinery of a totalitarian state. The host government assumes responsibility for almost all administrative arrangements, including the vital but potentially vexatious issues of accommodation, transportation, and the provision of interpreters. The Pakistani president, his entourage, and senior officials, were lodged in a luxurious palace, and the rest in the hotel where I was staying. The programme for the visit, prepared through mutual consultations, included the usual ceremonial events, meetings with the Romanian leaders, two shooting trips which Ayub enjoyed very much, and an evening at the opera which was much less enjoyable; the delegation left at the interval though sheer incomprehension and boredom, and I joined them happily because it was truly an appalling production.

The Romanian state visit followed Ayub's state visit to France, but since the runway at Bucharest's Baneasa airport could not handle the PIA Boeing that flew in from Paris, it was decided that the president's plane would land at Constanza and the delegation would immediately transfer to a Romanian VIP Ilyushin 18 aircraft which would then land at Baneasa for the official arrival ceremonies. It was arranged for Diana and me to receive the president in Constanza and accompany the delegation to Bucharest. Just as I thought that the plans for the visit were neatly and harmoniously tied up with the Romanians, we hit a glitch. The official arrival and departure ceremonies at the airport included the presentation to President Ayub of ambassadors resident in Bucharest, and also invitees to the official receptions. I pointed out to the Romanians that we did not want the Israeli and East German ambassadors, two countries with which Pakistan did not have relations, at either of these functions. I was told that the authorities had taken note of my views, a response that was repeated with an insouciance that aroused my suspicion at each level that I raised the issue; with the chief of protocol, head of department, deputy foreign minister, foreign minister. This led me to confront Prime Minister Gheorghe Maurer and obtain his assurances. Maurer was his usual forthright self, and said that since Romania had diplomatic relations with all these countries it was incumbent on them to invite all ambassadors present in Bucharest. He said that the two ambassadors affected would receive formal invitations but would be advised by the Romanian authorities informally not to attend. I thought this suggestion to be disingenuous, if not dishonest, and said so to Maurer, adding that the ambassadors were likely to follow instructions from their own governments and not suggestions from the Romanian Foreign Office. Maurer agreed, and came up with what he called the 'De Gaulle solution'. This was a device employed a few weeks earlier when President De Gaulle paid an official visit to Poland, where the ambassador of the German Democratic Republic, which was not recognized by France, was present at the Warsaw airport. Accordingly the General had not shaken hands with any of the ambassadors, but simply marched past the line of diplomats, his hand at the salute, imperiously intoning, in his own inimitable fashion, 'Bonjour, Messieurs les Ambassadeurs!' in a gesture that was clearly more a proclamation than a greeting. Maurer's proposal was not very satisfactory to me, but it had some merit, especially as Ayub had already left Paris and was in the air as we sat discussing the issue in Maurer's office. Finally, a contingency plan was hatched that I was to be informed, while flying from Constanza to Bucharest, if 'the two untouchables' were present at the airport, and President Ayub could then exercise whatever option he wished. The flurry of telegrams between the foreign ministry and the embassy in Bucharest had obviously crossed Ayub's desk, and he was quite aware of the situation. When I explained our 'De Gaulle solution' to him shortly after take off, he gave me an amused look, and said, 'If a man has the decency and courtesy to come and greet me at the airport, I am going to shake hands with him. Then let the bloody Foreign Ministry sort it out'. This was vintage Ayub Khan. And it made no difference that the Israelis did not show up.

Ayub Khan's state visit to Romania was a complete success. Despite their separate ideologies and systems, there were no political differences between Pakistan and Romania; if at all, there was a certain similarity in the manner in which both countries were adapting subtle changes in their orientation to international relations, loosening their ties with the superpowers, and asserting a neutrality without actually joining the Non-Aligned Movement. For both the countries their common diplomatic relationship with China was an added link, and was a topic that received much consideration in the discussions Ayub had with Ceausescu and Maurer. Both sides explained their well-known positions on the major issues; the Romanians stressing their 'positive neutrality' and strict adherence to non-interference in internal affairs, while Ayub gave an account of Pakistan's economic development and the difficulties encountered in our relations with India. A tentative attempt by the Romanians, particularly the garrulous Prime Minister Maurer, to interpose their 'good offices' in a mediation role in the Kashmir issue was ignored by Ayub with unmistakable firmness. The final communiqué expressed the usual sentiments of mutual goodwill and increased economic co-operation. The first was achieved without any difficulty, but the second never really got off the ground. The restricted, high-level talks provided an interesting contrast in the style, manner, background, and approach of the leaders of both sides. Ceausescu maintained a steely, cool and purposeful attitude throughout the talks, while Maurer displayed a loud and jovial manner throwing out ideas, suggestions and proposals like Santa Claus at Christmas. This good cop–bad cop tactic was the standard operating procedure in negotiations with the communists, and while Maurer was the one to put up trial balloons, the hard line was held by Ceausescu and the real decisions made by him. Both men had grown up, struggled, survived and hacked their way to the top in a closed, dark system that was one of the most repressive ever devised by man. Leadership in this society demanded a combination of duplicity, ruthlessness, and amorality of almost inhuman proportions. Their backgrounds were essentially working class and parochial, and much of their formative years had been spent either underground or in prison, or else as refugee revolutionaries under training in Moscow. Both Ceausescu and Maurer were working within limited parameters of ideas, but for objectives that were fully focused and immune to compromise.

Ayub Khan's background and mental outlook were of an entirely different nature. Born and brought up in a conservative, rural, oriental society, his values were essentially humane, and emanated from centuries of religious belief and custom. To this was added a dash of colonial tradition derived from Sandhurst, and a fundamental devotion to the service of God and country. By no means a highly intellectual man, Ayub Khan nevertheless possessed a liberal mind that was always receptive to new ideas and suggestions. He also possessed a native peasant shrewdness that guided so many of his practical measures and decisions. It was fascinating to observe, in Bucharest, the reaction between Ayub and Ceausescu, two men of such widely differing aspects and backgrounds, whose only common element was the possession and exercise of power. There was no real tussle between the two, since there were no contentious issues to discuss, but because of the differences in their personalities there was no empathy between them either. The result of their interaction was, I thought, essentially a standoff, with perhaps a touch of mutual, distant respect.

There were, of course, a number of high level and state visits by foreign dignitaries to Romania during my tenure in Bucharest, but apart from the visit of Ayub Khan the two that stand out most in my mind were those of the French President De Gaulle from the 14 to 18 May 1968, and by the US President Richard Nixon from the 2 to 3 August 1969.

In terms of popular acclaim, General De Gaulle received a tremendously positive reception, unsurpassed in the recent history of Romania. Throughout the duration of his stay, at all hours of the day and night, and along all the routes of his journey, whether in Bucharest or the provinces, De Gaulle was received with a welcome which was both genuine and enthusiastic. In turn, the president of France responded with the charisma that only he possessed in such masterful measure, and the result was an impressive amalgam of rolling oratorical cadences and a responsive popular acclaim. The latter part of the visit proceeded under the ominous cloud of the student uprisings in France, but in his public appearances, as well as his private talks, De Gaulle gave not the slightest indication of any of the preoccupations that he may have felt over the violent events in Paris. De Gaulle's visit went far beyond its lavish ceremonial aspect and carried two important political themes—the necessity for the creation of a European Europe, and for peaceful co-existence on the European continent. Much to the delight of Ceausescu and his comrades, De Gaulle said, 'You consider, just as we do, that this cold war which followed the division at Yalta can result only in an artificial and sterile division that, if not destructive, in the end is contrary to the very spirit of Europe.' In his speech to the Grand National Assembly, the French president emphasized the necessity for Europeans to be masters of their own destiny, adding that, 'Such an ample change in the actual conditions excludes any kind of foreign domination over the peoples of our continent. Yes, together let us give the example for unity on our continent.' Some substance was added to this rhetoric, and quite useful agreements were signed between the French and the Romanians.

During the reception hosted by the French ambassador, De Gaulle sought me out and had a brief conversation in which he enquired about the health of President Ayub, and expressed his appreciation of the recent meetings between him and the Prime Minister Aleksei Kosygin of the USSR. He urged the continuation of these contacts with a slightly Delphic observation, 'I agree; it is well balanced'. All the time that I was talking to De Gaulle about the Soviet–Pakistan relations, my mind kept harking to the ongoing news about riots and blazing fires in the streets of Paris and other French cities. Yet, I was convinced that the president was giving me his fullest attention and was entirely focused on the issue. I have frequently thought about this incident and my brief personal association with De Gaulle. It seems that I had just seen what leadership is all about, and that for a fleeting moment I was in the presence of greatness in all its grandeur.

President Richard Nixon's visit to Bucharest was short in terms of time, but obviously very substantive in terms of its political implications. The American president, who was no slouch when it came to accentuating the dramatic, seized the moment and commenced his speech on arrival at Bucharest's new Otopeni airport by declaring that 'This is an historic occasion, the very first visit by a President of the United States of America to Romania, the first state visit by an American president to a socialist country'. This also emphasized the immediate significance of the visit that it took place at all, that Ceausescu had invited Nixon and, in response, Nixon came. To that extent Romania had demonstrated her independent foreign policy and her avowed desire for friendship with all countries. One immediate consequence of Nixon's presence in Bucharest was the postponement of a visit by Brezhnev and Kosygin, but the Romanians took comfort from the fact that although Brezhnev did not come to Bucharest, he did not threaten to send his tanks either. Also the Soviet press had been, under the circumstances, reasonably restrained in its criticism of the Romanians.

The preparations for Nixon's visit to Bucharest included all the usual security precautions and also some unexpected ones, including the removal of all foreign students (Vietnamese, Korean, Algerian, etc.), from the capital. They were put into buses and sent on a compulsory tour of the distant provinces of Romania. Although the ovation received by Nixon was not as great as that accorded to De Gaulle, there was little doubt about the enthusiasm with which the ordinary Romanian regarded the presence of the American president in Bucharest. For the Romanian leadership, which was itself particularly and deliberately circumspect in its expression of warmth towards its visitors, the problem was not that of arousing the enthusiasm of its citizens but of controlling it. It was an open secret that the apparatchik cheerleaders in the crowds had been instructed to maintain vocal discipline, and the consistently controlled demonstrations which we saw during the two days of Nixon's stay in Bucharest, left an indelible impression on my mind of the efficiency and effectiveness of the disciplinary arm of the Romanian Communist Party machinery. It was only on the occasions when Nixon, in the manner of the expert politician, broke free of his escorts and rushed to mingle with the crowds, that their true enthusiasm manifested itself. And Nixon, who obviously knew what was going on, undertook this public relations exercise as often as he could.

The accolades accorded to Nixon were an expression of the approbation and desire of the Romanian people for the material affluence of the West. On this occasion, Nixon, basking in the superb technological success of the Apollo 11 mission, which had resulted in man's first walk on the moon, and which the Romanians had followed live on TV, had arrived in Bucharest at an incredibly opportune moment, and to the mass of Romanians he came as a political and economic Santa Claus. One Romanian worker to whom I spoke about the visit was quite confident that because of Nixon's visit to Bucharest, the Russians would not dare invade Romania. But at the same time the Romanian leadership continued to assert its impeccably orthodox communist policy, thus avoiding the fundamental schism with the Soviets, which Alexander Dubçek had perpetrated with his internal liberalization in Czechoslovakia, eighteen months earlier. Ceausescu had thus put Washington and Moscow on notice that he intended to maintain rigid communist orthodoxy at home, and hoped that the message got through to Moscow, for therein lay the security for Nicolae Ceausescu. Soviet–Romanian relations, conditioned as they were by history, geography, and not an inconsiderable element of temperamental difference, had always been somewhat tenuous, and Nixon's visit added to the mix in no uncertain fashion. A clandestine joke, heard in Bucharest at the time, concerned the appearance of a classified advertisement in a newspaper which stated: 'Advertiser wishes to exchange an excellent foreign policy for a better geographic location. Interested parties may please contact N. Ceausescu, Bucharest.'

One final note on the Nixon visit. The formal dinners were restricted to the two delegations, but there was a post-dinner reception to which heads of diplomatic missions and important Romanian officials were invited, and during the course of which both presidents circulated among the guests. It was on this occasion that both Nixon and Kissinger sought out Diana and myself, and engaged us in a very warm and friendly conversation. They had just flown in directly from Lahore, and it was clear that they were still in the glow of the goodwill generated by the hospitality accorded to them in Pakistan. Nixon took my hand in both his hands and said that he had had a 'very interesting and most useful talk with President Yahya, who is a very impressive person indeed. I am sure it will mean a lot to both countries. It has been most valuable.' Although I recall being pleasantly surprised at the effusive warmth expressed by both Nixon and Kissinger, I could never have imagined the reason. I was later to discover that it was at the Lahore meeting, in early August 1969, that Nixon and Yahya Khan had first discussed the epic idea of an opening to China through the good offices of Pakistan. It was a strategic initiative that would change the course of history, realign the geopolitical triumvirate of the superpowers, and create consequences, both intended and unintended, such as the destruction of Pakistan as we knew it, and the creation of Bangladesh.

Apart from the meetings during the visit of Ayub Khan, my meetings with the top Romanian leaders were very limited, and were confined to public ceremonial occasions. The one time that we saw and met them under comparatively informal conditions was the annual hunt, which was attended by the Romanian leaders and the ambassadors in Bucharest. These were lavish affairs, organized in an elaborate fashion with the full resources of a totalitarian state. Hunting equipment was provided, as well as jeeps and other forms of transport to carry the guests to the forest and fields. These had been well-stocked with birds and animals, reserved for slaughter on the occasion. Sumptuous meals, supplemented by the finest wines, were served in huge heated tents, and the dinners went on almost all night with singers and dancers merrily mingling with the guests. I had read accounts of shooting parties arranged in India by the viceroys and the maharajas during the colonial days, but none of those would have matched the elaborate and wasteful extravagance that went into the hunting parties laid on for the Communist Politburo in Eastern Europe. On these occasions it was possible to get a glimpse of the likes and dislikes of the top leaders inter se as they mingled with us and amongst themselves in varying degrees of inebriation, manoeuvring and manipulating, flattering and cajoling, and playing power games, with the usual blend of assertion and submission. It was as distasteful an experience as the unsporting destruction of wildlife that we had seen earlier in the day.

It was already clear by this time that the only two who counted amongst the Romanian leadership were Ceausescu and Maurer, in that order, and that the regime was embarked upon a course of vigorous internal repression. Hard line communist dogma was applied with increasing ruthlessness, principally organized and implemented by Elena Ceausescu, the president's wife, who surely and methodically established herself in leading positions, not only in the shadowy party hierarchy, but also in public life. Circumstances fortunately precluded me from having anything but the most formal contacts with this odious woman. There were, however, occasions when I was able to observe more of her husband and his manner of work. Nicolae Ceausescu was a small man with a thick shock of hair, and a face that frequently carried a smirk but almost never showed a smile. In my infrequent meetings with him, I was never able to look him in the eye; a soft, cold handshake was inevitably accompanied by a lowering of the eyes and the turning away of his head. Yet, despite the evasive nature of these gestures and mannerisms, his presence exuded a sense of power, reminiscent of a coiled snake, and a chilly, aura that discouraged any attempt at familiarity. I was left in no doubt that Ceausescu was a ruthless and effective operator, who had ascended to the top of a system in which determination, political savvy, and cold-blooded efficiency were sine qua non, and cruelty an added asset. In my meetings with him I found him to be a man of few words, thoroughly in command of his subject and his brief, cold though not unfriendly in manner, and exuding authority in the sinister fashion of a mafia godfather. This impression was embellished by the expressions of terrified sycophancy on the visages of the few aides who accompanied him.

During my tenure in Bucharest I saw with alarm, and fascination as well, the daily progress of the ruthless manner in which Ceausescu increased repression and terror within the country. At the same time he kept advancing his image as a brave, liberal leader determined to establish Romania's independence in the international arena, a concept to which the visits of De Gaulle and Nixon added credence. Nicolae and Elena Ceausescu kept this political duality going for almost twenty years after my departure, but in due course their foreign policy initiatives ran out of steam, whilst their internal repression and personal arbitrariness increased to intolerable proportions. The result was that, with the end of communism in Europe, the Ceausescus were the only leaders whose removal from office was accompanied by a sordid execution, carried out by a bunch of hate-filled partisans.

CHAPTER SIX

Bulgaria

Budgetary constraints prevented me from visiting Bulgaria as often and for as long as I would have wished, but by the end of my tenure we did manage to cobble together a trade agreement. This was not an easy task, considering that the obvious paucity of products and items that could suitably comprise a trade agreement was compounded by the difference in socio-economic systems. But a generous resort to barter proved very helpful, and more importantly, there was a genuine desire for achievement on both sides. Compromises were readily offered and accepted, so that conclusions were both possible and pleasant.

Like its neighbour Romania, Bulgaria possessed a natural beauty that was enhanced by the numerous monasteries and castles scattered all over the country, and by the white sands on the Black Sea coast. But the contrast in the political climate between Bucharest and Sofia could not have been more striking, notwithstanding the ideological bond of communism that provided the titular link to their systems. Bulgaria was firmly and fervently planted in the Moscow camp, and basked in a relationship that had been forged by both ethnic and historical bonds. During my travels all over Eastern Europe in the period of Soviet domination, I found that Bulgaria was the only country where the Soviet Union and the Russians were universally and genuinely popular. The Bulgarian monarch, King Boris, though his country was under Nazi occupation in the Second World War, had consistently resisted Hitler's pressure to join in the German attack on the Soviet Union, maintaining that no Bulgarian government could survive if it declared war on Russia. Soviet Marshal Fedor Tolbukhin, whose reputation in Warsaw was that of a ferocious oppressor, was revered in Bulgaria as a great liberator, and even had a city named after him. Within the bounds of the restrictions imposed by a communist society, the Bulgarians appeared to be a comparatively free people, and the sharp contrast of this relaxed attitude became evident from the moment one crossed the border into Bulgaria from the grim and sullen Romania. It was also significant that border-control procedures between Romania and Bulgaria, both Warsaw Pact allies, were far more stringent than those between Bulgaria and Turkey, who were Warsaw Pact–NATO rivals.

My first visit to Bulgaria took place in early December 1967, and lasted a productive and event-packed week. Apart from the presentation of credentials to President Georgi Traikov and its attendant ceremonies, I had substantive meetings with Ivan Basev, the dynamic Foreign Minister, and with Todor Jivkov, the Prime Minister and Secretary-General of the Communist Party of Bulgaria, and, therefore, the most important political personality in the country. At these meetings there was the usual presentation and elaboration of the elements of the respective foreign policies of Bulgaria and Pakistan, and then we got down to substantive issues, such as trying to utilize the obvious goodwill that existed between the two countries. This was necessary in order to overcome the formidable practical obstacles posed by the realities of distance and differing socio-economic systems. It was satisfying to recollect that our early efforts on that first occasion eventually led to the conclusion of a trade agreement. In our political discussions the Bulgarians displayed a great deal of interest in the Regional Co-operation Development (RCD), the pact which had just been established between Turkey, Iran, and Pakistan. Todor Jivkov told me that since Bulgaria was at that time actively engaged in improving relations with Turkey, the RCD was of particular interest.

Todor Jivkov struck me as being a classical example of the 'Communist Party leader', and one whose adherence to Moscow was absolute, based upon a combination of ideological orthodoxy and ethnic affinity. In his late middle age, he possessed a firm and decisive personality, backed by a confidence derived from his willing association with the USSR. He had the reputation of being an able administrator, and possessed an impressively detailed knowledge of the economic situation, not only in Bulgaria but in the Balkans in general. I had the feeling that some of his outbursts and tirades during our discussion were more calculated than emotional, and that in reality he was a reasonable statesman. For example, he was quite annoyed that some Arab students, who were being sheltered and educated in Sofia, had recently gone on a rampage and attacked the US embassy, causing some embarrassment to the Bulgarian government and considerable damage to its exchequer by way of compensation costs. 'Our Arab guests should show their bravery against the Israeli army and not attack peaceful residences in Sofia,' Tudor Jivkov groused, with some justification. He then went on to reiterate his earlier suggestion that I travel freely in the country and meet and talk to anyone that I pleased, giving me the impression that Pakistan was being warmly welcomed into a humble household. As I left the prime minister's office, the interpreter, who had been present and now accompanied me outside, apologized for any inadequacies in the execution of his duties, and pointed out that he was not a professional interpreter but was in fact a director on the Asia desk in the Foreign Ministry. We then had quite a lengthy conversation in Urdu, which he had learned at Moscow University on a two-year course, having spent the three previous years studying Hindi. His conversation was, therefore, a peculiar and amusing mixture of stilted, academic Urdu and Hindi. I recollect thinking at the time that this was a vivid illustration of the thoroughness of communist procedures in some fields. And yet, in the hotel where I stayed it was necessary to change rooms three times before I could find one in which heating, lighting, and plumbing were simultaneously operational.

In May 1968 I made another visit to Bulgaria, driving around the country and savouring the pleasant spring atmosphere, particularly as we went through the famous Valley of Roses. Here the scent of the flowers, delectable when one first enters the valley, becomes almost overpowering at the end of the fifty-kilometre drive. We were also able to visit the opera house in Sofia, a building of some architectural interest as it is a replica of the Wiener Staatsoper, for some concerts and an opera performed by excellent musicians. A short trip to the south of the country took us to the border with Greece, and enabled us to spend some time, en route, at the beautiful Rila Monastery. On the business side there were the usual meetings with officials, including two interesting sessions with Foreign Minister Ivan Basev, during which we reviewed the progress of our trade agreement, and I was able to get a slight insight into the schisms that were becoming visible in international communism. China continued to be the main bugbear, and provoked more Bulgarian venom than the American imperialists in Vietnam.

In early November 1969 I paid my farewell visit to Bulgaria, and was treated with considerable warmth and courtesy. I had long and substantive meetings with all the senior members of government, including Todor Jivkov, and our discussions covered everything from international affairs, notably Vietnam and the Middle East, and the Moscow Conference of Socialist States, where acrimony with China and Albania, had considerably intensified. More importantly, we discussed the recent events in Pakistan which had brought to an end the Ayub era, and the imposition of martial law by Yahya Khan. Foreign Minister Basev told me, somewhat reassuringly, 'We are not against military regimes, so long as they are not right wing'. We reviewed the progress of our bilateral relations during the two years of my tenure, and I was informed that in recognition of my personal efforts the Bulgarian government had decided to award me a high decoration, the Madarski Konnik. The conferring of this award apparently required a 'Ukase' or resolution from the Bulgarian parliament, which had already been secured. However, my formal acceptance had to await the concurrence of my government, which, following the usual bureaucratic red tape, duly arrived.

This was, indeed, a satisfactory conclusion to an assignment that I had rather enjoyed.

CHIAROSCURO

During a brief moment of relaxation while on his state visit to Romania, President Ayub and I took a stroll in the beautiful gardens of the official guest house on Sos Kiseleff in Bucharest, where the president and his entourage were lodged. Ayub was relaxed and in a reminiscent mood, exuding a grace and charm as only he could. He told me that two weeks earlier he had attended a dinner in his honour, given by the Parsi community in Karachi on the occasion of the Prophet Zarathustra's birthday. In his after-dinner speech the president of the Parsi community or Anjuman, had made three requests of the government on behalf of the community. The first was that citizenship be facilitated for Parsi girls from India who married Parsi boys in Pakistan. Ayub said he thought that reasonable. The second was that licenses should be readily issued for the import of sandalwood used for religious ceremonies in the Parsi fire temples. Ayub thought that too was a legitimate request. The third request was that, in view of a shortage of Parsi priests in Pakistan, the government should facilitate the issuing of visas for priests from India. Ayub, his eyes smiling with mischief, gave a deep chuckle and said to me, 'I said to myself, *O bevakufon!* You don't know how lucky you are! *Hum in salon ko door rakhne chahtey or toom oonko laney chahtey!'* (Oh idiots! You don't know how lucky you are! Here we are trying to keep these blighters away, and you want to bring them in!).

* * *

The presence of representatives from countries with differing political systems added sparkle to the daily diplomatic routine in Bucharest, especially as the Cold War and the Sino–Soviet confrontation were both particularly intense at that time. The representative from Spain was a senior ambassador but was designated as the trade representative, since Romania had not gone to the extent of a full diplomatic recognition of the Franco regime in Madrid. Upon arrival in Bucharest, the shrewd and able Ambassador Ricardo Arrau informed the Cuban ambassador, who was the doyen of the diplomatic corps, of his desire to establish personal relations with the ambassadors of all the socialist countries resident in Bucharest. However, since he did not wish to be rebuffed, he asked the doyen to ascertain, from his socialist colleagues, their reaction to this suggestion. In due course the doyen informed Ambassador Arrau that all except one of the ambassadors from socialist countries would be happy to maintain personal relations with him. The exception was Ambassador József Vince of Hungary who, since he had fought in the Spanish civil war as a member of the famous international brigade, would have nothing to do with a representative of the Franco regime. The two envoys accordingly kept their distance, in civilized fashion, until several months later, when they found themselves together in the same group of about eight ambassadors at a reception given in my embassy. Someone in the group complimented the Hungarian ambassador on his fluent Spanish, to which Ambassador Vince, responding darkly, said he had learned it in a hard school, and mentioned a particularly bloody engagement in the Spanish civil war.

Ricardo Arrau could not resist entering the discussion and said that he too had fought in that battle, and could never understand why the government forces had not mounted an offensive the very next morning. Vince replied by explaining their difficulties and from that moment onwards the two ambassadors broke away from the group, went to a quiet alcove in my reception room, and relived the whole Spanish civil war. Thirty-five years after they had been shooting at each other from the trenches in war-torn Spain, destiny, in a strange fashion, had reunited these two civilized and dedicated men, in Bucharest, Romania, and they were able to experience an exchange of past memories over a glass of wine. And on Pakistani soil, at that.

* * *

'How can a man, who has a walnut tree die unhappy?'
Romanian proverb

MEANWHILE IN PAKISTAN

My stay in the Balkans coincided with the early phases of a political convulsion that led inexorably to the destruction of the Pakistan that we had got to know and love so much. The years of the Ayub regime were brought to an inglorious and a messy end. The violence that erupted all over the country compelled Ayub to hand over power to the army chief, General Yahya Khan. As had happened once before in 1958, the imposition of martial law by Yahya Khan was, if not welcomed, certainly greeted with a sense of relief by the people of Pakistan, largely because it brought to an end the civil strife, strikes, and general turbulence that had prevailed all over the country. On a personal note, I felt that the change in government obliged me to tender my resignation, and I did so accordingly. But I was instructed to remain in service and to return home for a briefing prior to transfer to my next post, Moscow.

The Pakistan to which I returned was a country in a state of political turmoil. The feeling of comfortable stability that had existed over the previous decade had almost completely disappeared, and had been replaced by a mounting political agitation, skilfully orchestrated by Mujibur Rehman and his Awami League Party in East Pakistan, and by Zulfikar Ali Bhutto and his newly-established Pakistan People's Party in West Pakistan. The once invincible Ayub Khan now appeared to be floundering in an atmosphere of indecision, offering and making compromises that took him nowhere, and abandoned by his 'basic democrat' straw men, who were fleeing in droves. Above all, Ayub was by now suffering from a heart ailment that severely limited his activity and considerably damaged his political image. Unable to handle the agitation in the streets and powerless to control the countrywide demonstrations, protests and strikes that accompanied it, and which were beginning to cripple the economy, Ayub Khan handed over power to General Yahya Khan. It was a sad and inglorious end to what, in retrospect, was for a brief period as close to being a halcyon era as Pakistan has ever known.

Yahya Khan immediately took measures to stabilize the situation, and in the initial phase met with some success. He entered into a dialogue with all the political leaders and parties, gave assurances about general elections and a return to civilian rule, and dismantled the province of West Pakistan, the controversial 'One Unit', into its composite provinces of Punjab, Sindh, Balochistan, and the North West Frontier, thus restoring a sense of relief, and perhaps even goodwill, amongst politicians all over the country. There was also a shake up in the bureaucracy, and many stalwarts of the Ayub Khan era were either retired or replaced in the 'de-Stalinization' process that inevitably follows any major change in top leadership. But the calm that ensued from Yahya's early initiatives proved to be both deceptive and short-lived. Bhutto and Mujib had by now sensed that political power was not a distant dream, but a distinct and imminent possibility, and they each worked on improving their respective power bases in spectacular fashion. The Yahya government, composed of well meaning but un-enterprising senior politicians, retired army officers, and civilian bureaucrats, was rightly viewed as an interim phenomenon. It may be said to Yahya's credit that he left the civil administration largely to the civil service, without imposing an undue military component onto the functioning civilian bureaucracy. The result was that whilst the government fumbled its way through, the major political parties built up their resources and began to achieve substantial recognition amongst the population.

Much has been said and written about the fall of Ayub and the end of his era. This could perhaps be attributed to four main factors. The first was the failure in Pakistan to create, operate, and abide by the institutions of a modern democracy—a constitution, the rule of law, the independence of the judiciary and the media, and the acceptance of a change of government through the ballot box, following a free and fair election. Sadly, this major deficiency persists to this day. The second was the time factor. Without the facility of an institution for peaceful and credible change, eight to ten years is about the limit for the incumbency of a regime to exist in Pakistan, no matter how benign or beneficial. Our subsequent history (Bhutto, Ziaul Haq, and Musharraf) appears to reflect this time frame. In this connection, one is reminded of Voltaire's typically mischievous comment: 'The best form of government is a benevolent despotism, tempered by the occasional assassination'. The third element was Ayub's serious heart ailment, which gave public emphasis to his failing grip on events. The fourth element which, if not the most important, was certainly the one that precipitated the end, was the disastrous 1965 war with India and the Tashkent Agreement that followed.

I had very few personal discussions with Ayub, but at one of these he made an observation that left me with an indelible impression. He said, 'Kashmir is important to me, but not as important as Pakistan'. Considering the statesmanship of this policy, and its eminently realistic nature, I wondered how the hawks in Ayub's administration had managed to manipulate him into the ill-fated venture of 'Operation Gibraltar'. Years later, I discussed this issue with my good friend Altaf Gauhar, who had become one of Ayub's closest confidants. Altaf said that he had once put the same question to Ayub, and had received the cryptic response: 'My mistake was that I did not carry out a counter-syndicate'. This was Army Staff College terminology for exercises in which one syndicate plans an operation and a counter-syndicate subjects it to critical review. With the hindsight of many years, and after reading all that I could on the subject and speaking to many of those involved in these dramatic events, I have arrived at an assessment that remains, of course, subject to the stern verdict of history. Its origin is in the Rann of Cutch in 1964, where there was a border dispute between India and Pakistan over territory in the un-demarcated salt land marshes and creeks of the Indus delta.

This sparked off a small-scale military operation which was followed by a ceasefire, which in turn was followed by a mutually agreed international arbitration process to be held in Geneva. Using this as a precedent, the hawks in the Pakistan establishment, including Bhutto, Aziz Ahmed, General Akhtar Malik and some others, prepared a similar model for use in Kashmir. The objectives were to provoke an uprising in the territory, start a sharp but short conflict, and drag the Indians to the negotiating table thus breaking their intransigency on the issue. Once the operation began, it took a course of its own, as so often happens, and further blunders—military, political and diplomatic—were committed and compounded. This included the incredible assumption that an incursion across the ceasefire line in Kashmir would not provoke the Indians into crossing the international border in Punjab. And the rest, of course, is history.

My stay in Pakistan consisted of a series of intensive meetings, briefings and consultations. Firstly, there were the meetings in the Ministry of Foreign Affairs, where I had to familiarize myself with the dossier on the USSR, a formidable task in itself. The immediate issue, I gathered, was that of the steel mill, negotiations for which had broken down, largely because we had told the Soviets that we could get a better deal from the West. This was a tactless observation that predictably infuriated the Russians, who threw out our delegation and sent them home. It appeared that subsequently things had not gone so well with a Western consortium, and we now wished to restart negotiations with Moscow. Since the Soviets were well aware of what had happened, I reckoned that my situation, as a negotiator, was a trifle delicate to say the least. The background scenario, in terms of our relations, was however a very interesting one. The historic Indo–Soviet friendship, coupled with our equally long but less rigid alliance with Washington, were factors that clearly militated against us to a considerable degree. Add to this our firm friendship with China, at a time when the Sino–Soviet dispute was at its height, and we had a situation where an incoming Pakistani ambassador could, with some justification, feel himself entering uninvited into the lion's den. Yet the Soviets were not unaware of the recent policy initiatives taken by the Ayub administration to achieve some balance in our international posture, and had shown signs of a positive response. Apart from the Tashkent Agreement, to which Kosygin had attached much importance, there had been the recent highly successful visit of President Ayub Khan, during the course of which there had been encouraging talks about the supply of Soviet tanks for the Pakistan army. It seemed to me, therefore, that there was scope for some interesting diplomatic activity.

My other obligations in Pakistan included familiarizing myself with the new administrative set up, following the assumption of power by General Yahya Khan. The competent and extremely able S.M. Yusuf was now the foreign secretary, and handled the portfolio with a smooth efficiency that evoked the admiration of all those fortunate to have any dealings with him, either professionally or personally. A series of meetings with him, together with Tabarak Hussain, the cool and knowledgeable Director General for Eastern Europe, provided me with both background and instructions for my Moscow assignment. I also followed the routine requirement of calls on the governors of the provinces and some federal ministers, and the drill ended with a courtesy call on the President. I had first met Yahya Khan in Quetta in August 1947, when he was a major, and also the senior Muslim officer in the garrison at that time. We celebrated the independence of Pakistan at a tremendous party held at the Quetta Club, and Yahya made a speech entirely appropriate to the occasion. Since then, our contacts had been infrequent but always very pleasant, and so the meeting in the autumn of 1969, was the first time that I was able to have a substantial interaction with Yahya Khan. I immediately discerned that behind the bluff and hearty manner, coupled with an earthy soldierly bearing, there was an intelligent and highly perceptive mind. He gave a sober account of the situation in the country and had no illusions about the difficulties that confronted him. He gave me no specific instructions with regard to my forthcoming assignment, but said that he intended to visit Moscow as soon as he could. 'They were the first to give me an official invitation after I became President, and I intend to avail of it as soon as possible.' This seemed to me to be as good a reason as any, quite apart from the importance of the USSR itself.

Yahya Khan was in the first flush of his popularity at that time. He was being courted by all the politicians and political parties, and also had a large measure of popular support. It is a curious but noticeable phenomenon in the political process in Pakistan that martial law has always been welcomed at the time of its imposition, essentially because it restores law and order following a disruptive phase of political agitation. But the welcome is short-lived and the urge for the restoration of democracy soon manifests itself. I left Pakistan for Bucharest at a time when the Yahya Khan political honeymoon had just commenced, and the prevailing mood was one of cautious optimism. As events would soon show, this did not last too long.

PART III

USSR AND FINLAND

CHAPTER SEVEN

❦

USSR 1969

'The world is large. Russia is great. Death is inevitable.'
– The first sentences in a 19th century Russian primary school textbook.

'I cannot forecast to you the action of Russia. It is a riddle wrapped in a mystery inside an enigma. But perhaps there is a key. That key is Russian national interest.'
— Winston Churchill, radio broadcast on 1 October 1939.

Following a few departure delays caused by the weather in Moscow, we flew out of Bucharest in an Aeroflot Ilyushin 18 turboprop on a cold, snow-swept November night. As Niloufer had returned for the Michaelmas term to Oxford, where she was happily ensconced, Diana, Feroza, and I were allotted the four seats around a table in the forward section of the aircraft. This configuration was standard first class accommodation in most Soviet passenger aircraft of that era. The fourth seat was occupied by Simeon, the delightful blue roan cocker spaniel that we had acquired in Bucharest. My friend and colleague, Soviet Ambassador A.V. Basov, had told Diana that if we flew to Moscow by Aeroflot, then 'Simeon will travel first class and will travel for free'. So here he was, long black ears flopping, and soulful eyes gazing at us appreciatively as we shared with him our Aeroflot dinner, minus the vodka. This was the first instalment of the affectionate VIP treatment that Simeon received for the duration of his stay in the Soviet Union, not only from our friends but also our Russian domestic staff, as well as the KGB (Komityet Gosudarstvyennoi Biezopasnosti, Committee for State Security) security guards stationed at our embassy, and also in the VIP room at Sheremetyevo airport where Simeon and I were frequent visitors.

I was touched that despite the late hour and freezing weather, the officers and staff of the embassy had turned up in full force to greet our arrival. The previous missions in which I had served had been, quite rightly, sparsely staffed—two diplomatic officers, two Pak-based assistants, and limited local personnel. Moscow, of course, was different, and although we had a small staff compared to most others, it was satisfying that the Pakistan embassy was generally viewed as being lean and mean. The calibre of the officers I was fortunate to have in the Moscow embassy was absolutely first class. We had an adequate diplomatic section that included a minister, a counsellor, and two first secretaries, a military section headed by a brigadier, and a commercial section headed by a senior deputy secretary. I declined the somewhat persistent offers of an Information officer on the grounds that he could be much more useful in a country where control over the dissemination of news was less rigorous than in the Soviet Union. Furthermore, there was an excellent group of international journalists in Moscow, with whom we maintained constant contact and developed a mutually beneficial working relationship, and a great deal of friendly respect. These were men and women who were experts in their field, at the very top of their profession, and represented the leading print and electronic media of the world. We also had two junior Foreign Service officers who were borne on the books of the embassy, but went for language training to a grim institute at the University of Moscow, set up by the Soviet Foreign Ministry explicitly for foreigners. After graduating they were posted to the embassy which found much use for their newly-acquired skills. One of them told me much later, when he had acquired near-ambassador seniority, that 'Even now, when I go near that place I still get the creeps'. But for whatever reason, whether it was the harshness of the methods or the innate capability of the students, or a combination of the two, our Foreign Service managed to get some very fine Russian speakers.

The embassy was situated in the central part of Moscow, at Ulitsa Sadovaya-Kudrinskaya 17, and consisted of a splendid old Czarist era edifice, with a courtyard in the rear, at the end of which there had probably been the stables and servant quarters. These had been demolished and replaced by a dull contemporary utility structure, which had now become an office-cum-garage and was the official chancery, accommodating all the officers and staff in quarters that were as uninspiring as they were cramped. The residence, however, possessed a splendid interior, especially in the reception and the dining area of the ground floor. The property belonged to the Soviet government as did most other embassies. The Soviets were responsible for its maintenance, whilst the embassy paid the rent. We dealt with the ubiquitous UPEDEKA department of the Ministry of Foreign Affairs, which meant that we had probably the second-worst landlord in the world; the worst, in my view being the Ministry of Foreign Affairs in Islamabad. The popular legend prevalent in Moscow at that time was that these impressive residences had, during the Czarist era, belonged either to members of the Russian aristocracy or to rich merchants, and that some had been gifted by their wealthy owners to their mistresses. Sadovaya-Kudrinskaya 17 apparently fell into the latter category, but its farsighted recipient had turned it into an elegant tea room. The huge kitchen in the basement, equipped with a vast nineteenth century stove and oven, which we could never use, seemed proof of this. But a much more elegant testimony could be found in the enormous reception rooms, with beautiful malachite walls that extended thirty feet from the floor to the rococo plastered ceilings, the superb parquet floors and the elaborate oak banisters. Reportedly one of the regular visitors to this elegant establishment had been Feodor Chaliapin, one of the world's greatest basso singers, and sometimes when I gazed across the room, there was a little tingle in my spine at the thought of that superb voice booming off the high rafters. But then did Chaliapin really sing there, or only take tea?

Shortly after our arrival in Moscow, and even before I had presented my credentials, there was a visit by a high-level delegation from Pakistan, headed by the Foreign Secretary, S.M. Yusuf. Since Yahya Khan had not appointed a foreign minister, Yusuf was the de facto head of the ministry and was accorded ministerial protocol by the Soviets, a generous gesture that did not, however, put the slightest dent on the inherent modesty of their remarkable guest, who went through the visit with his intelligent comprehension and usual, modest, courtesy. Ayub Khan's earlier visit had initiated a favourable turn in Soviet–Pakistan relations, but the political turmoil in Pakistan associated with Ayub's departure had put a check on a promising momentum. This was particularly so since the Tashkent Agreement, on which the Soviets prided themselves and which had become an inflammatory issue in the hurly-burly of the newly emerging politics of Pakistan. Added to this was the perfunctory and abrupt manner in which Pakistan had unwisely broken off negotiations with the USSR over the acquisition of a steel mill, an action prompted by powerful domestic interests with ties to equally powerful suppliers in the USA and Western Europe.

At this point I digress from the chronological narrative to record the origins of the first, and the only one to date, steel mill in Pakistan, and do so because there has been a measure of distortion and turbulence in the function of this enterprise over the past quarter century. Serious negotiations for the project were commenced by Foreign Secretary S.M. Yusuf during his visit to Moscow in November 1969. Earlier negotiations with the Soviets had been suspended, as already stated, as a result of pressure from the Western countries. When talks with the latter proved unfruitful, the Government of Pakistan decided to reopen talks with Moscow.

As I read through the record of these proceedings, prior to my arrival in Moscow, it became quite clear that the Soviets were aware of our predicament, and in discussions with the foreign secretary and other officials of the ministry, we decided to adopt a strategy which would be realistic and dignified, devoid of both apology and bluster. Yusuf's calm and imperturbable temperament made him the ideal negotiator, and after our first few meetings with the Soviet officials there was noticeable progress. The tenor of our talks gradually moved from hostility to cordiality, whilst on substantive issues obduracy gave way to meaningful proposals. The bitter cold of a Moscow November, which had initially penetrated the conference room, now perceptively shifted from the chamber back to the snow-covered streets. Having restarted the negotiations for the steel mill and set them on course, Yusuf returned to Pakistan leaving us with his terse instructions to 'progress the case'. This was done over the following months, in both Pakistan and Moscow, by a series of specialized delegations comprising representatives from the ministries of finance, industries, and economic affairs, under the vigilant supervision of S.M. Yusuf back in Pakistan, who had by now been appointed as Chairman, Pakistan Steel Mills, with Sultan Khan replacing him as Foreign Secretary. Thanks to the former's effective initiatives, the framework of an agreement was in place by the time President Yahya Khan visited the Soviet Union in the summer of 1971.

Our negotiations took place exclusively with the Soviet State Committee for Foreign Economic Relations, whose chairman was S.A. Skatchkov. The State Committee was a powerful institution in the Soviet system which functioned as a ministry but possessed executive functions. The KGB was also a State Committee but in the case of the steel mill project, the Soviet State Committee undertook responsibilities for large-scale civilian projects like steel mills and power plants, and also for the supply of military equipment, such as tanks and aircraft. Our principal interlocutor was Vice Chairman V.A. Sergeev, an affable, able and skilful negotiator, who combined technical and administrative competence, with a frank and friendly disposition. Most of the Soviet apparatchiks that I dealt with tended to be dour and assertive, partly by training and partly by temperament. Vasily Sergeev was the delightful exception. Despite the long hours, days and nights that I spent negotiating with him, and despite the complicated issues that we were obliged to tackle, often under uncompromising pressure exerted by our respective governments, there were never any heated moments in the time that we spent together seated across the ubiquitous green and beige tables. There was always a smile on Vasily's face whenever one entered or left his office, no matter what may have happened in-between.

In January 1971 S.M. Yusuf signed the formal agreement on the steel mill, the document having followed the memorandum of understanding reached during the state visit of Yahya Khan to the USSR, the previous summer. The Soviet Union provided 180 million roubles (US$200 million) credit for the construction of a million tonne annual capacity steel mill, at Karachi, together with technical assistance and training facilities in Pakistan and the USSR. When we called on Kosygin after the signature ceremonies, the Soviet prime minister told Yusuf that facilities for expansion had already been incorporated in the Soviet blueprint and that Moscow would purchase any surplus production from the plant. My direct association with the steel mill project ended on this promising note. Subsequently a team of Soviet specialists visited Pakistan, and having selected a site north of Mauripur as the location for the steel mill, commenced preparations accordingly. However, when the PPP government assumed office in

1972 this location was rejected on environmental considerations strenuously expressed by J.A. Rahim, and further studies were carried out resulting in the choice of the present site at Pipri, forty kilometres east of Karachi. Kosygin correctly warned that the delay would have adverse consequences, particularly in terms of cost increases, but Rahim's objections prevailed, even though Bhutto had also joked with Rahim saying 'Why are you so worried? You will be dead by the time it is constructed!' Subsequent mismanagement only added to this initial reverse and the pristine promise of the viability and profitability of the project quickly faded. However, later measures have restored efficiency and improved the quality of output, and the project still retains its iconic status as the basic fulcrum of the nation's industrial growth.

To return to the narrative of the winter of 1969, our arrival in Moscow invoked a personal emotion which remains unforgettable. Our stays in Bucharest and Sofia had accustomed us to living conditions in communist societies, and we were, therefore, cushioned against the cultural shock that assails outsiders on their first exposure. But Moscow was different. What seized my impression, and I stress impression, was an unmistakable sense of pervasive and omnipresent power, and the indescribable manner in which it pervaded the senses. Perhaps it began with my first sight of the Kremlin, that dark repository of 'a riddle wrapped in a mystery inside an enigma', with its turrets, moats and great walls, encompassing and sheltering the vast 'marzipan' palaces and onion-domed churches in its courtyards. These beautiful domes, which radiated their defiance to the pale, winter afternoon sun, were reflected in a startling fashion by the colourful towers and domes of St. Basil's Church, that uniquely Russian edifice, situated just outside the Kremlin. From the few huge gates and drawbridges that punctured the grim Kremlin walls, there emerged at high speed the occasional black Zil or Chaika automobile, its curtains drawn and its barely discernible occupants wrapped in overcoats, scarves and shapkas. The apparatchiks were at work, ensuring that the latest writ of Moscow, as pronounced in the Kremlin, was expeditiously conveyed to the world at large. Indeed, as Soviet Foreign Minister Andre Gromyko had thundered at a session of the USSR Supreme Soviet in June 1968, 'The Soviet Union is a great power, situated on two continents, Europe and Asia, but the range of our country's international interests is not determined by its geographic position alone. The Soviet people do not plead with anybody to be allowed to have their say in the solution of any question involving the maintenance of international peace, concerning the freedom and independence of the peoples, and our country's extensive interests. This is our right, due to the Soviet Union's position as a great power. During any acute situation, however far it appears from our country, the Soviet Union's reaction is expected in all the capitals of the world.'

In the subsequent three years I was destined to visit the formidable and fascinating edifice of the Kremlin frequently, in all seasons and at all hours of the day and night. Sometimes it was to accompany important visiting delegations whilst on their guided tours of the magnificent Kremlin palaces and museums, with their display of priceless icons, paintings, and jewels, and the meticulous and reverentially preserved apartments where Vladimir Lenin spent his last years. On other occasions it was to go to the specially constructed great theatre where the superb Bolshoi Ballet staged its magnificent performances. Or less agreeably, to attend the equally meticulously staged celebratory gatherings of the Soviet leadership, to be subjected to the regulated format of socialist meetings, listening to an interminable list of achievements, and watching the expressionless faces of the ruthless men of the Soviet Politburo, whose combined years could easily carry them back to the Ice Age. But most memorable and impressive were the visits that I was privileged to make, either individually, or in small high-level delegations, to the power denizens of the Kremlin, Brezhnev and Kosygin, especially the latter. They sat in large rooms, modestly furnished with a desk and a bank of telephones where they did their work, and a large conference table, covered in the standard green cloth, for their occasional meetings. The only decorative objects in the room, if they could be called that, were the ubiquitous and regulation photographs of Karl Marx, Friedrich Engels, and Vladimir Lenin. During my tenure in Moscow these working meetings in the Kremlin, which were obviously always important and substantive, took place at all hours of the day and night, the more disagreeable ones being scheduled for shortly before midnight in a bitter Moscow winter, a tactic which, I suspected, was standard Soviet intimidation operation procedure.

I presented my credentials on 30 December 1969 to N. Yu. Shaumaskis, Deputy Chairman of the Presidium of the Supreme Soviet of the USSR, at an impressive ceremony in the Kremlin. Shaumaskis was from the Latvian Soviet Socialist Republic, and one of the Deputy Chairmen of the Presidium whose functions are largely ceremonial. Under the 'buggins turn' custom then prevalent, December had obviously been his duty month. He was assisted by M.P. Georgadze, a Georgian, who as Secretary of the Presidium was the hardy perennial for these occasions. The Foreign Ministry officials, headed by its sophisticated Deputy Foreign Minister, N.P. Firyubin, were in their full regalia uniforms. The exception was A.A. Fomin, the Head of the South Asia Department, who was in a business suit. The sartorial distinction was attributable to his seniority in the KGB, as I was to discover later.

The credentials ceremony was a very simple and dignified affair. There was no national anthem or guard of honour, but the brilliantly illuminated halls and corridors with their opulent furnishings from the Czarist era, coupled with the multiplicity of historical associations that inevitably assail the senses of any visitor to the Kremlin, provided a sufficiently impressive aspect. After the short speeches that accompanied the presentation of credentials, I was taken to yet another imposing salon for informal discussions with the deputy chairman, who was accompanied by Georgadze, Firyubin, and an interpreter. Dutifully complying with his protocol obligations, Shaumaskis commenced by talking about the cold weather in Moscow and the not as cold weather in Pakistan, so that I was obliged to gently redirect the conversation from meteorological matters to issues of more direct concern to my duties. As soon as I did so, Firyubin jumped in right on cue and took over the conversation, stating that relations between our two countries were 'moving in a positive direction', a common expression in the lexicon of Soviet diplomacy to indicate cautious optimism. During the official visit of President Ayub Khan to the Soviet Union the previous year there had indeed been a significant breakthrough, even to the extent of a very limited supply of Soviet arms to Pakistan, but this had ceased after Ayub Khan's departure from office. I told Firyubin that what had been a trickle had now completely dried up, and that a resumption on a modest scale would be seen as incontrovertible proof of Soviet–Pakistan friendship.

Firyubin responded by saying that the requirements of Vietnam had put a heavy strain on Soviet resources, and added that, in view of the Tashkent Agreement and the Soviet desire for peace in the subcontinent, 'providing you with military equipment might well be regarded as a negative consideration'. I responded by stating, somewhat dryly, that while their Vietnam obligation was perfectly understandable, the massive arms deliveries already effected to India made the current invocation of the 'Tashkent spirit' a trifle incongruous. Firyubin, being the true professional, refused to be provoked, and giving me a sly smile, took up the subject of the steel mill, and reiterated the promise of Soviet co-operation. There followed the usual homilies about the importance of peace with India and continuing our bilateral discussions. At the end of the ceremony my colleagues and I left the Kremlin in reasonably optimistic spirits, and in my report to the ministry I said that while goodwill for Pakistan existed in some measure, its manifestation and implementation would obviously be conditioned by, and be subject to, the priorities and vagaries of a Great Power.

I used to take my little cocker spaniel Simeon with me wherever I could. Apart from my office, this included trips to the airport whenever I went to see off or receive visitors. The security officers at the VIP room at Sheremetievo airport accordingly got to know Simeon well, and he became quite a favourite. On one occasion, after I had seen off a visitor and was leaving the VIP lounge with Simeon, a security officer who was obviously new on the job stopped me, and asked to see 'the import papers for the dog'. Before I could respond, two other security officers seated at a desk at the other end of the hall shouted out to their colleague, 'No! No! No! That is not a dog. That is Simeon!'

Some of my happiest memories of the Soviet Union emanate from the rich cultural life that exists for those fortunate enough to have access to it. Galleries like the Hermitage, the Tretyakov, and the Kremlin, to name only three, are so large and so rich that it was quite impossible to absorb their treasures during the period of my tenure. Much the same could be said about music, and I had no hesitation in pulling ambassador's rank and privilege in pursuit of these pleasures. Diana and I were regular visitors to the Bolshoi and spent many happy evenings at the superb performances of the opera and the ballet. With the help and encouragement of friends like A.A. Fomin, and the Soviet Minister for Culture (and Firyubin's wife) Ekaterina Furtseva, who knew our passion for music, we were privileged to make friends with a number of Soviet musicians, artists and composers. These included violinist David Oistrakh; cellist Slavo Rostropovich and his wife, the superb soprano, Galina Vishnevskaya; pianists Emil Gilels and Sviatoslav Richter; conductors Kyril Kondrashin and Gennady Rozhdestvensky; and the incomparable prima ballerina assoluta of the Bolshoi ballet, Maya Plisetskaya, and her composer-husband, Rodion Schedrin. A particular friend of ours was the Armenian composer Aram Khachaturian. Diana gave him the highly appropriate nickname of the White Rabbit, and at his request, I presented him with a set of tapes of Pakistani folk music which I especially obtained from Radio Pakistan. Shortly thereafter, Khachaturian met me at a reception, thanked me profusely with hugs and kisses, and rapturously exclaimed 'You have such a rich musical heritage! There is so much material there for every form of musical composition—symphonies, concertos, sonatas, oratorios! What is your Union of Writers, Artists and Musicians doing about this? They are so lucky!' I could only respond that we would be happy if he could use any of these themes in his own wonderful compositions.

One of the guests at our National Day reception, held in a hotel, was the General Officer Commanding of the Moscow Military District. An enormous man, almost seven feet tall, he came in full dress uniform, his barrel chest covered with medals and decorations. After the buffet dinner the senior guests and I adjourned to an adjoining salon for drinks and conversation. The General, however, decided to stay on in the dining room, taking station at the head of the table and attacking with gusto the plates of food and bottles of vodka that his aides had rapidly rearranged around him. Meanwhile, I delegated our very able Second Secretary, Riaz Khokhar, to act as the host, and ensure that the General's requirements were met. After a while Riaz returned to us looking like a defeated all-in wrestler, his impeccable suit crumpled, hair dishevelled, and a damp red face, with the Order of Lenin faintly imprinted on one cheek. It seems that the General's inebriation always triggered outbursts of lachrymose affection, which he bestowed upon Riaz in full measure. With loud and repeated sobs of 'Pakistan *Sovietski Soyuz Druzhba*' the General smothered Riaz in a series of bear hugs supplemented by a copious deluge of tears. And Riaz, who is a tall person, was just high enough to have his face squeezed against the General's chest to get the Order of Lenin imprinted on his cheek.

Apart from bread and milk, which were readily available, there was a perpetual shortage of food in Moscow, and the quality was always poor. Most embassies obtained weekly consignments of supplies from Helsinki, where a firm called Stockmann had established an efficient supply and delivery system. However, one exception was ice cream which was always available, and one brand in particular, 'Sever', which was deliciously rich. It was rumoured that when the Soviet Commissar for Trade Anastas Mikoyan visited Washington in the early 1930s for negotiations and the acquisition of patents relating to steel and power equipment he enjoyed the ice cream so much that he also added it to his package of acquired patents. This was the original 'Elsie, the Borden cow' recipe, loaded with calories and cholesterol, which the Americans had long since abandoned, but which the Russians continued to blissfully consume. Anastas Mikoyan had been the first member of the Soviet Politburo to have visited Pakistan, and although now in retirement he continued to maintain his interest in the region, and frequently sought me out at Kremlin receptions to talk about Pakistan. On one such occasion I moved to the subject of 'Sever' ice cream and sought his confirmation on the story. His deep, brown Armenian eyes twinkled, and with a crooked smile he said 'I, too, have heard that story.'

Our contacts with Soviet artists and writers had to be circumspect, as overexposure could cause them problems with the KGB. My association with Ilya Glazunov, a leading young painter, proved to be very agreeable, and we became good friends with him and his wife, who was a cousin of the distinguished British actor Peter Ustinov. Diana and I were frequent visitors to their studio, which was filled with icons, paintings and other beautiful Russian artefacts, and spent many happy hours in their company. Ilya had been in and out of favour with the authorities, spent some time in prison, and yet liberated on other occasions to travel abroad and paint portraits of the King of Sweden, Finnish President Urho Kaleva Kekkonen, and Indira Gandhi. He also painted my portrait, which is a prized personal souvenir, and the sessions spent sitting for him in his studio provided a welcome break in a particularly difficult and stressful period during my tenure.

My other association was with Alexei Rukhin, a large, untidy man with a red beard, who drank heavily, smoked constantly, and produced some astonishingly powerful modern work. A rebel by temperament and fearless in his opposition to the establishment, he was always at the receiving end in his constant battles with the KGB. Riaz Khokhar gave me a gift of one of Rukhin's paintings, bought on the pavement shortly before the KGB broke up the display. It is not a particularly remarkable work of art, but I cherish it essentially for the sentimental and tragic emotion that it invokes every time I look at it. Rukhin lived in a small and untidy dacha on the outskirts of Moscow. Riaz informed me that one night the KGB burned down the dacha, with Rukhin and all his paintings in it.

Soviet agnosticism was redeemed considerably, in my view, by the recognition and preservation of the artistic manifestations of the Russian orthodox church. Anatoly Vasilyevich Lunacharsky, the first Soviet Commissar for Cultural Affairs, later executed by the White Russians, had the sense to realize the historic and cultural value of the artistic decorations in the churches, and issued decrees prohibiting their desecration and ensuring their preservation. The result was that whereas most churches were closed down, and some turned into sobering up stations for drunks, the Russian orthodox church was permitted to practice, albeit under strict official control, and religious relics and artefacts were carefully preserved. One example of this manifestation was the annual Russian Easter Midnight Mass, which was celebrated at one of Moscow's few functioning churches. Not only did the orthodox priests conduct the service in full regalia and expressed it in the deepest religious devotion, but they were assisted in their rituals by a chorus from the Bolshoi. For me it was a night of extraordinary emotional incongruity. A large number of people would gather in bitter cold outside the church, and were prevented from entering it by groups of tough men, wearing red armbands on their overcoats. Selective in their approach, they allowed only the older people, mostly peasants from the countryside, to go into the church, and made quite sure that the many younger people were kept out. Diplomats and other foreigners were, of course, free from their attention and allowed in. Once inside, we foreigners were confined to the central part of the church, whilst the Russians were crowded into the four naves on the ground floor. The service was conducted by the impressive orthodox priests and the Bolshoi chorus from the first floor, and was a most moving experience, even to my agnostic temperament. Perhaps the most memorable moment was when the big Archbishop in his full regalia and his high mitre, moved to the centre of the enclave, swinging his huge bejewelled incense burner and proclaimed 'Christ has arisen' to the worshippers standing below him in each of the four naves, and each time the congregation, together with the Bolshoi chorus, would sing back his words 'He has arisen'. The Russians who crowded the church and participated in the service with such deep devotion, could have come out of any seventeenth century painting, as could the whole ceremony itself. But there was one disgraceful exception. Many of us foreigners, located in the centre of the church, came armed with cameras, tape recorders, microphones, and flash bulbs, which were used indiscriminately throughout the beautiful service. Some even had the disgusting temerity to thrust their cameras and recorders up to the faces of the Russians. They were met by the dignified bearing of the Russian devotees who looked up past the cameras to the glorious dome of the church and then, doubtless in their devotion, to God Himself. As we left the church we again encountered the men with the red arm bands, but this time I was far less intolerant of them, being convinced by then that their behaviour outside the church was far less reprehensible than that of the foreigners within.

Foreign Minister Andrei Gromyko's famous observation about the importance of the USSR in world affairs was no idle boast, and was reflected in the frequency and regularity of official visits, undertaken by the heads of state or governments from all over the world. These carefully orchestrated occasions were accorded the degree of ceremonial and protocol commensurate with the importance of the event or the degree of political importance that the Kremlin attached to the state the VIP represented. However, most state visits involved a reception given in honour of the visiting dignitary by the Ministry of Foreign Affairs at the House of Friendship, an ornate, 'marzipan' edifice of Czarist times, owned by the ministry, and used for its official receptions. The usual function was a midday event, at which the ambassadors were lined up and introduced to the guest of honour for a brief greeting and conversation. This was followed by a reception where we were served indifferent Russian champagne and superb Russian vodka and caviar.

One of these receptions was in honour of the Iraqi vice president, who at that time went by his full name of Saddam Hussain Tikriti. I did not know much about Iraqi politics, except that it had some fairly bloody undertones, but was told by my Arab colleagues that our distinguished visitor was the virtual ruler of Iraq, and that he was shooting his way up to total dictatorship. My meeting with Saddam was necessarily brief and almost monosyllabic. He spoke in Arabic, which his Soviet attendant translated into Russian, and I replied in very imperfect Russian hoping that the competent interpreter would convert it into intelligible Arabic. He extended his greetings to my president, government and the people, which I reciprocated, and congratulated him on the success of his visit to Moscow. I was struck by the powerful presence of the man, and the manner in which his sharp, piercing, dark brown eyes, never met mine, but darted from side to side. I felt that I was in the presence of a predator, on the constant lookout, either for a victim to pounce upon or an attacker to guard against. Despite the outward politesse, it was not an agreeable encounter, and I thought that I had earned the double vodka that I downed immediately thereafter.

The residence of the Tunisian ambassador, my good friend Mohammad Essafi, had at one time been the home of Lavrenti Beria, Stalin's bloodthirsty and sadistic Commissar for Internal Security and the Head of the KGB. It was an ornate, tiled and marble-floored, red building, of the Czarist days, with columns and high ceilings, and an elaborate, heated, indoor swimming pool. It also contained a deep basement which had been barred and bolted, and was not available to its current Tunisian occupants. Mohammad told me that the prohibited area of the basement contained cells where the barbaric Beria had incarcerated and tortured his chosen victims.

In autumn 1971 Mansur Ahmed joined the embassy as minister, on a transfer from Turkey. He and his lovely wife Safia brought with them a warm cordiality that suffused us all. Mansur was one of our ablest diplomats who went on to serve with distinction as our ambassador in Bangkok, Geneva, and Tokyo. Soft-spoken and low-key, Mansur is a highly intelligent man of great principle and courage, and his cool, perceptive presence was of immense strength to all of us in those difficult times. Two days after he arrived in Moscow and took over as deputy chief of Mission, I received a call informing me of a meeting with Firyubin in the Foreign Ministry at 9 p.m. The Soviets used to deliberately schedule nocturnal meetings when they wanted to be difficult, and after reflecting a little, I decided to take Mansur with me and throw him in at the deep end, as part of his initiation. As expected, the meeting was acrimonious and unpleasant. As we emerged from the Foreign Ministry building into the cold November's night air in Moscow, Mansur said to me, 'What a contrast from Ankara! There everyone greets us with a smile and a hug!'

On another similar occasion I was unable to take Mansur with me as the notice was short and he was at a dinner party. This time the meeting went on till about 11 p.m. and Mansur came over to the residence, in response to an anxious telephone call from Diana. 'Do not worry, *Begum Sahiba*', he reassured her, 'If it has taken so long then I am sure that everything will be OK. A declaration of war only takes two minutes.'

MEANWHILE IN PAKISTAN

Between my visit to Pakistan for consultations in the autumn of 1969 and the end of that year the political situation had undergone a considerable change, and was in the process of doing so on an almost continuous basis. As Shuja Nawaz has observed in his seminal book on the Pakistan army (*Crossed Swords*, Oxford University Press, 2008), 'Yahya's regime inherited a number of major unresolved issues from Ayub's eleven year rule. These included the growing disparity between East and West Pakistan.' The magnitude and consequences of this fundamental issue certainly dominated events during my tenure in Moscow. Much more significantly, of course, it led to the dismemberment of Pakistan.

A change in regime is inevitably followed by changes in policies, as well as the people who frame and implement them, and so it was after Yahya Khan's assumption of power. His declaration at the time he imposed the martial law was no different from that of his predecessor, or successors, for that matter, 'My sole aim in imposing martial law is to protect the life, liberty and property of the people, and put the administration back on the rails'. He then went on to take some very important political and administrative measures, the most significant being the dissolution of the 'One Unit' and the restoration of the four provinces of West Pakistan, an action that was applauded in both wings of the country. There was also the inevitable change of guard in the senior administration, and a number of senior officials were purged, including my friend, the redoubtable, Altaf Gauhar. Yahya's new team of close advisers was entirely from the armed forces. A close friend and colleague, General Hamid Khan, was promoted and made the Chief of Army Staff, and together with Admiral S.M. Ahsan, and Air Marshal Nur Khan, was named the Deputy Chief Martial Law Administrator (the latter two subsequently moved to other positions). Yahya's principal advisers however, were Lt.-Gen. S.G.M.M. Peerzada, who was nominated Principal Staff Officer, and Major General Ghulam Umer. Both these energetic officers took over the conduct of government; Yahya's laissez faire attitude being no impediment to their doing so. Peerzada was virtually the prime minister of the country.

Another very important early action taken by Yahya Khan, was the promulgation of the Legal Framework Order of 28 November 1969, which set the general elections for October 1970. This immediately set in motion a massive wave of political activity throughout the country, with the early vibrations of confrontational positions being discernible even to me, situated as I was in cold and distant Moscow in December 1969. Mujibur Rehman's 'Six Points' agenda had already gathered considerable support in East Pakistan, whilst Zulfikar Ali Bhutto's populist slogan of 'roti, kapra, makan' ('food, clothing, housing') found a tremendous response in West Pakistan. Both parties appeared to have already staked out maximalist positions, and the newly-found independence of the print and the electronic media helped them to propagate them on a scale and manner hitherto unknown in Pakistan.

These events were, of course, being closely followed in Moscow, and I was both intrigued and impressed by the depth of knowledge and understanding of these issues displayed by Fomin and his colleagues in the Soviet Foreign Ministry. They were extremely well-informed, and had closely monitored as well as clearly established their own effective links in Pakistan. Thus my meetings with Fomin in those days were not just briefing sessions, when I told him, or was instructed to tell him, about the evolving political situation at home. They almost always turned into exercises in political analysis, with my able interlocutor contributing his own information and insight to the issues. Those happy and stimulating intellectual encounters would change as time went on, sadly into realistic exercises in diplomacy, some of which would occasionally become acrimonious.

CHAPTER EIGHT

Finland

'(The desire) to have a real fatherland, to be a citizen of a State, and not a squatter in a rotten province governed by stupid asses and sly foxes.'
– Adolf Iwar Araisdo, early 19th century Finnish nationalist, and spokesman for freedom from Sweden.

In January 1970, Diana and I, proceeded to Finland for the presentation of credentials, travelling in a comfortable, well-heated, and well-furnished railway carriage, from Moscow to Helsinki. It was an overnight journey and the only inconvenience encountered was at the border, where the control procedures ensured that the train and all its occupants were given the most thorough and meticulous examination. Our diplomatic status was scrupulously respected by the Soviet border guards, and we were treated with the utmost courtesy on this, and every subsequent occasion. But for the other passengers we noted that it was a different matter. As we approached the Soviet–Finnish frontier we also observed a chilling sparseness of dwellings. An area of about fifty kilometres from the frontier on the Soviet side, had been cleared of its inhabitants, and only a few people, who had special permission and were under close scrutiny, were permitted to live in this veritable no man's land. Once we crossed the border into Finland however, we saw that the houses almost touched the border fences.

Helsinki was a refreshing and lively contrast to the grim surroundings of Moscow, for the several other diplomatic colleagues in the USSR, who had, like us, the good fortune, to possess concurrent accreditation to Finland. For those who did not, Helsinki still remained the easiest and most pleasant place for a short holiday. The freedom and affluent comfort that manifested itself upon arrival in Helsinki, after the grey and grinding reality of Moscow, was like spring after a dark, cold winter. The credentials ceremony was a simple one, but it did include the playing of national anthems on arrival at the gates of the Presidential Palace. In winter this involved precision in timing, because the honour guard and band had to remain inside the guardhouse until just before the arrival of the ambassador. Any exposure to the elements beyond a very limited time period would cause the instruments to freeze. Accordingly, the chef de protocol who accompanied me in the car from my hotel to the Presidency, remained in constant touch with the guardhouse by telephone, as cell phones did not exist at that time. In the event the timing was perfect, and Scandinavian efficiency ensured that everything went smoothly, including an impeccable rendering of the Pakistani national anthem.

President Urho Kekkonen, at the time that he received me, was already an established international leader, respected both in Moscow and Washington. In a noteworthy collaboration with his predecessor, President J.K. Paasikivi, he was the founder and executor of a brilliant and courageous cold war strategy, which came to be known as the 'Paasikivi–Kekkonen neutrality line'. The policy had its origin in the Paris Peace Treaty at the end of the Second World War, when five political commissions from allied countries were constituted in order to negotiate terms with the defeated powers. The commission that dealt with Finland consisted of the USSR, Byelorussia, UK, Canada, Australia, South Africa, pre-partition India, New Zealand, and Czechoslovakia. To the Finns it was clear that the only member of the political commission that would count was the USSR. The USA was not a member of the commission because it did not declare war on Finland, and was, therefore, not entitled to a seat on the commission negotiating the peace treaty. The prescient Finnish President, J.K. Paasikivi, therefore, sent specific instructions to the Finnish delegation at the peace talks in Paris to concentrate on, and maintain, the closest relations with the Soviet delegation, and that on no account should the Finnish delegation do anything that might cause the vigilant and mistrustful Soviet delegation to suspect that the Finns were plotting with the West against the USSR. The peace treaty, when concluded, imposed some harsh terms on Finland, which was forced, inter alia, to pay very heavy economic reparations, and to concede about 10 per cent of its territory to the USSR. But the Finns were spared an army of occupation, with all its implicit and manifest, burdensome, political and economic consequences. Moreover, the reparations that the Finns were forced to pay created an assured market in the USSR, which in turn helped to build Finland's important shipbuilding and light engineering industries. Kekkonen continued Paasikivi's policies in the post-war era, maintaining close links and pursuing confidence-building measures with Moscow, in both word and deed. He wisely and courageously eschewed substantial short-term gains by refusing all aid under the Marshall Plan, a decision which did much to advance the close personal relations that he was developing with the Soviet leadership. President Kekkonen told me that Finland must not only remain neutral, but she must be seen to remain neutral, and above all she must be able to convince Moscow of her desire as well as the ability to maintain this neutrality.

During my meeting with Kekkonen we discussed these issues in some detail. He was interested in knowing about Pakistan's relations with China and their impact on its relations with Washington. He was also intrigued by the recent announcement that a military ruler, Yahya Khan, was about to hold elections in Pakistan. I told Kekkonen what little I could about the fluid situation in Pakistan, and then we reverted to the subject of neutrality in international relations. Kekkonen was a big man, with a large, bald head, and piercing, blue eyes. His voice was a deep baritone, and he punctuated his frequent smiles with a loud laugh. Tremendously fit and mobile, he was reputed to be one of the foremost langlauf skiers in his country. Fluent in English, Russian, and German, as well as all the Scandinavian languages, Kekkonen was a most effective communicator. He told me that he made it a point to spend part of his summer, as well as winter vacations, with the Soviet leaders in different resorts in their vast country, and it was obvious that the personal relations that he had developed with them were unique, and quite beyond anything by any other non-communist leader. In 1969, when Sino–Soviet relations were at their worst, there was a story current that Brezhnev, Kosygin, and Nicolai Podgorny, had invited Kekkonen to a vacation in the Crimea (this much is true), and whilst there the Soviet hosts, burdened by their preoccupations over China, asked their guest for advice on 'how to co-exist peacefully with a powerful eastern neighbour'. When I mentioned this to Kekkonen all I got from him was a deep, throaty chuckle. Then turning serious, he said that at a time of political crisis it was very important to 'put oneself in Moscow and then see how things look from there'. Sound advice from the most accomplished of practitioners.

Relations between Finland and Pakistan had always been good, but geography posed obvious limitations on the scope for their further expansion. We had a lively honorary consul general in our office in Helsinki, and he used his business contacts to further trade. But success was limited to a modest sale of sports goods, frequently accompanied, I am afraid, by trade disputes over substandard supplies, and missed delivery deadlines. There was a small but very active Muslim community whom I enjoyed visiting in Helsinki. They were of Turkish origin, had been prosperous fur traders in the Kazan, and had emigrated to Finland after the Russian Revolution. They were now fully assimilated into Finnish society, practicing a number of professions and trades, notably in the carpet and fur businesses. On one of my visits they arranged a reception at which they provided a substantial donation for relief operations following the disastrous cyclone in East Pakistan. However, the main purpose of my visits to Finland was to benefit from the valuable advice and counsel of the Finnish officials on the course of events within the USSR, as well as its external relations. This was particularly relevant as Helsinki had just been designated as the venue for the important early Strategic Arms Limitation Talks (SALT) negotiations. There was a palpable feeling in that small northern capital that the immense dark cloud of a nuclear holocaust, which had suspended itself so ominously over the world for so long, might begin to lighten. In my extensive meetings in Helsinki with the president, the prime minister, the foreign minister, and other senior officials, the views expressed to me were always incisive and unbiased, and proved to be of immense value. They were also an essential part of the great gulps of oxygen that one absorbed upon arrival in Helsinki, far from the confines of Moscow.

CHAPTER NINE

USSR 1970

'Whenever your son is discontented in France, I have a simple remedy: tell him to go to Russia. The journey is beneficial for any foreigner, for whoever has properly experienced that country will be happy to live anywhere else.'

– Le Marquis de Custine

'Communists would like to be all the wicked things their opponents say they are. They would like to be subversive, unscrupulous and ruthless. In fact they are only unsuccessful.'

– A.J.P. Taylor

My first meeting with Prime Minister Aleksei Kosygin took place in January 1970, and was the start of a relationship, both official and personal, that I have always deeply valued. It had its vicissitudes, as was inevitable in view of the intensity and volatility that Soviet–Pakistan relations would undergo over the next two years, but I never discerned any anger or hostility directed either against my country or me, on Kosygin's part. On the contrary, there were many occasions when his very sound advice was tendered in the gentlest possible manner. Kosygin remains, without doubt, one of the most impressive world leaders that I have encountered.

The purpose of my meeting was to deliver a letter from President Yahya Khan to Kosygin on the anniversary of the Tashkent Declaration. I had requested an early appointment, and was received by him in the Kremlin within two days of his return to Moscow. It was a particularly busy period for the prime minister, as was evident in the anteroom outside his office, which was filled with Soviet officials, many shuffling papers, and all in varying attitudes and states of nervous tension. During my interview with Kosygin only Fomin and an interpreter were present. The former, in marked contrast to the many agitated aides in the anteroom, was as cool and self-assured as ever. Kosygin's opening remarks were as encouraging as one could wish. 'There is much speculation in the world about the present state of Soviet–Pakistan relations. I want to assure you that the Soviet Union will take all steps to improve and strengthen these relations.' The rest of the meeting proceeded in this agreeable manner, with Kosygin reiterating the Soviet desire to see peace and stability in the subcontinent. We did not discuss any substantive issues and no mention was made about our relations with China, either. My assessment of the meeting was quite positive. Most ambassadors did not get to meet Kosygin even once during their entire tenure, whereas I had been received by him, in a very reassuring fashion, within three weeks of my arrival. In my report to the ministry, I indicated that although meeting Kosygin at short notice during his very busy schedule was indeed a favourable event, we would need to temper our optimism. He was obviously interested in developing relations with Pakistan, but there was also an unmistakable indication of an intention to specify terms. As we drove out of the Kremlin onto snow-covered Red Square, I recalled the words of Niels Bohr, the famous Danish physicist, 'Every sentence that I utter must be understood not as an affirmation, but as a question', and felt that it would be prudent to apply the same criteria to Kosygin's remarks.

The favourable impression that I obtained at my first meeting with Kosygin is one that has remained with me forever. Compact and of medium build, his short-cropped grey hair, stern demeanour, and his slow deliberate movements, contributed to the general impression of Kosygin, as the classic Soviet apparatchik. He was always dressed in impeccable, though sombre, fashion, quite unlike some of his other colleagues, whose clothes were either outrageously flashy or downright sloppy. Extremely well read and highly intelligent, Kosygin was a first rate economist. He knew more about Pakistan's economy than I did. He clearly possessed a fine analytical mind that could immediately identify problems and propose solutions. Very soft-spoken and totally imperturbable, he exuded self-confidence and a sense of power ensuring compliance, without having to raise his voice. As far as I was aware, the only language he knew was Russian. Coming from Leningrad he spoke it with a purity worthy of that great rich language, and in a manner that always enthralled me. His eyes were a deep blue and lit up delightfully, as did the rest of his face, whenever he smiled, which was not very often. A photograph of Kosygin, presented to me by him at my request, shows him with this unusual smile, and I am told it was personally chosen by him as a gift to me. Kosygin had an attractive, dry and acerbic sense of humour, and was capable of a biting sarcasm that terrified his victims. This was a reminder that, notwithstanding his many admirable qualities, Kosygin was still a member of the collective leadership of a regime that inflicted the gulags on its people. Nor could he have reached the top ranks of a powerful communist hierarchy without exercising an element of ruthlessness. Nevertheless, Kosygin's brilliance, his modesty and courtesy, and the sheer force of his powerful personality were an immense attraction for me. His name was never associated with the personal excesses, such as drunken orgies, of the other senior party apparatchiks. On the contrary, as a reclusive widower, he was known to regularly visit his wife's grave bearing flowers. He was devoted to his scientist daughter Ludmilla; who was married to a capable nuclear physicist and whose seniority was based entirely upon merit.

Brezhnev and Podgorny were the two other members of the triumvirate that at that time composed the Soviet leadership. Although Podgorny was the President of the Supreme Soviet, the only time I met him was when, in that capacity, he welcomed and bade farewell to President Yahya Khan on his official visit to the USSR in the summer of 1970. Although a number of significant political actions and decisions were attributed to him, I was never quite clear about his political power, and did not know how far it went beyond his titular functions as head of state. His personality, from what little I could discern during my brief contact with him, was basically that of a high-level communist leader—domineering, brash, ruthless, and self-assured. I could not discern in him any of Kosygin's subtle refinement.

Within the Brezhnev–Kosygin–Podgorny troika, Brezhnev was by definition primus inter pares, it was clear that by virtue of his position as Secretary General of the Communist Party of the Soviet Union, Brezhnev was the leader of the country. Kosygin and Podgorny appeared to have comfortably settled themselves into this arrangement, and relations between the three leaders seemed to be smooth and harmonious. During my tenure in Moscow there were neither reports nor evidence of the intrigue and murderous infighting that had characterized previous struggles for leadership within the Kremlin. The only charge against its denizens, and one that was frequently mentioned, was the elderly and sclerotic composition of the Politburo.

Leonid Brezhnev was a big man, with large bushy eyebrows dominating a visage that was part-Slav and part-Mongol. In almost every aspect of his mannerisms he was a total contrast to Kosygin. Loud, ebullient, and expansive, he radiated authority like a drill sergeant on a barrack square. His speech possessed a slurred forcefulness, and he conducted himself with a rough, hearty swagger. He had a raucous sense of humour sometimes bordering on the clownish, but none of this could conceal a sharp intellect leavened with considerable peasant cunning. Authority and decisiveness permeated his strong personality, and on encountering Brezhnev one immediately felt that one was in the presence of the leader of the Soviet Union. Unlike the reclusive Kosygin, Leonid Brezhnev's private life was flashy and opulent. A bon viveur who loved parties and entertainment, he was also known for the lavish hunting trips that he indulged in all over the country. His daughter was a leading light in Moscow society, attending lavish parties dressed in the latest, often daring, fashion. Brezhnev himself had a passion for fast cars—it was said he owned a Jaguar and a Ferrari, but I knew no one who had actually seen these possessions—and a juvenile fascination with gadgets. He once proudly showed us a cigarette case, set to a timer, which opened only in accordance with his daily ration of cigarettes. There were many reports concerning his ferocious temper which, on two occasions at least, was implicated in international events. The first was when the unfortunate Czech leader Alexander Dubček was overthrown and brought under arrest from Prague to Moscow, where he was held in the Kremlin and humiliated by Brezhnev personally in the crudest and cruellest manner. The second instance was his outrage over the Afghan President, Sardar Dawood, whose persistent defiance eventually provoked the fierce outburst that preceded Brezhnev's decision to intervene in Afghanistan.

Andrei Andreyevich Gromyko was another senior member of the Politburo, whom I had met during my stay in Moscow, but never got to know very well. Grim and dour, he was a stubborn and uncompromising negotiator, and remained the textbook example of the Soviet apparatchik. To his high intelligence was added the richest possible diplomatic experience. This included participation in the Potsdam Conference, assignments as Soviet ambassador to the United States, and service as a senior official in the Soviet Foreign Ministry through the regimes of Stalin, Malenkov, Khrushchev, and Brezhnev. Gromyko's career was a tribute to his skills both as a professional and as a survivor. A rigid belief and adherence to communist ideology, and its efficacious promotion and practice in both international affairs as well as in his domestic conduct, ensured Gromyko's longevity. Notwithstanding his rich, fascinating historical experience, Gromyko has written the dullest possible of memoirs, filled with the same communist clichés and slogans he had already expressed all over the world, and this in a lifetime, in which he was a close or direct participant in events that had either shaped or altered, the course of history. The rigid fist of Marxist orthodoxy had, alas, finally prevailed, over the fascinating objectives of historical truth. I met Gromyko on one rare occasion after the Cold War was over, and formed the impression of him as a lonely old lion, lost and aimless in a forest that had suddenly become strange to him. The fire in the eye of the old warrior had been damped as surely as the conflict that no longer existed. Gromyko was lost without the Cold War.

Nikolai Pavlovich Firyubin was the Vice-Minister for Foreign Affairs and the senior most official, together with A.A. Fomin, with whom I did the most work, and with whom I had the most extensive contacts. I should add that my relationship with these two was among the most pleasant, memorable, and fruitful aspects of my tenure in Moscow. Of medium height, with greying dark hair and light brown eyes, Firyubin had a quick smile to go with his ready wit. His pale, blotchy face occasionally carried the puffy consequences of the previous night's carousing, which, though occurring at regular intervals, never seemed to affect the sharpness of mind and concentrated thoughts that he brought to bear on our morning meetings. Always impeccably dressed, polite, and well mannered, Firyubin was a professional to his elegantly manicured fingertips, was extremely knowledgeable, and never conducted a meeting without a complete command of his brief. It helped, of course, that as

Vice-Minister for Foreign Affairs he had been dealing with South Asia for over a decade and a half. This longevity in office was a standard custom in the Soviet bureaucracy, a practice which carried both advantages and disadvantages. As a result he had acquired an institutional memory of formidable proportions. He had known and dealt with some of my predecessors, whom I had hardly ever met. Firyubin was married to Ekaterina Furtseva, the dynamic, powerful, and controversial Soviet Minister for Culture, whom we got to know later on our own initiative, and through whose good offices we were able to meet a number of brilliant and fascinating Soviet writers, artists, and musicians. Firyubin spoke fluent French, and in due course, following cautious feelers, we developed a mutual understanding to use this language as a means to convey continuity of personal goodwill. There were, unfortunately, a number of sessions when we were obliged to forcefully express our respective official positions in Russian and in English, with the interpreters and other officials present seriously taking careful notes. Having satisfied, with due emphasis, our formal positions for the benefit of both governments (and also the microphones in the ceiling), Firyubin and I would, on reaching the exit door, give a firm handshake and whisper into each other's ear 'Mes homage à madame' (My respects to madame). It was a reassuring device with which to conclude an otherwise difficult, and frequently, an unpleasant session.

The Soviet official with whom I had the closest and most productive relationship was A.A. Fomin, Director of the South Asia Department in the Soviet Foreign Ministry. Shortly after I first met him I learned that Fomin was also a very senior officer in the KGB, a fact confirmed by a number of his actions, all positive and in support of my requirements, both official and personal, and by the quiet and tremendous confidence in his general manner and behaviour. This reticence, so contrary to the popular conception of the brusque and crude KGB bully, was a very effective undercover disguise. Tall and well-built, with a handsome face and large brown expressive eyes, Fomin was soft spoken, had a sense of humour and a ready smile. Exuding gravitas, he was always polite but never deferential; characteristics which he retained, I noted with appreciation, even during the course of our meetings with high officials like Kosygin and Gromyko.

Although firm in his convictions and the implementation of his duties, Fomin had none of the rigidity which many of his apparatchik colleagues possessed. He was the most regular interlocutor during my tenure in Moscow, and together we dealt with all kinds of situations, from the commonplace to the critical. We handled two presidential visits to the Soviet Union, and sustained, by the slenderest thread, the diplomatic ties between Pakistan and the Soviet Union at a moment when relations were under the greatest strain. Although my country had the closest friendship with China and the USA, two powers with whom his country had deep and substantial rivalries, and although the USSR was allied to India, a country with which we eventually went to war, the personal and official relations between Fomin and myself were as close as I had maintained anywhere else. I knew, even during the darkest days in Moscow, that Fomin and I had a profound understanding of each other. And I like to think that this extended to mutual respect. It should be remembered that Fomin represented a communist country which was at that time at its zenith as a superpower, whereas I represented a country which was a military dictatorship, undergoing a tortuous and tumultuous inner transformation. Yet we managed to find and nurture a civilized association that kept us together at the worst of times, thus enabling us to commence the process of rebuilding an important international relationship. Fomin's health was never robust, and after my departure from Moscow he answered the call of duty and went as the first Soviet ambassador to Bangladesh. There his health broke down completely; he was flown home to Moscow on a stretcher, and died shortly thereafter. The Soviet Union lost one of its finest diplomats and I a great and noble friend.

My activities in the USSR inevitably brought me into contact with a number of officials, including three Soviet officials with whom I worked quite closely in Moscow, and with whom I continued the happy relationship elsewhere. The first was Dmitri Polyansky, notable as being the youngest member in the geriatric Politburo, whose dynamism and competence were sometimes brought to bear on issues concerning South Asia. Polyansky was also the politburo member who escorted President Bhutto during the latter's official visit to Moscow in early 1972. Polyansky and I developed an amiable personal relationship during my tenure, and I thought that his comparative youth, coupled with his evident capabilities, would take him far up the Politburo ladder. But, somewhere in the dark recesses of the corridors of power in the Kremlin, he appears to have taken a wrong turn, and ended up as the Soviet ambassador to Japan. For Diana and me it was a delight to catch up with Polyansky and his charming wife in Tokyo, in 1976.

Another good friend in Moscow was Alexei Nesterenko, a nimble-minded Ukrainian whom we had known many years earlier when he was posted as the ambassador of the USSR at Karachi. Back in Moscow he was Director of United Nations affairs, and we maintained a constant contact which, though sometimes acrimonious, was generally productive. My sessions in his office, at the time of the Bangladesh crisis in December 1971, when the Polish resolution was being considered by the UN Security Council in New York, witnessed their fair share of tempers lost and found. Nesterenko spoke excellent English, and had a dry, sardonic, humour especially with spiced the tales of his extensive sojourn in the USA. It was a pleasure to meet him again as a colleague some years later in Dublin.

A junior Soviet official whom we got to know quite well was an attaché in the Foreign Ministry named Igor Khalivinski. Charming, gifted and intelligent, he was a knowledgeable and skilful diplomat, who sometimes acted as an interpreter as well, and with whom the junior officers in our embassy had excellent relations. His merit took him far in the Soviet Foreign Ministry, and specializing in United Nations affairs he later assumed important posts in the organization itself. It was Diana's lasting regret, and perhaps to Khalivinski's profound relief, that despite her best efforts and all her plotting she was unable to get Igor married while we were in Moscow. She repeatedly offered the embassy premises for the wedding reception.

One constant and stimulating aspect of diplomatic life in Moscow was the high calibre of the diplomatic corps. The list of ambassadors before, during, and after my time there, is a veritable galaxy of talent, skill, and experience. The enforced isolation of foreigners in communist capitals created social ghettos, but the high professional competence of the ambassadors in Moscow was some mitigation for this isolation. It certainly ensured a productive intellectual stimulus of high quality. I cannot recall any dull diplomatic party in Moscow. Much the same could be said of the foreign correspondents stationed in the USSR, who were amongst the most brilliant in their profession. Extremely well-informed about all aspects of the Soviet Union, they possessed excellent contacts, and by developing a mutual confidence, they worked with the members of the diplomatic corps in an admirable fashion.

The onset of spring in 1970 brought with it a welcome thaw in our relations with the Soviet Union. I had a very satisfactory meeting with Firyubin, followed by an official lunch offered by him in my honour, attended by senior members of the Foreign Ministry and our embassy. In his speech Firyubin addressed us as *tovarichi* ('comrades'), an honorific which customarily is used by communists only when they address one another. After reviewing with satisfaction the progress in our bilateral relations, Firyubin said that the Soviet government 'was working very hard' on the visit of President Yahya Khan to the USSR, and hoped to schedule it for the coming summer. In my reply, I first expressed our delight and honour at being addressed as *tovarich*, which we reciprocated in 'comradely' fashion, and also expressed the thanks of my colleagues for the splendid co-operation which we had received from Firyubin and his officials.

On 21 and 22 April 1970 Moscow embarked upon a grand celebration of the centenary of Lenin's birth. A two-day 'Solemn Meeting', held in the Kremlin's vast Palace of Congress, was attended by top level delegations of communist parties from all over the world, except China and Albania. The Russian poet Vladimir Mayakovsky's famous exhortation 'Lenin lived, Lenin lives, Lenin will go on living' was plastered on banners and thundered on loudspeakers all over the city. At the Palace of Congress the gathering was addressed by the secretaries general of all the participating communist parties and, as expected, Brezhnev made the longest speech, lasting three hours. In view of the solemnity of the occasion, there was an obvious attempt to eschew discord, and I found the tone of the celebrations to be nostalgic and valedictorial rather than revolutionary and purposeful. The Chinese chargé d'affaires contemptuously dismissed the entire event by remarking that Brezhnev's three-hour oration did not mention Cambodia once—'perhaps for him the problem does not exist'.

By late spring 1970 arrangements were well advanced for the official Pakistani presidential visit to the Soviet Union. Yahya was personally very keen on this, and told me during one of my preparatory meetings in Islamabad that, after he became president, the Soviet Union had been the first country to invite him to visit. The evolving political situation in Pakistan clearly had a major impact on our preparatory work for the visit, and was of equally important interest to our Soviet hosts. Accordingly it was decided in Islamabad that the president would give the Soviet leaders a full briefing and his own frank assessment of the situation. The other important issue was the interruption in the supply of Soviet military equipment, including tanks and spares. This military co-operation agreement, despite its modest scale, had been a diplomatic triumph justly associated with President Ayub Khan's last visit to the Soviet Union the previous year. However, its implementation had ceased almost simultaneously with Ayub Khan's departure from office. Immediately upon arrival in Moscow I had commenced a discreet examination of this issue, and my carefully conducted enquiries revealed that the Soviets had decided to suspend military deliveries to Pakistan until a clearer picture of the political scene emerged in the country after the elections. I accordingly recommended to the president, when I met him in Islamabad, that he eschew all reference to arms supplies, and that he concentrate on our economic requirements, especially the steel mill. Our delegation brief was accordingly prepared, and Yahya Khan followed it scrupulously, avoiding any mention of arms supplies either in formal meetings or in his informal conversations.

On his four-day official visit to the Soviet Union in June 1970, Yahya Khan was accompanied by a large and high-level delegation. This included the Finance Minister Muzaffar Qizilbash, Foreign Secretary Sultan Khan, former Foreign Secretary and now Chairman of the Steel Mills Corporation S.M. Yusuf, Chairman of the Planning Commission M.M. Ahmed, and General Ghulam Umer, a powerful and influential member of Yahya Khan's martial law staff. A number of other officials, as well as a large press contingent, completed the delegation. President Yahya Khan was received at Vnukovo International Airport by an impressive welcoming committee including President Podgorny, Prime Minister Kosygin, Defence Minister Marshal A. Grechko, Deputy Foreign Minister Firyubin, and a number of other officials. As I entered the cabin of the PIA aircraft to greet and welcome the president, I sensed that Yahya Khan and the accompanying officials were all a bit tense. This was unusual for the fearless, jovial and swashbuckling Yahya, but in fact was quite a normal sensation for anyone arriving for the first time in the grim city of Moscow of the 1960s and 1970s. I tried to put them at their ease, but things livened up of their natural accord once the distinguished passengers had disembarked and been greeted with bear hugs by their equally distinguished Soviet hosts. Yahya was whisked away in a large black Zil automobile accompanied by Podgorny, Kosygin, and an interpreter. Since the Kremlin apartments were under restoration, the delegation was lodged in a large, luxurious villa, in the suburbs of Moscow, where immediately upon arrival we were treated to an enormous and sumptuous meal. The atmosphere was lively and convivial, and Podgorny and Kosygin each took it in turn to toast Yahya with glasses of vodka. The Soviet leaders were of course aware of their guest's propensity for alcohol, and I was amazed and a trifle disgusted that these world leaders should start a state visit with such a cheap, shoddy prank. But Yahya, who was obviously aware of these tactics, turned up trumps and said, after the fourth toast, 'Mr President, Mr Prime Minister, I feel that this is not very fair. I know what you are trying to do, but there are only two of you against me, and that is not fair for you. I warn you that I can easily handle four of you'. At that Kosygin laughed, threw up his hands and promptly put his upended glass on the table. After that, conversation was resumed in a more serious manner.

The programme of the visit was a comfortable blend of business and pleasure. There was a formal dinner, hosted by Kosygin in the opulent splendour of the Kremlin's banquet hall and attended by senior Soviet officials and the Pakistani delegation. Conversation at the table was wide-ranging, but Yahya's formal speech did not completely satisfy Kosygin. In a quiet comment after the president had concluded his speech, Kosygin observed wryly that it contained a great many laudatory references to the Lenin Centenary, but barely made a reference to the Tashkent Declaration. The next morning there was an official meeting of both delegations in the Kremlin conference room. It was a businesslike affair during which Yahya gave a frank account of the prevailing political situation in Pakistan, and reiterated his determination to hold free and fair elections by the end of the year. Kosygin followed the presentation with interest, sought some clarifications and ended up by expressing strong support for Yahya's actions. On turning to bilateral relations Yahya said that his priorities were the development of political and economic relations between our two countries. He raised the issue of the steel mill, to which Kosygin responded in a positive fashion, and after a short discussion the Soviet prime minister made a formal commitment that the USSR would provide the credit, the equipment, and the technical expertise for establishing a steel mill in Pakistan. He added the assurance that Moscow would purchase any production that was surplus to Pakistan's requirements. A team of experts would shortly visit Pakistan to carry out a preliminary survey of the project. We next negotiated the broad outlines of a five-year trade agreement, and also reached an understanding on cultural exchanges. It had been a successful session, and Yahya had studiously avoided all reference to arms deliveries. As became apparent later, this omission somewhat mystified the Soviets. The rest of the delegation's stay in Moscow was spent in sightseeing, including the obligatory visit to Lenin's tomb and the wreath laying at the war memorial. My reception at the Pakistan embassy in honour of President Yahya Khan was attended by Soviet officials, the embassy staff, and the entire presidential delegation. With agreements on the steel mill and the five-year trade plan, and the establishment of a high-level political dialogue in place, President Yahya Khan's visit to the USSR was hailed both by the tightly controlled Soviet media, and by its less tightly controlled Pakistani counterpart, as being highly successful. In a typically flamboyant gesture, President Yahya Khan was kind enough to announce that I was being awarded the Sitara Quaid-i-Azam (SQA).

The next night we were taken to Leningrad in a luxuriously appointed special train for sightseeing. The programme included a performance by the magnificent Kirov Ballet. On boarding the train for the return to Moscow we were informed that Podgorny and Kosygin would meet President Yahya at the Moscow railway station the next morning and accompany him to the airport for his departure. Over dinner in the train that night Fomin approached me and said that the Soviets had been surprised that Yahya had not raised the issue of resumption of arms supplies with the Soviet leaders. 'Do you not think that important? If you do think it important then the President should be advised to raise it with the Soviet leaders when he meets them in the morning'. I immediately went to Yahya Khan's saloon, persuaded him to temporarily dismiss his coterie, and reported to him my conversation with Fomin. Just as I had finished, S.M. Yusuf came in to report a similar conversation that he had with Ambassador Rodionov, the Soviet ambassador to Pakistan. The president summoned Sultan Khan, and after a brief discussion it was agreed that Yahya would raise the issue with the Soviet leaders the next morning. In Moscow we moved in a convoy from the railway station to the airport as scheduled, but once there we encountered a long delay, with the presidential Zil parked near the aircraft steps, and the occupants of the car involved in deep conversation. Finally, the three smiling leaders emerged and following a hearty farewell, Yahya climbed the steps into the aircraft. I followed him into the cabin, where he thanked me again, told me that it had been a very successful visit, and that Sultan Khan would convey to me the gist of his conversations with Podgorny and Kosygin.

Two days later I received a cipher message from the foreign secretary that Podgorny and Kosygin had confirmed to the president the Soviet Union's decision to resume arms supplies to Pakistan, and that I should take immediate steps with the relevant Soviet agencies for its implementation. Our very able and active defence attaché, Brigadier Ghulam Hussain, accordingly contacted the State Committee, but was informed that as yet no instructions had been issued. I made enquiries, first with Sergeev and then with Skatchkov in the State Committee, but found that whilst work on the steel mill was proceeding smoothly, there were still no instructions on arms supplies. I then took up the matter at the political level, starting first with Fomin, and then going on to Firyubin and Gromyko, but at each stage there was the same bland unresponsive reaction. I finally obtained a meeting with Kosygin and confronted him both with my instructions and the reasons that prompted them. Kosygin was totally unmoved and neither confirmed nor denied his airport conversation with Yahya. Instead, he assumed his best avuncular attitude with the advice 'Do not accelerate this question'. In his view, Pakistan should first concentrate on solving the many urgent and difficult problems with which it was confronted, including political agitation, poor economic performance, and social disorder. I did not know it at the time, but President Yahya Khan, in the first flush of his return from the successful Moscow trip, had already informed senior officers at GHQ that Soviet supplies would soon be resumed. It is no wonder that my cipher telegram, reporting Kosygin's dash of cold water, produced shock waves of outrage and indignation that reverberated across Islamabad. The entire phenomenon has remained a mystery, and even though nearly forty years have passed it continues to puzzle me. I can find no clue or explanation for this bizarre episode.

Meanwhile life continued in Moscow at its exciting pace, and the many visits of heads of state and governments were a constant stimulant to diplomatic activity. The Sino–Soviet dispute, rivalry with the USA, the wars in the Middle East and Vietnam, the ethnic and proxy conflicts in Africa, and now the preliminary rumblings in South Asia, were issues which, in Gromyko's words, 'directly affected the Soviet Union as a great power', and which obliged us diplomats accredited to this 'great power' to carefully follow its reaction to this trend of events. Added to this was a new and important development, the rapprochement in Europe, the continent from which two World Wars had emanated.

Winston Churchill's clarion speech in Fulton, Missouri, in March 1946, had marked the start of the Cold War, and ever since, and with increasing clarity, the problem of Germany had emerged as being central to the issue, and needed to be addressed if the peace of the world was to be ensured. The arrival of Willy Brandt as Chancellor of the Federal German Republic, and his bold and imaginative policy of 'Ostpolitik', marked an important and substantive move towards reconciliation in Europe. His overtures evoked a positive response from the Soviet Union. At about the time that I arrived in Moscow in November 1969, Egon Bahr, an important State Secretary in the West German Foreign Ministry, and a confidant of Willy Brandt, had been invited by the Soviets to commence high-level discussions on a peace treaty. Thanks to the encouragement of Brezhnev and Brandt, these negotiations assumed a rapid momentum, so that by August 1970 a document entitled 'Treaty between the Union of Soviet Socialist Republics and the Federal Republic of Germany' was signed in Moscow. Although it was, in essence, a peace treaty ending the war between Germany and the USSR, it also established the permanence of frontiers as they existed in Europe at the end of the Second World War. It dealt with the vital question of a united Germany through an important clause in the Treaty which called for 'the Federal Republic of Germany to work towards a condition of peace in Europe in which the German nation attains its unity again in free self determination'. As I followed these events in Moscow, and studied the documents, I confess to being peripherally caught up in the euphoria that prevailed in the city at the time that Brandt and Kosygin signed the treaty. In retrospect, it seems logical to regard the USSR–Federal Germany Treaty of 12 August 1970 as an event that marked the beginning of the end of the Cold War.

At a gala reception in the Kremlin that evening, optimism bubbled like the vast quantities of champagne and vodka that was being consumed, and all those present were touched by the sensation of being witness to history in the making. Kosygin noticed me, and beckoning me over to him said 'Look, Mr Ambassador! They killed twenty million of our people, but today we are making peace with them. You must do the same with India'. Notwithstanding the veracity of both his assertion and his advice, there was something in his oft-repeated homily, this time in the presence of many others, that I found irritating. With Kashmir floating at the back of my mind, I responded with the utmost civility, 'Mr Prime Minister, they killed twenty million of your heroic people (I emphasized the adjective), but you threw them out of your country. If they were still in occupation of Ukraine, would we be drinking these toasts?' The temerity of my remarks, expressed in rudimentary Russian, evoked an audible gasp from one of the officials present. But Kosygin was as understanding and tolerant as ever. With a smile, and a twinkle in his eye, he raised his glass and said 'Let us drink to the health of your President'. Changing the subject, he asked how much I had travelled in the USSR. I said that with the kind co-operation of his government I had enjoyed my visits to a number of regions and beautiful cities, but as an amateur student of military history I was keen to go to Kursk to visit the battlefields where the world's greatest armoured encounters had occurred, and to see the sites where Marshals Georgi Zhukov and Konstantin Rokossovsky had achieved their historical victories. Kosygin gave me a long, thoughtful look, and instructed his aide to inform him immediately when a request from the ambassador to visit Kursk was received. He then abruptly turned away to talk to his other guests. Unfortunately, my request was never made because of my preoccupation with more important and urgent diplomatic commitments.

CHIAROSCURO

Vladimir and Suzdal are two towns from the Middle Ages, located within driving distance of Moscow. The Soviet government had, very wisely and creditably, designated them as heritage sites, and preserved and maintained them in all their pristine beauty. Diplomats were allowed to visit them, but since they were situated beyond fifty kilometres, prior permission had to be obtained from the Ministry of Foreign Affairs. This was readily obtained, once details such as the make and licence number of the automobile and the names of the driver and the occupants were submitted. However, the date and time of the journey, together with the route to be followed, was also prescribed. Equipped with this permit, Diana, Niloufer, Feroza, and I set off on a beautiful summer morning in the embassy's official car driven by our chauffeur, the gentle Volkov. The road was reasonable by Russian standards, but was also punctuated at regular intervals by the ubiquitous GAI (State Automobile Inspectorate) posts, manned by Soviet security officers in their forbidding green tab uniforms. Each time that we approached a GAI post, Volkov would slow down to ensure that the officers got a good look at the car's licence plates as well as its occupants. We had a very pleasant visit to Vladimir and Suzdal, where we admired the colourful orthodox churches and the ancient wooden houses that filled the town, and could well imagine ourselves in the heartland of ancient Mother Russia. On our way back home we passed a beautiful copse of green grass and silver birch trees, situated on the banks of a small lake, and I decided to stop at this bucolic spot for a short picnic. This alarmed Volkov, but he reluctantly obeyed my instructions, and we duly sat on the grass and unpacked our hamper. In a very short while there appeared a GAI car and two irate officers who berated the terrified Volkov for a breach of regulations. They had obviously been dispatched when after passing one GAI post, we had failed to appear at the next within due time. I intervened to tell the GAI officers that Volkov had very reluctantly obeyed my instructions to stop, and that the fault was entirely mine. I also offered to share our coffee and sandwiches with them, but they very politely declined, and equally politely suggested that it would be best for all concerned if we resumed our journey immediately. As we set off on our bumpy road home, I recalled the remarks of the eighteenth century Russian author, Nikolai Mikhailovich Karamzin, 'There are two troubles in Russia—roads and fools'.

I recounted this incident to Fomin some days later, and he capped my story with something even better. Fomin was an avid fisherman who pursued his sport in the numerous lakes and rivers in the vicinity of Moscow. He went one Sunday morning to a quiet spot where he had discovered a small lake in which the fish were plentiful and there were no fishermen except a few locals. Fomin kept its location as a fiercely guarded personal secret until one day, to his horror, his peaceful solace and enjoyment was interrupted by two GAI officers who told him to report forthwith to the Kremlin. There had been an emergency, the ministry had called his wife at home and had been told that Fomin had gone fishing but she did not know where. That information, together with the licence number of Fomin's car, was all that the KGB needed to trace his whereabouts within a 200 kilometre radius of Moscow. Fomin told me that the time that elapsed between the telephone call to his wife and his 'capture on my secret little lake' was about thirty-five minutes. A single resident, in a city of nine million people, had been traced by the KGB in a forest a hundred kilometres away, in less than three quarters of an hour. Fomin did not seem at all surprised by this extraordinary feat of detection, but he was furious that his carefully concealed fishing spot had now been revealed to predatory GAI anglers.

* * *

One day I saw on the back page of *Pravda* a small news item which reported that N.S. Khrushchev had died. The next day I called on Fomin at the Foreign Ministry and enquired as to whether there were to be any formal arrangements for a funeral, in which case I would need to alert my government. Fomin looked me in the eye and said slowly and deliberately, 'Mr Ambassador, I only know what I read in *Pravda*'. On my way back to the embassy, I tried to recall what I had read about the events of 15 October 1964 when, at a hastily summoned meeting in the Kremlin, Khrushchev's colleagues in the Politburo had confronted him with a series of charges. Familiar as he was with the ruthless methods of communist power struggles, Khrushchev realized that he had lost, but never being less than himself, had responded to his accusers, 'You gather together and splatter shit on me, and I can not object to you'. When he left the room he found that his bodyguard had been withdrawn and his opulent Zil automobile had been replaced by a humble Volga. On arriving at the embassy I sent a telegram conveying the news of Khrushchev's death, and suggested that no condolence message was necessary, as politically he had been dead for seven years. I sent a bouquet of flowers to his funeral, and later read, again on the back page of *Pravda*, a small news item which stated, 'Pensioner Khrushchev N.S. was buried in the Novodevichy (New Maiden) Cemetery'. It was commonly held that Khrushchev's political fall was due to 'the six Ks'. These were *Kitai* (China), *Kuba* (Cuba), *Kukkuruza* (Corn, i.e. failure of agriculture), *Kult Leechnosti* (personality cult), *Kuskinomat* (vulgar and rude personal behaviour), and *Kumovstvo* (nepotism). In any event, when the Soviets turn a former leader into a non-person, they do a thorough job.

* * *

During the state visit of President Yahya Khan we were treated to a superb performance of 'Swan Lake' at the Bolshoi. During the second intermission, we were taken to an opulent salon, which had been the Czar's private dining room, for an elaborate supper, and some relaxed, informal conversation. However, this suddenly turned serious when Kosygin demanded, in stentorian fashion, 'Mr President, when are you going to recognize the German Democratic Republic? You know that sooner or later you will have to do so.' Yahya, who was, until now, having a good time, went into prevarication mode and passed the question on to Sultan Khan who, in turn, mumbled something about the matter being under consideration. Just at that moment, as Kosygin was thinking he had Yahya on a skewer, Ekaterina Furtseva entered the salon and the conversation was disrupted by the greetings that she received, and the announcement that the curtain was rising for the final act of the ballet. As we were leaving for the concert hall Kosygin acidly remarked, 'Our Minister for Culture believes in attending only the last act of a performance'. Yahya, relieved by not having to say anything about East Germany, whispered in my ear, 'Who is that woman? Kiss her for me. That's an order!'

* * *

I once bought a painting at a small private exhibition, from a young Russian artist who was relatively unknown at the time and still remains so. It was not a particularly outstanding work of art but it attracted me nevertheless. I bought the canvas and gave it to my Russian secretary to have it framed. Valia suggested that I have it done in Helsinki because 'here it will take a lot of time'. On my insistence that it be done in Moscow she set about her task by writing a formal letter to the Ministry of Foreign Affairs giving details of the purchase and my request to have it framed. The Ministry of Foreign Affairs conveyed this request to the Ministry of Art and Culture, which in due course conveyed it to the Union of Artists and Writers of the USSR. Six weeks after the initial request Valia received a letter instructing her to go to Shop No. 71 of the Union from where the framed painting could be collected on payment of two roubles and fifty kopeks (approximately US$2). However, the picture just had a frame and no glass, and Valia's face fell when I insisted on having it with glass. So we went through the whole process again, and at the end of the exercise I had obtained a glass frame for my canvas at a cost of three months in time and three roubles and fifty kopeks in money. Poor, sweet Valia, long suffering but never complaining, had endured twelve weeks of frustration, and I had obtained a glimpse and personal inkling of the sclerotic nature of the Soviet system, and the stressful grind that it imposed on the daily lives of its citizens.

* * *

Secrecy and Security. All diplomats posted at Moscow were aware of the omnipresence of the KGB and the formidable efficiency of its surveillance systems. This was accepted and endured as a fact of life, rather like the long, dreary Russian winters. And just as we attempted to cope with the rigours of the climate through the use of overcoats, chapkas and snow boots, so we employed devices to shield us from the intrusions of the KGB. These varied, in terms of cost and effectiveness, in accordance with the resources available to each mission. We knew that all our Russian staff was obliged to report our daily activities to the KGB, and we also knew that our premises had been thoroughly bugged with the listening devices. Occasional sweeps, such as the one that discovered a microphone in the American eagle wall decoration in the US ambassador's office, provided a relief that was merely temporary. The more affluent embassies had constructed elaborate 'bubbles' in the basements of their premises, which were rendered secure by a series of sophisticated counter-intelligence devices, and were used for staff conferences as well as meetings with other 'friendly' ambassadors. We, of course, had no such facility and had to devise our own modest methods. I never dictated any of my cipher messages, or my secret special reports, but gave the handwritten drafts to either the cipher assistant or personal assistant for preparation and transmission. If there was any secret matter to be discussed we did it outdoors, either in the embassy yard or on the Leninski hill in Moscow's suburb, which also marginally helped us stay healthy. Niloufer and Feroza made it a point to include 'Mike', the listening device installed in their bedroom, in their 'goodnights'.

* * *

Faiz Ahmed Faiz was a regular visitor to the Soviet Union. A recipient of the prestigious Lenin Peace Prize, he was received with warmth by his Soviet hosts, and treated with the utmost hospitality and courtesy. It was always a pleasure to meet Faiz, and at the formal receptions that I gave in his honour, which were, of course, well-attended by Soviet officials as well as literary luminaries, we were able to observe with pride, the admiration and respect that Faiz evoked in these elite, intellectual, gatherings. Once the formal reception was over, Faiz would stay on with the embassy staff for informal conversation, and of course, a recitation of his verses. These sessions would last late into the night, as Faiz Sahib, glass in one hand and a cigarette in the other, a quiet smile and eyes half-closed, wove his magic and transported us into a fairyland of passion and beauty that only he could create. It is as shameful as it is incomprehensible that this literary giant and humanitarian, loved and honoured all over the world, and especially by the people of Pakistan, should have been relegated by successive establishments to the fringes of our society.

* * *

As part of their Cold War strategy, the Soviets had lured a number of young Pakistani boys with the promise of an education—an attribute that has always been and will be the most sought after in Pakistan—with the ultimate objective of communist indoctrination. They had entered the USSR without any documents and were lodged in the Patrice Lumumba University (now Peoples' Friendship University of Russia) together with other young people from Africa and Asia. After living under conditions of considerable oppression and hardship for over a year, they had acquired little beyond the rudiments of the Russian language and a dubious grounding in Marxism–Leninism, and most of them were thoroughly miserable and homesick. At the end of Yahya Khan's visit to Moscow, he graciously asked if he could do anything for me. I told him of the plight of these students and requested his permission to issue them Pakistani passports for their return home. Yahya's response was replete with typical generosity and expletives, 'Silly buggers! Give them their bloody passports and a kick on their arses at the same time.'

MEANWHILE IN PAKISTAN

Yahya Khan's Legal Framework Order of 8 November 1969 initiated a new dynamic in the politics of Pakistan. Based upon the principle of one man–one vote, it envisioned a National Assembly consisting of 169 seats for East Pakistan and 144 seats for the four provinces and the Federally Administered Tribal Areas (FATA) in West Pakistan. Elections were scheduled for October 1970, and the newly-elected assembly was given 120 days to frame a constitution. The nation thus being presented with a set of clear-cut objectives, the politicians commenced their activities with gusto. So much has been written about this turbulent period in Pakistan's history by competent experts that further detailed comment is superfluous. It would only be appropriate to record the transitory personal impressions obtained during my periodic visits from Moscow to Islamabad for consultations.

It became clear to me, almost from the start, that Mujibur Rehman, with his Six Points agenda, had effectively galvanized support in East Pakistan, and by combining a legitimate sense of economic deprivation with heavy emotional parochialism, had secured an obvious majority. Increase of this stranglehold on the province was evident on each of my subsequent visits. In the west there was less evidence of the predominance of any one political party at the start of the year. But in a very short time it was clear that Bhutto's dynamic political campaign, notably his stirring call for '*roti, kapra, makaan*', was taking effect. There was a certain amount of clandestine support for the religious and conservative parties, organized largely by Sher Ali Khan Pataudi, the Information Minister, and this may have led to complacency on the part of the government. In my briefings I was told that the Pakistan People's Party (PPP) would have very limited success, but from what I could see for myself, I was sure that this was the kind of wishful thinking that spooks invariably feed to their masters. A notable feature of this election period was the genuine neutrality displayed by the government-controlled media, both print and electronic. This scrupulous impartiality had never been seen before in Pakistan.

The election campaign was proceeding in full swing in both wings of the country, when suddenly East Pakistan was hit by a destructive cyclone in which over twenty thousand people were killed and large parts of the province devastated. The Soviet Union provided a fleet of helicopters for relief operations, and I made a number of visits to the Soviet Ministry of Defence urging more assistance. Marshal Grechko was most helpful and co-operative, and took upon himself the responsibility to both increase and expedite deliveries of the aircraft. Grechko had earlier developed an excellent personal relationship with Admiral S.M. Ahsan, our former distinguished Chief of Naval Staff, and one of the finest and most able public officials to have served Pakistan. When I told Grechko that Ahsan was now Governor of East Pakistan and working desperately on relief efforts in the province, the Marshal said that there could be no greater incentive for him than to help Ahsan.

The elections, which had been postponed from October to December, were held in a comparatively peaceful and orderly manner; transparency being assured by TV monitors placed all over the country, reporting results from polling booths as soon as they were received. The elections were universally regarded as the freest and fairest ever held in Pakistan, a record that stands to this day. The results that ensued were a veritable electoral revolution, with Mujib's Awami League securing 161 out of 169 seats in East Pakistan, and Bhutto's PPP securing 88 out of 144 seats in West Pakistan. Neither the Awami League nor the PPP secured any representation in the opposite wings of the country. The establishment, which had expected a very different outcome and anticipated the possibility of Yahya Khan manipulating a hung parliament, was clearly caught off guard. There is an account, probably apocryphal, of Henry Kissinger (then US National Security Adviser) observing to Yahya Khan when the results were known, 'Mr President, for a military dictator you run a lousy election'. The end of the year 1970 thus found Pakistan with a free, fair, and transparent election as a creditable accomplishment, but by some fiendish twist of irony it was an achievement that also brought the country to the brink of disaster. I recall Henry Kissinger telling me during one of our discussions, 'Everywhere else in the world elections help to solve problems; in Pakistan they seem to create them'.

During one of my consultation visits from Moscow to Islamabad, probably sometime in September 1970, Yahya Khan summoned me to his office in the presidency in Rawalpindi for a personal meeting. He said that the information that he was about to give me was extremely secret and not even an inkling was to be divulged to anybody. The only reason for telling me was because 'You are sitting on a bloody volcano and need to know about it'. He told me about the top secret initiatives that were underway for a US–China rapprochement, and of his personal role in this fascinating exercise. Yahya further stated that he was currently working on arrangements for a secret visit by Kissinger to Beijing. Yahya did not indicate to me the actual state of negotiations at that time, but did say that all communication between Nixon and him was through handwritten letters so that maximum security was ensured. He said it commenced in the Governor's House, Lahore, where Yahya and Nixon had their first meeting in August 1969. According to Yahya, Nixon said to him 'Mr President, both you and I have just taken office as president so I think that you and I can learn a lot from each other. Tell me, what do you think of our China policy?' Yahya's response was short and pithy, 'All bloody wrong. How can you ignore such a large nation with so many people?' In the discussion that followed, Nixon, Kissinger and Yahya planned the early modus operandi that first took Kissinger to Beijing, then Nixon to Shanghai, and eventually created a watershed in international relations that shaped the course of the second-half of the twentieth century. In its own tiny way that conversation in Yahya's office provided me with the explanation for the warm and effusive greetings that Diana and I received from Nixon and Kissinger in August 1969 at the Bucharest airport, where they had flown in directly from Lahore.

CHAPTER TEN

USSR 1971

'Men make their own history, but they do not make it as they please.'
    – Karl Marx

'Soviet power, unlike that of Hitlerite Germany, is neither schematic nor adventuristic. It does not work by fixed plans. It does not take unnecessary risks. Impervious to logic of reason, it is highly sensitive to logic of force.'
    – George F. Kennan, US diplomat and historian

'Russia is like an elephant which moves slowly in the forest, and feels the ground very carefully before it places its foot. But once it is planted the foot is very difficult to remove.'
    – Abdur Rehman, Amir of Afghanistan, on nineteenth century Russian expansionism.

The year 1971 was perhaps the most climactic in the history of Pakistan's relations with the USSR and merits a record of the events, particularly as they appeared at the epicentre, Moscow. Just outside the city of St. Petersburg (formerly Leningrad), at the famous Piskarevsky Cemetery, about half a million victims of the wartime siege of Leningrad lie buried amongst surroundings of sombre beauty. The war memorial carries a poem by the Leningrad poetess and diarist, Olga Berggolts, who herself endured those dark days of war and siege. The poem ends with the words:

'Let no one forget;
Let nothing be forgotten.'

Since the inception of Pakistan in 1947, our history has experienced periodic moments of turbulence, which has been the lot of most developing countries. But the events of 1971 were an explosive tragedy, in human as well as political terms, the consequences of which altered the course of South Asian history. From January 1971 until the first week in March, our relations with the Soviet Union were close, and even cordial. A delegation led by S.M. Yusuf, the Chairman of the Pakistan Steel Mills Corporation, signed a series of agreements with various Soviet organizations, and was granted a lengthy and friendly audience with Kosygin. The Soviet Union had signed similar agreements with countries all over the world, but their representatives were never received by the Soviet prime minister. Kosygin's meeting with Yusuf was, therefore, clearly a mark of friendship and interest in Pakistan. By the beginning of March, however, the Soviets began to manifest their concern over the development of political events within Pakistan, and the Soviet ambassador in Islamabad handed a note to President Yahya Khan informing him that, 'In Moscow friendly attention is being given to the situation developing in Pakistan. Though the deteriorating situation in Pakistan is mainly a matter of internal character, the tension of the situation in friendly Pakistan, which is a neighbour of the Soviet Union, can not but arouse the concern of the Soviet people, as in situations of this kind problems of internal character are often inseparable from matters of the outside political situation'. The note went on to request President Yahya Khan for his 'considerations regarding the situation and the prospects of its early development which the President would find possible to share with us.'

On 22 March, Fomin summoned me to the Foreign Ministry and told me about the conversations which had recently taken place between the president, the Soviet ambassador and Mujibur Rehman. The gist of Fomin's statement was that the Soviets were seriously perturbed about political developments in Pakistan, and that they sincerely hoped that a peaceful solution, based upon the unity of Pakistan, could be evolved. The president had apparently indicated to the Soviet ambassador his willingness to accept three of Mujibur Rehman's 'Four Points' but he could not agree to an immediate lifting of martial law. Mujibur Rehman, in turn, had apparently informed the Soviet consul general of 'an earnest desire to settle issues on the basis of a united Pakistan and would only opt for independence as a last resort and if force was used by the army. Fomin informed me that

Mujibur Rehman's views had been conveyed to the president of Pakistan, and also indicated that according to Soviet sources of information, both the president as well as Mujibur Rehman were under severe pressure from extremists in the army and the Awami League, respectively. Fomin also reiterated that while the Soviet Union was strongly committed to a peaceful solution of the East Pakistan problem on the basis of a united Pakistan, there were 'imperialist and other forces' which were working for fragmentation. It seems to me, in retrospect, that one of the most revealing aspects of this important conversation with Fomin, which took place as long ago as 22 March 1971, was the close interest which the Soviets had been maintaining in our internal affairs in general, and in East Pakistan in particular.

On 28 March 1971, the Soviet consul general in Karachi saw President Yahya Khan on the latter's return from Dacca, and communicated an oral message from Kosygin, the contents of which are indicated below.

The Soviet Government with anxiety met the news about the break off of the negotiations in Dacca and that military administration may possibly use armed forces against the population in East Pakistan.

Moscow does not have enough information about the reasons which led to this turn of events.

But to be quite frank we would like to express our opinion that Fratricidal conflict in East Pakistan will inevitably give rise to the sense of deep anxiety and negative reaction in the Soviet Union, and as we are sure, amongst all friends of Pakistan.

It is evident that extreme measures taken by the military administration and continuation of bloodshed in East Pakistan will not solve the existing complicated problems and will hinder their settlement and lead to new sacrifices and sufferings for the whole people of Pakistan.

It cannot be ruled out that imperialist circles and those forces in Asia which consider such turn of events to be in their favour, can use the existing situation in detriment to the collective interests and integrity of Pakistan.

The Soviet Government asks the President to take immediate measures for the cessation of bloodshed in East Pakistan and for the resumption of negotiation.

We have a deep conviction that in a situation like this not only every day, but every hour should be counted in order to prevent the loss of control over the events. Moscow would like to hope that the answer of

President Yahya Khan to this friendliness call will be positive. Moscow would be very thankful to the President if he considers it possible to give his opinion in respect of this call of the Soviet government.

The messages sent to us by the Soviets, quoted in extensio above, indicated that as early as March 1971, they had an active interest in the events unfolding in Pakistan and that they would not remain bystanders. On 1 April I received telegraphic instructions to convey President Yahya Khan's reply orally to Prime Minister Kosygin, and accordingly I sought a meeting with the latter. Before this could materialize, however, I was summoned to the Foreign Ministry on 3 April and handed a copy of a message from Podgorny to Yahya Khan, and at the same time I was informed that the Soviets intended to publish its contents in the press that evening. The message, cautionary in nature and admonitory in content, contained the standard homilies about peaceful negotiations, and evoked the expected adverse reaction in Pakistan. In a long meeting with Kosygin on 12 April I conveyed these sentiments to the Soviet prime minister, who while expressing a desire to normalize Soviet–Pakistan relations, categorically and frequently stressed that the Soviets had no desire to interfere in the internal affairs of Pakistan, and that Podgorny's message was not meant to convey that impression. As I reported at that time to the ministry, this was an obvious travesty, but the very fact that Kosygin said it might imply an easing of pressure on us. I also noted that during my long meeting with Kosygin there were a number of issues which he did not raise. These included China, which he did not mention at all, and neither did he mention Mujibur Rehman or make any reference to the arrest of political leaders. On the contrary, he stated at least five times during the course of the meeting that it was for the Pakistani leaders to themselves decide what kind of political system they wanted. As I left Kosygin's office in the Kremlin that evening I felt that I was now on the up side of the Moscow seesaw, but descent was inevitable, and one could only hope that the bump would not be too hard and painful.

On 17 April Kosygin sent another message to Yahya. It was somewhat cold and formal in tone and continued to stress the need for peaceful settlement, but for the first time made an ominous reference to 'the lawful wishes of the parties' and to 'the interest of the population of both West and East Pakistan'. Yahya did not respond to this message but sent instead a special envoy, M. Arshad Husain, a former foreign minister of Pakistan and also former ambassador in Moscow. He was received by Kosygin on 26 April, and although the meeting was lengthy and frank, it was by no means friendly. Arshad Husain had brought with him a map of East Pakistan and he pointed out the areas which had now been 'brought under control' by military action. Since this was precisely what the Soviets were cautioning us against doing, Kosygin's irritation at the exposition was palpable. However, the atmosphere improved when Arshad Husain mentioned our future political plans, which appeared to interest Kosygin, even though he studiously avoided comment, reiterating only the necessity for a peaceful settlement in East Pakistan and for peaceful co-existence with India. Kosygin then expressed his bitterness about the anti-Soviet press campaign in Pakistan. On this issue he was even more critical than he had been when he first raised it with me on 12 April, and he was pretty angry then. He said quite frankly and dogmatically that the press campaign was being artificially created and that it did not reflect the opinion of the majority of Pakistanis. In my report to the ministry at the conclusion of Arshad Husain's visit I stated that while it had checked the deteriorating trend in our relations, the Soviet position remained ambivalent, and by no means clearly committed to support the Pakistan government. They would, in the overall interests of peace and stability, prefer a united Pakistan, but they had doubts about our ability to bring the situation in East Pakistan under control, and feared that a continuation of instability would help Chinese interests to prosper in the region.

In May and June the diplomatic battle in Moscow continued, and the Indians pressured the Soviet Union by sending a number of unofficial delegations, including J.P. Narayan and Biju Patnaik. This was backed up by an official visit by Foreign Minister Swaran Singh who gained some mileage, so far as the Soviet position was concerned, by obtaining in the communiqué a reference to the necessity for restoring peace in East Pakistan and 'creating all conditions for the safe return of refugees'. At this stage, there were also some overtures from the Indian embassy to try and get some of our Bengali staff to defect, but this met with no success. I had taken particular care to ensure that the Bengali members of our staff received special consideration, knowing that they were under tremendous stress over the tragic events unfolding in their homes, and always made them participate in all the activities of the embassy, including access to top secret telegrams and attendance at all staff meetings. It is a matter of record, and my deep personal appreciation to the splendid Bengali officers and staff of the embassy, that whereas by now their colleagues in several other Pakistan missions had jumped ship, the Bengali members of the Pakistan embassy in Moscow only left the mission on the day after the Soviet Union had formally recognized Bangladesh.

Towards the end of June, there was a further exchange of messages between Yahya Khan and Kosygin which, apart from the intrinsic importance of exchanges between heads of government, were the last examples of purposeful seriousness, and a measure of polite understanding on the part of Kosygin. From July onwards Soviet messages became increasingly hostile, and so did our responses, resulting in a mutual contribution to deteriorating relations. On 22 June 1971, I had a long and very important meeting with Kosygin in the Kremlin, and conveyed to him the text of a message which President Yahya Khan had sent to a number of heads of government. The meeting, which lasted for just over an hour, was not only frank but was also informal and friendly, and Kosygin was, as usual, accompanied by Fomin and an interpreter. Although he 'used many sharp expressions', Kosygin's own phrase, the talks were entirely free from acrimony. I said at the outset that President Yahya Khan was committed to effecting a political solution in East Pakistan, and that he was also committed to restoring democratic processes and civil political rule in Pakistan. He was fully determined to implement these objectives, and the unhappy events of the previous March had deferred, but not in any way altered them. The second point which was very clear was that the restoration of democratic processes would be accomplished within a framework which would truly safeguard the territorial integrity of Pakistan. This was not only a precondition of the president's plan, but it was also in accordance with public opinion. In this connection, as the president had indicated in his message to Kosygin, a formal pronouncement was expected on 28 June.

At this point Kosygin interrupted me and enquired whether I was 'familiar with what the President was going to say on the 28th'. When

I replied in the negative, the Soviet prime minister said, 'I have asked this question because this is going to be a decisive public statement.

> If it is not successful it could bring about a conflict. It should be considered carefully otherwise it will have a negative effect. I would ask you to inform the President that this statement should be conducive to peace so that we could support it strongly, and so that all peace loving people could support it. It should be worded so that it helps in calming the situation between India and Pakistan. I am telling this to you as a friend of the President. The statement should help peace to be maintained and should avoid conflict.

Kosygin spoke with great seriousness, and with quite unmistakable feelings of sincerity and concern. He emphasized that he had no wish to interfere in our internal affairs, that he had raised this subject only because the president had himself mentioned in his message an intention to make a public statement on 28 June, and that this was the kind of advice that Kosygin would customarily tender to a friend.

Kosygin added,

> Please understand me, Mr Ambassador. The President will be speaking at an acute moment upon issues which are almost about war and peace. If the President's statement does not take into consideration the Indian attitude there will be a sharp response from the other side. If both sides make sharp public pronouncements then it would be difficult to control the situation.

As Kosygin said this, he consciously emphasized his agitation and concern by first forcefully placing side by side an ashtray and a scribbling block on the table in front of him, then holding one object in each of his hands, raised each hand in turn in a gesture of escalation. He continued by saying, 'The President's statement may be made in such a way that it brings about a situation which is in the interests of both India and Pakistan.' Kosygin again emphasized that he was only raising this question because in the oral message the president had not indicated what he was going to say on the 28th.

> It is not my invention; it is the President who has indicated that he will make a public statement, but he did not elaborate what he is going to say. This statement would perhaps bring about war, or peace. I am not talking

about harmonization—the interpreter issued the wrong term—I am suggesting that these statements should be such as to bring about peace. This could be done through diplomatic channels, that is through you, Mr Ambassador, and others.

Kosygin concluded by urging me to bear in mind that this was an unofficial conversation. 'We have got used to talking to your President unofficially and informally, and to exchanging our thoughts and ideas. Please convey this to the President.'

I replied that I had taken note of the prime minister's views, and also his concern, and said that I would convey them immediately to the president. I also thanked Kosygin for the lively personal interest that he continued to take in the affairs of the subcontinent and urged the continuation of his valuable efforts for maintaining peace in the region.

Kosygin then turned his attention to another issue, which he said was 'a matter of grave concern to us'. He said that the president had mentioned in his oral message that India had grossly exaggerated the number of refugees who had crossed the border and had also exaggerated the stories of atrocities. Kosygin said that

If people flee, it is because of abnormal conditions; they do not flee under normal conditions. No case in history can prove the reverse. If people are fleeing—four million of them or five million of them; numbers are not important—it is because such unbearable conditions have been created for them that they are forced to leave everything behind and to flee from Pakistan to India.

Kosygin went on to say that the Pakistani peasant is a conservative person who loves his land and his village. He knows that India is not a paradise, and that when he goes to India nothing awaits him except hunger and privation. Yet such has been the insecurity in East Pakistan, and so grave had been the threat to life, that millions of peasants were forced to leave their homes and lands and flee to India. Kosygin said to me,

How can you count on the world's sympathies when so many people are fleeing and are being killed on their way to India? Numbers are not important. Despite many peaceful pronouncements by the President, people are still going to India, even though they are aware of the difficult conditions there. India has difficulties with food and housing, yet your people are prepared to go there. Can this situation be called normal? This means that either the people in authority cannot cope with it or they are playing a double game. Our people do not and cannot understand this.

I reported this outburst, which was of considerable emotional proportions, fully and carefully. But even so, Kosygin spoke more in sorrow than in anger. It was clear to me that Swaran Singh had touched the Soviet prime minister on an emotional nerve and had fully exploited the situation. I decided to respond with some sharpness. I told Kosygin that nobody could feel the tragedy of recent events in East Pakistan more than the Pakistani people themselves. The Indians only exploited the situation; it was we who felt the pain and the impact. These unfortunate, displaced persons were *our* people, they were not Indians, and we wanted them to come back. I said,

> Mr Prime Minister, I want to make it very clear to you that nobody has done more than the President to restore democratic processes within the country. He has worked for it night and day, and it is the supreme personal tragedy for Yahya Khan that the results of his efforts have been frustrated by corrupt politicians who were in league with outside elements. But I can assure you, with every emphasis at my command, that everything possible is being done to restore peace in East Pakistan and to bring about democratic processes.

I forcefully indicated the measures that we had taken in order to encourage the displaced persons to return. I said that the president of Pakistan had made a public announcement a long time ago, urging all Pakistani citizens to return. We had declared a complete and general amnesty, had established reception centres all along the border and had arranged for the stationing of United Nations personnel in East Pakistan. The United Nations high commissioner for refugees had held discussions with our leaders, had visited the reception centres, and had expressed complete satisfaction with all our arrangements. It was now up to the Indians, who had aggravated the refugee problem in the first place, to suspend hostile activities on our borders so that the displaced persons could return in peace.

But Kosygin was still labouring under a gross misapprehension which had obviously been created by Swaran Singh. The prime minister said that we could hardly expect the refugees to return under the conditions that we had provided for them.

> They are afraid that you've set up some kind of ghettos for these returning people. You put them in camps and keep them surrounded. If there is no guarantee for their safety, and for the return of their possessions, they will not return. If you made these people leave the country, you must return their possessions. To make them return you must compensate them and guarantee their security. They are Pakistani citizens. They would be happy to return.

I replied,

> Mr Prime Minister, we are doing precisely that. We are not putting these people into camps, and we have no intention of doing that. Reception centres have been set up on our borders so that transport and other facilities are immediately made available to take the returning Pakistanis to their homes. These reception centres are not camps, much less ghettos or places of detention. The United Nations High Commissioner for Refugees himself has seen these reception centres and has expressed complete satisfaction with the arrangements. His representative and other United Nations representatives are permanently stationed in East Pakistan, and now that law and order has been restored in the province, we have allowed foreign newsmen complete freedom and access to the area. What else can we do? We have even suggested that our representatives should visit the Indian camp in order to facilitate the early return or our nationals to Pakistan. I am afraid, Mr Prime Minister, that your information is not at all correct.

Kosygin said that his information came from a number of newspapers, and then added, 'You should treat the persons humanely, you should assure them that you will return to them what they have lost. It is not easy to move a peasant from his home. He was given a choice to die or flee, so he fled. If a peasant moves from his native place, especially in India or Pakistan, it means there is danger.'

I told Kosygin that he was wrong again; there had been no movement in recent weeks from the interior. 'Movement has taken place only from the border areas where there is a sense of insecurity, created by the fact that the Indians are engaging in armed infiltration and shelling of these areas. These armed incursions must stop, so that the peasants can return to their homes in peace.' At this, Kosygin smiled and said to me 'I cannot agree that these people moved to India in order to be trained as saboteurs. Among them are women, children and old people. I don't think you yourself would believe that they could become saboteurs.' I replied, 'I did not say this. What I said was that saboteurs were being sent from India, we were hunting them down, and this created a sense of insecurity in the border area. Kosygin retorted, 'Then they should flee into the interior of Pakistan.' I replied 'In fact a lot of them have done exactly that.'

After this exchange Kosygin again smiled, and addressed me in a friendly but serious manner. He said,

> Mr Ambassador, I do not want to turn this conversation into a debate. You are not a defendant and I am not a prosecutor. We are both men of state who are discussing grave issues in a serious and friendly manner. I want you to know that we are very anxious for all disputes between Pakistan and India to be settled peacefully. Neither country is so rich as to be able to afford a conflict, and even countries much richer than you try to avoid conflicts. We say with all sincerity that Pakistan and India should resolve their differences without resorting to a conflict. We say it to you and we say it to India.

Continuing in the same vein, Kosygin reiterated two important points. First that the Soviet Union would continue its economic collaboration with Pakistan, and second that the Soviet Union had no desire to interfere in the internal political affairs of Pakistan. He said,

> We are interested only in the peace and welfare of Pakistan, and we will continue to assist you in all respects for this purpose. We have no profit motives, and we have no other consideration. We do not want to interfere in your internal affairs. This is for you alone to decide. We think a democratic government should find its legitimate rights. It will find it, sooner or later.

Kosygin then asked me to convey his greetings to the president and to thank him for the oral message which he very much appreciated receiving. He said, 'Please tell the President that we are very concerned about the developments in Pakistan, and would like to see a peaceful solution between Pakistan and India, and that we have no other consideration.' He then gave a very wide smile and said, 'Please also tell the President that this talk is not an official one. It expresses the friendship and concern that we have for you. I do not know what the President would have told me if he were sitting in your place just now, but if he would have told me all that you have said, I would have told him exactly what I have told you.'

I thanked Kosygin for the time that he had spared for me, and the continuing and genuine interest that he took in Pakistan's affairs. I said I hoped he did not misunderstand the motives behind any of my sharp statements, but when he very kindly used the expression 'tovarish' at the beginning of our discussion, I decided to take him at his word and be quite frank and friendly. Kosygin replied, 'You were absolutely correct and used no sharp words. Perhaps my statements seemed sharp, and that is why I told you what I did.' I remarked that we had a situation where sometimes sharp statements were necessary, and Kosygin was kind enough to say, 'In fact, I think our talk will prove very useful. What is important is the essence and not the words. As far as you are concerned, you have been very honest and we respect you.' After that we got up from the table, and as I was taking leave of Kosygin, he again asked me to convey his best wishes to the president. The prime minister appeared to be in a very friendly mood. He smiled as he shook hands with me and said, 'I want to tell you that your mission is not an easy one.'

I have related the above conversation in some detail, partly because I think that any conversation with Kosygin needs to be recorded in detail, and partly because I wish to try and convey the mood of the Soviet leadership towards our problems at that time. The details of this meeting with Kosygin are based upon the personal notes that I recorded at the time, in the belief that they might, in due course, help in the compilation of a historical record of these momentous events.

On 24 June, following my long meeting with him, Kosygin sent another message to Yahya Khan, hammering away at the same themes of refugee problems and the danger of interference by internal and external forces. But he now added an ominous new dimension. Quoting the instance of 'the problem of Palestinian refugees in the

Middle East' he warned that 'in no case shall we allow a similar problem to lie like a heavy weight on Pakistan–Indian relations which are not simple as they are.' At the same time, Moscow sent as its new ambassador to Pakistan an able and senior diplomat A.A. Rodionov, whose last assignment had been Minister of Foreign Affairs of the Russian Socialist Federal Republic, and was much more influential than his predecessor. His entry on to the stage could not have occurred at a more critical juncture. Until the middle of July it was clear that although the Soviets were worried about the course of events in the subcontinent, and had expressed their reservations in both public messages and private statements, their attitude was one of disagreement or disapproval over a particular issue, and not one of open hostility. It had been my constant and desperate endeavour to persuade our Soviet interlocutors, from Kosygin downwards, to maintain the Tashkent concept of neutrality in the subcontinent and not to put all their eggs into the Indian basket. To a certain extent this worked, and the Kremlin attempted to maintain a semblance of balance between India and Pakistan. The controlled Soviet press was, for example, much less anti-Pakistan than the free press in the West.

All this suddenly changed however, with the news of Kissinger's visit to Peking (now Beijing), and of Nixon's forthcoming visit to China. In the closed atmosphere and society of Moscow the reaction had no dramatic manifestations, but was a much more menacing one of muted fury and concern. I reported at the time that we must expect a hardening of Soviet attitudes towards us, but I hoped that we might be able to keep Soviet–Pakistan relations 'on an even keel'. This hope unfortunately proved to be far too optimistic. The reality was the fulfilment of Yahya Khan's earlier prediction about my 'sitting on a bloody volcano'. In my meetings with Soviet officials there were almost no emissions of sound and fury, but there was instead a disquieting attitude of deep suspicion bordering on betrayal. No awkward questions were asked of me, and I was reminded of André Malraux's incomparable description of a difficult meeting that he had once had with the formidable General De Gaulle: 'his silence was an interrogation.'

It was not possible to overstate the grave significance that the Soviets attached to a Sino–American detente. For the Kremlin it was almost like waking up from a bad dream and finding, to its consternation, that reality was no different from the nightmare that preceded it. Hitherto the international situation had been seen as an equation of tripartite mutual distrust: the Soviets had differences with the Americans and the Chinese, the Americans had differences with the Chinese and the Soviets, and the Chinese had differences with the Soviets and the Americans. Now suddenly the Soviets were confronted with the painful fact that this comfortable balance of hate had been disrupted by a potential détente between their two major foes. Pakistan's role in this development was noted with the deepest resentment, and was singled out for punishment. Later in the year, I had a discussion on Soviet–Pakistan relations with Professor Yuri Gankovsky, Head of the Pakistan Desk of the Institute of Asia and Africa, USSR Academy of Sciences, who was a good and sincere friend of Pakistan. He said, 'The turning point in our relations was when Kissinger went to Peking from Pakistan. My dear Marker, why did he have to go from Rawalpindi? He could have gone from Hong Kong, or from Bangkok, or from anywhere else, but not from Pakistan. It had the same effect in Moscow as when the U2 flew from Peshawar.'

By August it became clear to me that prospects of a Sino–American détente would stimulate Indo–Soviet co-operation, and *Pravda* gave prominence to Swaran Singh's statement that 'The Indian Government will be careful of any negative effects of Nixon's visit to Peking and we will take all measures for the defence of India'. Events moved rapidly and Indo–Soviet collaboration shifted into high gear. D.P. Dhar, who had been Indian Ambassador in Moscow and was now Chairman of the Policy Planning Commission in New Delhi, made a sudden visit to Moscow on 4 August, to be followed by an equally sudden visit by Gromyko to New Delhi on 7 August. The outcome was the Indo–Soviet Friendship Treaty of 9 August 1971, and from that moment onwards, despite frequent Soviet assurances to the contrary, Moscow and New Delhi set themselves on an increasingly hard and antagonistic course against Pakistan. The Friendship Treaty was a powerful document, which included a clause obliging the parties to come to each other's aid in case of a military attack on either. In response to Dhar's demands for meaningful support, the Soviets appeared to have insisted on a proper treaty, such as the one they had proposed before. The draft of this treaty had apparently been dormant in the archives in New Delhi since 1969, having been consigned to cold storage under murmured Indian platitudes about non-alignment. This draft was now revived and formed the basis of the Friendship Treaty of 1971, and was, in a sense, the quid pro quo that the Soviets extracted as diplomatic tribute. In my discussions with Firyubin and Fomin I was given the official party line that the Indo–Soviet Friendship Treaty was not directed against any third country and was a device to ensure peace in the subcontinent. Firyubin added that Soviet objectives in the treaty 'were not to encourage India but to restrain her'. Firyubin did not respond when I said that even he would find it hard to really believe that. In a lengthy, wide-ranging, and much more fruitful discussion with Fomin I said that I had no doubt that the treaty would considerably increase Indian intransigence, but whatever else the treaty might imply, it had made the Soviet Union the prime arbiter of war and peace in the subcontinent. I vividly recall Fomin's face as he smiled and mopped the perspiration off his face on a hot Moscow August afternoon. 'In that case, Mr Ambassador, you can be sure there will be peace.'

Fomin's assurances notwithstanding, it was at this time that a new and ominous element began to emerge in our relations with the Soviet Union. Although mutually acrimonious and belligerent statements had been emanating from New Delhi and Islamabad since March, and war hysteria had been on the increase in both India and Pakistan, the Soviets had begun to take the view that Pakistan was likely to initiate hostilities with India in order to divert world attention from the internal disorder in East Pakistan. A timely suggestion that the foreign secretary visit Moscow to demonstrate the importance that we attached to our relations with the Soviet Union was readily accepted, and Kosygin being away on vacation, a meeting with Foreign Minister Gromyko was set for 6 September. Unfortunately an incident occurred in the region that was to have a profound impact on the tenor of our meeting with Gromyko. There had been rumours that some elements of the Mukti Bahini, the Bengali liberation army, with active encouragement from India, might seize a bit of territory in East Pakistan and declare it as 'Bangladesh'. Yahya Khan had very unwisely overreacted to this rumour by making a pompous and belligerent public declaration that if anything like this were to occur, then Pakistan would attack India in order to reclaim this territory 'and let the world take notice'. The meeting with Gromyko, who was not the most gentle of persons and at his best when he could bully, did not therefore take place under the most auspicious of circumstances. Both sides reiterated their known positions, but the Soviets had by now considerably hardened theirs, and Gromyko told Sultan Khan, 'One gets the impression that certain circles in Pakistan are not against a military clash with India.' We then entered into one of the most bizarre and unpleasant episodes in my diplomatic experience. Speaking in Russian, Gromyko said that the Soviet leadership had taken note of Yahya Khan's statement and warned 'Please do not take any action that would oblige us to fulfil our obligations to a country with whom we have a Treaty of Friendship.' At this point Gromyko stopped the interpreter, and looking long, hard and directly at Sultan Khan, he said in English 'The interpreter did not interpret me correctly. I did not use the word "please". I think you understand my meaning.' In a diplomatic career that spans over thirty years, this was as close as I got to receiving a declaration of war. Unfortunately, somewhere in the process of transit, the full purport of this important and menacing exchange did not get to Yahya. However, in retrospect one wonders whether the threat would have made any difference even if it had been conveyed as it was said.

The mood of the rest of the meeting was not very different and Gromyko demanded from Sultan Khan the answers to three specific questions. First, could he report to the Soviet government and leadership President Yahya Khan's assurance that he would not take any measures to launch hostilities against India? Second, 'Could you briefly tell us of the position of China in this problem?' He added that the Soviets had an idea of the Chinese position, obtained from their own sources. Thirdly, could he be informed of the measures that the Government of Pakistan intended to take to defuse the situation? Sultan Khan gave an adequate response to the three questions, stressing the importance of restraint on the part of India, and informing Gromyko of the Indian rejection of our proposal to involve the United Nations, particularly in the matter of refugee repatriation.

The visit of the Indian Prime Minister Indira Gandhi to Moscow from 27 to 29 September brought the Soviets and the Indians into an even closer relationship than before. I speculated that this was probably the occasion when the Kremlin and New Delhi arrived at a tacit understanding that the situation in East Pakistan had reached the stage where armed Indian intervention, with full Soviet material and diplomatic backing, was a possibility to be considered. This assessment was motivated by a significant paragraph in the joint statement which read:

> The Soviet side took into account the statement by the Prime Minister that the Government of India is fully determined to take all necessary measures to stop the inflow of refugees from East Pakistan to India and to ensure that those refugees that are already in India return to their homeland without delay.

When I raised this issue with Fomin, I was given the bland response that the Soviets had merely taken note of what the Indians had said. But I persisted in my interrogation, stating that a clarification of the Soviet position was a matter of the greatest importance to me. Although Fomin appeared a little uncomfortable he was still quite firmly evasive and said, 'Mr Ambassador, this sentence was included on the insistence of the Indian Prime Minister. It is beyond my knowledge and my competence to tell you anything more on the subject.' As he said this, he knew and I knew that he had said enough. My worst suspicions had been confirmed.

By the autumn of 1971 there was a general deterioration in the situation in all areas—on the ground in East Pakistan, in Indo-Pakistan relations, and in our relations with Moscow. The Soviet press had become increasing venomous and strident in its approach to Pakistan, and whilst Kosygin and Yahya still continued to maintain contact, the content and language of the messages exchanged had worsened sharply. The Soviets continued to maintain that the massive deployment of Indian forces on our borders was a defensive move, and continued to express the darkest suspicions about our intentions. Kosygin's letter to Yahya Khan, dated 7 October 1971, expresses this view in stark fashion,

> One cannot but express grave concern in connection with the official statements of Pakistani representatives, that the expansion of activities of the forces of resistance in East Pakistan will be considered by the Pakistani Martial Law Administration as an attack by India against Pakistan. In fact it means that you shift off the responsibility of the struggle inside Pakistan

onto India, to which we cannot agree. It means that the Martial Law Administration of Pakistan reserves the right to launch armed action against India at any time. The initiative in unleashing military action against India, with which the USSR is bound by lasting friendship, will meet with the most resolute reaction in the Soviet Union.

By early October the deterioration of the situation in South Asia had been both rapid and extensive, and had become the major preoccupation of the Soviet leadership. Indian and Pakistani troop build up and deployment was increasing on the borders; within East Pakistan resistance and repression were continuing in gruesome fashion and were reported in lurid terms in the world press; Mujibur Rehman remained in detention and under threat of execution; and Indira Gandhi had set off on a tour of the major capitals to prepare world leaders for her aggressive intentions which few could now doubt. Moscow was a focus of attention during this crisis, which had by now drawn into its whirlpool the other major powers, notably the USA and China. I vividly recall a discussion I had during those hectic days with my friend Ambassador Alexei Nesterenko, who at that time was Chief of the United Nations Department in the Soviet Ministry of Foreign Affairs. Surveying the current unsatisfactory state of our bilateral relations, which he said was a cause of concern for him as a true friend of Pakistan, Nesterenko urged me to show restraint, and was convinced that this difficult period would soon be over. He then made the curious observation that 'You are the victims of what we call an objective situation. Just now a game is being played for very high stakes, and it has not so much to do with you. Objective conditions have forced us to make some statements, and you should understand the situation, as well as our position.'

In the midst of this turmoil in Moscow there suddenly appeared a glimmer of hope. The Shah of Iran had arranged the lavish and opulent ceremonies celebrating the coronation of Cyrus the Great and the establishment of the Iranian monarchy, at the site of the ancient ruins of Persepolis. Among the large number of heads of state and government invited to this extravaganza were Presidents Podgorny and Yahya Khan, and a meeting between the two was arranged for 15 October. I had high hopes that the occasion and the atmosphere might be conducive to some understanding, but although there was a certain amount of drama and posturing by both sides, nothing of substance emerged from the meeting.

By the end of October the drum beats of war were sounding all over the world. Indira Gandhi was on her whirlwind tour of Western capitals, and the Soviets and Indians commenced a series of well-publicized high level consultations under Article IX of the Indo–Soviet Friendship Treaty. This was the article that called for mutual consultation in order to remove the threat of attack to which either party was subject and to take appropriate measures to ensure peace and security. Article IX took Firyubin and Marshal P.S. Kutakov, the Soviet Air Force Chief, on separate occasions, to New Delhi, and brought General Sam Maneckshaw, the Indian Chief of Army Staff, to Moscow for consultations. Pakistan, for its part, sent a high level delegation to Peking, led by Z.A. Bhutto, which included a senior military component. This visit was briefly reported in the Soviet media, without any comment, but it was clearly a matter of great concern to the Soviets. Although the officials were very guarded in their talks with me, they were much more outspoken in their talks with other ambassadors. Much more outspoken in their misgivings of Sino–Pakistan collaboration, they regarded the visit of the Bhutto mission to Peking with the gravest suspicion. For me, personally, there was an interesting bit of symbolism linked to this event. I recollect a long conversation that I had with Soviet First Deputy Foreign Minister V.A. Kuznetsov on 7 November, as we found ourselves standing next to each other for over two hours on a freezing, snowy morning in Red Square, watching the impressive Revolution Day military parade. Our conversation was wide-ranging and rather friendly. Then just as the fearful, sleek and powerful Soviet Intercontinental Ballistic Missile Launchers came into view, Kuznetsov growled, 'So Mr Bhutto has visited Peking.' It seemed to me that the remark, with the symbolism of the threatening military might rumbling before us, was quite deftly timed. The shift in the tone of the conversation, from affable to gruff, was also typical of Kuznetsov, who was regarded as one of the Kremlin's foremost diplomats and trouble shooters. I replied that we were very satisfied with the visit and regarded it as being an extremely important one. As the first deputy foreign minister was no doubt aware, his having led the Soviet team in the Sino–Soviet negotiations that had lasted some months, negotiations in Peking constituted one of the more important aspects of international relations these days, and our contacts were part of a long standing association which would help to advance the cause of peace in Asia.

The United States had by no means been a bystander in the evolution of these events, and I had maintained regular contact with Ambassador Jacob Beam, a cool, phlegmatic, and highly intelligent professional with an immense knowledge of the Soviet Union. The other western ambassadors whom I constantly met were Robert Ford of Canada, one of my closest friends, a poet, and one of the foremost experts on the Soviet Union, Duncan Wilson of the United Kingdom, Gunnar Jarring of Sweden, Roger Seydoux of France, and Helmut Allardt of the Federal German Republic. Iranian Ambassador Ahmed Mirfenderski, Mohammed Essafi of Tunis, the redoubtable Murad Ghaleb of Egypt, Ahmed Chorfi of Morocco and Rheda Malik of Algeria were other colleagues whom I met constantly and who were a great source of strength and support in those difficult days. Although Peruvian Ambassador Xavier Pérez de Cuéllar and I were colleagues in Moscow, we did not really get to know each other at that time. Our friendship developed much later in our professional lives at the United Nations. The information and advice that I received from these splendid colleagues was of the greatest value to me and provided a vast reservoir of support and encouragement. But devoid of any personal hostility, they naturally also counselled the prevailing view of their governments, that a military solution in East Pakistan was erroneous and the manner of its imposition repugnant. The interference by India was recognized and generally deplored, but all of this was overshadowed by apprehensions about an approaching conflict.

During the course of a routine meeting with US Ambassador Jacob Beam on 16 November he told me, 'As you know, your President has agreed to negotiate with some of the Bangladesh leaders who have been in touch with us, and we are hoping that there can be talks that will lead to a political settlement.' Ambassador Beam was instructed to inform the Soviets of this development because 'We do not want them to think we are intriguing behind their backs and so want to keep them fully advised, and are also hoping that they will restrain the Indians.' I had, of course, known nothing about these developments, and though somewhat irritated was not at all surprised. After all, that was the way we did, or did not do, things. In terms of communications between ambassadors and the government, it was about par for the course. Beam told me that he had conveyed this information to Kuznetsov, who was apparently quite supportive, but made no response to the suggestion that Moscow should restrain New Delhi. However, these developments were overtaken by the Indian invasion of East Pakistan, which commenced on 21 November 1971. On my own initiative I flew to Islamabad for three days of hurried consultations, which included a most useful session with my Doon School friend General Ghulam Jilani Khan, the Director General of Inter Services Intelligence (ISI), who gave me an admirable briefing on the military situation in East Pakistan. This was conveyed to Fomin immediately on my return to Moscow, stressing the urgent necessity for an immediate ceasefire and troop withdrawals before the conflict escalated. But Fomin was both defensive and evasive, and insisted on the immediate release of Mujibur Rehman and the installation of an Awami League government in Dacca. The conversation was far from friendly, and Fomin continued by expressing his concern over anti-Soviet propaganda in the Pakistani press and the anti-Soviet demonstrations all over the country. When I managed to get the discussion back to the much more serious problem of the Indian invasion of East Pakistan, Fomin finally conceded that the situation on the Indo–Pakistan border was very tense, and he formally expressed the Soviet hope that 'there would be no incidents on the West Pakistan border which would result in a general conflagration.' I replied that we hoped that peaceful conditions could be established on all borders, west as well as the east.

Shortly after I returned to the chancery we heard the news over the wireless of the outbreak of full-scale hostilities. While the war was being fought in the subcontinent I remained in constant contact with the Soviet Foreign Ministry and was summoned there at odd hours on some occasions to review the current political situation, and at others either to be given a protest about anti-Soviet demonstrations in Pakistan or else to request assistance in the evacuation of Soviet nationals from the country. I was never sure whether I was going to have a 'smile session' or a 'snarl session'. But notwithstanding the nature of the discussions that took place at these meetings, the Soviets always maintained a high standard of courtesy and correctness of behaviour. The visits made at my initiative were essentially political, as I tried to break down some of the Soviet intransigence. Needless to say, my endeavours were completely unsuccessful, and I was compelled to observe, at first hand and entirely helplessly, the dismal spectacle of the Soviet Union fiercely, and with characteristic ruthlessness, pursuing the objectives of its hegemonic interests entirely at the expense of my own country. As an experience it was both frustrating as well as mortifying, particularly when the Soviets applied their veto against the Security Council ceasefire resolution, and thus ensured the continuation of the war in East Pakistan. This attitude brought to my mind one of the Kremlin's most infamous decisions during the Second World War. This was the decision to halt the advance of the Red Army at the gates of Warsaw until such time as the Nazi occupation forces had completely crushed the Polish resistance movement within the city. The Polish resistance fighters had committed the two cardinal errors of not being pro-Moscow and of attacking the Nazis in anticipation of helping the Soviet forces to capture Warsaw.

During the period of the war in East Pakistan I also maintained close contact with a number of ambassadors of friendly missions, notably Canada, USA, China, UK, Turkey, Iran, France, Algeria, Afghanistan, and Ceylon (now Sri Lanka). The general impression that I received was that the Soviets were 'playing it alone', and neither wanted nor encouraged any form of advice or consultation. Until the fall of Dacca, an objective for which the Soviets were becoming increasingly desperate, it was impossible for most diplomats to get anything out of the Soviet Foreign Ministry except the rigid pro-Indian party line. After this aim was accomplished, the Soviet attitude once more turned into that of the bland peacemaker, ready to discuss anything with anybody.

The events unfolding at the United Nations in New York were obviously both actively directed by, and closely followed in Moscow. The powerful speeches of the US and Chinese delegates were not reported in the Soviet media, nor of course was the brilliant oratory of Zulfikar Ali Bhutto. George Bush, Sr., the United States Permanent Representative at the time, and later President of the United States, described Bhutto's intervention as one of the most moving speeches ever heard in the Council Chamber.

The Soviets were clearly not pleased with these developments, and the aggressive activities of the newly arrived Chinese in the Security

Council, evoked much anger and bitterness in Moscow. But the Soviets had long ago ignored any slight compunction that they may have had in the exercise of their veto in the Security Council, and this occasion was no exception. For the Kremlin, a much more serious situation was created by the massive vote that followed the debate in the General Assembly. Although this was reported in the Soviet news media in terms of linguistic sophistry that would have provoked the admiration of the most skilful Jesuit pamphleteer, it nevertheless failed to satisfy large sections of the Soviet public. It even left Soviet officials disturbed by the realization of the extent of the Indo-Soviet diplomatic isolation. An extraordinary propaganda campaign was initiated, both internally and externally, to mitigate the moral censure implicit in the massive General Assembly vote. All the shibboleths that the Soviet propaganda machine had churned out over the years—the inadmissibility of settling disputes by force, of not occupying territories by force, of not violating settled international boundaries—were conspicuously ignored in the case of the Indian attack and occupation of East Pakistan. Instead, the Soviet emphasis was on the support of the freedom struggle for Bangladesh.

The war and turbulence that prevailed in East Pakistan compelled me to make an effort to cajole and pester the Soviet officials as much as I could, but as I sat through meetings in the Kremlin and the Foreign Ministry I was acutely aware that my presence was entirely peripheral. In a meeting with Fomin on 11 December I was told that General Farman Ali's proposal, something of which I was totally unaware at the time, represented the only realistic approach, and that some of our 'other friends' were thinking on these same lines. I immediately reported this in a telegram to the ministry, and in the deafening silence that ensued I got a follow-up report from Fomin stating that the proposals that had originally emanated from General Farman Ali had subsequently been rescinded upon orders from the president. In another meeting, at about the same time, Firyubin mentioned the 'Polish Draft Resolution' that was before the Security Council, and commended its acceptance. Since I knew nothing about this one either, I did not respond. This document has, of course, been the subject of much heated public debate since the dramatic moment when Bhutto tore it up with a flourish during his tearful speech, and stormed out of the Security Council chamber.

In the cool and collected light provided by hindsight, a great utilitarian device for historians, it is possible to make a realistic assessment of the issue. In the first place, the Pakistan delegation had decided to reject the Polish draft, even before entering the Security Council chamber. I believe this decision to be correct on two counts, even though it could not have been an easy one to take in the tense and surcharged atmosphere of uncertainty that prevailed at the time. First, only someone like Bhutto could have had the combination of statesmanship and courage to push it through. Secondly, the paper that Bhutto tore up and threw on his table was not, in fact, the draft resolution document, but a piece of paper containing his rough notes and some doodling. But that too is alright, because it helped create the requisite drama. As for the substance of the draft resolution (United Nations Security Council Document S/10453/Rev.l, Poland: revised draft resolution, Original: English, Security Council 1614th Session, 15 December 1971), it envisaged a ceasefire and the immediate installation of an Awami League government in East Pakistan, to be followed by troop withdrawals and the repatriation of West Pakistanis, without specifying the timing and modalities for implementation. This meant, in reality, that the Government of Pakistan would formally accept and legally endorse, in an international forum, the forcible occupation of a large part of its territory, a commitment unprecedented in history. In my view, such a formal abdication of national sovereignty is as demeaning as it is unthinkable and unacceptable. Finally, we need to look at the sequence of events connected with the introduction of the Polish resolution. Viewed with the benefit of hindsight, it emerges as one of the quirks that one finds dotted about in the history of all nations. The ceasefire in Dacca had commenced at 1700 hours local time on 15 December 1971, and the surrender was signed the next morning. The UN Security Council took up consideration of Draft Resolution S/l0453/Rev.1 at its meeting that commenced at 1210 hours EST (New York time) on 15 December 1971. By this time the ceasefire had already gone into effect in East Pakistan, and the members of the UN Security Council, as they took their seats and assumed consideration of the 'Polish Resolution', were blissfully unaware that the break-up of Pakistan, one of the United Nations' member states, was already a fait accompli.

After the inglorious surrender in Dacca and the outrage in West Pakistan that followed it, Yahya Khan was forced out of office, and Z.A. Bhutto, flown in from New York, was sworn in as the President and the Chief Martial Law Administrator. True to form, he took a number of political and administrative measures that immediately established his dynamic stamp and fired the spirits of his demoralized countrymen who were desperately looking for leadership, and enthusiastically supported him in the Herculean task of 'picking up the little pieces' as he graphically described the situation. India, quite obviously, was the first country to recognize Bangladesh but prompted by the Soviet Union a number of East European communist countries did the same, to be followed by a number of Commonwealth countries. Bhutto reacted by immediately breaking diplomatic relations with any country that recognized Bangladesh, and also withdrew Pakistan from membership of the Commonwealth. I became a little concerned that as Bhutto went about severing diplomatic relations left, right, and centre, he might also include the USSR in his frenzy, due to its inevitable recognition of Bangladesh and warned against such action, as Moscow was much too important for us to abandon. I need not have worried, because the far-sighted Bhutto had not only taken this into account, but was already thinking about ways to involve the Soviet Union in the solution of our problems. Consequently, it was not long after Bhutto assumed power that I received indications from Islamabad that he was angling for an invitation to visit Moscow.

In the meanwhile, towards the end of December, I received a summons for a meeting with Kosygin. By this time I was accustomed to the vagaries in the moods and manners of reception in the Kremlin, but this time I was taken by surprise. Normal meetings with Kosygin were always very businesslike, the only refreshment being a bottle of mineral water surrounded by a few glasses placed in the centre of the table. This time there was tea and biscuits, as well as a bottle of pepper vodka, which Kosygin said would cure my cold (he was quite right). Kosygin welcomed me, said that we had not met for some time and that much had happened since then. He wanted to know what I had been doing, and what should we now be doing, I replied that I had just endured one of the most difficult periods of my life, standing by helplessly as I observed my country being invaded and torn apart. With time on my hands, I had gone through the archives in my embassy and found records of the exchange of telegrams in 1965 between President Ayub Khan, Indian Prime Minister Shastri, and Prime Minister Kosygin. Shastri was now dead and Ayub Khan had been forced into sequestration, but Prime Minister Kosygin continued to be a key player in the drama of South Asia. I noted that in the 1965 telegrams and messages that Kosygin sent to the South Asian leaders there was a passionate call for peace and a demand for an urgent ceasefire. Kosygin had said that this was not the time to apportion blame, or to ascertain who fired the first shot, or even made the first provocative action. This was the time to immediately stop the fighting. Any delay in a ceasefire could only add to the death and destruction that had already occurred. I said that I frankly failed to understand how the same Prime Minister Kosygin, who so passionately and correctly pleaded for peace in 1965, should now, in 1971, not once but twice, veto a ceasefire resolution presented at the Security Council of the United Nations. What had changed? Why should the killing and destruction continue now? This action was entirely contrary to the peaceful intentions so often expressed by Moscow over the past two years, which we regarded as genuine. They could not be reconciled with Soviet active military and diplomatic aid to India, as a result of which my countrymen were being killed and bloodshed continuing perhaps even now as a consequence of the Soviet veto in the Security Council. I said that in 1965 Kosygin had written to Ayub and Shastri stating that whatever may have been the original cause, the first objective was to stop the killing. But today the Soviets, for reasons of their own, had done everything possible for the continuation of bloodshed and the break-up of Pakistan. Knowing that I had nothing more to lose, since the Soviets had already done their worst, I went on to include sharp comments such as remarking on Soviet encouragement for the violation of international borders, and of Soviet interference in internal affairs. I said that Pakistan had done nothing to harm Soviet interests, tongue in cheek over the Kissinger trip to Peking, and had always worked for good relations with Moscow, but all this had been rejected by the Soviets in favour of India. I said that in the life of nations, as well as men, there comes a time when dignity and honour become as important as survival, and remain inseparable. Pakistan was going through this phase, and it was something which the prime minister, as a Russian, with a knowledge and personal experience of his own glorious history, would surely understand.

Kosygin listened very calmly to my tirade and displayed no emotion whatsoever. He replied at some length, but despite the provocative nature of my remarks he did not become either indignant or polemical. He patiently recalled how, in this very room, he had urged us to find a political solution to the problem of East Pakistan, how he had cautioned us about the mounting consequences of a failure to seriously attend to the problem caused by the refugees. These were the issues that were the root cause of the problem and he reiterated that the Soviets had consistently stated that this could only be solved by a political act that took into account the lawful interests of the people of East Pakistan. Turning to the future, Kosygin said that the Soviet Union continued to maintain the greatest interest in Pakistan and wished to have the best of relations with us. The Soviet leadership was following events in Pakistan closely with a view to furthering our friendship. I suggested that if this was really his wish then he should consider inviting Bhutto to visit Moscow at an early date. I was sure that the suggestion would be received in a positive manner. This was a gross understatement, because knowing Bhutto's state of mind at that time I was certain that an invitation would be accepted with alacrity. Kosygin said he would give the matter some thought, and then said abruptly, 'I hear that you will be leaving us shortly. When will that be?' I was at that time under orders of transfer to Madrid, but not sure of my departure date. When I told the prime minister that I expected it to take another six weeks, he nodded his head and said quietly 'We will see what we can do.' Before I left his office Kosygin insisted that we drink a toast in his special pepper vodka. As we did so, Kosygin said to me that he was deeply conscious of my remark that nations can only survive with honour.

Some time after my meeting with Kosygin, I received a message from Islamabad, which indicated that Soviet Ambassador Rodionov had delivered a message to President Bhutto containing an invitation for an official visit to Moscow. I was instructed to stay on in Moscow until after the visit, and my posting to Madrid had been cancelled, although this was for other reasons.

At the end of 1971, I reported to the ministry my assessment of how the situation appeared from Moscow. The Soviet presence in South

Asia was far greater than it had ever been before, and the Kremlin intended to keep it that way, if not expand it. This attitude was not something new, and was a fundamental manifestation of Russia's sense of itself as an expansionist power, which had nothing to do with ideological considerations and which constituted the principal motivation for all Russian foreign policy, whether directed by the Czars or the Politburo. Any foreigner who has lived in the country for more than a few weeks can hardly fail to be impressed by the innate sense of aggressive pride which every Russian feels within himself, and the massive, jingoistic confidence, with which they regard their country's relationship with the rest of the world. Neither the shortages of goods and long queues at every shop, nor the shabbiness and difficulties of daily living, can detract from this fierce, expansionist pride, that seems part of the Russian subconscious. This was not something new, and was not something that was instilled by the communist system. It was basic to the Russian character, as so poetically described by one of Russia's greatest sons, Nikolai Gogol, in *Dead Souls*:

> And thou, Russia, art not thou, too, rushing headlong like the fastest troika that is not outdistanced?... What is the meaning of this awe inspiring onrush?... Russia, whither art thou speeding? Answer me! She gives no answer... Everything on earth is flying past, and the other nations and states, eyeing her askance, make way for her and draw aside...

CHIAROSCURO

In October 1971, when the Soviets had begun to heat up their propaganda war against Pakistan, I was told by Fomin, at the end of a routine meeting in his office, that the military repression in East Pakistan had aroused much indignation amongst the Soviet people. As a result, he continued, there were representatives from some factories and other institutions in Moscow, who wished to meet, me and present petitions to my government. I responded that I would be happy to meet them, provided that his KGB guards posted at my gate would permit them to come into my office. I was not going to meet them on the pavement. Ignoring this sarcasm, Fomin said that one delegation would call on me the following Monday morning, another that afternoon, and some more later during the week.

I decided to prepare a paper stating the Pakistani position, and had it ready in its Russian translation by the time the first delegation arrived at my office. Six men and two women duly arrived on the Monday morning, frowns on their faces and feigned indignation in their bearing. Refusing the refreshments that I offered them, the spokesman launched into a diatribe expressing the indignation of the workers in his factory at the repression being carried out by the army in East Pakistan. He handed me a sheet of paper carrying the declaration of his colleagues, and asked that it be conveyed to my government. He added that another copy of this declaration had been posted on the official notice board at their workplace. I thanked the delegation for their visit and for the interest that they had taken over the difficulties in my country, and I briefly explained to them the Pakistan position with the request that they convey it to their comrades. Just to simplify their task, I too had prepared a paper which indicated the factual position prevailing in East Pakistan. I suggested that they study this paper and then post it on their factory notice board alongside their own declaration, so that everybody got an opportunity to see both sides of the picture. This set the cat amongst the pigeons, and sent the delegates into a virtual flurry. The spokesperson, to whom I gave my note, acted as though I had handed him a grenade with the pin pulled out. One of the other members muttered that their instructions had been to deliver the declaration and nothing else. I ostentatiously put their declaration on one side of my table and assured the delegation that it would be forwarded to my government by the next diplomatic bag, but this would only be done after one of my diplomatic officers had visited their factory and seen my statement posted alongside their declaration on the factory notice board. Until then their declaration would remain on the corner of my desk, where they saw it now. After some consultation amongst themselves, they requested the use of my telephone, and after making the call trooped out of my office without my statement.

That afternoon there was a repeat of the morning's performance. But there were no further visits and the quota for the week that Fomin had indicated remained unfulfilled.

In early November 1971, when Indo–Pakistan tensions were at their highest and the Soviet anti-Pakistan propaganda was at full blast, there was a visit to Moscow undertaken by General Sam Maneckshaw, the

Chief of Staff of the Indian army. This consultation, it was loudly proclaimed, was in accordance with Clause IX of the Indo–Soviet Friendship Treaty. Diana and I were attending a ballet at the Bolshoi that evening when we saw General Maneckshaw arrive at the theatre, accompanied by an escort of Soviet generals in full uniform. Since Sam was an old family friend we decided to try and meet him during the intermission, and were able to catch him just before he was taken into the Czar's private salon for refreshments. Sam was delighted to see us and we greeted in oriental fashion by throwing our arms around each other, followed by two loud moustache fringed kisses which he bestowed on Diana. With the two countries on the brink of war, the sight of the Pakistan ambassador and the Indian army chief hugging each other in the foyer of the Bolshoi Theatre in Moscow must have appeared incongruous, to say the least. The astonishment evoked amongst Sam's hosts was totally undisguised, but added to this was the fact that Sam and I carried out a short but totally innocuous conversation in Gujrati, our mother tongue. This obviously slipped past the Hindi-speaking officer whom the Soviets would inevitably have inducted into Sam's entourage, and added to the general consternation.

The next morning, at the end of my meeting with Fomin, he remarked that he heard that I had met the Indian chief of army staff the previous evening. I told Fomin that Sam and I had been very good friends all our lives, and that we greatly enjoyed meeting each other again. He asked me what we had talked about, and gave a sly smile when I replied, 'Didn't your people tell you?'

* * *

There was the usual National Day reception at the embassy of Finland in Moscow, which this particular year took place the day after we got news of the fall of Dacca. Diana and I attended the function with a very heavy heart, and did so only because as ambassador to Finland it was a diplomatic obligation, and also because we were determined to carry on as normally as we could. The chief guest at the Finnish reception was Dmitri Polyansky, the youngest member of the Soviet Politburo. He was an attractive person, whom we had got to know and like. After the main toasts had been raised to Finland and Soviet–

Finnish friendship, Polyansky sought out Diana and raising his glass, asked her to drink a toast with him. It was an unnecessary act of bravado which Diana instinctively rejected. Holding firmly on to her glass she refused to raise it, and said with the utmost firmness and dignity, *'Sevednoye nyet'* ('Not today'). Resisting his further attempts to drink a toast with him, she finally and with great grace, acquiesced to perhaps do so on a future occasion, and Polyansky withdrew equally gracefully. I was never so proud of my wonderful Diana, and so were the numerous guests who witnessed the incident. We apologized to our host, the ambassador of Finland, for any embarrassment that may have been caused to him, but he forgave Diana in most generous terms of understanding and admiration.

Some weeks later we again found ourselves closely quartered with Polyansky. He was the Politburo member designated to escort Bhutto on his presidential visit to Moscow, and at one stage during the proceedings Diana had the opportunity to talk to Polyansky alone. She said that she owed him an apology for her behaviour to him at the Finland embassy reception. Polyansky graciously responded, 'Madame, I could never be offended by your patriotism and your dignity.' So when we met the Polyanskys some years later as colleagues in Tokyo, we were able to continue a friendship that was already well-established, and one that had survived the vicissitudes of diplomatic fortunes.

MEANWHILE IN PAKISTAN

Historians will argue for a long time over the causes of the break-up of Pakistan. Just as the creation of the state was a unique political phenomenon so, in its own way, was the political separation of East and West Pakistan. To describe East Pakistan's action as 'secession' is an oxymoron in terms of political science, for the reality was that the majority had 'seceded' from the minority. East Pakistan had become Bangladesh, West Pakistan had become simply Pakistan and the necessary cartographic amendments were incorporated in the maps of South Asia and the world. But beyond this of course, and what really mattered, was the massive nature of the human tragedy, the death and destruction, the separation of families and friends, and the mortal trauma inflicted on the fabric of a society hitherto composed of nearly 200 million souls. The standard view now prevalent, and one with which I am in general agreement, was that the main responsibility for the disaster rested with three men—Mujibur Rehman, Z.A. Bhutto, and Yahya Khan—the first two because the compulsions of their fascist character precluded the compromise and sharing of power implicit in a democratic polity, and the third because he completely lost his earlier political acumen, and committed strategic blunders of the highest magnitude. Other long-term considerations, such as economic and political disparities, and the debilitating geopolitical presence of a hostile India situated between the two provinces, were also major factors that led to the dismemberment of Pakistan. But this is neither the place, nor have I the competence, to attempt a complete historical analysis of these definitive events.

In Pakistan, Bhutto was faced with a multitude of overwhelming problems; the major ones being that of having to recover over 90,000 persons designated as 'prisoners of war' and held in camps in India, and also to recover territory in West Pakistan that was under Indian occupation. His major assets in this dire situation were his own indomitable strength of will and his charisma, and above all, the spirit of the people of Pakistan who gave him a blank cheque and told him to do with them as he wished because they were fully with him. In the background also, was the support of the United States, and of Nixon and Kissinger in particular, whose regard for the country had prompted the famous 'tilt towards Pakistan' remark.

Bhutto embarked upon a whirlwind tour of friendly countries that took him to China and a number of Muslim and Arab nations, in order to galvanize support for Pakistan, and he achieved a considerable measure of success. In the meanwhile he also defused a potential domestic crisis, removing General Gul Hasan, the Army Chief, and Air Marshal Rahim Khan, the Air Force Chief, who had earlier been two of his main supporters. Dramatically accusing them of 'Bonapartism', he dispatched them as ambassadors to Vienna and Madrid, respectively. This was part of the exercise that Bhutto commenced to bring the administration under his control and to seize firmly all the levers of power.

So far as the USSR was concerned, we had maintained diplomatic relations, as noted earlier, and with the invitation to visit Moscow in the spring, Bhutto had fast approached his moment of truth, and the opportunity to address the major problem with which he was confronted—the post-conflict situation that prevailed in South Asia.

CHAPTER ELEVEN

USSR 1972

'Perché! sempre una mutazione laschiae lo addentellato per la edificazione dell altra.'
('For one change always leaves an indent for the edification of the next.')
– Niccolo Machiavelli, *The Prince.*

For us the New Year commenced with a splendid party thrown by the Canadian Ambassador Robert Ford, one of the ablest and greatest ambassadors to have served in Moscow after the Second World War, and his charming and vivacious wife, Theresa. For a few short but happy hours spent among close friends, Diana and I were able to largely overlook the tragic events back home. But once the festivities were over and reality returned with the break of dawn, I was reminded of a passage in Thomas Mann's lovely work *The Magic Mountain*: 'Time has no division to mark its passage. There is never a thunderstorm to announce the beginning of a new year. Even when a new century begins, it is only we mortals who ring bells and fire off pistols.' As I surveyed it in the first weeks of 1972, the reality was that Pakistan had been dismembered and 90,000 of its brave soldiers and citizens were held prisoner in India. That the political and economic future of what was left of Pakistan was dubious to say the least, and the Indo–Soviet predominance in the subcontinent was overwhelming. The Indo–Pakistan war of 1971 had provided the Soviet Union with considerable, immediate, political advantages. It now had a massive political presence in India, and an overwhelming one in Bangladesh. If Tashkent marked the initiation of Soviet influence in South Asia, then the Bangladesh war of 1971 could be regarded as the definitive consolidation of that presence, for the Soviet gains in the region, in practical terms, were infinitely greater than anything acquired at Tashkent. Bhutto instinctively understood the changed scenario, and had the vision not only to adapt to the new realities, but to seek a modus vivendi for the future; hence his anxiety to meet the Soviet leaders in Moscow. The Soviets, in their usual cautious manner, took some time to respond, first consolidating their gains in South Asia and then preparing the ground for the next stage. Kosygin invited (summoned?) Mujibur Rehman for a meeting in Tashkent, and the symbolism of the encounter was manifest. They drew up the outlines of their future co-operation, and the talks also provided Kosygin with background material for his forthcoming meeting with Bhutto.

News and reports of the drastic changes that were taking place in Pakistan were flooding my desk in Moscow and formed the topic of our staff meetings as well as, occasionally, and with due precautionary diligence, our meetings in the Soviet Foreign Ministry. We were, of course, totally unaware at that time of the dramatic events that were unfolding in Pakistan. A group of enraged army officers, at the level of brigadiers and colonels, had called for Yahya Khan's resignation, and their threatened putsch was held off, as Army Chief Gul Hasan and Air Force Chief Rahim Khan, hastily made arrangements for Bhutto to return to the country and take over power. Bhutto was on his way back from the meeting of the UN Security Council in New York, and was nervously marking time in Rome waiting for events to unfold in Islamabad. A special aircraft sent by Gul Hasan and Rahim Khan brought Bhutto from Rome to Islamabad, where at a hastily convened ceremony late at night Yahya Khan resigned as president and handed over power to Bhutto as President and the Chief Martial Law Administrator.

Yahya was almost immediately placed under house arrest, where he remained in incarceration until his death a few years later. A number of the senior most officers in the armed forces were either dismissed or compulsorily retired. These included Generals Peerzada, Hamid, Umer, and Mitha; 'fat and flabby generals' as Bhutto contemptuously referred to them in a public statement. A new chief of naval staff was appointed, whilst Gul Hasan and Rahim Khan retained their posts. This arrangement did not last very long, and following a conflict born out of mutual distrust, Bhutto removed the two service chiefs and sent them off as ambassadors. He continued this purge by retiring a number of senior military officers, including most of those who had originally led the revolt against Yahya Khan, and were instrumental in installing him as president. He also attempted to discredit the army through the widespread display of the humiliating surrender ceremony in Dacca, but strong opposition from the military obliged him to curb this campaign. This development, coupled with the appointment of the controversial General Tikka Khan as Chief of the Army Staff, were perhaps the first seeds of the conflict between Bhutto and the army, that eventually led to devastating consequences for the former.

Bhutto then established a commission to carry out a judicial enquiry into the causes of the military defeat. Headed by Chief Justice Hamoodur Rehman, an eminent Bengali jurist, the commission examined a large number of witnesses, including former president, Yahya Khan, and in due course produced a voluminous report. But the Hamoodur Rehman Commission Report was immediately suppressed and was never released to the public. Several years later the document was leaked under mysterious circumstances, and was only made public after its contents were already known, with the time long past for taking any effective measures.

Bhutto's next move was a blast of a storm that had an impact on us in Moscow. In a brutal style that was soon to become the hallmark of his administration, there was an announcement on the TV and radio of the termination of service of over a hundred civil servants. Many of these were senior officials with several years of honourable and dedicated service to the country, and included federal secretaries and ambassadors. No causes were assigned nor reasons stated for the dismissals. A senior minister of the government just came on to the TV and read out the names of the victims. The fascism in Bhutto's character was no longer latent, nor was there any further doubt about the nature of the government he intended to impose upon Pakistan. As I read through the list, seated at my desk in Moscow, I could find no reason for either the inclusion or the exclusion of my name. I had submitted my resignation as ambassador to the USSR as soon as Bhutto had taken office, and had been asked to remain at my post, but that really did not mean anything under the prevailing circumstances. An unsubstantiated account, repeated to me by someone who claimed that he was in Bhutto's presence when he was told about my resignation, stated that Bhutto was furious, and said 'Who the hell does he think he is, offering his resignation to me?' When told that it was the correct procedure, though not always followed, he still remained furious and said, 'Then why aren't all the other bastards doing it?' You could not win with Zulfikar Ali Bhutto.

President Bhutto's visit to Moscow lasted from the afternoon of Thursday, 16 March, to the forenoon of Saturday, 18 March 1972. He was accompanied by his wife Nusrat, and son, Murtaza. Bhutto also brought with him an impressive official party; a substantial group of party-senators and members of the National Assembly along with a large press contingent which included senior and respected journalists, including Mazhar Ali Khan. The official delegation consisted of Presidential Adviser Rafi Raza; Foreign Minister Aziz Ahmed; Foreign Secretary Sultan Khan; M.M. Ahmed, the Chairman of the Planning Commission; Said Ahmed of the State Bank of Pakistan, and Ambassadors Aftab Ahmed Khan; and M.A. Bhatti from the Foreign Ministry. Among the parliamentarians was my good friend, the indomitable Nawab Akbar Bugti, from Balochistan, who stayed on with me as a personal guest at the end of the visit in a gesture of warm companionship that was never forgotten. The brief visit was necessarily crowded, and included one substantial meeting with Kosygin at the Kremlin in the morning, which was attended by both of the full delegations. On the afternoon of 17 March there was a meeting with Brezhnev at the office of the Communist Party of the Soviet Union. In accordance with Soviet protocol, this was a very restricted meeting, attended by only three persons on either side, whose names had been designated by the hosts. On the Pakistani side it was the president, the foreign minister and the ambassador, and on the Soviet side it was Secretary General Brezhnev, Foreign Minister Gromyko, and Ambassador Rodionov, the Soviet ambassador to Pakistan. The rest of the programme consisted of the obligatory visit to Lenin's tomb, the laying of a wreath, a performance at the Bolshoi, and a banquet hosted by Kosygin in the Kremlin. Separate arrangements were of course made for the parliamentarians and the press, and as usual the Soviet authorities had taken care of all the logistical requirements. These excellent backup facilities provided by the administration in totalitarian states is always heartily welcomed by the resident ambassador during an official visit.

The composition of the Pakistani delegation was a great relief to me, because it did not include General Tikka Khan as Bhutto had initially wished. During my meetings with Soviet officials it became very clear that they harboured a strong dislike of the General and viewed his appointment as the army chief with extreme suspicion and distrust. The officials became almost hostile when they heard from their sources in Islamabad that he might accompany the president to Moscow. I conveyed this to the government in my telegrams, and gently suggested that his inclusion in the delegation would be counterproductive. Kosygin, especially, appeared to be fiercely allergic to Tikka Khan, and it was evident that during his recent Tashkent meeting with Mujibur Rehman, whose animosity to the General was much greater than that of Kosygin, the Bangladeshi leader had succeeded in adding much fuel to the fire. The Soviet prime minister was unusually graphic and dramatic, when he told me that Mujib had trembled, wept, and had almost broken down at the mention of Tikka Khan during their talks. Some of Mujib's melodrama had obviously rubbed off on to the otherwise quite phlegmatic Leningrader, and this prompted the insistence in my advice to exclude General Tikka Khan from the delegation. I do not know how Bhutto reacted to my suggestions, as he was quite notorious for his fury at being crossed on even minor matters. But any misgivings that he may have had on this issue should have been cleared by Kosygin's brutal frankness at their first meeting.

Kosygin commenced the meeting in the Kremlin on 16 March by welcoming President Bhutto and his delegation to Moscow, and said that he looked forward to a productive outcome of the visit. The greeting was by no means effusive, and reflected the extreme, personal reserve with which Kosygin regarded Bhutto. Podgorny had earlier told Yahya Khan that 'Kosygin has hitched his star to Tashkent', whereas Bhutto's immediate past had included an election campaign which contained, as a major component, some fierce denunciations of Tashkent. Consequently, there was a bit of unpleasantness that would need to be cleared up. Kosygin took his seat after briefly stating that it was customary to first offer the floor to the visitor. Bhutto began by thanking Kosygin for his invitation, and immediately launched into a veritable panegyric about the importance that Pakistan, and he personally, attached to relations with the Soviet Union. He admitted that there had been misunderstandings and obstacles in the past, but he was here to remove them and to urge that we establish a new relationship based upon trust and friendship. Bhutto was, of course, a superb orator, and possessed a personal charm that was almost impossible to resist. On this occasion, he combined both attributes and beamed them at the stony-faced Kosygin in megawatt doses. At one point Bhutto interrupted his peroration, walked around the table, and shook Kosygin's somewhat limp hand in a theatrical gesture of his vintage. He urged Kosygin to peruse the PPP manifesto which outlined his plan of action and his commitment to peace. Bhutto concluded by stating that as a token of its earnestness and goodwill, Pakistan would immediately accord diplomatic recognition to the German Democratic Republic.

Kosygin, who appeared to have been inured to Bhutto's powerful charm offensive, commenced his response in a stern manner that he maintained throughout its presentation. He said that the Soviet Union had first advised and then warned Yahya Khan against military action in East Pakistan, and had always urged a political solution. Unfortunately the Pakistani authorities had disregarded this advice and embarked upon a course that led to the disaster which Moscow had predicted. Linking this with the issue of Tikka Khan, Kosygin said that the former 'would be torn to pieces in Dacca', and went on to deplore the fact that he had just been chosen as the new army chief. 'Your appointment of Tikka Khan as Army Chief of Staff has created a strong reaction with Mujib, who believes that this means the end of all relations, and the Indian reaction is similar.' Kosygin softened his position a little when responding to Bhutto's proposals for improving relations, and said that the Soviet Union would always reciprocate 'any positive measures taken by Pakistan'.

He was almost contemptuous as he tossed aside Bhutto's announcement of establishing diplomatic relations with East Germany, saying that was entirely Pakistan's affair, and that sooner or later 'you would have to do so anyway'. Kosygin concluded with the categorical assertion that, 'If these events are repeated, and we are once again confronted with the same situation, then I tell you that we will act in exactly the same manner as we have done.'

Turning to the issue of the steel mill, Kosygin said he was concerned that we had rejected the Mauripur site chosen by the Soviet survey team, which had carefully viewed all the factors, including environmental aspects, before making their decision. He said that the delay caused by a review of location would have serious financial consequences and unfavourably alter the economic assumptions of the project. Bhutto responded that he had been compelled to oblige his Senior Minister, J.A. Rahim, whose objections on environmental grounds had been very vehement, 'even though I told him why are you worried, you will be dead by the time the steel mill is built'. The atmosphere of the meeting gradually improved as we talked about other issues of mutual concern, and Kosygin even allowed himself a slight smile as we took our leave.

The next afternoon we had a substantive meeting with Brezhnev at the office of the Politburo of the Communist Party of the Soviet Union, and the results that ensued had a crucial bearing on the history of South Asia. The severely restricted meeting was attended only by Brezhnev, Foreign Minister Gromyko, and Ambassador Rodionov. The Pakistani representatives were President Bhutto, Foreign Minister Aziz Ahmed, and myself. The only other person present was Viktor Sukhodrev, the brilliant Soviet interpreter, who had almost become a legend during his lifetime. Viktor had spent his boyhood in England and the USA, and had adapted his considerable and unusual skills to speaking with a flawless English or American accent, depending on the background of the interlocutor. We had become good friends while in Moscow, and were able to continue this association many years later when Viktor worked at the United Nations in New York as Special Adviser to the Secretary General.

Brezhnev, who obviously had none of Kosygin's personal reservations about Bhutto, greeted his guest very warmly, and as we took our seats at the table the atmosphere had none of the chill of the previous day, and in fact seemed quite congenial.[1]

The secretary general of the Communist Party of the Soviet Union started by asking how the talks of the day before had proceeded, and Bhutto said he thought we had made a good beginning, but perhaps Gromyko could testify to that, whereupon Brezhnev said that he only agreed with Gromyko 50 per cent of the time, except when it came to peace, where they both were in full agreement. I thought that this kind of friendly banter was a pleasant way to start negotiations, and a good omen. Brezhnev said that he knew that Bhutto was confronted with many complex problems and wanted him to regard the present meeting as one for consultation and mutual advice. The conversation should be frank—'I am no diplomat,' he said. Bhutto thanked Brezhnev for his invitation and his hospitality, and said that although the talks had gone well so far, he was seeking not only Soviet advice but also help and co-operation from Moscow. He said that previously we had some intractable problems with India but now they had assumed a triangular dimension. He added that he had taken the very difficult decision to release Mujibur Rehman, but recognition of Bangladesh would still take some time.

So far as India was concerned, Bhutto said that he had given a pledge to the Indian prime minister for a 'turning over of a new leaf', and he was now repeating the same pledge to Brezhnev. The history of the past centuries could not be overturned immediately, but the new generation had the courage and vision to turn the page and establish new traditions. The Pakistan government intended to stand by its commitment to peace in the subcontinent, as time would show. Bhutto added that the Soviet Union could be of positive help in making peace, and as an example cited the instance of the release of Mujibur Rehman, which had been prompted not only by objective considerations but also in response to Soviet demands. Bhutto said he was severely criticized by the army for releasing Mujibur Rehman without first recovering Pakistan's prisoners of war. The opposition, in fact, was so serious that he was compelled to dismiss his army and air force chiefs. Although Bhutto did not mention it, these were the two service chiefs principally involved in the manoeuvring that had brought Bhutto to power, but Brezhnev was doubtlessly aware of this.

Bhutto described how the problem of the prisoners of war was becoming increasingly serious, adding to the difficulties of Pakistan which was already forced to negotiate from a position of weakness. He addressed Indira Gandhi's complaint that Pakistan was in the process of raising four new divisions and said he was compelled to maintain a minimum-force strength. Bhutto reiterated his commitment to genuine attempts at peace—'my assurance to a great power' and said that the POW issue was a constant impediment to his efforts. India could not exploit this situation indefinitely, as international conventions and other objective realities, would compel their return. Positions would only harden if Indira Gandhi thought that by prolonging custody of the prisoners of war she could impose a humiliating peace. Bhutto added that he was prepared to offer a formula to advance the peace process.

Brezhnev said that there had been much international speculation about Bhutto's current visit to the USSR, and that China and the USA had been particularly concerned. However, the basis of a solution remained between Pakistan, India, and Bangladesh. He warned Bhutto that he should beware of outside interference as both China and the USA had their own agendas. The USSR was only concerned with a policy that was 'in accordance with the interests of the people', and that the strongest and best policy was that which was 'based on realism'. Brezhnev expressed 'deep satisfaction that you deemed it necessary to visit the USSR, and regarded it not as a status seeking visit but as a business visit'. Under the circumstances Brezhnev said he felt deeply conscious 'of the responsibility for the advice or the recommendations that we give you'. Starting with the issue of Soviet–Pakistan relations, he said he wanted them advanced in all fields, economic, cultural, and political. Brezhnev said that this was not only his personal view, but he was speaking in the name of the state and the party. There should be a spirit of accord between Pakistan and the USSR, 'as we are prepared to go as far as possible and are bound by nothing'. Waxing theatrical, and expanding the geographic range of his vision, Brezhnev said, 'We would like decisions taken and solutions found which would lay the foundation stone of permanent peace in all three countries.' Referring to the prisoners of war, Brezhnev said that he fully understood the feelings of the Pakistani people and appreciated their anxieties. He also fully accepted Bhutto's assurances that once returned these persons would not be used for war. 'But that is not for me alone. I am not Indira Gandhi. That is the basis of the difficulty.' However, he noted with satisfaction that Bhutto and Gandhi were prepared to meet.

Bhutto agreed and said that what was important was the result that emerged from the meeting. If there was no agreement, then it would be a great setback. The outcome would be either a case of complete success or still greater tension. Brezhnev agreed and asked Bhutto for his views on 'a meeting which would conclude with an agreement on non-use of force and non-interference in each other's internal affairs'. The Soviet Union would be prepared to contribute in all possible ways, and the treaty would mark a radical turn in developments, fostering peace between India and Pakistan. Brezhnev said that such a step would require courage, 'but we already know that you have always had that'. He added that the views which he had just expressed were entirely his own and had not even been discussed with his colleagues. However, if he could receive Bhutto's 'positive attitude' he would try to 'lead India in that direction'. He urged Bhutto to be frank in his response 'as we sincerely want to be good neighbours and friends'. On the subject of Bangladesh, Brezhnev urged Bhutto to be realistic. History could not be reversed as, forty nations had already recognized Bangladesh, and that USA and China would soon follow suit. Brezhnev urged Bhutto to recognize Bangladesh as early as possible, but there would be no offence taken if he did not follow this advice. Brezhnev then embarked upon a long dissertation on the necessity for normalizing relations with India and of how much the USSR could help in this process.

Bhutto thanked Brezhnev for his ideas and suggestions and said that since many of them were new, his reactions were tentative. Sensitive to the delicacy of the situation, Bhutto told Brezhnev that any thoughts conveyed to Indira Gandhi should be 'treated as objective considerations and not conveyed as emanating from me'. Hurriedly providing forthright reassurances, Brezhnev said, 'We will be very cautious in presenting them to Indira. Clumsy handling will spoil the best proposals.' Bhutto suggested moving from simple to more difficult problems. As a 'creature of the people and an elected leader, not a military dictator', he would go by the sense of public feeling, and 'slowly push it or take great leaps forward', depending on the situation, using political methods to educate the people. Whatever the progress, big or small, it should not be played as a victory or a defeat, since the Indian and Pakistani public, as well as press, tended to dramatize events. Similarly, although involvement of the Soviet Union was vital to the process, they should not give the impression of big power involvement. Bhutto said that a settlement of the dispute through a treaty or declaration was an extremely difficult problem, and neither Jinnah nor Liaquat, nor their successors, had been able to do it. He added that with the help of the Soviet Union and the blessings of his people, he would make a genuine search for a solution, and then in an unforgettable bit of Bhuttoism, said 'If I fail, then I hope the Secretary General will send a wreath to my grave.'

Brezhnev continued to press his idea of an agreement or memorandum, but Bhutto deftly deflected it by saying that he could agree to an understanding renouncing the use of force, but in order for it to be effective it should contain some mechanism for the peaceful settlement of disputes. The discussion had by now reached agreement by both parties on the necessity of a peaceful solution of the problems of South Asia, but there were differences on the issue of the approach. Brezhnev urged speed saying, 'I am a man of action', while Bhutto stressed caution. He said that relations with India, and the Kashmir question in particular, were not susceptible to 'a declaration in a vacuum'. In outlining his step by step approach he suggested that an initial measure could be to change the name of the 'Ceasefire Line' and to call it a 'Line of Control' instead. The change in nomenclature would perhaps more accurately describe the existing realities. This radical proposal, slipped into the discussion in a manner that was more deliberate than casual, was to have significant consequences and became a landmark in the regional geopolitical developments that ensued. It needs to be placed on record, therefore, that it was at this memorable meeting in the Kremlin on 17 March 1972 that the phrase 'Line of Control' entered the lexicon of South Asian geopolitics and replaced the term 'Ceasefire Line', which had been hitherto used to describe the disputed Indo–Pakistan border area in the north. Brezhnev, of course, seized on the suggestion with alacrity, and appreciated it both as a recognition of reality and a gesture that would help the process of negotiations.

On Bangladesh Bhutto remained firm, stating that he had already given Brezhnev a declaration of intent, but insisted on keeping the timing at his discretion—forty countries may have recognized Bangladesh, but Pakistan had been dismembered.

Returning to the issue that was obviously uppermost in his mind, Brezhnev posed a direct question to Bhutto, 'May we start work on India? Do you think the time is right?' Bhutto replied in the affirmative, adding the caveat that it should not delay the return of the prisoners of war. In an excited fashion Brezhnev said, 'My head is already busy with what steps can be taken to bring action to fruition.' He added that he would keep Bhutto fully informed of developments. Brezhnev concluded by saying that he was very pleased with the meeting, a sentiment which Bhutto warmly endorsed by declaring it as having 'a turning point nature'. My own impression, as we left the room in a plethora of handshakes and back thumping, was that the proceedings had gone far better than I had dared to hope, and that we had indeed crossed a watershed.

Later in the evening, as we were reviewing the events of the past two days, the president asked me how I thought the visit had gone. I replied that in the meeting with Kosygin the best that could be said was that the ice had been broken; there was too much baggage, in the shape of past suspicions and damaged egos, for the early creation of genuine new goodwill. We would need to work on it a great deal more, as Kosygin was by nature a cautious and reserved man, steeped in the sclerotic tradition of the communist apparatchik. On the other hand, I described the meeting with Brezhnev as being a unique and unqualified success. I added that this was, in large measure, due to the president's assurance to the Soviets of a gradual, but nevertheless substantive, change in our policy. Given the turbulent historical background of our relations with India, I hoped that the president would be able to effect the transition in a smooth manner. The response that I received was, once again, vintage Bhutto.

> You are only a bloody diplomat. *Tum yeh siasati kaam nahin samajhtay ho* (You do not understand the workings of politics). I shall take a delegation of sixty or seventy MNAs with me to India. In New Delhi their wives can go shopping for saris while they go whoring. In the meanwhile I shall make whatever agreements I like with Indira. Then we will see if any of them dares to criticize me in the Assembly.

I was not, of course, present at the historic conference that took place later in Simla, but its origins can clearly be traced to the Bhutto–Brezhnev meeting in Moscow in March 1972. And from what I could tell from this distance in time, its structure also appears to have received a shade of the Machiavellian aspect alluded to me at that time.

As for the Simla Conference itself, there is no doubt in my mind that it was a diplomatic triumph (success is too weak a word) for Zulfikar Bhutto. Starting from a position of greatest possible disadvantage and weakness, Bhutto had few cards to play except his own intellectual brilliance and innate diplomatic skill. Yet he managed to extricate his prisoners of war and recover his lost territories without conceding anything of substance to the triumphant and dominating Indians. This tour de force stands in sharp contrast to the Arabs, who are still engaged in a bloody struggle to recover their lost territories. Bhutto's major role in the conflict that resulted in the dismemberment of Pakistan, and the war that led to the mess that necessitated Simla, is perhaps undeniable, but these are issues on which judgment is best left to historians. What cannot be ignored, however, is the skill and finesse that characterized Bhutto's performance at Simla and the substantive results that he achieved despite all odds. Did he make verbal promises to Indira Gandhi regarding Kashmir, as Indians sometimes allege? In my personal opinion, knowing Bhutto, it is just possible that he smooth talked her with some kind of assurances, but if so, and again knowing Bhutto, he made quite sure that they did not find their way into the written record. In the final analysis, what has been achieved is a general understanding that the Simla Agreement stands on a par with the United Nations Resolutions for the purpose of settling the Indo–Pakistan dispute over Kashmir.

The official visit of President Bhutto to the USSR brought to an end my tenure in Moscow. Kosygin was kind enough to tell me, 'We have highly valued your work here', and wished me future success. He also kindly responded to my request and sent me an unusual portrait of a smiling Kosygin, which I am told he had personally selected. At a farewell lunch in my honour at the Ministry of Foreign Affairs, Deputy Foreign Minister Firyubin announced that his ministry had requested the mayor of Moscow to retain the names of my family and myself in the list of residents of the city. This would enable us to live in Moscow at any time we wished without having to comply with the formalities associated with this residential permit. This was a much coveted privilege for Soviet citizens at that time.

For me a far greater satisfaction was that the next resident of Sadova Kudrinskaya 15 would be my close and dearest friend Samiullah Khan Dehlavi, an ambassador of outstanding ability and one of the giants in the Pakistan Foreign Service.

Following an emotional farewell at Sheremetievo airport from a large group of friends, we flew out of Moscow on a lovely spring day in 1972. As I looked out of the window of the aircraft I saw the beautiful meadows and fields of Russia and its lush forests of fir, beech, pine and oak trees. As it gently faded from view it was a sight that was soothing to the eyes. But my mind and emotions were elsewhere, as I thought of Pakistan, battered and truncated by the turbulent events of the past year. What went wrong? The questions kept racing through my head, even though I felt I knew the answers. I felt myself sharing Ghalib's despair:

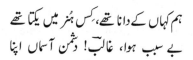

CHIAROSCURO

One of the embassy's Russian drivers was named Gubin. Cheerful and polite, efficient in his work and always willing to help, he was a great favourite with all of us. His appearance was pure Russian, with blond hair, blue eyes, and a pale face. But his commercial instincts were those of a Levantine in the darkest souk and he was always on the lookout for a trade, whether in cigarettes or automobile spare parts. I was convinced that, left unhindered, he was capable of single-handedly converting the entire Russian system from a state-controlled command economy into a capitalist free market. He was also well read and followed current affairs closely, so we would have many agreeable and enlightening discussions. At one time we were talking about the state-sponsored campaign against the famous writer and Nobel Laureate, Alexander Solzhenytsyn, and I found Gubin's views to be as astonishing as they were forthright. He failed to understand Solzhenytsyn's problem. Did he not have plenty of money from his writing, an apartment in Moscow, a dacha in the country and the possibility to travel abroad? What did he have to complain about? It was people like Gubin who had to work so hard to make ends meet, to live under restrictions, and suffer from food shortages, who were entitled to complain, not Solzhenytsyn. Altering the subject slightly, I said that we were talking about a great Russian writer and I wished that my Russian was sufficiently advanced to be able to read him in the original text. Gubin's response was dismissive, 'Who can find time to read books in Russia?'

* * *

Diana and I were walking on a snow-covered pavement in Moscow, and passed a group of old women (*babouchka*) who had been employed by the city authorities to sweep the snow off the footpaths. They were cheerfully going about their work, using their large tree branches, as we exchanged greetings. Suddenly one *babouchka*, giving a loud shriek, grabbed a fistful of snow and smeared it over my cheek. She had spotted the first signs of frostbite, and disregarding all formalities, had employed the traditional Russian antidote with the alacrity that the symptom demanded. This was a typical example of the spontaneous warmth of the Russian people. Refusing all offers of compensation the *babouchkas* urged us to get home as soon as possible. On this occasion the cure worked and I had no ill effects, but the next time I was not so fortunate. Standing for four hours in Red Square, as I attended the celebrations for the Great October Revolution, I was exposed to a frostbite which has left me with a scar that I will carry as a souvenir for the rest of my life.

MEANWHILE IN PAKISTAN

Zulfikar Ali Bhutto moved swiftly and decisively to consolidate his political power. The changes that he made in the top levels of the armed services have already been indicated. Riding on the mandate of popular support that he had received from a despairing nation, ready and hungry for redemption, he stormed around the country making a series of dramatic appearances at well-attended public meetings, and spread a message of determination and hope. He also undertook a whirlwind trip abroad, visiting a number of friendly countries and urging their cooperation at this time of need for Pakistan.

Focusing on the internal affairs of Pakistan, he nationalized a number of important industries, often subjecting the previous owners to public humiliation, and threatened to continue the process even further. He turned on the civil service with a devastating assault that severely damaged an institution whose structural function should have been the solid framework of a country's administration. Not only were competent officers removed from service, without cause or enquiry, but they were replaced by incompetent party hacks, whose only qualification was personal loyalty to Bhutto. As time went on, Bhutto's latent fascist inclinations became increasingly pronounced, and there

With President Kwame Nkrumah of Ghana, April 1965.

Place De La République, Tombouctou, Mali—during the morning rush hour. Photograph by author, July 1966.

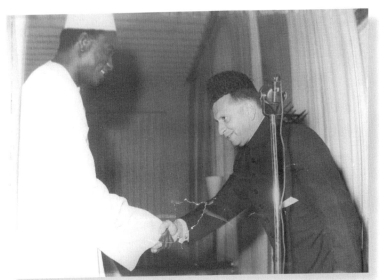

Presenting credentials to President Modibo Keïta, Bamako, Mali, 1966.

President Ayub Khan surrounded by a happy crowd in Romania,
October 1967.

resentation of credentials ceremony in the Kremlin, Moscow, on 30 December 1969. Seated
rom left to right: Secretary of the Presidium Georgadze, Jamsheed Marker, Deputy Chairman
f the Presidium N. Yu. Shaumaskis, and Deputy Foreign Minister N.P. Firyubin.

Receiving the Sitara-e-Quaid-i-Azam from President
Yahya Khan, December 1970.

Diana's address at a UN Women's Conference, Moscow, 1970.

Diana and Simeon, Pakistan Embassy, Moscow, 1970.

Diana and I receive Faiz Ahmed Faiz at the Pakistan Embassy, Sadovaya-Kudrinskaya, Moscow, April 1970.

Reception in honour of Faiz Ahmed Faiz, Pakistan Embassy, Moscow. With V.A. Sergeev, Vice Chairman State Committee for Foreign Economic Relations, April 1970.

With Faiz Ahmed Faiz at a reception in his honour at the Pakistan Embassy, Moscow, April 1970.

Meeting in the Kremlin, June 1970. Clockwise from left: Prime Minister Kosygin, President Podgorny, President Yahya Khan, Finance Minister Muzaffar Qizilbash, Sultan Khan, M.M. Ahmed, S.M. Yusuf, Jamsheed Marker, General Ghulam Umer.

S.M. Yusuf and V.A. Sergeev, signing the agreement for collaboration on Pakistan Steel Mills, Moscow, January 1971.

Diana with Valentina Tereschkova, the first woman cosmonaut, Moscow, 1971.

S.M. Yusuf, Chairman Pakistan Steel Mills Corporation with Prime Minister Kosygin at the Kremlin, after the signature of the steel mill agreement Moscow, January 1971.

Meeting at the Kremlin during the visit of President Bhutto to Moscow. Front row L to R: Foreign Minister Gromyko, Prime Minister Kosygin, President Z.A. Bhutto. Back row L to R: Dr M.A. Bhatty, Aftab Ahmed Khan, Rafi Raza, Said Ahmed, Qamr-ul-Islam, Jamsheed Marker, Sultan Khan, and M.M. Ahmed, Moscow, March 1972.

A historic and crucial meeting at the office of the Communist Party of the Soviet Union held on 17 March 1972. Secretary General Brezhnev is assisted by Foreign Minister Gromyko, and Rodionov, the Soviet ambassador to Pakistan. President Zulfikar Ali Bhutto is accompanied by Foreign Minister Aziz Ahmed and Jamsheed Marker. Viktor Sukhodrev (back to the camera), is the ubiquitous and superlative interpreter.

Presentation of credentials to Governor General Roland Michener of Canada, Ottawa, May 1972. Also present John Halstead, of the External Affairs Department.

With Governor General Arthur McShine of Trinidad and Tobago Port De Spain, December 1972.

Reviewing the Guard of Honour, East Berlin, July 1974.

Presenting credentials to Willi Stoph, President German Democratic Republic, East Berlin, June 1974.

Diana performing the earth breaking ceremony for the construction of the chancery building in Tokyo, 1977.

Arnaz Marker

With President Ziaul Haq, General K.M. Arif, and Ambassador Niaz A. Naik at the Non-ligned Conference of heads of state and government, Havana, Cuba, November 1979.

President General Mohammad Ziaul Haq presiding over the conference of Pakistan ambassadors on its second day at the Foreign Office in Islamabad on 10 December 1979. L to R: Jamsheed Marker, Sahibzada Yaqub Khan, General K.M. Arif, General M.G. Jilani, Agha Shahi, President Ziaul Haq, Ghulam Ishaq Khan, and S. Shah Nawaz.

With President Julius Nyerere of Tanzania, Arusha, June 1979.

My parents with Professor Dr Langmann, President of Merck Corporation, Darmstadt, Germany, July 1981.

With the Premier of Bavaria, Franz Josef Strauss, in Munchen, September 1981.

Flag hoisting on National Day, Pakistan Embassy, Bad Godesburg, August 1981.

Arnaz meets Franz Josef Strauss, the Premier of Bavaria. A dynamic and colourful personality, popularly called 'The Uncrowned King of Bavaria', and a great friend of Pakistan, September 1981.

Presenting credentials to Mr Amadou-Mahtar M'Bow, Director General of Unesco, as the new Permanent Delegate of Pakistan to the Organisation, Paris, July 1982.

Reviewing the Guard of Honour, Belfast, Ireland, November 1982.

Presenting credentials to President Hillery of Ireland, November 1982.

Arnaz with Omar Sharif and La Duchesse de La Rochefoucauld at a dinner at the Pakistan Embassy, Paris, November 1982.

With Prince Sadrudin Aga Khan, dinner at Aiglemont, September 1985.

Presenting credentials to Secretary General Pérez de Cuéllar, United Nations, New York, August 1990.

With Secretary General Boutros Boutros-Ghali at the United Nations, 1992.

In the office of the President of the Security Council, United Nations. L to R: Alamgir Babar, Haroon Shaukat, Mansur Sohail, Jamsheed Marker, Sher Afghan Khan, DPR, New York, April 1993.

Security Council votes to strengthen sanctions against Federal Republic of Yugoslavia (Serbia and Montenegro) as of 26 April, unless Bosnian Serbs agree to a peace plan and end attacks, UN New York, 17 April 1993. View of Jamsheed Marker (right), President of the Security Council, conferring with Madeline K. Albright (second from right), Permanent Representative of the USA, while David Hannay (front left), Permanent rep. of the UK, looks on. Credit UN photo 182869/J. Isaac.

A difficult and stressful moment as Jamsheed Marker meets the international press correspondents after presiding over a late night session of the Security Council. His press counsellor, Mansur Sohail is by his side. Pakistan, which had been a co-sponsor of the 'Safe Havens' resolution on Srebrenica, had abstained on the vote because it believed that the force provided for its implementation was inadequate. The large massacres that occurred soon after provided cruel and brutal justification for its concern.

Holding press briefing with members of the OIC, 24 June 1993. View of Jamsheed Marker (left), Permanent Representative of Pakistan, responding to a question from a correspondent. On the right is Ahmed Snoussi, Permanent Representative of Morocco. Credit: UN photo 183201/M. Grant.

Security Council calls 'unacceptable' decision by Bosnian Serb party not to permit further humanitarian aid delivery to Srebrenica. United Nations, New York, 3 April 1993. View of Jamsheed Marker of Pakistan, President of the Security Council, addressing the meeting. Also in the photograph, Kofi Annan, Under Secretary General and Alvaro de Soto, Assistant Secretary General. Credit: UN photo 182854/J. Isaac.

Security Council calls for deployment of fifty military observers to Abkhazia, Georgia, following effective ceasefire. Sir David Hannay (left) of the United Kingdom, President of the Security Council, conferring with Diego Arria (centre, back to camera), Permanent Representative of Venezuela; Yoshio Hatano (centre, facing Ambassador Arria), Permanent Representative of Japan; and Jamsheed Marker (right), Permanent Representative of Pakistan. Credit: UN Photo 183315/M. Grant, 9 July 1993.

In the office of the President of the UN Security Council, with Prime Minister Ghulam Mustafa Jatoi of Pakistan, and Ambassador Yuli Vorontsov of Russia, an outstanding diplomat and a close personal friend.

Informal and obviously friendly consultations with Jean-Bernard Merimee, Permanent Representative of France in the Security Council Chamber, March 1994.

Arnaz with Joseph Verner Reed, the dynamic and colourful Chief of Protocol at the State Department, Washington, D.C. The inscription reads 'To Arnaz. A Superstar!'

was a growing disillusionment with his government. Things seemed to bear a striking similarity to the situation that had arisen in Ghana during the Nkrumah regime.

NOTE

1. Since there were no secretaries present at this meeting, Aziz Ahmed asked me to take notes as fully as possible. I did so, and prepared the minutes of the meeting which were shown to both Bhutto and Aziz Ahmed and approved by them, before the president's departure from Moscow. I had two copies of the minutes prepared, numbered them, designated them 'Top Secret', and forwarded one copy to the foreign secretary in Islamabad, retaining the second for the archives of the Pakistan embassy in Moscow.

   Some years later, during an informal conversation with General K.M. Arif, the formidable Chief of Staff to President Ziaul Haq, I mentioned this meeting, and gave him a verbal account as well as the location of the two copies of the top secret minutes. General Arif got back to me later and informed me that neither copy of the minutes could be traced.

   My account of this historic encounter is based largely on memory, aided to some extent, by the discovery in my personal papers of the remnants of some scribbled notes that I took at the time for the preparation of the minutes.

PART IV

CANADA, GUYANA, AND
TRINIDAD & TOBAGO

CHAPTER TWELVE

Canada

'*Mon pays n'est pas un pays, c'est un hiver.*'
(My country is not a country, it is a winter.)
French Canadian folk song

We could not go directly from Moscow to Ottawa, as my predecessor needed extra time to wind up his affairs. We accordingly spent a very agreeable interlude in Bonn with our dear cousins, Jumbo and Khorshed Kharas, where the former had been posted as Pakistan's ambassador to the Federal German Republic. The Kharas's warmth, affection and generous hospitality were the perfect antidote to nerves frayed by prolonged exposure to the unremitting crises that we had endured during our difficult sojourn in Moscow. Like us, they had suffered the recent torment of helplessly witnessing the rupture of our country, and the few weeks that we spent together provided an opportunity for the mutual consolation and solace that only close affection can provide. It was, therefore, with batteries recharged and spirits considerably restored that we boarded the Air Canada aircraft at Frankfurt for the trip to Montreal. It was early spring as we flew over Quebec, and the landscape below, of forests interspersed with patches of snow, reminded us a little of the Russian taiga. However, all similarity to Russia ended as soon as we touched down at Montreal's brisk, bright, and shiny Duval airport. We were greeted cheerfully by the Canadian protocol officers and rapidly transferred to our connecting flight to Ottawa, where we received a more formal but equally cheerful reception. Diana and I, together with our dog Simeon, who appeared in good form despite the long flight, soon found ourselves in our very comfortable new home, situated in Rockcliffe Park, one of Ottawa's elegant residential areas.

The only resident diplomatic officer in the embassy was First Secretary Touqir Hussain, a bright and capable career diplomat who combined high intelligence with due modesty, and who was typical of the excellent professional service that we possessed at the time. Unfortunately this superb cadre was about to suffer some depredations, as a result of Bhutto's decision to induct a number of so called 'lateral entrants', on the basis of party affiliation, regardless of either qualification or competence. Touqir gave me a quick rundown of the major political issues we faced. Apart from the residual bitterness over Bangladesh there were no basic problems, and all we had to do was to develop a good working relationship into a better one. This was a change, to say the least, from our recent work in Moscow. Diana was even more pleased with Touqir's report on the ready availability of items for household consumption and on the facilities that made living in Ottawa so very agreeable. We had, for the first time in our diplomatic life, moved into the First World.

Robert Ford, the Canadian Ambassador in Moscow, and one of the leading Western experts on the Soviet Union, had been both my mentor and one of my dearest friends. He and his vivacious and dynamic Brazilian wife, Theresa, had formed a close relationship with Diana and me, and we had spent many happy and stimulating hours together in Moscow, in a friendship that had continued for many years. Like Diana, poor Theresa was also later struck down by cancer, whilst Robert, who had earlier been disabled by polio, suffered a series of strokes and eventually died in his retirement villa in France. Robert, who was a living legend in Canadian political, diplomatic, and literary circles, was delighted when I told him about our posting to Ottawa. With typical generosity Theresa and Robert took it upon themselves to inform their many Canadian friends about our forthcoming stay in Ottawa and sought their help in making us feel at home in our new surroundings. Since these friends of the Fords were amongst the most important and influential in the land, we were assured of a considerable fund of valuable goodwill even before we had arrived in Canada.

I presented my credentials to Governor General Roland Michener at a simple ceremony in which the only protocol requirement was the wearing of decorations. Since Bhutto had precipitously pulled us out of the Commonwealth, I presented my Letters of Credence as Ambassador and the Letters of Recall of my predecessor, a High

Commissioner. The governor general was a distinguished and polished political figure, whose varied experience had included an assignment as high commissioner to India. Although his constitutional role was strictly ceremonial, his vast experience and political perception provided the background for a most interesting conversation which covered the subcontinent, which he obviously knew very well, and also important issues relating to the Cold War. Kosygin had recently concluded a very successful visit to Canada, and since Ottawa had always maintained an active mission in Peking, Michener was keen to receive an evaluation of the newly-established relationship between Washington and Peking, following the famous Kissinger visit. Diana also accompanied me to Government House for the credentials ceremony and was received by Mrs Nora Michener in a private salon, where she was given refreshments and shared a very pleasant conversation.

Canada has always been known for its dynamic and liberal policies, both domestic and foreign, and this has made it one of the major donors of financial, economic, and technical assistance to the developing countries. From its earliest days, Pakistan has been a major partner with Canada in economic development, and the Warsak Dam near Peshawar, which was the first major hydroelectric project following independence, is a prime example of this co-operation. Subsequently, Canada provided the reactor and other equipment for the Karachi Nuclear Power Plant (KANUPP), which was Pakistan's first nuclear power station and made a substantial contribution towards meeting the country's growing energy requirements. Co-operation relating to a number of other projects has continued over the years, and most of these were supervised by the Canadian Agency for International Development (CIDA), a dynamic and efficient autonomous body created by the Canadian government. During my tenure in Ottawa I spent a great deal of time working with CIDA, under the most congenial and productive conditions.

Pakistan's nuclear activities had just begun to ring alarm bells all over the world, with the result that our nuclear co-operation with Canada, particularly in terms of supplies of fuel and spares to KANUPP, were subjected to increasing scrutiny and suspicion. One of my major responsibilities was to ensure the continuity of the nuclear relationship in general, and more importantly that of the supplies.

Munir Ahmed Khan, the competent and effective Chairman of our Atomic Energy Commission, was a frequent and regular visitor to Ottawa. He had many friends there and had also built-up excellent connections with the Canadian nuclear establishment, both on a bilateral basis as well as a result of his work as a senior member of the staff of the International Atomic Energy Agency (IAEA) in Vienna. Nevertheless, we were working in Canada in what was clearly a second place position to India. Canada and India, under Lester Pearson and Jawaharlal Nehru, had developed a very warm and friendly relationship reflected not only in their bilateral relations, but over the whole range of international affairs.

Indian and Canadian co-operation in the nuclear field, in those early days, formed a particularly important element in this cosy companionship, and one that was pursued with outstanding results by Dr Homi Bhabha, the brilliant physicist who headed the Indian nuclear programme, and was closely supported, both personally and professionally, by Jawaharlal Nehru. Bhabha's scientific genius was, of course, acknowledged all over the world, but outside of his own country it was perhaps in Canada that he was most admired by his scientist peers, and with whom he and his colleagues had developed a close and productive relationship. Dr Homi Bhabha was tragically killed in an air crash over the Alps, but before his death he had firmly established the Indian nuclear programme and set it on its predictable course. His prestige in the Canadian nuclear establishment had remained as high as ever, and even though this was several years after Bhabha's death, I saw his photograph in the offices of some of the officials with whom I had worked. Later on, after the Indians had conducted their nuclear test in 1974, the starry-eyed Canadian nuclear collaboration with India was to suffer a profound and indignant disillusionment. But in 1972 our nuclear collaboration with Canada was less easy than it was in other fields, and the main reason was obviously because of the strong relationship that had already been built-up between the Canadian and Indian nuclear establishments, and the priority that both sides attached to it. Fortunately, our co-operation with the Canadians in the nuclear field, albeit in second place, stayed on course during my tenure. But there were occasions when we would hit crises which were not easily overcome.

We went about our diplomatic duties in Ottawa in conditions that could hardly have been better. The Canadian political leaders, parliamentarians and officials were capable, friendly and helpful, and much the same could be said about the media, academics, and other members of civil society, with whom we were associated. Our diplomatic colleagues were of the highest calibre, and it appeared as though the congenial atmosphere in which all of us worked had also found reflection in the inter se relations of the diplomatic corps. The Pakistani community in Canada in the early 1970s was of modest proportions and consisted mostly of doctors, professionals, academics, and students. But this was all about to change, and I was able to observe, with considerable fascination, the initiation of the early amendments in the administrative and legislative measures designed to liberalize Canadian immigration policies and procedures. The influx of immigrants from the subcontinent, which commenced just about the time of the termination of my tenure, has, with the induction of a large multiethnic and multicultural element, transformed the Canadian society, in what appears to me, to be an entirely positive and productive fashion.

As already indicated, our relations with officials in the Department of External Affairs, in CIDA and other ministries were, as friendly and cordial as they could be, with business being conducted mostly on a first-name basis and often including our families. Ministers, senators and members of parliament were likewise friendly and helpful, and above all easily accessible. The governor general and his wife honoured us with their presence at a dinner at the embassy. It was a most enjoyable evening, with protocol at the barest minimum, and security measures that were entirely unobtrusive.

The Prime Minister was Pierre Eliot Trudeau, a dynamic leader who, at a comparatively young age, had swept into power on a wave of popularity, and had brought with him a fresh breeze of informality that had blown the cobwebs out of the staid, old, neo-colonial atmosphere, still lingering in the halls of the government. Trudeau's thinking and politics carried a trace of the attitudes of the vocal, anti-Vietnam, newly-enfranchised, young generation of that era, the flower children, flaunting their freedom with their guitars and songs. In this he was well ahead of his time, and in the motivation of his policies and actions there was clear evidence of his anticipation of the environmental movement that would shortly overtake the globe. There was little wonder that a popular book of the time was the *Desiderata*, a tract written by an obscure Indiana poet named Max Ehrmann and based upon inscriptions found in an old Baltimore church. 'You are a child of the universe, no less than the trees and the stars: you have a right to be here, and whether or not it is clear to you, no doubt the universe is unfolding as it should.'

My meetings with Trudeau were, alas, infrequent and were restricted to brief, friendly but inconsequential conversations at official receptions. The only time that I had a substantive discussion with Trudeau was during the mandatory official call that an ambassador pays on the prime minister. This lasted for about an hour and covered a wide range of issues, mixing matters pertaining to the affairs of state with literary speculations on the origins and impact of the *Desiderata*. Trudeau had by this time lost a considerable amount of the popularity that had first brought him into power, and was in fact in the midst of a troublesome domestic political crisis, such as those that constantly occur in democratic societies. His features were zestful and youthful as ever, if somewhat weather-beaten, and his eyes sparkled with cheerful intelligence. Unlike many of my other contemporary interlocutors, he did not waste time in deploring our actions over Bangladesh, and preferred to talk about the future of Pakistan and the subcontinent. He assured me of Canada's fullest co-operation with Pakistan in all areas, regardless of the fact that we had quit the Commonwealth, which he thought was a mistake. He admired the manner in which Bhutto had overcome the deep crisis after the surrender at Dacca, but expressed considerable apprehension and disquiet over the arbitrary manner in which Bhutto now appeared to be acting. I surmised that this opinion was the result of a combination of the reporting telegrams from the able Canadian ambassador in Islamabad, as well as the personal relationship that had recently developed between Trudeau and Bhutto. I concluded the meeting with the customary invitation to the prime minister to visit Pakistan. Trudeau accepted this with grace, and then said it would not be his first visit to the country. It seems that in his reckless youth Trudeau and some of his bushy, long-haired friends had taken the overland route to India, and had been arrested as they crossed the Afghan border into Pakistan. They had spent the night in a Peshawar police lock-up and been released the next morning after receiving a punitive haircut. Pointing to the thinning hair on his head, Trudeau gave me a mischievous grin and said 'They couldn't do that to me now!' I left the prime minister's office with a strong feeling that it was my discomfiture that triggered the twinkle in his eye.

The linkage between national demographic and geographic features is unique in Canada. Almost the entire population is located on the southern border with the USA, whilst the rest of the vast land to the north remains sparsely settled. The tremendous gravitational pull exerted by the USA on Canada, especially in socio-economic terms, is manifestly evident. North–south connections are far more pervasive than east–west links, and the daily lives of the residents of Vancouver in the west are far more closely linked with Seattle than they are with either Toronto or Montreal in the south-east, much less with the far east in St. John's, Newfoundland. This applies to everything from road communications, and TV and radio stations, to shopping centres and holiday plans. Yet, notwithstanding these US-loaded economic compulsions, there is a distinct Canadian persona, both political and public, which is felt and exercised with quite legitimate national pride. It is not so much a spirit of anti-US defiance as it is of Canadian self-reliance, and it has been very successful in sustaining an identity separate from the United States. This is particularly remarkable in the field of human rights, where Canada has created a much more tolerant and humane society than its powerful southern neighbour. Other outstanding examples are Canada's bilingualism, and its medical care and old age protection systems, which are far more humane and efficient than those of the USA. Along with the constant emphasis on Canadian identity, there is a commendable and pragmatic accommodation of economic realities. I asked the governor of British Columbia, who came from a strong and distinguished trade union background, how he reconciled his publicly proclaimed views of an independent Canadian identity with the fact that almost the entire Canadian trade union organization was affiliated to the US trade unions such as the American Federation of Labor and Congress of Industrial Organizations (AFL-CIO), and the Teamsters Union. I was told that since the major industrial enterprises in Canada were either owned, or controlled, by large United States corporations, the Canadian trade unions' own resources were insufficient to meet the requirements of collective bargaining with those powerful employers, and so it made good sense for the Canadians to associate themselves with the strong US trade unions.

We took every opportunity to travel in Canada, and to see as much of this vast and beautiful country as we could, combining official calls with radio and TV talk shows at each of the provincial capitals that we visited. A particularly memorable expedition was the one organized for members of the diplomatic corps by the Department of External Affairs in conjunction with the Department of Indian and Northern Affairs and the Government of the North-west Territories. The visit lasted from 2 October to 7 October 1972, and we flew in a Royal Canadian Air Force Cosmos twin turboprop aircraft, especially adapted for operations in the Arctic. The trip, which took us from Ottawa to Frobisher in Baffin Bay, Resolute Bay, Cambridge Bay, Inuvik, Tuktoyaktuk, and Yellowknife, covered the North and West Arctic regions. Thanks to the superb organization of the Canadian authorities, we travelled in great comfort, despite the fact that we were in some of the world's most inhospitable areas. Resolute Bay, situated in the Arctic Circle, was the northernmost part of our journey. It is icebound for over ten months of the year, has a population of 400 people, two Mounties, and an indeterminate number of husky dogs. The temperature when we arrived was -28 degrees Celsius, and we were told that it was a warm day. Subsequently, we flew through the Western Arctic back to Ottawa. A conversation with Captain Jennings, our aircraft commander, and Major Poidre, the navigator, gave me a little insight into the specialty of Arctic navigation. For one thing, there is a considerable distance between the location of the geographic and magnetic North Poles, and for another, when you are flying directly above the North Pole every direction is South. The lonely, cold outposts that we visited existed for two reasons only—oil and defence. The latter consisted of radar-tracking stations for the early detection of any airborne or other missile attacks, emanating from the USSR, and for the monitoring of signals from the considerable radio traffic in the region. As for oil, the activity was multifarious including exploration, extraction, and delivery through the oil pipelines. The hardy individuals who lived and worked in these inhospitable surroundings came from all over the world. They usually stayed for short spells of time, the longest being six months, had virtually no expenses and earned very large salaries which they then either blew in Las Vegas or remitted to buy a comfortable home in some Third World country. I met a tractor operator from Pakistan, whose father had worked with the Canadian civil engineers on the Warsak Dam, and then followed them to Labrador. The son had continued his father's occupation and was now 'making good money' in the Western Arctic.

In October 1972 I was instructed to join the Pakistani delegation at the United Nations General Assembly in New York, where Iqbal Akhund had just taken over as the Permanent Representative. His predecessor, Agha Shahi, was now our Ambassador in Peking, but had also been instructed to join the delegation, which was led by Raja Tridev Roy, a minister in Bhutto's cabinet. Tridev Roy, who was the Chief of the Chakma tribe in East Bengal, was an ardent and patriotic Pakistani, had been a member of the National Assembly, and a vehement political opponent of Mujibur Rehman and the Awami League. The events that led to the break-up of Pakistan were a particular torment for this honest and upright gentleman. Even more soul-searing was his decision to remain in Pakistan, since it meant perpetual separation from his people, the Chakma tribe, who were so dear to him and for whom he had devoted a lifetime's service. Tridev Roy served as a Cabinet Minister and later did a long stint as Ambassador of Pakistan in capitals in Latin America. On arriving in New York it was a particular delight to meet Ambassador Huang Hua, an old friend from Accra days and one of the world's most able diplomats. He had been appointed as the Permanent Representative of the People's Republic of China as soon as his government had won its rightful place at the United Nations and he was busy establishing his mission in New York when we met.

The basic brief for the Pakistani delegation was to prevent the admission of Bangladesh to the United Nations on the grounds that it was created as a result of armed intervention by one UN member state against another. For us it was an uphill battle since, in the first place, the ground reality of the existence of Bangladesh and its recognition by a number of states could not be ignored. Secondly, there was a considerable and growing sympathy and support for the Dacca regime. For me, personally, it was extremely sad, and a trifle distasteful, to find myself in conflict with, and lobbying against, diplomats who had been our former colleagues, and with many of whom I had maintained a personal friendship. The General Assembly session concluded without taking a decision on the admission of Bangladesh. But notwithstanding our extensive and vigorous lobbying, I felt sure that we would have lost had there been a vote in the General Assembly. Our success, if it could be called that, was entirely due to the position adopted by the delegation of the People's Republic of China in the Security Council. China indicated that it would veto the admission of Bangladesh to the United Nations, since it remained under foreign military occupation, and that this position would be maintained so long as Indian troops were stationed in Bangladesh. Initially this development was seen by Dacca as both a disappointment and a setback, but since there can be no doubt that the Chinese veto provided an incentive for all concerned to withdraw foreign troops from Bangladesh, it served to expedite the process, and to that extent was beneficial for the country.

The matter which triggered the Chinese decision is both an interesting and important background issue, and merits record. It was recounted to me many years later by Agha Shahi, and I recollect being most forcefully struck by the nature of the narration. It was in a manner that was simple and straightforward in its recollection and recounting of facts, and was entirely devoid of any hint of self-promotion. It will be recalled that Agha Shahi, in his capacity as ambassador in Peking, had been appointed as a member of our UN delegation, and used to visit Islamabad in order to keep Bhutto informed of the situation in New York and to carry his orders back to the delegation. On one such occasion in Islamabad, Shahi approached Bhutto with the suggestion that we request China to exercise its veto and maintain it so long as Indian troops remained in Bangladesh. Shahi said that he had barely commenced his suggestion when Bhutto said to him, 'Stop! Stop! Stop! Why didn't I think of this? You have lost none of your brilliance. Go immediately to Peking and take a letter from me to Chou En-lai!' The rest, of course, is history, and universally known, but what needs to be recorded is this fascinating little background vignette. Not only is it vintage Bhutto, but it also casts a light upon his volatile relationship with Agha Shahi. Both men were, of course, master practitioners of Pakistani diplomacy.

Our very pleasant tenure in Ottawa came to an end well before it should have. I received a letter from Iftikhar Ali, the Foreign Secretary, expressing his profuse apologies and saying that health and family reasons had compelled him to seek a posting to Canada, and that I was being transferred to East Berlin, where I was to open a new mission, following Pakistan's recognition of the German Democratic Republic. Foreign Minister Aziz Ahmed sent me a very nice letter of apology for the personal inconvenience caused to me.

Accordingly, we left Ottawa in the summer of 1974, and crossing the Atlantic once again, found ourselves behind the Iron Curtain, this time in East Berlin.

CHAPTER THIRTEEN

Guyana

'Daylight come and I wanna go home.'
– Harry Belafonte, West Indian Calypso.

Pakistan's envoy to Canada was entrusted with two concurrent accreditations: as High Commissioner to Guyana, and High Commissioner to Trinidad & Tobago. On checking the records I noticed that Caribbean problems always seemed to raise their ugly heads between the months of November and March, compelling the high commissioner's absence from snowbound Ottawa and his presence in the sun-drenched Caribbean. The compulsion became all the more powerful if, as was frequently the case, there happened to be a cricket test series at the time. I am glad to say that I followed this worthwhile practice during the two winters of my tenure, and thus maintained an excellent tradition. It was the most agreeable of experiences to look out of the aircraft window as the snow ploughs cleared the runways at Toronto airport and, a few hours and a few cocktails later, to walk down the gangway at Barbados and feel the sun blazing into one's eyes and the humidity making the shirt cling to one's back. The first time that I landed at Barbados airport was also the first time that I had set foot on West Indian soil, and as we waited in the transit lounge I gazed at the green hills, the blue sea and sky, and the rich dark brown earth. My mind went back to the days of cricket commentary and I recalled the names and faces of all those giants— Frank Worrell, Gary Sobers, Clive Walcott, Everton Weekes, Rohan Kanhai, Sonny Ramadin, and Alfred Valentine. This is where they all came from, and so, as we walked back to the gangway to board the aircraft, I bent down and picked up a fistful of West Indian soil, quite sure that it contained a speck of the magic ore that produces great cricketers. I did not care to explain this gesture of lunacy to my astonished fellow passengers, since that would have meant trying to explain the magic of the lunacy of cricket. And who has ever succeeded in doing that?

Our destination was Georgetown, Guyana, where I presented credentials to President Arthur Raymond Chung at a simple ceremony followed by a small reception which was also attended by Diana, and a few members of the cabinet, including the dynamic Foreign Minister Shridath Surendranath 'Sonny' Ramphal, who was also attorney general. The leading political figures at that time were Dr Chedi Jagan and L.S. Forbes Burnham who had together fought to free Guyana from colonial rule, and had fallen out, as so often happens, once independence was achieved. Chedi Jagan's origin was Indian, whilst Forbes Burnham's was African, and the inclusion of the Chinese-origin President Chung, provided an insight of the multiethnic composition of the population of Guyana. The professionals, traders and businessmen, who constituted the middle class, had a large Asian component, whereas the proletariats were for the most part of African origin, and this ethnic faultline sometimes manifested itself in explosive fashion, as had occurred in the civil disturbances shortly before my arrival.

My discussions with President Chung were mostly of a formal nature, in accordance with the constitutional requirements of his office, but I did, at his request, give him an account of the current political situation in the subcontinent. My substantive discussions took place with Prime Minister Forbes Burnham and Foreign Minister Ramphal. Both were men of formidable political insight, and Sonny Ramphal, in particular, had a global vision that eventually took him well beyond the Caribbean onto the international stage. He became a leading environmentalist, writing books and numerous articles on the subject, and provided me with tremendous help and guidance almost ten years later when as the chairman, I negotiated on behalf of the Group of 77 at the United Nations Conference on Environment and Development at Rio de Janeiro in 1992. Later, as Sir Shridath Ramphal, he conducted a highly successful tenure as Secretary General of the Commonwealth.

I found the political situation in the Guyana of 1972 to be considerably polarized on both ideological as well as on ethnic lines. Dr Chedi Jagan, who was the country's first prime minister, had started off with socialist policies but had moved significantly further to the left. His high profile American wife Janet had been a card-carrying member of the Communist Party, and the couple brought rhetoric and flamboyance to the politics of Guyana, drawing it into the orbit of the Cold War. Forbes Burnham assumed office after Jagan's electoral defeat and in turn moved a moderately conservative position into a perceivably anti-communist one. I heard the story, probably apocryphal, that when Forbes Burnham was asked by the Foreign Office to approve the appointment of an incoming Soviet ambassador, he remarked that Moscow did not need an ambassador in Guyana so long as Chedi Jagan was in the country.

In my first meeting with Forbes Burnham we both expressed the necessity and value of good relations between Guyana and Pakistan, whilst also recognizing the obvious limitations imposed by objective geographical circumstances. But we did have a substantive discussion on the international political situation, and I received an inkling of the strong views of this fiery West Indian. A firm believer in non-alignment, he nevertheless had his preferences, which in his case was being anti-Moscow rather than being pro-Washington. In this he was no different from most of the leaders that I met or knew in the Non-Aligned Movement. They were one step either to the left or the right of the non-aligned line. To my regret, I had no further opportunity to react or work with Forbes Burnham or to develop a relationship that seemed full of promise. I also regretted not being able to meet Chedi Jagan during my infrequent visits to Georgetown since he was out of the country. All the indications were that he was just as dynamic and intelligent as Forbes Burnham, but was a much more charismatic figure. However, it was with Sonny Ramphal, the Foreign Minister, that I developed a friendship. Highly civilized and intelligent, Ramphal had a global perception that was both tolerant and wide-ranging. His bright eyes and lively smile reflected his gentle sense of humour, and discussions with him were always as pleasant as they were rewarding. His subsequent careers, as a foremost environmentalist and as secretary general of the Commonwealth, were a tribute to his out-standing ability, but above all he remained a great humanist.

Since there were no political problems between Pakistan and Guyana, my efforts were concentrated on maintaining good relations between the two countries and trying to develop some trade. I was very successful in my first objective, mostly because of the friendly attitude of the Guyanese government and its people. But this was not enough to overcome the barriers imposed upon us by economic and geographical realities, and despite my best efforts I could not identify any areas of possible commercial co-operation. The result was that my few visits to Georgetown were essentially goodwill missions and my time was spent interacting with some very attractive people in a beautiful little country.

CHAPTER FOURTEEN

Trinidad and Tobago

'As the governor of Barbados stated, the Barbadian planters found by experience that three blacks work better and cheaper than one white man.'

– Eric Williams, Capitalism and Slavery

'Why Bacchra no do what King bid him?'
West Indian slaves' protest at planters' refusal to implement the Emancipation Act 1833, passed in the British Parliament.

– Eric Williams, Capitalism and Slavery

I presented credentials to Sir Arthur McShine, the Governor General of Trinidad and Tobago, at Port of Spain in mid-December 1972. It was a simple ceremony, followed by a short conversation of pleasant generalities, in accordance with his constitutional role.

Trinidad was in a happy mood at the time, with calypso steel bands playing all over Port of Spain, practicing for the forthcoming carnival festival. I was told that the West Indian calypso steel band originated in the Second World War, when the US air force maintained aviation fuel stockpiles for refuelling aircraft before their flights to Europe. The abandoned empty fuel drums were then taken over by the locals and turned into musical instruments that have since delighted the world with their unique combination of cheerful lyrics and fabulous rhythms. As elsewhere in the West Indies, the amalgam of Afro–Asian culture was pervasive, but here the South Asian element appeared to be more prominent and there were quite a few mosques as well as Hindu temples. Our honorary consul general was Ahmed Kazem, a friendly and energetic businessman with an attractive wife, who participated in an admirable fashion in his business and social activities. They had a variety of friends, which gave us a certain amount of exposure to the lively and amiable Trinidadian social scene.

The internal politics seemed to be reasonably tranquil at the time we were there, and this was largely, if not entirely, due to the firm but enlightened manner in which affairs of the state were being handled by the Prime Minister, Dr Eric Williams. He was kind enough to grant me an audience on both occasions that I visited Port of Spain. Pakistan–Trinidad relations were quickly disposed off, since we were both friends but neither could find any avenues to develop this asset in concrete terms. However, our discussion on other issues was most productive, and we talked about the Cold War, US influence in Latin America, and the Caribbean, the Non-Aligned Movement, which Eric Williams firmly supported without being starry-eyed about it, and the North–South economic divide. Eric Williams was a leading historian who had taught at Howard University, Washington, D.C., and was an authority on colonial history. As I already had the good fortune to have read both of Williams' books, *History of the People of Trinidad and Tobago* and *Capitalism and Slavery*, these conversations became both meaningful and fruitful. A short, stocky man with close-cropped hair, Williams spoke softly, which is unusual for a person who wore a prominent hearing aid, and possessed a sharp, dry wit. I never got to see his eyes because he wore thick, dark glasses, but in the aggregate two hours that I spent with this impressive man I discovered that his conversation, which could sometimes be acerbic but was always clear and concise, conveyed his thoughts with precision. There was no doubt about his deep ideological motivation, but at the same time he had a realistic approach to political life, as epitomised in the views expressed in his book, 'Where your treasure is, there will be your heart also.' Unlike many other leaders that I have met, particularly in the Third World, there was nothing messianic about Eric Williams. Not once did he mention to me his ambitions for his country, nor were there any bombastic declarations about opposing exploitation and creating a free and equitable society. He preferred that I saw things as they were, and that what I saw was what I got. As I left his office he proffered me one last piece of sardonic advice, 'Go and see the un-Islamic fashion in which we celebrate Carnival.'

I took the prime minister's advice, and went with Diana, Niloufer and Feroza, to a number of spots where we saw happy and carefree

Trinidadians enjoying themselves, filled with beer, steel band music and calypso dance. The blend of a rhythmic body and a joyful soul is impossible to describe and just as impossible to forget.

CHIAROSCURO

The high commissioner's official car in Ottawa was an enormous black Oldsmobile, imposing and overbearing in appearance, which was tended by our quaint and fastidious chauffeur, George, with loving pride and joy. A proud and loquacious native of Ottawa, George was a big, florid man who was an institution not only in the Pakistan High Commission, but in the entire diplomatic corps. I am sure he would have been doyen of CD chauffeurs, if such an entity had existed. A confirmed and fastidious bachelor, George's loyalties were to Ottawa, the Oldsmobile, Pakistan, Canada, and the Royal Canadian Mounted Police, in that order. He had a visceral dislike of the Quebecois, and kept muttering 'city of sin' from the moment we approached Montreal until the time we left its municipal limits. As for me, I was always uncomfortable riding in the huge, ostentatious Oldsmobile, but had no choice, especially when on official duty. George would love to drive through the part of town where he grew up, and proclaim it as 'my happy old stomping grounds' each time that we traversed the territory, and would try to make a detour via his stomping ground whenever he could. It was situated in a peripheral working class district, and on one occasion as we drove through it, I happened to be smoking a cigar. To a bunch of rowdy young boys lounging on the street corner, the combination of big, black Oldsmobile and big Havana cigar was an obvious provocation, and somewhat to my amusement I heard a loud yell, 'Capitalist bastard!' But for the staid and proper George it was a matter of acute embarrassment that such an indignity should have occurred on his old stomping grounds, and I could see the colour on the back of his chubby neck turn from pink to red, and then to an explosive purple, 'You shouldn't mind them sir, these boys must be from out of town.'

* * *

The high commissioner's residence on Coltrin Road in the exclusive Rockcliffe Park area of Ottawa, possessed a large garden which was tended, in somewhat desultory fashion, by a young American who had come to Canada as a draft dodger from the Vietnam War. I believe that the inevitable ideological conflict between him and George had been settled earlier on and by now relations had assumed a surly neutrality. I did receive the occasional snide reference from both sides, but was not called upon for any serious conflict resolution. However, the garden did suffer from neglect, and one sunny Sunday afternoon I decided to do a bit of lawn mowing. The effect on the lawn was peripheral, but the exercise left me feeling vigorous and virtuous. These feelings of self-satisfaction increased tremendously on Monday, when Diana told me that she had received three telephone calls from the neighbours complimenting her on finding a gardener to work on a Sunday, and asking for his name and telephone number.

MEANWHILE IN PAKISTAN

Bhutto's dynamic activities were imposing an enormous imprint on the country. Having eased out General Gul Hasan and Air Marshal Rahim Khan, the two service chiefs who had in effect brought him to power, he appointed the ruthless but obedient Tikka Khan as the army chief. On the political front he negotiated a deal with the National Awami Party and the Jamiat Ulema-e-Islam (JUI) whereby these parties would form coalition governments in the North West Frontier Province (NWFP) and Balochistan, and then, under an interim constitution approved by the National Assembly, Bhutto took a formal oath as the President and the Civilian Chief Martial Law Administrator (CMLA) of Pakistan.

In July 1972, Bhutto returned in triumph after signing the Simla Agreement with Indira Gandhi. This secured the recovery of Pakistan territory, re-established diplomatic relations with India, and formally changed the name of the 'Ceasefire Line' in Kashmir to 'Line of Control'. The prisoners of war still remained in Indian custody, but Bhutto had correctly assessed his priorities—recovery of territory before recovery of prisoners—knowing that India could not hold on to 90,000 prisoner of war indefinitely, and that it is easier and more productive to organize international public opinion in favour of the return of prisoners than it is to get support for the return of territory. The Simla talks were something of a cliff hanger, and it was not until the last moments that Indira Gandhi uttered the pre-agreed code words for success, *'Larka hai!'* ('It is a boy!'). The code words for failure *'Larki hai!'* ('It is a girl!'), were fortunately, not used. Bhutto returned to Pakistan, together with his daughter Benazir, who had accompanied him to Simla and had been a close observer of the negotiations. Bhutto declared the Simla Agreement a victory for both Pakistan and India, thus securing its approval in the National Assembly.

Bhutto's next triumph, in April 1973, was the drafting and passage through the National Assembly, of a new Constitution of Pakistan, which changed the nation's government from a presidential to a parliamentary system. All executive power was vested in an elected prime minister with the presidential functions being purely ceremonial. Whilst maintaining a strong centre, the constitution nevertheless allowed for substantial provincial autonomy. But despite its many attractive features, the 1973 Constitution reflected the many concessions that Bhutto had been forced to make, and which were the early steps in the Islamization that would become much stronger in the years to come. It declared Pakistan an 'Islamic State' in which only a Muslim could be its president or the prime minister, and established the Council of Islamic Ideology, charged with the task of Islamization of laws over the next seven years. In the closing days of his regime, and in a desperate but forlorn attempt to survive, Bhutto made further concessions, such as the prohibition of alcohol, the declaration of Friday as a weekly holiday, and a parliamentary motion declaring Ahmadis as non-Muslims. Perhaps most damaging of all was the fact that, shortly after the near-unanimous adoption of the constitution by the National Assembly, Bhutto's imperious lust for power drove a hole in the document large enough to drive a coach and horses through it. He dissolved the NWFP and Balochistan provincial assemblies in the NWFP and Balochistan, imposing the governors' rule from the centre in each province, and mounted a repressive action in Balochistan that haunted the rest of his term in office.

Perhaps the highlight of Bhutto's many successes in international diplomacy was the holding of the Islamic Summit of the Organization of the Islamic Conference (OIC) in Lahore, in 1974. This was a tour de force, almost entirely orchestrated and driven by Zulfikar Ali Bhutto, which proved to be a resounding success. Not only did it restore the image of Pakistan in the comity of nations after the disastrous East Pakistan debacle, but was also the occasion when, with a stroke of deft and daring diplomacy at which Bhutto was so masterful, the new state of Bangladesh was simultaneously recognized by Pakistan and admitted to the membership of the OIC. This in turn led to the liberation of the 90,000 Pakistani prisoners of war held in India, who were given a warm and rapturous reception on their return to their homeland. The entire episode of the Islamic Conference at Lahore and its ramifications was a masterstroke of inspiration, conception, planning, and deft and detailed implementation, driven with enthusiasm and firmness by Bhutto. It brought a sense of pride to all the people of Pakistan, who participated enthusiastically in all the events and manifestations of the conference. It was perhaps the highlight of Bhutto's career in a lifetime that had in it the fullest measure of triumphs and tragedies.

But there were other developments that were both discomforting and ominous. Bhutto's attitude and actions had by now moved from being authoritarian to the downright repressive, and there was a foul stench of fascism in the air. Secret camps were established where political opponents were held incommunicado, and a paramilitary force known as the Federal Security Force (FSF), was created on the lines of the SS and SA of Nazi Germany. The Dr Jekyll of Zulfikar Bhutto's Simla and Lahore was being increasingly replaced by the Mr Hyde in his FSF and in the moody whims and caprice of his daily conduct, both official and personal. He savaged the bureaucracy, which despite its occasional failings was an honest, and certainly competent, institution. 'God willing, and Waqar living, I will sort out the CSP' was one Bhutto aphorism that was frequently quoted. He brought into the civil service a large number of party hacks, most of whom were both corrupt and incompetent. On the economic front, the rampage of nationalization continued at full speed, eventually extending to the absurd inclusion of the smallest agricultural enterprises, such as cotton ginning and rice mills, and causing immense damage to the nation's financial and economic structure.

In April 1973 a group of army officers was arrested on charges of plotting a coup against Bhutto, and was subjected to severe interrogation in the Attock fort. A military tribunal, named the Attock Conspiracy Tribunal, was established and was headed by Major General Ziaul Haq, who was then commanding an armoured division in Multan. He had earlier served with distinction in Jordan, and had developed a close friendship with the Jordanian royal family. It was during Prince Hassan of Jordan's visit to Pakistan that General Ziaul Haq first got to know Bhutto. He must have created a favourable impression on the prime minister, who then chose him to head the Attock Conspiracy Tribunal. From all accounts General Ziaul Haq conducted the tribunal in a totally fair and impeccable manner, but it did manage to bring him into close contact with Bhutto, who was following the proceedings closely. Impressed by Ziaul Haq's deferential manner, and in cognizance of his background as a refugee from East Punjab, with no links to the Jhelum–Attock camaraderie that so strongly prevailed in the officer corps of the Pakistan army, Bhutto decided to appoint Ziaul Haq as army commander when Tikka Khan retired in April 1976. Subsequent history has revealed the far-reaching consequences of this decision for both of the powerful personalities involved.

By now, Bhutto's imperious posture, both in his lifestyle and in his relations with his political friends and foes, had begun to cast a dark shadow over the country, and tales of his arrogance and vindictiveness were legion. In retrospect, it seems to me that this was the spring in which he sowed the seeds of the disaster which he was to so tragically reap in the autumn.

PART V

GERMAN DEMOCRATIC REPUBLIC
AND ICELAND

CHAPTER FIFTEEN

The German Democratic Republic (GDR) 1974–1976

'Sliced houses will always remind me of East Berlin.'
– Diana Marker

'Berlin is like the testicles of the West. Every time we give it a squeeze, they howl.'
– Nikita S. Khrushchev, Secretary General of the Communist Party of the USSR

'I love Germany. I love it so much that I am glad there are two of them.'
– Francois Mauriac

On arrival at East Berlin's Schoenfeldt airport we were received by protocol officers of the GDR Foreign Ministry and Mohammed Tayyab Siddiqui, the First Secretary of the Embassy who, together with two assistants and a security guard, formed the Pakistan-based component of the mission. This was my first meeting with Tayyab, and was also the beginning of a close and lifelong friendship that my family and I cherish very much. Highly intelligent, well read and articulate, Tayyab had a penetrating facility to size up character and motivation, an ability which was a tremendous professional asset. He was also very outspoken; a tendency which, coupled with his ironic sense of humour and irreverent attitude to authority, produced a somewhat bumpy ride through his career. I was told later that mine was the first good Annual Confidential Report (ACR) received by Tayyab, but whether that was true or not, I always had the highest regard for his ability, patriotism, and loyalty, and was proud of his friendship. In a previous posting at Jordan he had developed a close friendship with Pakistan's Military Liaison Officer to the Kingdom, a certain Brigadier Ziaul Haq This was an association that obviously appreciated in political value when the latter became the President of Pakistan, but one that Tayyab never exploited, in a career that followed the normal course of postings and promotions.

The situation on the ground, as explained to me by Tayyab, was not very different from the one that I had encountered upon arrival in Bucharest. Premises of a spartan nature had been obtained for the chancery, but as yet there was no residence and the possibilities of obtaining one in the near future were not very bright. This feeling intensified as we drove into East Berlin from the airport, and it was obvious that the economic miracle (*wirtschaftswunder*) that had turned the war-shattered Federal Republic of Germany into an economic giant, had left the East Germans far behind. The devastation caused by the Second World War was still very much in evidence; piles of crumbled masonry shared empty plots with the standing remnants of buildings and houses, and bumpy cobbled streets were bordered by decrepit pavements. It was only when we reached the centre of the city that one discerned signs of reconstruction. But here too there was disappointment, because the architecture and quality of construction reflected the soul-destroying nature of socialist reality. Most depressing of all was the sight of the infamous Berlin Wall which we approached as we neared the city centre. This monstrosity was to become a part of our lives over the next two and a half years, and even though we were to transit through it on numerous occasions, sometimes five times a day, one never quite overcame a disagreeable and distasteful sensation as one did so.

We were lodged at the Hotel Unter den Linden, a newly-constructed building on the avenue famous for its beauty and the historic events immediately associated with its name. It had been completely destroyed at the end of the Second World War, like the rest of Berlin, where every street and alley had been a battleground, but the GDR authorities had embarked upon an effective reconstruction programme, starting with the lovely linden trees that gave the avenue its famous name. The remnants of the older edifices had been restored in their original style, such as the famous Staatsoper, and new buildings had replaced those that had been completely destroyed. Our chancery occupied one floor in a new block of office buildings on Otto-Grotewohl-Straße, which also accommodated a number of other foreign embassies. The location was superb and from my office window I could see, across a wasteland of rubble which bordered the wall, the heavily damaged but still impressive Reichstag building in West Berlin, and the majestic Brandenburger Tor, that formed part of the border between East and West Berlin. Following the spate of recognitions that followed the USSR–Federal Republic of Germany Treaty, the GDR authorities, with customary German efficiency, had embarked upon the construction of a number of buildings suitable for use as embassies in the select Pankow region of East Berlin. In my negotiations with the GDR authorities I was anxious to avoid this diplomatic ghetto existence, and was lucky enough to obtain a property in Niederschönhausen, on the north-western tip of East Berlin. It was a house with a small garden, and although it was entirely surrounded by ten storey residential flats, I preferred indifferent German citizens to inquisitive diplomatic colleagues as neighbours.

The credentials ceremony was quick and simple. Following an inspection of a guard of honour whose uniforms I thought looked remarkably like those worn by the *Wehrmacht*, I was received by Willi Stoph, the President, who was accompanied by Deputy Foreign Minister Claus Willerding. Discussions were a combination of pleasantries coupled with the known positions of both sides on the major political issues, and I was given the usual promises of co-operation. Looking back on the issue of economic relations I recollect that we did manage to advance this to a certain extent during my tenure, particularly after Pakistan's participation in the famous Leipzig trade fairs. But objective realities, including our closeness to West Germany and the substantive nature of their credits, precluded the development of major economic relations with East Berlin. An air traffic agreement backfired after a while, when it was discovered that the Schonefeldt airport in East Berlin was being used as a transit point for illegal immigration.

As we settled in, life in East Berlin became increasingly interesting, despite the fact that the scope for the development of bilateral relations between Pakistan and the GDR had its obvious limitations. The presence of West Berlin with its accessibility to diplomats relieved us of the problems of the shortage of domestic necessities that had plagued our lives in other communist capitals. But more than that was the fascination of finding oneself at the epicentre of the international confrontation between East and West at the height of the Cold War. Washington and Moscow never seemed to be distant, for whatever transpired in these capitals had a perceptible and almost immediate impact in Berlin; the artificially created geopolitical barometer of Cold War relations. Diplomats stationed in East Berlin used to have regular working lunches in the comfortable cafes and restaurants in West Berlin, conscious of the fact that even though there might be no microphones concealed under the tables or in flower pots, there was always the possibility of alert waiters infiltrated by different secret services ready to report to their masters for ideological or pecuniary considerations. Although the GDR, with its known rigid adherence to the USSR, was in itself a political dead end, the spate of recognitions and the consequent establishment of foreign missions in East Berlin in the mid-1970s rendered the whole of the divided city into a unique listening post of limitless diplomatic activity and interest.

I had followed and studied German history of the twentieth century with the deepest interest, and found it fascinating to visit the sites of the events that had so dramatically created history in this city, which had not only itself witnessed so much violence, but initiated it throughout the world in two devastating wars during the century. There was the reconstructed balcony of the Imperial Palace from which Karl Liebknecht and Rosa Luxemburg had proclaimed the communist state at the end of the First World War, and then met their violent ends; the working class district of Wedding where the Nazi and Communist thugs had fought their street battles before Hitler imposed his *diktat*; the imposing Reichstag building which marked the rise and fall of the Nazi regime, first when the contrived fire provided the excuse for the Nazi takeover, and later when the Soviet soldiers had triumphantly hoisted the Red Flag on its dome at the end of the Second World War; the forlorn glory of Goering's Air Ministry, still standing; the rubble of Hitler's chancery and the dreaded Gestapo headquarters; the long, wide boulevards that encompassed the Victory Monument and most imposingly the Brandenburg Tor, designed not for the flow of urban commercial traffic but to carry massive columns of armoured troops and tanks as they marched through the city in reviews of military might. By contrast, there was the *embarras de richesse* of the cultural life still available in the Berlin of the 1970s. There was the Museumsinsel, which held the Pergamon and other magnificent museums where I spent many happy hours in East Berlin and the rich Staatsmuseum in West Berlin. For music, which was my great passion, the choice was as rich as it was limitless. Two magnificent orchestras, led by Herbert von Karajan in West Berlin and Kurt Masur in East Berlin, the traditional Staatsoper where Hitler listened enthralled to his favourite Wagner, and the famous Komische Oper in East Berlin, and to the Deutsche Oper in West Berlin. In addition there was chamber music galore of the highest quality. One of my favourite pastimes was to drive along the famous Avus racing track to the Sanssouci Palace in Potsdam for a chamber music concert, and follow it up by a civilized dinner in a restaurant in West Berlin before returning home via Checkpoint Charlie. All these delectable pleasures were available to the diplomats stationed in East Berlin, for whom transit through the Berlin Wall was just a matter of a routine border check. But for the Germans it was a totally different situation, and while a lucky few managed to escape, many died in the attempt to get through this monstrous man-made creation in order to join their loved ones. Although I had passed through all the checkpoints in the Berlin Wall many times, I was never able to overcome a sense of sadness and revulsion each time that I did so.

Shortly after I arrived in East Berlin, relations between the two Germanys hit a crisis which was much more serious than the ones that periodically afflicted relations between the East and West Germans, and it was one that caused the indefinite postponement of ceremonies when envoys from both countries would be formally accredited. The reason was the sensational discovery that Günther Guillaume, a close associate of Chancellor Willy Brandt, and the Personal Assistant for Party Affairs in the Office of the Chancellor, had been an East German spy, infiltrated into the Chancellor's office and confidence by the Stasi, the infamous secret state police of the GDR The arrest of Guillaume and his wife and their subsequent trial revealed the sinister, long-term methods employed by the Stasi, and the brilliant successes that they achieved. Although the course of detente between Bonn and East Berlin continued after a while and there was an exchange of ambassadors, the Guillaume incident dealt a crippling blow to the political career of Willy Brandt, who was obliged to resign from office and was succeeded as Chancellor by Helmut Schmidt, his able and competent deputy, who was also a brilliant economist.

Lenin once said, 'Whoever controls Berlin will rule Germany; whoever controls Germany rules Europe', and it seemed to me, when I arrived there in the spring of 1974, that Berlin was, in many ways, the manifestation of Lenin's prophetic words. The city, despite the grotesque impact of its partition, remained the symbolic as well as strategic barometer of European peace, and indeed the exercise of peacekeeping in Europe over the previous thirty years inevitably implied the manifold considerations regarding the status of Berlin.

On 7 October 1974, while the West Berliners maintained a normal working day and attempted the studious expression of an unconcern which they clearly did not feel, the East Germans celebrated the twenty-fifth anniversary of the foundation of the German Democratic Republic with due pomp and an enthusiasm that occasionally appeared contrived. The chief guest for the anniversary celebrations was Leonid Brezhnev, the First Secretary of the Communist Party of the Soviet Union, who was accompanied by Foreign Minister Gromyko, Defence Minister Marshal Andrei Grechko, and the legendary Marshal Vasily Ivanovich Chuikov, the Commander of the Soviet 8th Guards Army which had defended Stalingrad in 1942, and then went on to capture Berlin in 1945. I very much wanted to meet Marshal Chuikov, for whose military achievements I have always had the greatest admiration, and although I did get to shake his hand, no conversation was possible, partly because of the constraints on his speech brought about by old age, but mostly because he was surrounded by many people seeking his attention.

The ceremonies included a commemorative meeting where laudatory speeches were delivered, a sumptuous reception in the Palace of the Peoples, and a military parade, where I found myself standing next to the Spanish ambassador. He told me that he had stood in the same place thirty years before, and witnessed a similar parade. At that time he was a young military officer cadet in the Franco regime sent as part of a delegation to one of Hitler's Nazi Party manifestations. I asked the ambassador whether he saw any difference between then and now. His laconic response was, 'Only the slogans on the banners.' In addition to the parade, the ceremony included the laying of wreaths at three of the war memorials to Soviet troops, located in different parts of East Berlin. As we trudged from one memorial to another, commemorating what was officially designated as the '*Befreiung*' (liberation) of the GDR, the Egyptian ambassador said to me, 'I have never seen a manifestation of people celebrating their defeat with so much style and enthusiasm.'

But there was more than a ceremonial aspect to the celebration of the twenty-fifth anniversary of the founding of the GDR. In his address to the Sozialistische Einheitspartei Deutschlands (SED, Socialist Unity Party of Germany), its Secretary General, Erich Honecker, introduced a number of important amendments to the constitution, the most significant of which was the elimination of all previous references to 'the entire German nation' and of the intention 'to overcome the division of Germany'. Instead, the constitution formally renounced any desire for the reunification of Germany. Foreign Minister Oskar Fischer made the new situation entirely clear in a speech in which he said,

> Today there are, on German soil, a socialist state, the German Democratic Republic, in which the socialist state is developing, and the capitalist Federal Republic of Germany, in which the capitalist nation exists. Between socialist and capitalist nations there can only be relations of peaceful coexistence, the principles of which can safely be assumed to be known everywhere.

The West Germans were obviously not happy with this development, but did not let it impede their growing diplomatic and other relations with the GDR. At this moment Chancellor Helmut Schmidt made the significant observation, 'One cannot, with a stroke of the pen on a piece of paper, dissolve centuries of German history and culture.' This wise prophecy was fulfilled, almost exactly fifteen years later, when on 12 November 1989, the Berlin Philharmoniker, under its famous conductor Daniel Barenboim, performed a free open air concert for the people of East Germany in the shadow of the infamous Berlin Wall which they had just torn down. To rapturous applause from a highly charged and emotional audience, consisting of residents of both East and West Berlin, the Philharmoniker played Beethoven's First Piano Concerto and his Seventh Symphony. Helmut Schmidt was so right; indeed German history and culture had not been destroyed.

In March 1975, there was minor diplomatic consternation in Berlin when it was suddenly announced that Soviet Ambassador Mikhail Timofeyevich Yefremov, a comparatively benign and jovial personality, was being recalled to other duties—he subsequently went as ambassador to Vienna—and was being replaced by Pytor Andreyvitch Abrassimov. Not only was this change unexpected, but it was accompanied by additional changes in the Soviet embassy in Berlin, the minister, counsellor and military attaché all being recalled with the ambassador. Such simultaneous top level changes were obviously unusual, and Abrassimov brought with him, as Minister Counsellor, Anatoly Gromyko, the son of the Soviet foreign minister, who I thought looked absurdly like his father. Abrassimov had been Soviet Ambassador in Berlin from 1962 to 1971, and was also Chief Soviet Negotiator for the Four Power Agreement on Berlin. During the course of these negotiations he is reported to have told his American counterpart, 'You look after your Germans, and we will take care of ours.' Abrassimov's other accomplishments included an active and successful intervention in the Politburo of the GDR in 1966, resulting in the appointment of Erich Honecker as First Secretary of the SED in place of Walter Ulbricht, the long-standing and dedicated communist leader who had spent the Second World War in the Soviet Union. Ulbricht was a hardliner and had been difficult over the matter of Soviet-inspired detente with the Federal Republic of Germany. The average East German viewed the announcement of the return of Abrassimov with a foreboding something akin to the renewed visitation of a pestilence from the east. Although those apprehensions were not entirely fulfilled, there was no doubt that Abrassimov's firm hand on the tiller was required for the purpose of ensuring that the GDR remained on course for two important ongoing international negotiations.

The first of these was the Conference on Security and Co-operation in Europe (CSCE), which had just concluded with the signing of the famous Helsinki Declaration and its principles of 'peaceful co-existence'. Moscow had ensured that the role of the GDR in the CSCE was anything other than subservient, reflecting an East German's witty and malicious description of the Soviet attitude towards Erich Honecker: 'Confidence is good, but control is better'. In the final analysis, so far as Berlin was concerned, the objective and geographic realities were changed neither by the CSCE nor the Helsinki Declaration. For the West the city remained potentially vulnerable, and for the East it remained a potential and disruptive hazard within its borders.

Abrassimov's second and equally important mission was to employ his formidable diplomatic skills, and even more formidable powers of persuasion, on the East Germans as they negotiated a new Friendship Treaty with the USSR. Here too, in his capacity as a virtual *Gauleiter* of the GDR, he delivered. The treaty was an extensive document that covered a large number of issues, but its main political content was the GDR's decision to finally abandon all talk of German reunification and replace it with the decision to link the GDR 'eternally' with the Soviet Union. On the economic front there were some positive gains for the GDR, as opening of trade with the Federal Republic of Germany provided the East Germans with access not only to the lucrative West German market but also to the equally lucrative European Common Market.

The remainder of my tenure in East Berlin remained quiet and uninterrupted by any events of significance. The Helsinki Declaration and the renewed Friendship Treaty with the Soviet Union had set the parameters of the political existence of the GDR, and the country settled down to working on its economy, which was by far the most robust in Eastern Europe. It also, now, had to cope with the social consequences implicit in living alongside but separate from the Federal Republic of Germany, which had by now become the powerhouse of Western Europe.

Unlike other countries in the European communist bloc, which were separate from Western Europe by linguistic differences as well as geographical barriers, the GDR was tied to the Federal Republic of Germany in every possible fashion. The Wall could hold the people in physical confinement, but it could not restrain the flow of news and ideas that streamed from west to east. Bonn did not need to bother with mounting an official propaganda exercise. Regular commercial broadcasts over the West Berlin radio in German, from a department store like Neckermann offering its clients a variety of consumer durables at affordable prices, was sufficient evidence of a superior life in the west. And if situated in East Berlin on a cold and foggy November day, one heard, as I often did, on West Berlin radio, an advertisement by Neckermann offering a two-week vacation in the sunny Canary Islands for a modest cost, the effect could be quite devastating. Every East Berliner would know that cousin Otto on the other side would be vacationing in the sunshine while he was confined to Berlin's notorious cold and damp fog. The GDR authorities tried to counter this by propagating the concept that the consumerism in the west could not compensate for the social security, such as the medical care and the old age benefits, which were provided in the east. Whilst this idea found some favour amongst the older population it was firmly rejected by most East Germans, particularly the youth.

On visits to Berlin in the 1990s, well after the Berlin Wall had been torn down, I was intrigued to note that its consequences were still apparent and that considerable differences existed in the attitudes of the East and West Berliners. As the Berlin novelist Peter Schneider had observed in 1981, 'It will take us longer to tear down the "*Mauer im Kopf*" ("wall in the head") than any wrecking company will need to remove the Wall that we can see.'

During my tenure in East Berlin I was accorded two assignments outside of my jurisdiction. The first was a conference of Pakistan envoys held in Rome in the summer of 1974 and chaired by Prime Minister Bhutto. Attended by about forty ambassadors from all over the world, it was an extravaganza that achieved success in its original objective of providing a boost to Bhutto's ego, and had little else to show for it. We were lined up at the Rome airport to receive the prime minister; but there were two absentees, our ambassadors in Madrid and Vienna, Air Marshal Rahim Khan and General Gul Hasan, Bhutto's earlier nemeses. For this lapse, Agha Shahi, who had just taken over as Foreign Secretary, got a rocket from his boss. Bhutto chaired the conference and we were regaled with an account of his accomplishments, impressive up to a point, and were given instructions with regard to the direction in which he intended to take Pakistan. We were then set to work to prepare a paper on the foreign policy of Pakistan, and this was reviewed in plenary after it had been drafted. There was a banquet at one of the finest restaurants in Rome, and the food and wine served were of the highest quality. Two events of considerable international consequence occurred during the course of our conference. The first was the news of the Indian nuclear explosion, with the now famous, and cynical, codeword 'The Buddha is Smiling'. The second was the coup d'etat in Kabul by Prime Minister Sardar Dawood, which removed the king who, like us, happened to be in

Rome at that time. These issues were mentioned in our conference and duly noted, but were never discussed in a meaningful way.

My second foray out of East Germany was a trip to Geneva and Divonne les Bains in the spring of 1976, to attend a conference on nuclear proliferation, organized by the Carnegie Institute. The recent Indian nuclear explosion had added an element of urgency to the issue, and was hotly debated by the delegates. We produced a report which may have had some relevance at the time, but by now has been overtaken by events, and is justly relegated to the closet of dusty records.

It was in the spring of 1975 that we were struck with a devastating personal tragedy. A routine medical check revealed that Diana had cancer, and following intensive further tests, she underwent surgery at the Klinikum Stegliz in West Berlin, where she remained in the care of the foremost experts in Europe. The courage and optimism that Diana displayed as she went through her ordeal elicited the admiration and affection of all her friends, and above all, of the medical staff that attended her, from the distinguished Professor Hürmann, to the house surgeons, and the entire nursing staff. On release from the hospital, after surgery and radiation, she was declared to be in remission. But the doctors warned that the next two years would be critical. Notwithstanding the fact that she had just emerged from a serious and life-threatening surgical procedure, Diana resumed her diplomatic activities in full measure, and never let her affliction detract her from her duties and obligations in any way whatsoever. It was on this note of personal uncertainty, coupled with a sense of hope that Diana had put the worst behind her and that her recovery would be complete, that we departed from East Berlin. We took a short holiday in Karachi and then proceeded to our next assignment in Tokyo.

CHIAROSCURO

The newly arrived ambassador of Bangladesh made a courtesy call on me in April 1974. Bashir-ul-Alam was a lawyer who had actively participated in the political movement that led to the creation of Pakistan. Like many of his compatriots, his disillusionment had motivated his subsequent political struggle for Bangladesh. As soon as he was seated beside me on a sofa in my office, he saw the portrait of the Quaid-i-Azam on the wall opposite, and was clearly very moved. Clutching my hand, he requested that we refrain from commencing a conversation and said, 'I have not seen that picture for a long time. Let me gaze at it for a while.' After a short time, still clutching my hand and still in a state of high emotion, he said, 'If that man had lived a little longer, then either you would have been here or I would have been here. Both of us would not have been here together.'

* * *

Simeon, our sweet little cocker spaniel, died while we were in East Berlin. Once we had got over his loss, the customary Marker obsession for canine companionship reasserted itself, and we obtained from England a superb Clumber Spaniel. His domed head, blue-green eyes, white fur, and solemn appearance, convinced me that he would one day write a dark Russian novel, so we named him Feodor Dostoevsky. Highly intelligent and temperamental, Feodor lived to be fifteen years old, travelled all over the world with us, and quite literally left his mark wherever he went, because his unpredictable nature could provoke him into biting friend and foe alike for reasons known only to him. In mitigation, as I tried to explain to a frequently distraught Arnaz, Feodor never held a grudge and always forgave his victim after the bite. I took Feodor in my car whenever I could, which was frequently, and as we were constantly passing through Checkpoint Charlie and the other Berlin Wall checkpoints, the security guards got to know Feodor quite well and there was always an exchange of friendly greetings on these occasions. However, I noticed that Feodor seemed to get extremely agitated as soon as we got to within three hundred yards of the border. After considering and eliminating all other causes for this unusual conduct, I concluded that Feodor, who had been bred as a gundog and had a very strong sense of smell, was reacting to the cordite in the mines that were placed in the border fences. This strip of no man's land, known as the *Todesstreifen* (Death Strip) consisted of a series of lethal devices, including watchtowers, barbed wire and landmines, and was collectively known as the *Mauer* (Wall).

Our embassy residence in Niederschönhausen, in the north-west of East Berlin, was located very close to the Wall, and there were nights when we would sometimes hear the explosion of a detonated mine. I tried to reassure Diana by saying that it was probably a rabbit that triggered the mine. But there were times when the explosion was followed by the sounds of police and ambulance sirens, and I had no answer to Diana's legitimate query, 'Police and ambulance for a rabbit?'

* * *

The diplomatic corps was invited by the GDR government to a hunting trip in the region of Erfurt. We were taken by a special train and provided with a sumptuous dinner, before being lodged for the night at a very comfortable hotel. The next morning, following a substantial breakfast, we were taken to the hunting area, which soon turned into a killing field of disgusting proportions. Some of us who did not hunt went for a walk in a different area and enjoyed the beauty of forests and fields of a German countryside, still unspoiled by the autobahns and industrial complexes, that had by now taken over the West German landscape. On our return to the elaborate campsite for lunch we saw a mass of dead rabbits and birds that literally overpowered our senses. It seems that this area had been designated as a reserve for the shoots of high party officials, and the game was, therefore, well stocked, and plentiful. Our hosts, clothed in the traditional German hunting green outfits, had blazed away at the unsuspecting wildlife that had been specifically preserved for the day's slaughter. They then rounded off the event with a boisterous evening of heavy feasting and drinking. No *shikar* in colonial India could have matched the lavish scale of these communist orgies.

* * *

The human tragedy of separation caused by the Berlin Wall was evident almost every day as one saw divided families tearfully waving to each other across the checkpoints. But there were two instances, involving my East German staff that came to my attention. The first involved my social secretary, Frau Kraft, who told me that all her family were in West Germany. Her own house in East Berlin had been destroyed by bombs during the war and she had moved to the West to live with the rest of her family. One day, before the Berlin Wall had been constructed and when movement between east and west was comparatively free, she and her husband revisited the site of her destroyed residence and saw some daffodils growing amongst the ruins. This beautiful, symbolic rebirth beckoned the Krafts into rebuilding their home. Before they could complete this task the Berlin Wall had gone up, and the husband and wife found themselves trapped in the East, and separated from the rest of the family in the West.

Our staff car driver had been provided to us, as was customary, by the Dienstleitungs Amt, the service department of the Foreign Ministry. Herr Klopsch was a large, shaggy, kindly man with the appearance and gait of a big Old English sheepdog. He was eagerly looking forward to his retirement, which was due in six months time, so that he could apply for residence with his family in West Germany. The GDR authorities were lenient about releasing older citizens, thus transferring the burden of old age security to the West, and Herr Klopsch, having made it known to all and sundry that he intended to avail himself of this facility, had refused all other offers of employment. A year later I found a disconsolate Herr Klopsch washing cars in the garage of the GDR Foreign Ministry, and learned from him his sad story. It seems that there was a rule that forbade transfer for a five-year period to any GDR citizen who had worked for a USSR organization in East Berlin. Three months before his retirement Herr Klopsch had been assigned a short appointment in a Soviet commercial enterprise, and this had deferred his move to the West for another five years. Quite clearly, Herr Klopsch's intentions had come to the attention of some apparatchik in the Dienstleitungs Amt who, with the petty, mean, and vicious spirit, so common to that species, had gleefully exercised his authority.

CHAPTER SIXTEEN

Iceland 1975–1976

The Ministry of Foreign Affairs, Government of Pakistan, was known on occasion to combine, in its administration decisions, common sense with justice in the due distribution of its meagre and very limited resources. One such instance was the allocation of concurrent accreditations in the Nordic countries. Our embassy in Moscow was allotted Helsinki, our embassy in Stockholm was also responsible for Oslo and Copenhagen, and Reykjavik was assigned to East Berlin. In the latter case, the mild incongruity of concurrent accreditation to a Warsaw Pact capital and a NATO capital appeared to have been overlooked in Islamabad. But East Berlin and Reykjavik appeared to have displayed similar indifference, leading me to surmise that, if the thought ever occurred to anyone in either capital, the conclusion would be that a harmless ambassador from the Islamic Republic of Pakistan was unlikely to tilt the balance in the ongoing confrontation between NATO and the Warsaw Pact.

Since there were no direct air connections between Berlin and Keflavik, a visit to Iceland involved a stopover in either London or Copenhagen, neither of which was a hardship. My first visit to Iceland for presentation of credentials was in early May 1975, and in my subsequent visits, which were undertaken both in the depth of winter and the height of summer, I had an opportunity to live under twenty-four hours of both darkness and daylight. Iceland was originally under Danish sovereignty, but assumed a wide-ranging autonomy in 1918. Situated almost exactly half way between Moscow and New York, and dominating the approaches to the North Atlantic sea lanes, Iceland possesses a geopolitical location of the utmost strategic importance. In the Second World War the British and Americans carried out a military occupation of the island in order to forestall a German invasion, but withdrew their forces in June 1944, following a plebiscite in which the Icelanders declared their complete independence from Denmark. Subsequently, during the Cold War, Iceland became a member of NATO, and possessing no armed forces of its own, accepted a considerable US naval and air presence in Keflavik. Only a quarter of the island is inhabited, and the population of 240,000, about the size of a single *mohalla* (neighbourhood) in Karachi, is occupied in the fishing industry, supplemented by some sheep farming and light industry.

I presented credentials in a simple ceremony to President Kristján Eldjárn, a scholarly archaeologist and historian, who was one of the foremost authorities on Viking history and culture. He headed a left of centre, coalition government, with a cabinet consisting of a prime minister and seven ministers. It was as compact an institution as everything else in Iceland. The entire Ministry of Foreign Affairs consisted of six officers, of whom two were away on mission almost every time I visited Reykjavik. Apart from its normal departments, the Ministry of Foreign Affairs also had a special division to deal with defence matters and the lease with the US base in Keflavik.

A drive from the airport at Keflavik to the capital reveals the inhospitable but sombre beauty of Iceland. The rugged volcanic soil, whipped by strong polar winds, combined to provide a landscape of striking harshness, black terrain interspersed with white snow, a few green pastures dotted with grazing sheep, and stark, deep blue, rivers and fjords. Particularly noticeable was the total absence of trees and shrubs anywhere on the island. The volcanic soil and fierce polar winds combined to ensure that no trees could either grow or survive in these inhospitable conditions. There are a number of volcanoes on the island, some of them active, and earthquakes are a common occurrence. But the most striking geological features are the numerous geysers that proliferate on the island and shoot out volumes of steam and scalding water at frequent intervals. The ubiquitous presence of these geysers and the total absence of trees were my first and lasting impressions of Iceland.

The innovative and industrious Icelanders had put to fullest use the availability of the subsoil steam, treating it as a prime natural resource and harnessing its properties for everything from power generation to domestic heating. Hence the only oil that Iceland imported was for use in its fishing fleet, and since all industry and power generation was based upon subsoil steam, the island's atmosphere was free of pollution, with the result that the air of Reykjavik possessed a sparkling champagne quality unknown in any other capital in the world. Coming from East Berlin, with its smog-laden atmosphere formed by the use of its disgusting brown coal, the contrast was particularly sharp and exhilarating.

Following the recent renewal of the defence treaty with the USA, the Icelandic government seemed to be satisfied with its status in terms of its foreign policy objectives, and was not confronted with any major foreign policy problems. The occasional violations of air and sea space by Soviet units were dealt with by routine notes of protest. On the economic front, however, Iceland was faced with major issues. The country literally functioned on fishing, and in this activity it was confronted by two formidable constraints: the increase in oil prices, which adversely affected the cost of running the fishing fleets, and the restrictions that were increasingly being placed upon the industry as other countries preserved their fishing stocks. Icelandic diplomacy was, therefore, naturally concentrated on dealing with these two issues.

My discussions with Icelandic officials were necessarily briefing sessions, at which I told them about the prevalent situation in South Asia, and they briefed me on conditions in Scandinavia and the North Atlantic region. Since their expertise was much greater than mine, I thought that I got the better of that deal. It was not without significance that the five permanent members of the UN Security Council all had as resident ambassadors in Reykjavik, diplomats who were both competent and senior in their profession. The Icelanders were by no means unaware of this situation, and although they had no defence forces of their own and were totally committed to NATO, they nevertheless appeared to conduct their foreign policy, and their relationship with the big powers, especially the USA and USSR, with a vigorous assurance and cheerful independence. I found this attitude quite refreshing, particularly after my exposure to the stultified, moribund, and predictable pronouncements, that were churned out from the GDR Foreign Ministry with monotonous regularity in Berlin. The American ambassador in Reykjavik, while expressing considerable satisfaction that the Base Agreement in Keflavik had at last been 'sewn up, sealed, signed and delivered', nevertheless observed, with more than a touch of peevishness, that 'these guys, the Icelanders, tend to get very soft with the Russians'. He thought that the Icelanders' excessive dependence upon Soviet energy supplies placed them in a difficult position with Moscow, and that the only time the Icelanders 'tell the Soviets to go to hell is when the Russians raise the subject of the Keflavik base'. The Chinese ambassador, not unexpectedly, told me that his advice to the Icelandic leaders, as well as the public, was that it was in Iceland's interest to remain in NATO and to maintain the US base at Keflavik, since Iceland was too small to look after its own security and would inevitably be overwhelmed by the Soviet Union. Ambassador Thorsteinson, the Secretary General in the Icelandic Foreign Ministry, told me that the Chinese embassy had behaved with impeccable conduct in Iceland, and were very correct in all their dealings. One member of the embassy, a female diplomat, had spent eight years in the University of Iceland, spoke and wrote correct Icelandic, and was most probably responsible for the copious literature, almost all of it anti-Soviet, which emanated from the Chinese embassy.

Dealings between Iceland and the USSR had always been rather tense, particularly because Iceland was so heavily dependent on Soviet oil. The Soviet embassy, already the largest in Reykjavik, was substantially augmented during my visit, and Deputy Secretary General Helgassen told me 'their staff are crawling all over the country, doing silly things like removing the CD plates from their cars as they go round snooping and talking to our people'. Helgassen also said that the Soviets were interfering a great deal in Iceland's internal affairs, both by overt means, such as lavishly financing friendship societies and public meetings, and covertly, through provoking industrial unrest. The new Soviet Ambassador to Iceland, Gergui N. Farafanov was a Scandinavian specialist; he told me that he had spent over thirty years in the region, and he spoke fluent Icelandic and Swedish. Shortly after his arrival he became an unwilling *cause célèbre* when his name appeared in a book published at that time in the USA, entitled *KGB*, which gave a list of the agents and senior officials in that notorious organization. This revelation naturally provided the right wing press in Iceland with a field day. Whilst Farafanov was understandably irate about this, I had the distinct impression that the officials in the

Icelandic Foreign Ministry viewed the episode with a shade more amusement than embarrassment.

Since there were no political problems between Iceland and Pakistan, nor were any foreseen for the future, my visits to Iceland were essentially goodwill missions. But they enabled me to benefit from the expert and impartial assessments of the capable Icelandic diplomats on a number of international issues, especially those that pertained to the Cold War, then at its height. Looking back upon those days and nights in the company of the gentle, friendly people of Iceland, I regard the time spent with them with nostalgic appreciation. It was, indeed, a very pleasant interlude in my diplomatic life.

MEANWHILE IN PAKISTAN

The forceful imprint of the policies and personality of Zulfikar Ali Bhutto had by now been manifest for over four years, and his domination over the affairs of state was complete. His achievements had included the Simla Agreement, the passage of the constitution in the National Assembly, where he dominated the proceedings during his infrequent attendances, and above all, the Islamic Summit in Lahore.

But behind these triumphs there lurked the dark shadows of fissures. Within days of the passage of the constitution in the National Assembly, Bhutto violated both the letter and spirit of the document by dismissing the National Awami Party (NAP) provincial governments in both the NWFP and Balochistan, and imprisoned his political opponents in both provinces. In a very short time this led to an insurgency in Balochistan that involved the army in a campaign of brutal repression which continued till the end of the Bhutto regime.

At the same time the ideological fissures that had always existed within the PPP had by now turned into a gaping chasm, as its leader reduced his reliance on the support of its pristine elements, such as J.A. Rahim, Mubashir Hasan, and Sheikh Rashid, and brought into prominence members of his own class of feudal landlords. Moreover, I discerned a perceptible shift in Bhutto's position from reliance on his party to reliance on the army and the bureaucracy—a paradigm shift that was doubtless motivated by his fatal hubris; his belief that he would be able to simultaneously manipulate and control all three institutions. As if to provoke matters further, Bhutto decided to establish the Federal Security Force (FSF), a paramilitary force ostensibly for use in quelling public disturbances, but really intended as a kind of praetorian guard which would be gradually extended, and acted directly under Bhutto's command, free of the constraints of the army's increasing reluctance to suppress political protests. He also decided to continue the campaign in Balochistan. The army of course viewed the FSF with the deepest suspicion, if not hostility, but the fatally flawed decision was compounded by the appointment of Masud Mahmud as its commander. A police officer with a notoriously pompous, brutal, and sadistic record, Mahmud was also known for his sycophancy and fickle loyalty; characteristics that he was shortly to reveal in full when he turned over and became a leading witness in the trial that led to the execution of Bhutto.

A major development, the significance of which I did not notice at the time, was the appointment of General Ziaul Haq as Chief of the Army Staff (COAS). General Tikka Khan had retired in April 1976, and Bhutto, in the exercise of his powers under the constitution, ignored the seniority of six generals and appointed General Ziaul Haq as the COAS. There has been much speculation since that time about this fateful move; the consequences of which have the air of a Greek tragedy. The general impression is that Bhutto was taken in by Ziaul Haq's seeming submissiveness, added to which was the fact that the latter's origins in East Punjab put him outside the Attock–Jhelum region that had traditionally provided so many general officers of the Pakistan army. These two elements combined to reinforce Bhutto's assumption of domination over the military and created the hubris which led to an appointment that would change the course of history.

This was the general state of affairs, as I saw it, upon my arrival in Karachi from East Berlin in the summer of 1976. But what struck me with even greater force was the atmosphere of personality cult that seemed to have pervaded the whole society. After ten years in Eastern Europe, the phenomenon was by no means unfamiliar to me, but it was nevertheless a source of great discomfort to see it manifested in my own country under the guise of a parliamentary democracy. Not only was the Press and Publication Ordinance vigorously enforced, but the print and electronic media seemed to have become institutions

Diana duck netting at the Imperial Wild Duck Preserve, Japan, Spring, 1977.

Diana, Niloufer, and Feroza having fun at the Pakistan Embassy, Tokyo, 1977.

With Mr Yoshio Ishibara, Chairman, Export-Import Bank of Japan, following signature of the Yen Credit Agreement, Tokyo, February 1978.

Charles Hernu, Defence Minister of France, at an embassy reception, Paris, 1980.

Arnaz with Katharine Graham, President, *Washington Post*, and Samina Kureishi Shepherd at an embassy reception, Washington, D.C., 1980.

th HH Aga Khan IV and Princess Salimah Aga Khan, Karachi, 1983.

naz with President Francois Mitterrand at the farewell lunch in our honour at the Elysée
lace, Paris, September 1986.

With Arnaz and Feroza at the ceremony of the presentation of credentials to President Ronald Reagan, the White House, Washington, D.C., 24 November 1986.

Jamsheed Marker presenting credentials to President Ronald Reagan, 24 November 1986. 'Happy Birthday, Mr Ambassador!'

With Prime Minister Mohammad Khan Junejo during an official visit to Washington, 1986.

A happy gathering in Detroit, Michigan, November 1987, after a concert by *Malika Taranum* Noor Jahan. Also in the photo is my friend Roedad Khan, who was Secretary General, Ministry of Interior at the time. He recalled that during our college days in Lahore, Noor Jahan was known as 'Baby Noor Jahan'.

Prime Minister Benazir Bhutto arrives to lay the foundation stone at the new chancer Washington, D.C. Also in the photograph is Tariq Fatemi (extreme left), Deputy Chief Mission, June 1989.

Prime Minister Benazir Bhutto at the foundation stone ceremony of the Pakistan Chancer Washington, D.C., June 1989.

With President George Bush, Sr. and First Lady, Mrs Barbara Bush, the White House, Washington, D.C., June 1989.

With President George Bush, Sr. and First Lady, Mrs Barbara Bush.

With Arnaz, Feroza, Niloufer and Lady. St. Petersburg, Florida, 1989.

Our closest and dearest friends Maestro Zubin Mehta and Nancy Mehta.

'Security Council declares Sarajevo, Tuzla, Zepa, Bihac, Srebrenica and Surroundings as 'Safe Areas'. United Nations, New York, 6 May 1993. View of Yuli Vorontsov, President of the Security Council, being congratulated by Secretary General Boutros Boutros-Ghali at the end of the evening's meeting. Benon Sevan (extreme right), the dynamic Cypriot Assistant Secretary General and Jamsheed Marker, collect their papers for future action. Credit: UN Photo 182996/M. Tzovaras.

Nelson Mandela autographs his book for Jamsheed Marker, Pretoria, South Africa, August 1997.

Greeting Secretary General Boutros Boutros-Ghali at the commencement of a meeting of the Security Council.

Charlie Wilson and his war. The inscription on the photo: 'To Arnaz and Jamsheed, from their friend and his friends—Charlie.'

With the SR-71 at the Lockheed Corporation, Burbank, California.

Secretary General Kofi Annan meets with Jamsheed Marker, former Permanent Representative of Pakistan to the United Nations. The meeting led to Mr Marker's appointment as the Secretary General's Personal Representative for East Timor.

With Paloma Picasso (centre) and Prince Amyn Aga Khan (right) at a reception at the Pakistan Embassy, Paris.

With President Ronald Reagan and Sahibzada Yaqub Khan, Foreign Minister of Pakistan, in the Oval Office at the White House.

Arnaz having fun at Marrakesh, Morocco, during a visit by the wives of UN ambassadors.

With General Jacques Mitterrand and his wife Giselle at an embassy reception in Paris.

Arnaz with President Ziaul Haq at Orly Airport, Paris. Also in the photograph, M. Iqbal, Consular Assistant, at the embassy.

Francois de Grossouvre, Special Adviser to President Mitterrand and Nicole Alheinc, at an embassy reception, Paris.

Begum Om Habibah Aga Khan and Yasmin Aga Khan at an embassy reception, Paris. Arnaz is in the background.

Ceremony at the Embassy of Pakistan, Washington, D.C., for award of the Hilal-e-Imtiaz to Senator Charles Percy and Mr Marshall B. Coyne.

Receiving the Hilal-e-Imtiaz from President Pervez Musharraf.

with the single objective of projecting and promoting Zulfikar Ali Bhutto. There were widespread reports of illegal detentions and of forceful methods being employed against dissidents and opposition politicians. Activities such as telephone taps and raids by the FSF added to the aura of an increasingly oppressive police state. At the same time I discerned evidence of a strong undercurrent of opposition to the regime, an opposition that was not limited to politicians alone but appeared to prevail amongst the general public. Fear and hatred, the two forces most inimical to the stability of a regime, had not yet become pervasive. But they were clearly discernable at the time that Diana, Feroza, Feodor, and I, boarded a Pakistan International Airlines (PIA) aircraft at the Karachi airport for our flight to Tokyo in July 1976.

PART VI

JAPAN

CHAPTER SEVENTEEN

❧

Japan

'We learned the eloquence of spaces in painting, the philosophy of the unexpressed, of nothingness, of transiency. An eighteenth century Japanese priest compared this world to "the white wake of a ship that has rowed away at dawn". This passionate passivity of the Japanese can, however, be sharply broken by the flash of a sword. The duality in the Japanese character has been an eternal enigma for foreigners. Part of it may have to do with the Japanese concept of death, Mishima's "beauty is death". Falling cherry blossoms symbolize the beautiful death of the samurai.'

– John K. Emmerson, *The Japanese Thread.*

As we winged our way through Bangkok and Manila to our destination, Tokyo, I pondered over this profound yet concise characterization of the people and the country in which I was destined to live and work over the next few years of my life. John Emmerson was a distinguished United States diplomat, with whom I had become very friendly during his stay in Karachi in the 1950s when he was the charge d' affaires at the embassy. Our shared passion for western classical music, history and literature, combined with the Emmersons' easy informality, brought our families together in a close friendship. John was an orientalist in the true sense of the word, having served in China during the Second World War, and in Japan, during the early years of the occupation. A skilled professional, his expertise was clinical, unbiased and motivated by humanitarian considerations. He was castigated during the McCarthy era, but emerged from the ordeal with his honour intact and his dignity enhanced. I thought a great deal about John as I proceeded to my new assignment, and regretted that I had not talked to him more about Japan during the period of our association. But in those distant, happy days in Karachi who could have foretold our destinies?

I reflected also on my personal association with the Japanese, of my days in Burma when we had fought them during the Second World War, and I often feared them as formidable foes but never got to hate them as people. Then, in the summer of 1953, Diana and I visited Tokyo, Osaka and Kyoto on a business trip and I signed an agreement with Dainippon Seiyaku, a leading Japanese pharmaceutical firm, for the supply of semi-processed ephedrine hydrochloride manufactured by our family concern, Marker Alkaloids, in Quetta. Japan had just embarked upon the massive economic drive that would make it one of the world's leading industrial powers, and I was intrigued to observe a facet of their early methods. In the mornings I would hold negotiations with our Japanese partners, and in the afternoons we would go together to the government offices of the powerful Ministry of International Trade and Industry (MITI) to report on the progress of the negotiations, and receive any instructions that MITI thought necessary. The most important one that I received was to provide an undertaking for not supplying our product to any other pharmaceutical manufacturer in Japan. The policy of allocating monopolies was designed by MITI to build up Japanese industries.

On arrival at Haneda airport we were received by the protocol officials of the Ministry of Foreign Affairs (Gaimusho) and by our embassy staff headed by Shujaat Hasan Khan, an experienced foreign service officer, and other members of our staff. As we drove from the airport to the residence I recalled that one of my first impressions during my previous visit to the country was one of almost total illiteracy. The signs on all the roads and shops were in the Japanese script, beautiful to behold but totally incomprehensible to me, and I thought how terrible it must be to go through life without knowing how to read and write. Twenty-two years later the same sense of inadequacy reappeared; the only redeeming difference being that this time there seemed to be many more Japanese who spoke English.

Our residence was situated in Motoazabu, one of the more elegant districts in Tokyo, and was a beautiful, modern, Japanese-style building ingeniously designed to blend the interior living spaces with the small garden on the outside. Its architect was Jiro Matsumuro, a gentle and cultivated man, who was also a leading architect, and with whom we became very good friends. Next to the residence was a spacious plot with a ramshackle old building which had once been the chancery but was now too rickety for occupation, and so our chancery was situated in a disagreeable commercial building located above a petrol pump. It also had the demerit of an exorbitant rent. As soon as I could, I obtained our government's permission to construct a new chancery building on our own plot next to the residence, and entrusted the task to Jiro Matsumuro. After the usual bureaucratic hassles, during which Jiro displayed much more patience than I did, the excellent new building was constructed at a cost of one million US dollars, with no overrun either on the time or cost estimates. Land values in Tokyo were as phenomenal as could be expected, and I asked Matsumuro to estimate the value of our property. He replied in terms of yen per tsubo (3.3 square metres), and after I asked him to translate it into figures intelligible to me, he took out his calculator and said, 'About seven US dollars for a postage stamp.' This property had been purchased by Mian Ziauddin, our first ambassador to Japan, and so I wrote him a letter commending the judgment and foresight that had provided the Government of Pakistan with such a valuable asset. I also told him that his son, Mian Qadruddin, who was one of the bright stars in our foreign service but was then with the United Nations, was now living in our neighbourhood. Mian Sahib wrote me a gracious reply saying that although he had bought property for the government in three different capitals, I was the only successor to have expressed appreciation. He also said that Qadruddin had not written to him for some time—'Kindly pull him up'. I conveyed this admonition with considerable relish.

At this time I had become concerned about Diana's health and wanted a specialist to give her a check-up as soon as possible. The officials in the Gaimusho were most helpful, and arranged an appointment with Professor Nakayama, one of the world's leading oncologists. He studied her records, gave a thorough clinical examination, and pronounced her to be in complete remission. Our relief was enormous, but alas would prove to be sadly short-lived.

In Tokyo, as elsewhere, I once again had the good fortune to find a first class group of officers posted to the embassy. The Deputy Chief of Mission was Counsellor Shujaat Hasan Khan, a bustling, energetic, and efficient officer who was also an able and meticulous administrator. Shujaat's ability at bridge coupled with his recently acquired familiarity with and enthusiasm for Sumo wrestling, enabled him to maintain some very useful contacts with the Japanese. Just towards the end of my tenure, Shujaat was replaced by Ashraf Jehangir Qazi, an old family friend from Quetta, and one of the brightest stars in the Pakistan Foreign Service. Much more deserves to be said about Ashraf, but that would need a book. My Second Secretary was Shahid Malik, an able, soft spoken and highly intelligent officer who was also a Japanese speaker. We would later catch up again in Washington, where he was my counsellor, and being another high flyer, he went on to become high commissioner in Ottawa and New Delhi. The Commercial Counsellor was Ziauddin Ahmed Malik, an energetic, competent, and knowledgeable professional who ably discharged what was clearly the main burden of our embassy in Tokyo. He had built up useful contacts in the financial and textile sectors, and kept himself well aware of the general economic situation. His presentations were frequently the high point of our staff meetings. Our Press Counsellor was Amanullah Sardar, a senior official in the Information Ministry whose wide experience was useful not only in his dealings with the local media, but would also provide us with the background on the political events in Pakistan. These had already started to show signs of disquiet.

The language barrier made it incumbent upon us to have a large Japanese support staff, and I got to know the qualities of hard work, patience, politeness, and loyalty that have come to be associated with the Japanese race. The most outstanding amongst the staff was Kato-san,[1] the chauffeur who had been working with the embassy for many years, and who lived with his lovely wife and daughter on the embassy premises. Kato-san, who spoke very good English, was full of initiative and became one of the most devoted, pleasant, and useful companions that I have known. We took to him from our very first encounter, delighted by his informal, friendly, behaviour, and moved by the instinctive dignity that emanated from his noble Samurai ancestry. Added to this was the deep and affectionate bond that grew between Kato-san and Feodor. Calling him 'my brother', Kato-san would unfailingly take Feodor on his daily evening jogs, and was constantly solicitous about the dog, spending nights sleeping on the floor with Feodor when the latter was recovering from surgery. When we left Tokyo on transfer, Kato-san, with Feodor's head cradled on his lap, was weeping buckets all the way, as he drove us to the airport.

Shortly after our arrival, Foreign Secretary Agha Shahi, accompanied by Director General Shaharyar Khan, visited Tokyo for the fourth round of the Pakistan–Japan bilateral consultations. Japanese protocol, which was rigid and formal in terms of procedures relating to the Imperial Court, was eminently practical in other matters, and permitted ambassadors to carry out their duties before the presentation of credentials. The foreign secretary's visit, therefore, provided me with an early exposure to senior officials in the Gaimusho, to know them personally, and to ascertain their working methods. The bilateral discussions followed the usual pattern, with the first session being devoted to international affairs, the second to Asian issues, and the third to bilateral subjects. The first two sessions on international and Asian issues followed the standard pattern of each side presenting its largely predictable positions. Agha Shahi's excellent presentation, combining facts and analysis, greatly impressed his Japanese interlocutors, and Vice Minister Hachirō Arita later told me that it was one of the best bilaterals held in the Gaimusho in recent times. The Japanese were particularly interested in Prime Minister Bhutto's recent visit to Pyongyang and his talks with Kim Il Sung. On bilateral matters we had some minor success in getting yen credits for the railways and for oil exploration, but the Japanese politely reverted to other matters when we contrasted the quantum of their aid to Bangladesh to that of Pakistan and suggested a more equitable allocation to us. However, the main subject of our talks with the Japanese related to the official visit of Prime Minister Bhutto to Japan, which Tokyo viewed with great anticipation. The original proposed date of April 1977 was amended at our request to September, but as it happened, other events intervened and the visit never took place.

We were received by Foreign Minister Kiichi Miyazawa and Vice Foreign Minister Arita, and they provided me with an early glimpse of the formidable prowess of Japanese diplomacy. It seemed to me that they almost never expressed an outright refusal to a suggestion or proposal, but in due course I was able to discern the polite prevarication that conveyed dissent.

Foreign Minister Kiichi Miyazawa, who shortly left office in a cabinet reshuffle, was one of the stalwarts of the Japanese political establishment, with a decisive impact on Japanese foreign policy. Always impeccably dressed, he was a short man with a ready smile, and was restrained, polite, and courteous in his manner and demeanour. He was also an extremely sophisticated individual, with a razor sharp mind and a broad perception of international affairs. Since he spoke perfect English it was possible for me to get to know him quite well and to benefit from his good-humoured wisdom. The Vice Minister for Foreign Affairs was Hachirō Arita, another able professional with a taciturn manner who always seemed to listen more than talk. At the conclusion of most of my meetings with him I came away with the somewhat disconcerting feeling that he had obtained more from me than I had got out of him. But that was alright, because I learned early in my dealings with him that he was genuinely interested in developing relations with Pakistan. The two senior officials in the Gaimusho, whom I got to know best, and with whom I became good friends, were Yoshio Okawa, the Director General of the United Nations Bureau, and Yosuko Nakae, the Director General of the Asia Bureau. Both were outstanding diplomats with keen perception and understanding, and both had an unemotional and rational approach to problems and situations. Okawa's fluency in English and Nakae's in French were of considerable help in my getting to know them.

Two events of interest occurred shortly after my arrival in Tokyo. The first was a crisis that grew over the defection of a Soviet air force officer, Lt. Viktor Belenko, who landed his MIG 25 jet fighter at a small civilian airport in Hokkaido, and sought political asylum, which was immediately granted by the Japanese and the US authorities. Invoking their Security Treaty with the US, the Japanese brought in American technicians to dismantle and inspect the MIG 25. The Soviets found themselves doubly embarrassed by the defection of an elite member of their air force, as well as the fact that the Americans had obtained an intact model of one of their most modern frontline aircraft. Diplomatic relations between Moscow and Tokyo took more than a metaphoric nosedive, as Foreign Ministers Gromyko and Zentaro Kosaka had a disagreeable meeting in New York, high level economic consultations were postponed indefinitely, and ministerial meetings cancelled. But both sides were conscious of the lucrative trade that had by now developed between Japan and the USSR, and in due course the incident was allowed to end quietly. But it had its amusing moments while it lasted, such as a tentative Japanese bureaucratic demand for penalty charges for an unauthorized import. The level of apoplexy that this suggestion provoked in the bureaucracy at Moscow is not known.

The second event of interest was a political crisis within the ruling Liberal Democratic Party, which had affected the office and the person of Prime Minister Kakuei Tanaka. The election was, of course, conducted in an orderly and civilized manner, but the outcome had been the result of a crisis of a long duration and of major political ramifications. It occurred to me that in many Asian countries a crisis of this length of time and magnitude would have shaken the edifice of the state. In Japan it caused hardly a ripple in the daily life of the people and at no time did one have the impression that one was living through a crisis. All the institutions of the state remained unruffled and continued to function as quietly and efficiently as ever. Whilst the politicians argued and bickered, industry, commerce, the trade unions, the banks, the courts, the press, and the powerful and competent bureaucracy, continued their smooth functioning and maintained the vigorous tempo of this virile country. At that very time in the United Kingdom, a strike by the Seamen's Union had sent the sterling into a downward slither but in Tokyo, despite a prolonged crisis that involved the office of the prime minister, the yen achieved such upward gains that the Bank of Japan was obliged to intervene in order to preserve a modicum of restraint. This was a tribute not only to the essential soundness of the Japanese institutions—the courts, the press, the economic organs, and the bureaucracy, that held them together—but also to the good sense, discipline, and political maturity of the Japanese people.

I presented credentials to Emperor Hirohito in a ceremony that was overlaid by protocol. There are a number of similarities in the protocol of the Imperial Court in Tokyo, and the Court of St. James in London. These include the uniforms and regalia worn by all the participants in the ceremony, from the Grand Chamberlain, to the coachmen and footmen, who accompany the Imperial State Coach which takes the ambassador to the Palace. The ambassador, together with his senior staff, assemble at the Palace Hotel, a well known hostelry, situated in the proximity of the Imperial Palace, where he is greeted by a marshal from the Imperial Court, and photographed as he boards the state coach for the short ride to the Imperial Palace. The members of the embassy staff follow in automobiles and the entire party is received by the Grand Chamberlain on arrival at the Palace. The state coach, with the emblem of the imperial chrysanthemum emblazoned on its doors, naturally attracted the attention of people on the footpaths, and while many of them waved in friendly fashion, I noticed that several performed the graceful Japanese ceremonial bow to the royal emblem on the coach. The protocol for the actual presentation of credentials was both very short and meticulously scripted. I bowed before the emperor and conveyed the greetings of the president of Pakistan as I handed over the letters of credence and recall. The emperor accepted the documents, welcomed me to Japan and asked me to convey his greetings to my president. He then wished me a successful stay in Japan and counselled me to take good care of my health. I requested the emperor's permission to withdraw, it was granted, and the ceremony was over. The Grand Chamberlain then escorted me to another hall, where the members of the embassy and officials of the court, and the Gaimusho were served refreshments. This ceremony, meticulously scripted and redolent of tradition, made a memorable impression. However, I was informed of one occasion when the customs of ancient pageantry unexpectedly conflicted with those of contemporary commerce. The British ambassador told me that the day of his credentials ceremony coincided with a business convention being held at the Palace Hotel. Consequently, the official photograph that depicted the occasion showed Her Britannic Majesty's ambassador in full diplomatic regalia, complete with decorations, sword and cocked hat, boarding the imperial state coach, with Japanese footmen, also in full regalia and bowing in salute. Above the coach there fluttered a banner which read 'Welcome Honda Dealer'.

My only meetings with Emperor Hirohito took place on my arrival and departure, and during formal ceremonies such as the New Year's Day, so that I never had the opportunity to converse with him. But we did have the honour of hosting dinners at the embassy for his brother Prince Mikasa, and his son Prince Hitachi, both of whom were charming and gracious guests, and who carried their royal presence with an informal dignity that was truly memorable. During our stay in Japan we got to hear many accounts of Emperor Hirohito's activities. He was a marine biologist with an internationally recognized reputation. Also well known are the dramatic instances of his first broadcast 'The Voice of the Crane', that brought an end to the Second

World War, and of his first meeting with General Douglas MacArthur, one of the great pro consuls of all time, and his refusal to permit the reconstruction of the Imperial Palace, after it had been destroyed during the war, until the homes of all the citizens had been rebuilt. But a less well known story about Hirohito, and one that appealed to me the most, was an account of an early post-war visit to an industrial enterprise where the workmen, many with communist affiliations, called out to him demanding that since he was no longer a deity he should come over and shake hands with them. The Emperor's escorts, fearing the prospect of some humiliation, attempted to steer him away from the workers, who were now showing signs of militancy. But Hirohito, resisting their attempts at restraining him, walked up to the workers and suggesting that they greet each other in the Japanese tradition, went into a deep bow. The immediate response was a large collective bow.

I pursued the usual activities related to ambassadorial duties, with an emphasis on economic issues. My visits to various industrial enterprises revealed some of the innovative methods that in 1977 had enabled Japan to achieve a trade surplus of $15 billion and a current account surplus of $10 billion. For example, at the Honda factory I was shown that the vessels which had been constructed specifically for the transport of automobiles to the USA, were equipped with facilities for the last four days of finishing work required on the vehicles. This economized on storage space at the works and delivery dates at destination. On another occasion, Akito Morita, the Chairman of the Sony Corporation, in reply to my query told me that the firm's percentage budgetary allocation for research and development was on a par with similar international enterprises. The difference was that Sony actively associated its sales staff with its research staff. The portable recorder/player was the result of proposals that emanated from market surveys that anticipated a public demand. The President of the Japan–Pakistan Friendship Association was Hiroki Imazato, a major industrialist, who was also the chairman and board member of several Japanese corporations. A burly man, whose imposing businesslike appearance, and bearing concealed an essentially kindly person, with a lively sense of humour that was presaged by a sly wink in his sparkling eyes. Imazato-san was a great friend and did much to bring Pakistan to the attention of Japanese business. Above all, he steered me through the corridors of the Keidarnen, the formidable collegium of major Japanese industrialists and financiers. Among his many attributes was a capacity to down a bottle of Johnnie Walker Black Whisky over lunch, whilst conducting a conversation that remained flawless in content and delivery.

The Imperial Court hosted three functions each year which were the delight of the diplomatic corps. The first was the New Year's luncheon offered by the emperor and empress, when we were assembled in formal attire at the Imperial Palace and presented individually for a bow to their majesties. We then repaired to a banquet hall where a sumptuous Japanese meal was spread on a buffet table. After the first toasts were raised, the immaculate waiters, dressed in white ties and tails removed the food and, with efficient white gloved hands, packed it into delicate lunch boxes which were presented to the guests to take home. Another gentle activity organized by the Court was a duck netting expedition at the Imperial Preserve. Members of the royal family usually attended this function, at which the guests were provided with poles to which was attached a net, and these were used to catch the ducks as they flew over the estate. The birds were then released with a ceremonial gesture, and the guests duly proceeded to a very pleasant outdoor lunch. A third activity was that of cormorant fishing, which took place on a river at night. Guests were seated in narrow boats, each with a flaming torch on the bow and a few cormorant birds in the stern. The flame attracted the fish, which were then pounced upon by the cormorants. Subsequently we came ashore to an elegant Japanese dinner. The gentle nature of these pastimes to which the diplomats were exposed were a major contrast to the bloody, brutal, and inebriated hunting parties that I had seen in Eastern Europe.

In the fall of 1977 I was nominated as a member of the Pakistan delegation to the UN General Assembly in New York, and relished this second opportunity to participate in what has been described as 'the greatest indoor game in the world'. One of the highlights of this experience was working with the diplomats that staffed our permanent mission. It was a virtual powerhouse of whirring dynamos. Their enthusiasm matched their professional skill, and it was a matter of pride to note the respect with which delegations from all over the world regarded the Pakistan mission. Unlike the last occasion when I was in New York in 1972, when we fought a bitter diplomatic battle over the admission of Bangladesh to the UN, there were no major problems so far as Pakistan was concerned, and we played our accustomed productive role on the hardy perennial issues, such as the Middle East, the North–South dialogue, and of course, Kashmir.

Shortly after our return to Tokyo in March 1978, we suffered a devastating personal blow. Diana developed some disturbing and very painful symptoms, which Dr Nakayama diagnosed as a metastasis, and immediately commenced chemotherapy and radiation. She endured this in her usual stoical fashion, and insisted on carrying on with her diplomatic duties, including hosting and attending diplomatic dinners and receptions, attending all types of public functions, and taking care of the numerous delegations from Pakistan that visited Tokyo. Above all, she continued her solicitous attention to our embassy staff and their families, and to the small Pakistani community then resident in Japan. All through the year she fought what I helplessly thought was a losing battle, but one that she was determined to overcome. As time went on, I found that my frequent bouts of internal despair were invariably overcome by the flaming courage that was constantly displayed by this most remarkable lady.

The visits from Pakistan by numerous delegations punctuated the tempo of our routine. These were mostly economic and commercial delegations, but there was also a visit by a team from the National Defence College. Thanks to the goodwill and efficiency of our Japanese hosts these visits were generally very successful. However, there was one task that fell to my lot early in my tenure that I found to be most disturbing and difficult. I had not been told about this during my briefings in Islamabad, so the problem came as a bit of a shock, when Ziauddin told me about it shortly after I assumed office. It seems that there had been a long-standing commercial arrangement whereby semi-finished textiles from Pakistan were exported for final processing in Japan. The trade was handled by a number of medium-sized trading houses in Osaka who negotiated the purchase from various textile mills in Pakistan and sold the product to major manufacturers in Japan. Prices, which were negotiated in advance, included the export duty. The Bhutto government, in one of the reckless decisions that became characteristically frequent in its last months, arbitrarily imposed a heavy increase on the export duty on these semi-finished textiles. A delegation of Japanese buyers came to Pakistan in order to find a solution to this sudden wrecking of a perfectly smooth trading relationship, and was treated in a most reprehensible manner. They were kept waiting a week in Karachi for a meeting with the minister concerned, and then packed off to Islamabad where they waited another week before receiving a brusque ministerial brush off. The immediate consequence was that a number of these medium-sized import houses went into bankruptcy. I was told that there had even been one suicide, but could not verify this. The major long-term effect was, of course, that the Japanese buyers gave up trading with Pakistan and turned instead to Hong Kong. I did the rounds in Osaka in an attempt to retrieve the situation, but my efforts were both painful and fruitless.

Apart from this one incident our economic relations with Japan proceeded in satisfactory fashion, and we were able to negotiate some useful yen credits. Since these were under constant and meticulous donor scrutiny, bureaucratic lapses, which were not infrequent on our side, constrained the disbursement of funds.

The lynchpin of Japanese foreign policy was the Security Alliance with the USA. Secure under the nuclear umbrella provided by Washington, the country was able to emerge from the ravages of war, and by maintaining minimum defence expenditure, was able to concentrate on economic and industrial development, an objective that was achieved in a spectacular fashion. The main compulsion of the Gaimusho, apart from the tinkering needed to keep US–Japan relations on an even keel, was Japan's relations with the USSR and China. Whilst both Moscow and Tokyo valued and nurtured their considerable economic ties, political relations remained almost frozen. The cause was, of course, the Soviet occupation of the Kuril Islands at the end of the Second World War. There had been occasional talks about a peace treaty, but Soviet occupation of the islands remained the basic obstacle to political reconciliation.

The issue of relations with the People's Republic of China was very much on the front burner during my stay in Tokyo, and one that I followed with the greatest interest. The improvement of Japan's relations with China had been held captive by two powerful elements, the influential Taiwan lobby in the ruling Liberal Democratic Party (LDP), and the US hostility to the People's Republic of China. The latter obstacle had been removed by Nixon's recognition of the Peking government, so that by the time I arrived in Tokyo there had already been early signs of a Sino–Japanese rapprochement, one hint of which had been a declaration that China regarded the Kuril Islands as Japanese territory. There had also been a number of visits by important Japanese political and industrial leaders to Peking, and an observation by Foreign Minister Miyazawa that 'The Japanese are emotionally more pro-China than pro-Soviet', was given the prominence that it merited.

Negotiations between Tokyo and Peking proceeded in a cautious manner throughout 1977, and there were reports of an exchange and circulation of drafts of a Friendship Treaty. Meanwhile the USSR stepped up its blandishments and warned against any deviation by Japan from its current policy of neutrality between Japan and the Soviet Union. Moscow offered a Peace and Friendship Treaty as an inducement, but the Japanese steadfastly maintained their position that a Peace Treaty that included a settlement of the Kuril Islands occupation must precede a Friendship Treaty. In February 1978 Prime Minister Fukuda publicly stated that Japan would formally announce its intention to reopen treaty negotiations with China. He then dispatched a high-level delegation to Peking and negotiations commenced in earnest.

Yosuko Nakae, the intelligent, urbane, and competent Director General of the Asia Bureau in the Gaimusho, had been associated with the China Peace Treaty from the outset, and had kept me informed of developments. He told me that there had been an occasion, during the cloistered series of negotiations in Peking, when he sensed a slight but perceptive shift in the Chinese position. He had decided at this point that Japan must respond in a positive and constructive fashion, convinced that this was one of those moments in history when opportunities could either be seized or lost. He, therefore, did his best to soften the Japanese position on the vexed issue of hegemony, a shibboleth which was as sacred to Peking as it was profane to Moscow. During one of our tête-à-tête lunches at the Palace Hotel in Tokyo, he informed me of this development and said that as things then stood there was a 55 per cent possibility that the treaty would go through by next spring. But he added, with a rueful smile, 'Just now I am carefully watching the other 45 per cent'. As we sipped our coffee, we observed from the windows of the restaurant the magnificent sight of the Imperial Palace, its moat and courtyard, resplendent on a sunny spring afternoon in Tokyo, and I commented on the sheer beauty of the spectacle. Nakae agreed and then added, 'It was not always like this. Just after the war it was a very depressing place because so many Japanese would come to this courtyard and commit Seppuku in front of the emperor's palace as atonement for defeat. We would not like it to happen again.' I was once again reminded of the deep psychological compulsions that motivated the modern Japanese passion for neutrality. As for the Friendship Treaty with China, it was successfully concluded on 12 August 1978, and signed by Chairman Hua Kuo-feng of China and Japanese Foreign Minister Sunao Sonoda. Nakae-san had successfully watched 'the other 45 per cent.'

During the summer of 1977 the work of the embassy was largely devoted to the preparations for the forthcoming visit of Prime Minister Bhutto to Japan, scheduled for the coming September. We had prepared all the position papers and been in constant touch with the Foreign Ministry in Islamabad and the Gaimusho in Tokyo. Arrangements were so far advanced as to include the prime minister's substantive as well as protocol commitments, and the provisional lists of delegations. I took these working papers with me to Islamabad for finalization, and prepared a summary for the prime minister's approval. But when I arrived in Pakistan it was clear that the country was once again in the throes of a major political crisis. My request for a meeting with the prime minister was put on hold whilst he carried out his desperate negotiations with the leaders of the various political parties, and it became increasingly clear that an official visit to Japan was unlikely. After waiting for almost two weeks in Islamabad, without meeting the prime minister, I was instructed to return to Tokyo and request a postponement of the visit sine die. I stayed overnight in Karachi and woke up the next morning to hear the news that General Ziaul Haq had declared martial law and that Bhutto and a number of other political leaders had been taken into custody. I returned to Tokyo the next day and shortly after my arrival received a signal from Islamabad instructing me to remain at my post. Whilst I continued to be the ambassador of Pakistan, the regime that I now represented was an entirely different one.

Towards the end of my tenure Counsellor Shujaat Hasan Khan was transferred and replaced by Ashraf Jehangir Qazi who, with his wife Abida, had been old family friends from Quetta. Since Ashraf was one of the brightest of a brilliant group of foreign service officers, and had also been in charge of the East Asia desk at the ministry, he moved into the assignment with the smoothness of the automatic transmission of the best Japanese automobile. Ashraf's star-studded career later took him to highly successful ambassadorial assignments in Syria, East Berlin, Moscow, Beijing, New Delhi, and Washington; a collection of high profile capitals that invokes considerable admiration. He then went on to become the UN Secretary General's Special Representative in Baghdad and later in Khartoum. I could only regret that our time together in Tokyo was so short.

In the autumn of 1978 I was informed of my transfer to Geneva as the Permanent Representative of Pakistan to the European Office of the United Nations, and accordingly commenced the formalities for my departure. By now Diana's health had deteriorated considerably, but she still insisted on carrying out her duties and obligations, including a farewell call on the emperor and empress, and attending our various farewell receptions. She continued with her treatment of chemotherapy and radiation, but it appeared to be a losing battle to everyone except her. Her indomitable spirit appeared to increase with each setback to her health, and courage and determination radiated like flames from her bright eyes.

We flew from Tokyo to Karachi, where I left Diana with Feroza and her parents, and went to Islamabad for briefing and consultations. This was my first encounter with General Ziaul Haq, the Chief Martial Law Administrator, as he then was. He received me in the drawing room of the Army House, an austere enclave that never changed its spartan simplicity throughout the many years that I subsequently visited it. I was accompanied by Foreign Secretary Shah Nawaz, and as we entered the room Ziaul Haq rose to give us a very friendly greeting. The heavy, dark moustache, and hooded eyelids, made a somewhat sinister initial impression, but behind the thick eyeglasses there sparkled a pair of bright brown eyes filled with intelligence and affecting warmth. Although clad in uniform, his body language was totally devoid of swagger, and seemed to suggest an innate modesty. Our conversation was pleasant rather than profound, and after a short while we took our leave, with Zia wishing me success in my mission. My first impression of Ziaul Haq was most favourable, and I thought that working for, and with him, should be an interesting experience.

CHIAROSCURO

The official crockery used in our embassies had originally been supplied by a well known British firm, Crown Derby, but as time went on the ministry was having trouble obtaining replacements. Apparently small orders for replacements were refused and delivery periods became increasingly lengthy. General Reza, the Secretary General Administration, and an iconic figure in the Pakistan diplomatic establishment, suggested that I should ascertain whether a Japanese firm could assume the supply of crockery for our missions. Responding to my request, two representatives of Noritake called at my office. Giving them samples of our official plates and cups, I explained our requirements, indicating that orders could be large or small, and that delivery periods should be short. Above all, the crockery that they supplied would have to exactly match the samples that I had provided, because we could neither discard our current sets nor have a mismatch on the dinner tables. The representatives gave me the necessary assurances and said that they would shortly provide me with a sample of their product for approval. Just as they were about to leave my office they commenced an earnest and agitated conversation among themselves, which I did not of course understand. They then said to me, in English, 'Sorry, Mr Ambassador, we can not make it exactly like your sample.' In exasperation I said to them that if so they had wasted their time and my time; I had quite clearly indicated my requirements, they had given me their assurances, and were now backing off. With eyes half closed and heads bowed, they sat in polite silence until I had blown off all my steam. Then, turning over the sample plate that I had given them, they pointed to the manufacturer's mark and said very politely, 'Here we must write Noritake, we cannot write Crown Derby.' To this day I wish that my shame-filled assent could have been more contrite than it was.

* * *

Feodor, our highly intelligent and temperamental clumber spaniel, used to ride with me in the car whenever possible. As soon as we came in the vicinity of our residence he would get happy and excited. Noting this, Kato-san said to me 'Ambassador, Feodor knows we are coming home. How does he know? Is it smell or computer?'

* * *

The newspapers once carried a sensational story about a young police officer who followed a young female teacher to her apartment, where he raped and killed her. The culprit was arrested within hours of committing the crime and would doubtless receive a life sentence in prison. But before the public outrage could become widespread, a number of senior police officials tendered their resignation. These included the head of the police station where the culprit was posted, the head of the police precinct of that district, the head of the police academy where the policeman had been trained, and finally the chief of the Tokyo Metropolitan Police Force. Newspapers showed photographs of these senior officials, many with over thirty years of meritorious service, presenting themselves at the home of the victim's parents, bowing before the latter in tearful apology and asking forgiveness for a lapse for which they considered themselves responsible. I was most impressed by this public display of contrition and collective responsibility, and expressed my admiration of this demonstration of Japanese character and honour to my friend, the distinguished Imazato-san, who was, of course, very much a representative of the old school tradition. His response was a snort of contempt and four curt words, 'Not even one Seppuku'.

* * *

I received a letter from Sahibzada Yaqub Khan, then our ambassador in Washington, requesting that I meet Edward R. Downe, a friend who was on a visit to Tokyo. We lunched at the Palace Hotel, and thus began a close and lifelong friendship. Both Ed and I later agreed that of all Yaqub's many kindnesses to both of us, his gesture in bringing us together was amongst the most valuable. Ed is the quintessential New Yorker, warm, outgoing, and friendly, with an insatiable desire to help people. A wealthy financier, with monumental successes and setbacks, which never affect his equanimity and optimism, he and I struck up an immediate friendship that has grown over the years. Edward Downe had a wide and eclectic range of friends, which included politicians, artists, and businessmen, and he opened the doors to an influential and privileged society which proved to be of immense value to me, both in terms of diplomacy as well as human relationships. He possessed a love of contemporary American painting and sculpture, and his discerning eye and taste helped many struggling artists to attain fame and fortune. He insisted on lending me some paintings from his private collection, and I hung them in our embassy salons with pride and pleasure.

MEANWHILE IN PAKISTAN

Two elements were emerging in the politics of Pakistan during the period 1976–77, each with increasing force, and as inimical to each other as fire and water. The first was Bhutto's grip on the country and its institutions, which he was increasing in relentless fashion until it had almost become a stranglehold. The second was the opposition to the regime, scattered and fractured at first, which had gradually coalesced and was beginning to display signs of meaningful resistance. At first the fire appeared irresistible, as Bhutto's megalomania manifested itself in all spheres of national activity. All opposition in the media was effectively muzzled, with the officially controlled press, radio, and TV devoted to the sole objective of projecting Bhutto. The headlong pursuit of nationalization had devoured even the smallest of industries, such as rice milling and cotton ginning, and had extended into the field of education, where it brought into the ambit everything from primary schools to colleges and institutions of higher learning. The law courts appeared to become increasingly ineffective in the face of the security services' tyranny and secret detention camps. At the same time, living standards for the population remained as low as ever. Public apprehension had become pervasive, and political conditions in the country had now reached a stage when the earlier popularity of the regime had dissipated, and the balance between support and opposition had reached a tipping point.

Confident in his grip over the country, Bhutto held the general elections in January 1977, in anticipation of obtaining a majority large enough to enable him to amend the constitution according to his wishes. He set up a special cell 'Operation Victory', designed to conduct the elections, but at the same time he made a public promise of 'a free and fair election.' To the surprise of many, including possibly Bhutto himself, the hitherto scattered opposition, galvanized by the prospect of an election, managed to get together a nine-party coalition under the banner of the Pakistan National Alliance (PNA). Although Bhutto contemptuously derided it as 'a cat with nine tails', it was clear that it possessed some electoral substance, and that the confrontation between the fire and the flood had commenced. The elections that ensued were blatantly rigged and provided Bhutto with an implausibly large majority. The Pakistani genius for humour, always present in moments of crisis, manifested itself in a current joke, which quoted Indira Gandhi's congratulatory message to Bhutto and also proposed handing over Kashmir to him in exchange for his chief election commissioner. The sad irony is that in view of most of the political observers, the PPP would have comfortably won a truly free and fair election, and had no need for the clumsy rigging carried out by a heavy handed bureaucracy.

The announcement of the election results immediately triggered a countrywide protest which grew bigger each passing day. A massive protest march by Air Marshal Asghar Khan was a signal that the flood was turning into a tsunami. Disturbances broke out in major cities and the army was called out in aid of the civil power. This in turn led to an ominous situation where in some cases officers refused to order their troops to fire on protesting crowds. Air Marshal Asghar Khan sent an open letter to the service chiefs stating that 'Bhutto has violated the constitution and is guilty of grave crimes against the people. Answer this call honestly and save Pakistan.' As the situation deteriorated, Bhutto adopted increasingly desperate measures, starting with the standard bogey of 'a foreign hand' wishing to destabilize Pakistan. In this case it was the USA, which was opposed to his independent nuclear policy. He then entered into a series of tortuous negotiations with the opposition leaders, and in the process of appeasement, he made a series of concessions to the religious parties, starting with the declaration of Friday as the weekly holiday, and going on to the imposition of alcohol prohibition all over the country. But most egregious of all was his parliamentary legislation, in 1974, declaring the Ahmadis a minority.

When I was in Islamabad awaiting a decision on the prime minister's visit to Tokyo, I was able to observe, by watching TV and talking to some of the participants, the tense and bitter atmosphere that prevailed during the course of these tortuous negotiations. One could clearly sense the predicament of the cornered prime minister. Each concession that he made seemed only to whet the appetite and increase the demands of his tormentors. I was reminded of the old, dramatic Russian folklore, depicted in words as well as pictures, of a terrified man riding through a snowstorm in an open sleigh, desperately trying to save himself by throwing, one by one, his cherished provisions to the pack of wolves howling behind him in unceasing pursuit.

NOTE

1. 'San' is the most common honorific in Japanese and is a title of respect similar to 'Mr' or 'Ms'.

PART VII

UNITED NATIONS EUROPEAN OFFICE, GENEVA

CHAPTER EIGHTEEN

※

European Office of the United Nations, Geneva, Switzerland 1978–1980

'The word you have spoken is your master.
The word you have not spoken is your slave.'
Arab proverb

As we left Karachi for Geneva in the late summer of 1978, my personal thoughts and emotions were an amalgam of anticipation and anxiety. Multilateral diplomacy had always fascinated me and the prospect of active participation in the work of the United Nations in Geneva was indeed exciting. But Diana's health had by now deteriorated alarmingly and the days ahead seemed filled with dark clouds. As we drove along Drigh Road from our home in Bath Island to the airport, I remember thinking to myself in despair that this was probably the last time that my dearest Diana would see her beloved Karachi.

The United Nations in Geneva is the workhorse of the organization and the nerve centre of some of the most productive and effective of its institutions. First of all there is the International Labour Organization (ILO), which, together with The International Court of Justice at The Hague, is one of the two charter bodies that survived the demise of the ill-fated League of Nations to metamorphose into the United Nations. It was also an institution with which I was somewhat familiar, having previously participated as an employers' member of the Pakistan delegation to three of its annual conferences. In addition to the ILO, there is a plethora of UN institutions, based in Geneva, to which our Permanent Mission is accredited. In many cases, such as the World Health Organization or the World Meteorological

Organization, the mission is not involved in the day to day work. Experts from the capital attend annual or special meetings invoked by these organizations. Other institutions, such as the Committee on Disarmament (CD), the United Nations Conference on Trade and Development (UNCTAD), the Human Rights Committee, the United Nations High Commission for Refugees (UNHCR), the General Agreement on Trade and Tariffs (GATT) now the World Trade Organization (WTO), needed constant attendance and monitoring by the Permanent Mission, and kept us very busy.

I found on my arrival in Geneva that in the matter of officers in the staff my good fortune had not deserted me and that those in the mission were of the highest calibre; intelligent, energetic, enthusiastic, and, above all, full of initiative. The Deputy Permanent Representative was Dr Humayun Khan, formerly of the Civil Service of Pakistan and now a senior member of the Pakistan Foreign Services (PFS), whose subsequent distinguished career would include postings as the High Commissioner to Bangladesh and India, plus service as the Foreign Secretary, followed by a senior post in the Commonwealth Secretariat. Humayun was later replaced by Munir Akram whose record as a UN specialist is legendary. Counsellor Khalid Saleem and Commercial Counsellor Mohammed Hamid were the other senior officers whose professionalism brought distinction to the mission. Our junior most officer was Salman Bashir who, at the time of writing of this book is the Foreign Secretary.

I immersed myself in my work with a great deal of enthusiasm and found it fascinating to interact with skilled diplomats from all over the world, with varying cultural, ethnic, and religious backgrounds. Officials of the UN staff were invariably friendly and helpful, even though there was a marked variation in the individual levels of their quality, intelligence, and industriousness. Some were highly intelligent, competent, and hard working, but there were others who were lazy duffers, foisted into the UN system by persistent governments. Unfortunately the latter category were far more numerous than was desirable.

The international repercussions of the events in Afghanistan had just begun to manifest themselves, and the first refugees from that unfortunate country were flooding into Pakistan. The Mujahideen had begun a resistance to the Soviet occupation, but it was still scattered and uncoordinated, and the Ziaul Haq regime in Pakistan had taken the decision to support the resistance movement. Like many others at the time, I did not then realize that we were entering into an epoch whose consequences would extend far beyond the attainment of immediate objectives, transforming itself, and swelling into an explosive political phenomenon that would bestride the history at the turn of the millennium. Did any of us know then that we might be creating a Frankenstein's monster? At that time, my efforts were part of a general move to persuade friendly governments to support Agha Shahi's endeavours for organizing a meeting of Mujahideen leaders designed to forge their unity. We managed to persuade the Swiss government to provide facilities for a conference at Mont Pelerin, a small resort tucked away in the Swiss Alps, where the Mujahideen leaders met for three days. I had a chance to meet some of these representatives, from the elegantly clad Gaylani in his three-piece suit, to others such as Hekmatyar, Burhanuddin, and Saif, in *shalwar*, *kameez*, long frock coats, and *kulla safas*. Since my duties were administrative and not political, my meeting with these leaders was necessarily brief and sporadic, and whilst impressed by the obvious evidence of their courage, I remained dubious about their intentions. A declaration stressing unity and determination emerged from the meeting. But who remembers Mont Pelerin today?

My work at the UN continued during the autumn, being concentrated mainly on the Committee on Disarmament (CD) and activities in UNCTAD. I made a number of interventions on important issues in the CD, and served on some committees and contact groups in the latter, particularly on the financial and debt issues. The constant negotiations that are a necessary component of these activities, would, under normal circumstances, have been an intellectual stimulant. But by now I was becoming increasingly concerned about Diana's health.

Shortly after our arrival in Geneva, she had seen an eminent oncologist who, after careful examination, had made the ominous prognosis that she had only a few months to live. She continued her treatment, and was in and out of the hospital, displaying her cheerful courage and fortitude all the while. Then, in early December, the dread disease struck its penultimate blow, and she was moved to the Geneva Cantonal Hospital, where further treatment was gradually discontinued and she was placed under sedation to ease the horrible pain and discomfort that had now seized her. My parents, who were in Europe at the time, came to meet Diana. Her sister Nancy Cowasjee, and my brother Minoo, were constant visitors. Our cousins, Dr Eddie Bharucha from Bombay, and Jumbo and Khorshed Kharas from Rome, also came to see Diana during her last days in the hospital. My darling daughters Niloufer and Feroza joined me in a constant vigil at Diana's bedside as she slipped in and out of a coma. She remained unconscious on 1 January 1979, but the next day she woke up looking amazingly bright-eyed and lively. I asked her if she would like some juice or coffee, but she replied, with a wicked wink of her beautiful brown eyes, 'Why not champagne? It's New Year's Day!' We cracked a bottle of Dom Perignon, hastily retrieved from the residence, and drank a toast, joined by her doctors and nurses, whose misty eyes were brimming in admiration of her spirit and courage. This was my darling Diana's last conscious act, gracefully moving out of this world with the same élan with which she had sparkled and blazed throughout her life. She slipped into unconsciousness shortly thereafter and died on the morning of 4 January 1979. There were dark clouds in the sky and heavy snow began to descend on Geneva as Niloufer, Feroza, and I left the hospital holding hands. We felt that all of nature had joined us in our sadness at Diana's departure. 'When beggars die, there are no comets seen. The heavens themselves blaze forth the death of a prince.'

Diana had a favourite uncle, Minocher Dinshaw, who had been the doyen of the business community in Karachi, and a man whose munificence had been as quiet as it had been extensive. Between Diana and her Uncle Minoo there had been a bond of love, understanding, and affection that had been perhaps even greater than her ties with her parents. Diana had been heartbroken when he died while on vacation in Brunnen, a small town in the Swiss Alps not far from Zurich, where he had been buried. In accordance with Diana's expressed desire to be buried next to her Uncle Minoo, we made the necessary arrangements through the cooperative Swiss authorities, and held a simple funeral ceremony with Jumbo Kharas leading the prayers. Some years later, our family was struck by another devastating tragedy when our darling Feroza was killed in a car crash, and she now lies next to her mother. Since then, we have made an annual pilgrimage to this site, breathtaking in its peace and beauty, and a resting place that befits three wonderful beings who had themselves provided so much joy and beauty to so many.

It was not easy to live without Diana, and it was only the love, support and devotion of my daughters that eased the burden of bearing the unbearable, even as I knew that their grief and bereavement was as great, if not greater, than mine. Every Sunday we used to take the train to Zurich for a visit to Diana's grave in a ritual that provided both a healing touch and a sense of continuity of association. The speed, efficiency, and comfort of the Swiss railways, with its opportunity for contemplation as we sped through the beautiful countryside, was also an unobtrusive form of therapy, and a signal that life had to go on.

My work at the Palais des Nations kept me involved in a number of issues, and the leading role that the Pakistan mission had carved out for itself in this fiercely competitive environment prior to my arrival, ensured that my days, and frequently evenings and nights, were fully occupied. Debates, discussions, and the drafting of resolutions and negotiating them to a conclusion, were activities that could be both frustrating and exhausting. But on the whole I found it to be heady stuff. Above all, it helped to ease the pain of my bereavement. Niloufer returned to Canada, but Feroza stayed on with me in Geneva and found work in her profession as an occupational therapist in a local institution. Gradually, as we found a new and more comfortable residence, we began to settle down in our new surroundings, carrying out the entertainment that is an essential part of diplomatic life, and hosting the various delegations from Pakistan that visited Geneva. I travelled on mission on a number of occasions, one of which included a week in Arusha, Tanzania, on a PrepCom (Preparatory Committee) for the forthcoming UNCTAD session. The proceedings were pretty much routine, but the extra curricular activities comprising visits to the wildlife sanctuaries were fabulous.

In the summer of 1979 I was appointed to a Committee of Experts, commissioned by the UN secretary general, to prepare a report on nuclear weapons. I had acquired a degree of specialization on disarmament issues, particularly in respect of nuclear weapons, and had been very active on the subject in the Committee on Disarmament. I presumed that this record, coupled of course with my government's nomination, led to my membership of this committee. Not surprisingly, the five nuclear powers designated in the Nuclear Non-Proliferation Treaty refused to have anything to do with this committee, and declined the secretary general's invitation to its membership. It used to meet for ten-day sessions once every three months in New York, and finally produced its findings in July 1980, unobtrusively entitled 'Report to the Secretary General', and subsequently issued as a UN publication. One of its more startling conclusions was the finding that at the time of the publication of the report, we had estimated that the combined nuclear arsenals of the USA and the USSR, had the destructive capability of about thirty-four tons of TNT for each man, woman, and child on earth. My appointment to this committee did much more for me than provide an opportunity to work with some first class minds and leading experts on an issue as vital as the continuation of civilization as we know it. The mundane logistics that entailed the convocation of the meetings on an intermittent basis in New York led to my meeting with Arnaz Minwalla, of which more later.

A conference of the UNCTAD was held in Manila, the Philippines, in the summer of 1979, and ended a three-week session with the usual high-sounding declaration of good intentions. On the vital issues of financial commitments and debt reduction there was no agreement, despite several late night sessions, of which the last one extended into the dawn of the day of the ceremonial closing. Since I was the leader of the Group of 77 negotiating these issues, the outcome was obviously a disappointment, but there was some redemption in the fact that the talks were conducted in a civilized manner and no blood was spilled on the plush carpets of the ornate conference chambers. Gamini Corea, the urbane Director General of UNCTAD, together with the President of the Conference, the ebullient little Philippine Foreign Minister General Carlos P. Romulo, were the competent helmsmen who steered the conference through some turbulent waters. My principal interlocutors on behalf of the G8 were Chuck Meissner of the USA, and Stephane Hessel and Michel Camdessus of France, with whom I remained in almost constant confrontation during the negotiations, but spent the evening hours in convivial camaraderie, and became lifelong friends thereafter. Chuck was later killed in a tragic air crash in Sarajevo whilst working on a mission to bring aid to the Bosnians, Stephane went into honourable retirement in Paris and wrote an exemplary book on diplomacy, and Michel, after a stint as Governor of the Bank of France, served with signal success for two terms as Managing Director of the International Monetary Fund in Washington.

The Philippine government spared no expense or effort to make the conference a success, and in the process injected a fair amount of the Marcos personality cult. The elaborate opening and closing ceremonies were conducted with great pomp by President Ferdinand Marcos and his haughty wife Imelda, and the couple hosted a number of lavish receptions for the visiting delegations. Accommodation, transport and facilities for relaxation were plentiful, and Manila appeared to be in a highly festive mood, with the achievements of the Marcos regime advertised at all times, and in every fashion. The Pakistan delegation was led by Ghulam Ishaq Khan, who was at that time the Finance Minister, Minister for Economic Affairs, and the Commerce Minister, as well. Heavily burdened by this triple charge, his stay in Manila was necessarily brief, and he left shortly after making his formal statement in the plenary, leaving me in charge for the rest of the session. I had been friends with Ghulam Ishaq Khan for many years, and greatly admired and respected him for his brilliance, his dignified competence, and his fierce loyalty for his country. These public attributes were, of course, widely known, but what I enjoyed most in his company was to observe his razor sharp mind at work, and the dry humour that often reflected it. I was sorry that his brief sojourn in Manila deprived me of the opportunity to spend more quality time with this giant among men, and to savour those rare personal attributes.

Late one night I received a telephone call in my hotel room from a presidential aide, inviting me to a golf party hosted by President Marcos at a new resort on an island in Manila Bay. I was requested to board the presidential yacht, berthed in the harbour, at 7 a.m. the next morning. After checking that the call was genuine and not a prank by one of my playful colleagues, I duly presented myself at the appointed time and place, and was immediately swept into an atmosphere of cordial and luxurious hospitality. Marcos arrived, with sirens screaming and shouted salutes, just as we had commenced our champagne breakfast, and the splendidly appointed yacht slipped into Manila Bay and headed for our island golfing paradise. The guests were three or four colleagues from the delegations and about half a dozen of Marcos' cronies, clad in designer golfing kit, oozing prosperity and smug satisfaction. After arriving at the opulent club I teed off in a disastrous fashion, my mulligan taking my Topflight ball directly into the South Pacific ('Planning to return to Geneva, Ambassador?' 'No Mr President, but thinking of going back to pub crawling.'). Nine holes later we were treated to a superb lunch, and then took a detour on our return to the harbour so that Marcos could point out the islands and jungles where he claimed to have led his guerrilla forces during the Japanese occupation in the Second World War. He was a superb raconteur and kept us fully receptive as he recalled his exploits and adventures. The American ambassador later told me that most of this was fanciful, and had been woven into the assiduously cultivated Marcos myth. Even so, a bit of Arabian Nights seemed to go quite well with a flute of champagne sipped at sunset over the blue waters of Manila Bay.

I spent the most part of autumn 1979 in New York, working partly with the Nuclear Weapons Experts Group and partly serving on the First Committee of the UN General Assembly. Both occupations were fascinating, and whilst we made slow but appreciable progress in the Experts Group, the results in the First Committee were predictably less satisfactory. Our major effort in the First Committee was devoted to obtaining a resolution creating a South Asia Nuclear Weapons Free Zone, an objective that was doomed from the start, likely to incur the fiercest Indian opposition and was further debilitated by the reluctance of the superpowers to give it anything beyond a token approbation. This was a hardy perennial on the agenda of the First Committee, and a cursory review of the records would reveal little variation in the names and numbers of the delegations that had previously participated in the debate, and an even lesser difference in the contents of their respective interventions. For Pakistan, however, the sponsorship of the draft resolution was an important public assertion of our commitment to nuclear non-proliferation, and we pursued it with vigour. Our position was never very convincing, and became less so with the increase both in our clandestine nuclear activities and the public innuendos that reported them.

I was temporarily detached from duties in the General Assembly for a two-week stint as a member of the Pakistan delegation to the conference of heads of state and government of the Non-Aligned

Nations in Havana, Cuba. This was the first time that Pakistan had participated as a full member of this amorphous organization which, in view of the continuing Cold War, still retained its relative importance in international affairs. The closing of the American base at Badaber and the departure of foreign forces from Pakistani soil, had removed the last obstacle to the membership that had hitherto been so relentlessly and implacably expressed by India. Our high powered delegation was accordingly led by President Ziaul Haq, accompanied by General K.M. Arif, his Chief of Staff, and Foreign Secretary Agha Shahi. Ambassadors Iqbal Akhund, Abdullah Saeed, Najmul Saqib Khan and I, together with senior officers from our Foreign Ministry comprised the rest of the delegation. This was the first of my several visits to Havana, and I had the opportunity to juxtapose my experience in Eastern Europe with what I immediately discerned as communism with a Latin beat. All the trappings and impediments of a totalitarian society were very much in place, but the Latin temperament with its remarkable multiracial acceptance seemed to have survived the crushing pervasiveness of Marxist–Leninist ideology. Besides and the general population, though obviously suppressed, seemed to be far less sullen than those that I saw in Europe. I thought, also, that the 'campanero' was a little more affable than the 'comrade', 'tovarich', or 'genosse'.

The conference, in accordance with established tradition, was to signal the assumption of the presidency of the Non-Aligned Movement by Cuba, the host nation. However, it was clear from the start that Fidel Castro intended to use his considerable influence to shift the focus of the movement firmly to the left, and there was talk of introducing a declaration into the final document to the effect that the Soviet Union was the natural ally of the Non-Aligned. Marshal Josip Broz Tito of Yugoslavia, one of the founding fathers of the Non-Aligned Movement was aware of this and deeply regretted the move, as well as his inability to prevent it. The opening session of the conference was an elaborate and opulent affair, filled with the spectacular display which only totalitarian regimes can produce, and involved a long and fiery speech by Castro, complete with orchestrated interruptions of applause. In a gesture that I thought was the epitome of hypocrisy, Tito was provided with an enormous, throne-like chair right in front of the speaker's lectern where, dressed in an immaculate white uniform sparkling with decorations and sashes, Marshal Tito nodded through the Cuban president's interminable address. After that, the vigorous young Castro strode from the lectern and in a dramatic bow received from the old warrior's hands the ceremonial gavel of office. It brought to my mind a famous photograph of the early 1930s, showing a fawning Adolf Hitler in a frock coat and carrying a top hat, bowing before Field Marshal Paul von Hindenburg seated in full dress uniform replete with decorations, and receiving from him the seals of the office of Reichskanzellor.

There were two major political issues before the Non-Aligned Conference, and although it was the new kid on the block, Pakistan's participation was both vigorous and effective. At our morning and evening delegation meetings, President Zia was kept fully briefed of the developments, which he followed with much interest and in turn provided us with encouragement more than instructions. He also carried out a number of bilateral meetings with other heads of state, and the few sessions that I attended gave me an opportunity to observe his working methods. He was obviously a quick learner and went to each meeting fully briefed and prepared. His unique brand of humble courtesy did the rest, and every leader he met in Havana came away pleased as much as impressed. On the acrimonious issue of the declaration of the Soviets being the natural allies of the Non-Aligned, we voiced our opposition in the plenary, in committees and in the corridors. Apart from Pakistan, the countries most active in this regard were Sri Lanka, Singapore, Senegal, Côte d'Ivoire, Egypt, and a number of other Arab countries, Yugoslavia, and latterly India. Finally, we succeeded in blocking this move and thereby saved the integrity of the Non-Aligned Movement.

The other issue was much more complicated and much more heated. This was a move, spearheaded by a number of Arab countries strongly supported by the communist states, to expel Egypt from the Non-Aligned Movement for having signed the Camp David Accords with Israel, leading to the recognition of the latter. Notwithstanding the fact that Egypt, together with Yugoslavia, India, Ghana, and Indonesia was one of the founders of the movement, the reaction to this volte-face was both strong and extensive. The Egyptian delegation, led by its Deputy Prime Minister, the redoubtable Boutros Boutros-Ghali, was under constant and heavy attack, and although they did receive support from moderate delegations like ours, it was essentially the skilful and defiant diplomacy of the Egyptians under the able leadership of Boutros-Ghali that prevented expulsion and confined condemnation to a statement. In his memoirs there is a telling passage in which Boutros-Ghali recalls a meeting with President Anwar El Sadat during the course of which he reported to the latter the extent of the rancour encountered by the Egyptian delegation at Havana. They were seated in Sadat's office in Sharm el Sheikh, and walking to the window, the president pointed out the Sinai to Boutros-Ghali and said that no amount of Non-Aligned Movement resolutions would have been able to give Egypt the land that had been recovered under the Camp David Accords. The fact that shortly thereafter Sadat paid for this with his life is a matter for reflection by both philosophers and historians.

I returned from Havana to New York and stayed there until the end of a not particularly noteworthy General Assembly session in mid-December. In the meantime however, my personal affairs had suddenly entered a new and exciting phase. Dr Nafis Sadik, the Director General of the UNFPA, who was a dear family friend for many years, invited me to a dinner party at her apartment. There I met Arnaz Minwalla (I later discovered that Nafis had planned the evening for this purpose, bless her), who had been living in New York for a number of years as a businesswoman. She was one of the daughters of Cyrus Minwalla, a prominent Karachi businessman, philanthropist, and proprietor of the legendary Metropole Hotel. I had known Arnaz in her Karachi days, as a beautiful young girl with a sparkling personality, but had much closer associations with her parents, and her mother Mehra had been a particularly good friend of Diana. In a very short time, Arnaz and I developed a mutual attraction, and I was captivated by her beauty, charm and the spontaneous generosity of her heart and soul. I was also struck by her courage and optimism, and the cheerful determination with which she moved through a life which, though still young, had not been without its setbacks. 'I am a survivor,' she said to me with a lively wink of her lovely hazel eyes, in the early days of our acquaintance. I had been blessed with a long and very happy marriage, and its cruel termination had left me hurt and bitter. The love, care, and attention bestowed upon me by my darling daughters Niloufer and Feroza, were a source of strength and comfort, without which I could not have survived, but yet there remained an inner loneliness that could not be assuaged. Meeting Arnaz in New York was for me a veritable *coup de foudre*, and the love, care, and understanding that she lavished upon me from the very start of our relationship turned the course of my life. I recalled the words of Cervantes, at that time, 'God, who sent the wound, has also sent the cure.' For Arnaz also, our whirlwind courtship had implications that were momentous. Her lifestyle, freewheeling, radiantly unattached, and limitless in options, would now be linked with the destiny of her husband, and include the demands of his profession. I responded to her tentative concerns about coping with the obligations of being an ambassador's wife by telling her to be herself. This was the soundest advice and also the most obvious, and Arnaz slipped into the role of ambassadress with style and elegance. She had a working knowledge of Spanish, but spoke French and Italian fluently, whilst her graduate degree from the prestigious École Hotelière de Lausanne, Switzerland, provided her with impeccable qualifications for the variety of social commitments that are a necessary component of diplomatic life. But above all it was her intelligence, beauty, and vivacious personality that made her such a success, and brought me so much pride and joy. Her impact and panache are remembered in some of the most important metropolises of the world—Geneva, Bonn, Paris, Washington, and New York. A photograph of Arnaz, taken with Joseph Verner Reed, the Chief of Protocol at the State Department, and also the United Nations, a flamboyant personality who could have come straight out of central casting in Hollywood, is signed by him with the caption, 'To Arnaz. A superstar!' That says it all.

I returned to Geneva in January 1980, and took stock of the events relating to our mission that had occurred in the past year, which by any reckoning had been a memorable one. At the routine level, Dr Humayun Khan had been transferred early in the year to Dhaka as Pakistan's High Commissioner, and replaced by Munir Akram as the DPR. It was a change of personalities only, for the level of professionalism and the quality of personal friendship remained at the same high degree. Transfers in the diplomatic service are seldom as smooth and satisfactory as this one was for me, and I was glad that my good fortune, in terms of having congenial colleagues in my mission, had continued. However, there was another factor, not directly concerned with the work of the mission, that had cast dark clouds over us during the previous spring. Concern had been expressed over the fate of Zulfikar Ali Bhutto, whose impact on the international scene had of course been considerable. Many questions had been asked of us, and I had the feeling that even more had been unasked. After his execution in April 1979, we had received a few expressions of personal shock, but these feelings tapered off fairly quickly, largely due, I suspect, to the muted reaction to this traumatic event in Pakistan itself.

Activities in Geneva proceeded in normal fashion during the first half of 1980, and towards the end of June, I was once again in New York for the last session of the Nuclear Weapons Experts Group. This lasted a little longer than expected because it was devoted to the final preparation of the report, and I availed myself of the opportunity to do something useful, and get married to Arnaz. We both wanted an unobtrusive civil marriage, and she went about making all the arrangements in her usual brisk and efficient manner, so that we were duly wed in a simple morning ceremony at her New York apartment on 12 July 1980. It was, of course, a civil marriage, and only Arnaz could have found and persuaded a very pleasant and cooperative Jewish judge to come to her home on a Sabbath to conduct the ceremony. The only others present on the occasion were Niloufer and Feroza, Mitzie, and Khurshed Birdie (Arnaz's sister and brother-in-law), Arnaz's twin sister Aban Jamall and her daughter Naila, and my old friend and colleague Tayyab Siddiqui, who was then serving in our UN Mission in New York. The previous day, the meeting of the nuclear experts group had extended late into the night, and the chairman had decided to call a Saturday morning session to conclude our work. Ambassador Andors of Sweden was kind enough to condone my absence when the reasons were conveyed to him in my leave application, wished me well, and added that he had never before received a request of this nature. We left the next day for Geneva, but were back in New York during the autumn and had a second marriage ceremony, this time under Parsi rites in order to satisfy Arnaz's mother, who was in beaming attendance.

By the summer of 1980 I found myself increasingly involved in the crisis following the Soviet invasion of Afghanistan, an activity which included not only a series of diplomatic initiatives at the UN, but also frequent trips to Islamabad for consultations. A special session of the OIC was convened in Islamabad in order to mobilize opinion and map out a course of action. The Foreign Ministry, true to form, had organized the meeting with a smooth efficiency that was wholly admirable, and the main purpose of the conference was achieved. I came to the conclusion that President Ziaul Haq's personal interest and involvement in this crisis were clearly manifest, and that the issue would henceforth become the focus of Pakistan's foreign policy. My own activities thus extended to meetings with the US congressional and other delegations which visited Pakistan from time to time, but more importantly, I was being summoned for consultations at the highest levels of our government. I had now tentatively commenced attending the informal late night meetings that Zia held with his close advisers in the drawing room of Army House. It was an association that would grow in time and last over the coming years. It would also enable me to observe, and work with, this truly remarkable personality.

In the autumn of 1980 I received orders appointing me as the ambassador to the Federal Republic of Germany, and accordingly made the short trip from Geneva to Bonn, leaving the former city with a feeling of regret and arriving in the latter with a frisson of anticipation. My stay in cosmopolitan Geneva, from the professional standpoint, had been most interesting and also reasonably successful. In personal matters it was a place where I had experienced great sadness, tempered at the very end of my tenure, with a promise of much happiness. It was also a post where, for the first time since Moscow, my work was beginning to include direct interaction with the policy-making institutions in Islamabad.

CHIAROSCURO

The series of crises and recoveries that Diana went through during her last weeks seemed to have had an uncanny effect on Feodor, who used to be left at home at the times that we visited her in hospital. He would be morose and despondent each time that she went through a crisis, and cheered up once she had overcome it. On one occasion, I left the hospital to go home for a shower and a change of clothes, with Diana sitting up and cheerfully having lunch with Feroza in attendance. I arrived home to find Feodor looking sad and sullen, and told him to cheer up, as all was well. Just then I received a call from Feroza asking me to rush back to the hospital because Diana was suddenly in a crisis. Feodor had been right once again.

On that sad, last snow-driven morning, as we returned home from the hospital after Diana's death, we found Feodor frisking around in happiness. Somehow he knew that now, at last, Diana was free from all pain.

During the dark, gloomy days that I passed with Diana in the Geneva clinic, as she approached the end of her beautiful, noble life, I was sustained by the love and care of Niloufer and Feroza. Equally comforting was the presence of my youngest brother Minoo, who always appeared by my side in times of difficulty and torment. Minoo and I are brothers in soul as much as we are brothers in flesh, bonded by some mysterious intuitive instinct. We have a shared love of history, of adventure, and of dogs, and a sense of humour that might appear to some as a bit warped. Ours is a relationship that is so close because it is so charged with understanding and comprehension. We both, obviously, have many faults, but neither of us can ever see them. The only difference between us is that Minoo has been a lifelong bachelor, whereas I have been blessed with two long and happy marriages.

* * *

The topic of the environment was beginning to assume increasing importance and figured on agendas for discussion in the various multilateral institutions in Geneva. Linked with this was, of course, the subject of pollution and 'energy', the rubric for coal and oil. As was to be expected, the Organization of the Petroleum Exporting Countries (OPEC) was particularly sensitive to this issue and maintained a fierce, sustained and effective campaign to ensure that environmental resolutions did not contain clauses that might impinge on their production activities. Since most members of the OPEC were also members of the Group of 77, this caused us some difficulty in maintaining group unity and was one of my major preoccupations when I was leader of the Group, both in Geneva and later during the Environment Conference in Rio de Janeiro. I was amused to note the inflammatory impact of the word 'energy', when seated next to an Arab delegate during the course of a long and rather dreary plenary debate. He was peacefully sleeping off the effects of the previous evening's activities in the nightclubs of Geneva, when the speaker at the rostrum urged the delegates to deal with the problems of debt relief with vigour and energy. This triggered an alarm bell in my neighbour's subconscious, 'What did he say about energy?' I was glad to note that my reassurances restored his somnolence.

* * *

The Non-Aligned Conference in Havana was organized on a lavish scale; however, the best plans and intentions can sometimes go astray. At the opening plenary session the foreign delegates were seated on the ground floor of the assembly chamber, whilst the rent-a-crowd Cubans were packed into the galleries, and punctuated Castro's long speech with their frequently hollered applause on cue. The delegates were of course much more restrained in their enthusiasm. The TV cameras were focused on Castro on the rostrum, and the heads of state and government were seated with their delegations on the ground floor. Viewers of the proceedings, on their TV sets in their homes, in hotels and in the public squares, were, therefore, treated to the hilarious experience of the sounds of stormy bursts of applause emanating from a noticeably sedate, if not silent, audience. Thanks to the length of Castro's speech the technicians were, in due course, able to correct the incongruity. But for the considerable time that it lasted, it provided Niloufer with much amusement, as she watched the proceedings on the TV set in our hotel room. And I am sure that she was not the only one.

* * *

One of the characteristics of Ziaul Haq, which I was delighted to note during the very early stage of our association, was his ability to tell a damaging tale about himself. Shortly after landing at Havana airport, whilst we were in the VIP lounge, and Castro, with his lady interpreter, had received and greeted Zia, the president said to me, 'Marker Sahib,

I have just dropped a brick. I asked him if that was Mrs Castro, and he said to me "There is NO Mrs Castro!" Then Zia gave me a rueful grin.

* * *

An envoys' conference was convened in Islamabad, presided over by Zia and directed by Agha Shahi, who had by then become the Foreign Minister. The format for the conference was a plenary opening session, followed by syndicates that discussed different issues and reported their findings to the closing plenary session of the conference. At the inaugural plenary a number of ambassadors made their presentations, with each one including laudatory references to Agha Shahi's stewardship. When it was Air Chief Marshal Zulfikar Ali Khan's turn, he commenced by narrating an incident that once occurred in an air force mess. Four or five officers had gathered around the bar one evening when the squadron commander arrived and generously offered to buy them a round of drinks. Knowing that the commanding officer was fiercely opposed to the consumption of alcohol, the flight lieutenants and senior flying officers ordered juices and cokes. A very junior pilot officer, when it was his turn, said, 'You have had a cheap round so far, Sir. I shall have a double Scotch.' Citing this precedent, Ambassador Zulfikar said that Agha Shahi had had a cheap round so far, and proceeded to make a forceful presentation. I could see that this not only delighted Zia but also twisted an embarrassed smile out of Shahi. It was little incidents like this one that enlivened the otherwise lugubrious tenor of these meetings. One of the personal benefits that I derived from the envoys' conferences was to meet and spend time with Sahibzada Yaqub Khan. Our mutual interest in literature and languages brought us together, and turned what was initially a friendship, into a long-standing and affectionate bond.

MEANWHILE IN PAKISTAN

The coup of July 1977, which had removed Bhutto from office, presented General Ziaul Haq with a twofold dilemma. The first was that Bhutto still retained a considerable degree of popular support, as was evident from the substantial attendance at his public meetings. The second issue was that of the legitimacy of Zia's action, highlighted by a suit filed by Begum Nusrat Bhutto which challenged the validity of the martial law and accused Zia of treason by violating Article 6 of the 1973 Constitution. Zia dealt with the first of these problems by arresting Bhutto and then activating a First Information Report (FIR) for murder filed against Bhutto by Ahmad Reza Kasuri when he was the prime minister in 1974. Kasuri was an erstwhile, maverick PPP politician. The issue of legitimacy was deftly dealt with by Zia and his legal adviser Syed Sharifuddin Pirzada, a brilliant lawyer known for his dexterous abilities in the field of constitutional law. They invoked a 1954 decision of the Supreme Court whereby the concept of the 'Doctrine of Necessity' was propounded as justification for the dismissal of the National Assembly by the then Governor General Ghulam Mohammad. This was, therefore, conveniently used as a precedent for a further similar decision by the Supreme Court in November 1977, to justify the imposition of martial law by Ziaul Haq. The stark reality of military rule, which the country had by now come to accept in any case, and had in fact been welcomed by those who had been opposed to Bhutto's fascist tendencies, had thus been granted a legal status, and this landmark decision was now beyond challenge. Zia had succeeded in covering his military iron fist with the velvet glove provided to him by the Supreme Court.

In his first public statement after the coup in July 1977, Zia said, 'Pakistan, which was created in the name of Islam, will continue to survive only if it sticks to Islam. That is why I consider the introduction of an Islamic system as an essential prerequisite for the country.' The actions that he took during 1978 and 1979 were to prove that his words were not mere expressions, and that he meant what he had said. Each time that I visited Pakistan during that period I was able to observe these changes, and the manner in which they were being implemented. In all government offices there were statutory provisions for the allocation of both time and space for daily prayers, which heads of department were encouraged to lead. The dress code of the bureaucracy had changed, almost overnight, from ties and three-piece suits to *achkans*, *shalwars*, and waistcoats. Also, the public display of piety had become a major component of the insidious code of obsequiousness that has always plagued our society.

In his personal conduct and deportment Zia always remained polite and low key. He was no Savonarola breathing fire and brimstone in the cause of religion. I often heard him say, 'What is between you and God is your personal affair, and has nothing to do with me or anybody else.' But in the domain of public policy his devotion to Islam was meaningful and unequivocal. During my intermittent visits to Pakistan I was able to observe the manner in which Zia was increasing his hold over the country, and what I saw was not entirely comforting. He postponed elections in 1977 as well as in 1979. He referred to this, in a personal conversation with me some years later when we had got to know each other quite well, and wryly admitted, 'I know I do not have a very good track record as far as elections are concerned.' Furthermore, he introduced and implemented a series of draconian martial law regulations and punishments, including the barbaric system of public floggings.

Zulfikar Ali Bhutto's fate was a matter of great public concern throughout 1978 and the early part of 1979. The dramatic proceedings in the Lahore High Court and later in the Supreme Court were followed, in the nation as well as abroad, with the greatest interest. A number of eminent foreign counsels came to Pakistan and followed the hearings, but were unable to assist Bhutto in the trials because of an earlier law—ironically promulgated by Bhutto himself—that prohibited the participation by foreign lawyers in Pakistani courts. For his part, Zia went through the gamut of the formalities of the entire legal process in his cool and methodical manner. Following the death sentence unanimously pronounced by the Lahore High Court in March 1978, the case was heard in appeal by the Supreme Court. Of the nine-member bench, one retired during the course of the hearing, and another withdrew because of illness. A split decision, with three judges siding with Chief Justice Anwar-ul-Haq, confirmed the sentence passed by the Lahore High Court. In conformity with statutory requirements, a mercy petition was submitted and rejected, respectively, by the ministerial cabinet, the Punjab governor and the martial law administrative council. Messages from several world leaders urging clemency were ignored. In an interview with Gavin Young of the London *Observer* on 1 October 1978, Zia had said, 'If the Supreme Court says "Acquit him", I will acquit him. If it says "Hang the blighter", I will hang him.' On 4 April 1979 Zia proved to be true to his grim promise.

For me in Geneva this was a difficult period, and the conduct of diplomacy was by no means simple. The imposition of martial law, the draconian manner of its implementation with arrests and floggings, and finally the execution of Bhutto, had combined to almost turn Pakistan into an international pariah. However, the unexpected calm that prevailed in the country conveyed the impression abroad, rightly or wrongly, that Bhutto's execution was not a major political trauma, and the absence of civil turmoil, and the consequential absence of adverse media coverage, gave us a breathing space in which to recoup and mend fences.

Conditions remained in this state of limbo until December 1979, when the Soviet invasion of Afghanistan presented the world with a fait accompli which reflected an unexpected and entirely unforeseen international menace. The sudden appearance of an aggressive USSR took the international community by surprise, and the newly-christened 'Brezhnev Doctrine' had driven a coach and horses through the delicate fabric of the détente that had been so carefully nurtured after the Helsinki Accords. Therefore, towards the end of my tenure in Geneva, my activities were dominated by the flurry of meetings and negotiations that had been triggered by Moscow's blatant military intervention in Afghanistan.

As the nations were beginning to come to terms with what was rightly regarded as an ominous development, they awaited, as usual, some signs of leadership from Washington. But the first response from the Carter administration was both muddled and pusillanimous. It cancelled US participation in the forthcoming Moscow Olympics. In a telephone call, President Jimmy Carter offered Pakistan an aid package amounting to $400 million, which Zia promptly rejected as 'peanuts'. Whether the implication of the reference to Carter's previous occupation as a peanut farmer was inadvertent or deliberate is not clear, but there was no doubt about the impact of the message and the alacrity with which it was flashed around the world. Pakistan had decided to use its own meagre resources to cope with the flood of Afghan refugees, and was at the same time prepared to enter into a diplomatic confrontation with the mighty Soviet Union.

Shortly thereafter a change occurred in Washington's policies, motivated largely by Zbigniew Brzezinski, the Head of the National Security Agency, who asserted his authority and his expertise on the

USSR to assemble a credible resistance to the Soviet action, to increase diplomatic cooperation with Pakistan, and also to provide the country with more substantive assistance. Delegations from the USA and Western Europe began dropping into Islamabad like rotten fruit, and Ziaul Haq and his team of advisers formulated a most effective routine of receptions, briefings, and hospitality that sent the visitors home happy and charged with fervour for the cause. The impact of these activities was reflected in Geneva, where I was involved in meetings and consultations that dealt not only with the pressing practical issues of the Afghan refugees, but also with the diplomatic efforts to maintain and garner political support for our policies.

The vagaries of world affairs were about to transform Pakistan from an international pariah to an international poster boy. The man who foresaw this, and trimmed his sails to catch the winds of opportunity for his country, was General Ziaul Haq.

Shortly after taking office Ziaul Haq displayed an act of bold and imaginative statesmanship which, unfortunately, has not been either recognized or remembered these days. A bitter and bloody insurgency in Balochistan had commenced immediately after Bhutto's orders of arrest and imprisonment of the Baloch leaders, including Bizenjo, Ataullah Mengal and a number of others. A ruthless campaign had been carried out by the army, under Tikka Khan, against the Baloch people, resulting in widespread casualties on both sides, and had already gone on for a number of years. Overcoming the objections of some of his senior generals (in itself an act of courage in the early years of his regime), Zia called off the military action and entered into negotiations with the Baloch leaders. Meeting them in person, Zia ordered their release, proclaimed them as free and loyal citizens of Pakistan, and ordered the recall of troops to their peacetime stations. He did all this as he sat and had lunch with the Baloch leaders at their place of detention in Hyderabad jail. He also arranged for Ataullah Mengal to be sent to Europe, at government expense, for treatment of his heart ailment. Balochistan returned to peace, and Zia never had a problem with the province for the next eight years of his regime.

PART VIII

FEDERAL REPUBLIC OF GERMANY, FRANCE, AND IRELAND

CHAPTER NINETEEN

Federal Republic of Germany

'*Wer den Dichter will verstehen Muss in Dichter's Lande gehen.*'
('To understand the poet, you must visit his country.')
– Goethe

We moved to Bonn on transfer in mid-November 1980, but I had already made a brief trip the previous month, as a member of the delegation accompanying President Ziaul Haq on his official visit to the Federal Republic of Germany. This was most helpful, and a very good way to jump-start my mission, as it enabled me to participate, as the ambassador designate, in the high level discussions that took place between Zia and Chancellor Helmut Schmidt, and also to get to know the senior Federal German officials. It also gave me an early insight into Bonn's positive attitude towards Pakistan's position on the Afghan situation.

Bonn had been designated as the 'provisional' capital of the Federal Republic of Germany in anticipation of a return to Berlin, the historic German capital, following the reunification of the country. At the time of my arrival I thought that it was a valid but distant dream, never imagining, in my turn, that it would be accomplished as quickly as it in fact was. The town of Bonn, situated as it was in the fields, hills, and vineyards on the banks of the Rhine, was surrounded by a number of picturesque little townships of which Bad Godesberg was the one in which our chancery was located, whilst the embassy residence was in Köenigswinter, which lay across the river. The commute between the residence and the office required crossing the Rhine by ferry, an activity that always pleased me very much, regardless of the weather. It was said that John le Carré, who was once a British diplomat stationed in Bonn, wrote much of the manuscript of his first book, *The Spy Who Came in from the Cold*, whilst in transit on this ferry.

The chancery building was a lovely piece of classical Westphalian architecture—grey stone, polished timber, and red roof, with comfortable and well-appointed rooms for offices, as well as a conference room and reception salon for visitors. The residence was spacious and comfortable, and had originally been built for Robert Ley, the Reichsminister for Labour, who was one of the most disgusting of Hitler's band of thugs. Apart from its lavish and commodious accommodation, the only remnant of Nazi association was the swastika design on the iron grills of the ventilator windows. There was an enormous garden, studded with magnificent oaks, horse chestnut and fir trees, which stretched down to the banks of the Rhine. By day we could see the variety of boats and barges that formed the river traffic, and by night the sounds of their horns and sirens provided a comforting soporific. My parents came to live with us for a while, as they did in most of the other capitals where we were posted, and I recall with considerable pride, pleasure, and nostalgia my mother's words of shy gratitude. She said that it had been her lifelong dream and desire to live on the banks of a river, and she graciously thanked Arnaz and me for its fulfilment.

I presented credentials to President Karl Carstens on 16 December 1980, and in my speech recalled the successful outcome of President Zia's recent October visit to Bonn, and the fruitful decisions reached after his extensive discussions with President Carstens, Chancellor Helmut Schmidt, and Foreign Minister Hans-Dietrich Genscher, including the decision of the Federal German government to provide Pakistan with both diplomatic and economic support. By mentioning Allama Iqbal's stay and studies at the universities of Heidelberg and Munich, I tried to associate the influence of the great German philosophers on Pakistan's ideologue. Carstens's response was as positive and reassuring as one could wish, and he said, 'You are now the bastion of the free world in one of the most sensitive regions, and all are looking to you to stand firm.' I felt that I was off to a good start.

The federal nature of the West German constitution, with the widespread autonomy and powers vested in the various *Länder* (states) that composed the republic, made it incumbent upon ambassadors to travel all over the country and visit the provincial capitals. This provided us with an escape from the 'cabin fever' of sustained residence in Bonn, while our task was simplified by the presence in Bonn of the accredited representatives of each of the *Länder* who made appointments and arrangements for the official visits It was all helped by the superb German road and rail systems which made travel all over the country both rapid and comfortable. Thus was possible for us to savour some of the riches of this great country, which historically had been at the heart of Europe and was now also the economic dynamo of the continent. From the bustling port of Hamburg on the cold North Sea, through the picturesque towns and villages that nestled on the banks of the Rhine, to the sophisticated city of Munich and the beauty and solitude of the Bavarian Alps, the industrial cities of Frankfurt, Stuttgart, and Essen spewing fumes and churning out automobiles, chemicals, and heavy industrial equipment, to the baroque towns of Hanover and Nürnberg, carefully restored after their destruction in the Second World War, and finally to the glitz and glitter of West Berlin, surrounded by the grim Wall, our travels provided us with a picture of current energy framed in a background of profound history and culture. My thoughts frequently turned to my stay in East Berlin and the feeling of stark contrast that it always evoked. I thought that the reality was not the geographical division imposed by different political systems, but rather the inevitability of one people getting together again. Nothing could be more ridiculous than the attempts made in East Berlin to claim that Bach, Beethoven, Goethe, Schiller, and of course Marx, were theirs, whereas Hitler and the Nazis belonged to the West.

Working with the Federal German authorities was always pleasant and productive. Foreign Minister Genscher had the reputation in his ministry as being a bit of a tyrant, but in my frequent dealings with him I received nothing but courtesy and co-operation. Unlike the senior officials in his department who were completely bilingual in German and English, Genscher was more comfortable in his own language. The Staatssekretär in the Foreign Ministry was Graf von Staden, an experienced diplomat of the classical old school, whose sharp mind was shielded by an innate courteous dignity and immaculate bearing. He and his charming wife Wendy, who had just written a best-selling book on her early life in wartime Germany, became very good friends with us, and I greatly valued not only von Staden's professional guidance but also the wide-ranging conversations that we had on history, music, and literature. This was a friendship that was as warm as it was instructive. The Chief of Protocol was Graf Fink von Finkenstein. When I first heard the name I thought it would be hard to conjure up anything more Teutonic. The Graf and his wife also became our very good friends. They exuded a hearty Bavarian goodwill and were immensely kind and helpful to us. Our desk officer in the ministry was another Bavarian, Graf von Pfetten, who was, in addition to being a superb diplomat, both outgoing and fun loving. Bertie and Gertie, as he and his wife came to be known in Bonn's close diplomatic circle, were amongst the most popular of our colleagues. This trio of German aristocrats, with their warm and courteous ways, made living and working in Bonn a most pleasant and memorable experience.

On one occasion, while in the reception area of the Foreign Office, I ran into Ambassador Mathias, the West German Ambassador to the UN European Office in Geneva, who was back in Bonn for consultations. After exchanging pleasantries, my former colleague asked me how I liked working in Bonn, and hoped that I did not find it too dull after the excitement, glamour, and glitter of the bright lights of Geneva. I responded by recollecting the long negotiating sessions, sometimes stretching up to two o'clock in the morning, that we used to jointly endure at the UN. I said that after arguing with him and his colleagues in the G8 for hours, I would emerge satisfied if I had been able to convince them to remove the square brackets from three sentences in a draft resolution. Here in Bonn I had just come out of a meeting that had lasted a little over forty-five minutes, and was walking away with a credit for fifty million Deutschmarks: he could draw his own conclusions. Ambassador Mathias roared with laughter, and I was told that an account of our conversation had done the rounds of the entire *Auswärtig Amt* (Foreign Office) by that evening.

During my tenure in Bonn a major issue in foreign affairs was, as always, West Germany's relations with the USSR, actively linked to Bonn's relations with East Berlin. Chancellor Willy Brandt's imaginative Ostpolitik had leapt over the GDR and concluded the famous Peace Treaty with Moscow, but this breakthrough had brought in its train a number of complications with the East Germans, including the Gunther Guillaume affair, in which the Stasi officer had penetrated the cabinet of Willy Brandt, resulting in the resignation of the

Chancellor. This time, however, there was a direct confrontation between Bonn and Moscow, arising out of the West German decision to permit the deployment of the American 'Cruise' and 'Pershing' missiles on its soil as part of the NATO force. These were tactical nuclear weapons designed to serve as force equalizers to the overwhelming superiority of the Warsaw Pact's conventional weapons. During an official visit by Leonid Brezhnev this issue formed the major element of contention, but the Germans stood firm, even though the Soviets carried out their threat to withdraw from the arms control negotiations in Vienna. They came back to the talks after a decent interval, and Helmut Schmidt both kept the missiles and survived what was believed to be the communist sponsored public agitation against the deployment. It was on this occasion that Schmidt made his dry observation that Moscow's concept of settled frontiers was to have Soviet troops stationed on both sides of the border. Chancellor Helmut Schmidt, while agreeing to deploy the 'Cruise' and 'Pershing' missiles on German territory, had at the same time, commenced negotiations with the Soviet Union for the balanced reduction of missiles in Europe. This *Doppel Beschluss*, or double track, decision had been the cornerstone of Schmidt's policy and one that he pursued with vigour.

Two other issues dominated the discussions between Brezhnev and Schmidt—Poland and Afghanistan. On the former, considerations of historic violence, coupled with the high emotions that were provoked by the ongoing Solidarity Movement of Lech Walensa, compelled Schmidt to tread a very cautious and circumspect path. However, on Afghanistan the Soviets adopted an extremely intransigent attitude and said that Germany, as a regional power, had no right to interfere in the Afghan question, that El Salvador would also need to be brought into the discussions if Afghanistan was to be considered, and that on no account would the Soviets permit any mention of Afghanistan in the joint communiqué. Brezhnev frankly stated that 'the Afghan Revolution was irreversible and no outside forces would be allowed to change it'. Nevertheless, both sides expressed satisfaction at the end of the Brezhnev visit, with the German cabinet stating that the talks had made an important contribution to international security and a commentary in *Pravda* declaring that the meeting had exceeded all expectations. But Pakistan had clearly been a fly in the Soviet ointment. When I spoke to Ambassador Zorin at a farewell reception for Brezhnev hosted by the Germans, the Soviet ambassador was blunt and hostile. When I congratulated him in Russian, at the success of Brezhnev's visit, he growled back in German, that relations between the USSR and West Germany were very good, but relations between the Soviet Union and Pakistan were very bad, 'Es gibt krieg' ('this is a war').

The embassy in Bonn was a large mission, comprising in all fifty-five officers and staff members, most of the local staff being Pakistanis. Initially the DCM was Abdul Wahid, a career foreign service officer, who was later replaced by Brigadier Sardar Ahmed. The defence, commercial, press, inspection, and technical divisions were headed by counsellors, whilst we had in the political section Counsellor Cheema, from the Intelligence Bureau, and First Secretary Shafqat Kakakhel. Once again I had the good fortune to be surrounded by an excellent group of officers, intelligent, keen, and enthusiastic. Two of the most distinguished were our Defence Attaché, Colonel Mohammed Asad Durrani, who spoke fluent German and had undertaken a course at the German War College. He later came back to Bonn as an ambassador and went on to become the Director of Military Intelligence, and also Director General of the ISI. Shafqat Kakakhel had a distinguished subsequent career with the United Nations in Nairobi. Shafqat was dynamic and enthusiastic, and was constantly taking initiatives that would exercise his bright intellect. Asad Durrani was cool and low key, with a quick grasp of issues and very sound in his judgment. Khalid Amin was our able and dedicated commercial counsellor who delivered fully on the high priority that was accorded to his duties in our embassy. We also had Ikram Khan, whose designation as procurement minister was meant as a cover for his work connected with our nuclear programme. He combined initiative, efficiency, and discretion to produce results that were quite outstanding. With such a splendid collection of talent, our staff meetings were always stimulating and I looked forward to them every day as I crossed the Rhine on the way to my office.

Our Honorary Consul General in Munich, Dr Hecklemann, was extraordinarily active in support of Pakistan, and devoted considerable time, attention, and expense towards this end. A wealthy entrepreneur with worldwide interests, he had great influence in the Christian

Democratic Union (CDU), the conservative political party that governed the state of Bavaria. He introduced me to its leader, the dynamic and flamboyant Dr Franz Josef Strauss who was also the Prime Minister of Bavaria, and with whom we became very good friends. A forthright and unabashed conservative, Dr Strauss regarded Pakistan's opposition to the Soviet occupation of Afghanistan as something very close to his heart. His unequivocal public call for defence assistance to Pakistan was the first such statement made by a high ranking German politician in many years, and although the Federal German constitution severely limited military assistance to foreign countries, Strauss backed his rhetoric with substantial quantities of aid, in cash and kind, from the Bavarian exchequer. We visited him in Munich for a ceremony marking the dispatch of relief goods for the Afghan refugee camps in Pakistan, and made a token inspection of the heavily loaded trucks before a group of press and TV reporters. As we walked through the streets in Munich, Franz Josef Strauss was constantly greeted by enthusiastic citizens, some of whom followed us into a modest *bierhalle*, wished to pay for our lunch, and sent steins of beer to our table. There could be no more vivid testimony to Strauss's reputation as the uncrowned King of Bavaria. He was a big, heavy man with a shock of dark hair and bright blue eyes that sparkled with intelligence and humour, and exuded the hearty bonhomie and assurance of the determined and successful politician that he was. He later led a delegation to Pakistan, accompanied by his wife and some senior members of his cabinet. They visited Islamabad, Lahore, Peshawar, and Karachi, held meetings with the president, the foreign minister, and other senior officials, and backed strong statements of political support for Pakistan with substantial economic and financial contributions.

The schedule of Strauss's delegation included the customary visit to Landi Kotal with lunch at the Khyber Rifles' mess and a meeting with the tribal elders, who were to present Strauss with a sheep. Strauss, having taken note of my earlier briefing that it was a token presentation, and that he was expected to return the animal to its donors, dutifully performed the ritual. However, an additional event was unexpectedly included in the schedule, and much to his delight Strauss was taken to the Army Remount Depot where he was presented with a splendid horse. On his return to Munich the Ministerpräsident gave me a glowing account of his trip to Pakistan, concluding with the observation that while he had given up the sheep he intended to keep the horse, and could we please arrange for its delivery in Munich? PIA had agreed to my request to carry the animal in its weekly freighter service to Frankfurt, but local veterinary rules prevented its disembarkation. Strauss responded with an oath when I conveyed this to him, and suggested that the aircraft land in Munich instead of Frankfurt. Another expletive followed when I informed him that our bilateral air agreement restricted PIA to Frankfurt. However, following intensive negotiations with his colleague, the prime minister of Hesse, and elaborate veterinary arrangements at the Frankfurt airport, Ministerpräsident Franz Josef Strauss was finally reunited with his trusty steed.

Another great friend of Pakistan was Dr Annemarie Schimmel, who was a Professor at Heidelberg and Bonn universities, and also a visiting scholar at Harvard. A poet and philosopher, she was steeped in the Sufi tradition and possessed an extensive knowledge of Pakistani folklore, particularly that pertaining to Sindh. But her specialty was Allama Iqbal, on whose work she was one of the world's leading authorities. Our frequent conversations with Annemarie, whether at conferences or at social evenings in our home, were always delightful and instructive. My predecessor, Iftikhar Ali, had said that Dr Annemarie Schimmel could close her eyes and talk about Iqbal for fifteen minutes, or half an hour, or an hour and a half. He was so right, and she could rivet our attention every time she did so.

My assignment in Bonn provided me with a peripheral involvement in the nuclear field, firstly through my association with Ikram Khan, our procurement minister, and through that channel to both the scientific and political establishment in Islamabad. I was instructed to also continue these duties when I was transferred to France. For obvious reasons this is a topic upon which elaboration is neither permissible nor possible. Suffice it to say that notwithstanding the moral and legal sanctions publicly invoked by their respective governments, there was no shortage of suppliers from industrial countries worldwide wishing, and even eager, to do business with us, provided that the price was right and a modicum of discretion was exercised. The concept of realpolitik, which in some form or another becomes a concomitant of diplomacy, necessarily affects its practitioners. But the combination of hypocrisy and greed that went with these exchanges was truly a revelation to me, and invoked a cynicism that I did not think I had hitherto possessed.

Economic cooperation with the Federal Republic of Germany had been a significant element in our bilateral relations, and as I noted from the records at the time of my arrival in Bonn, we had received economic assistance amounting to DM 2.4 billion from the West Germans since 1961, the loans being on International Development Association (IDA) terms, and generally untied. In May 1982 we negotiated a bilateral agreement which provided a loan, under the same easy conditions, for DM 130 million. This was a very satisfactory matter on which to complete my tenure in Bonn, as I had just received orders for transfer to Paris. My stay had been of less than normal duration, but had been particularly enjoyable, as it had been professionally quite productive. More importantly, I had been able to travel all over the country and savour every aspect of German life and tradition, with recollections of many happy hours spent at the Wagner Festspiele in Bayreuth, or consuming fresh asparagus and white wine in charming little restaurants on the banks of the Rhine and Mosel rivers.

In the summer of 1982, while my personal staff and our clumber spaniels Feodor and Lady travelled by car, Arnaz and I took the short flight from Köln to Paris, filled with happy memories of Bonn, and looking forward to the challenges and excitement of Paris.

CHIAROSCURO

Shortly after our arrival in Bonn we located a veterinarian close to our residence in Köenigswinter, and took an unwell Feodor to him for treatment. It was not a pleasant experience for the dog, and less so for us. The veterinarian was surly and uncouth, and I could see that his rough and perfunctory examination had evoked much more than Feodor's usual class enmity towards vets. The latter could see that we were foreigners, but when he heard that we were also diplomats, he embarked upon a loud and forceful expression of political views that would gladden the heart of Changez Khan. After he had concluded by saying 'Not everything that Hitler did was bad', we took our leave and found ourselves another veterinarian. This was the only neo-Nazi that

I encountered during all the years that I spent in both East and West Germany.

* * *

Over a quiet dinner in Munich, Franz Josef Strauss related, with considerable relish, his role in the defection of Maxim Shostakovich, the young Soviet conductor and son of the famous composer Dmitry Shostakovich. It seems that Maxim, who was on a tour of West Germany with the Moscow Philharmonic Orchestra, had sent signals indicating his desire to defect to the West. He was, of course, under close and constant surveillance by two or three KGB guards who accompanied him everywhere. At a performance in Munich, Strauss had arranged for Bavarian security officers to be posted in the concert hall as ushers and toilet attendants. During one of the intervals, for the few moments that Shostakovich left his KGB guards watching the door outside the toilet, the Bavarian usher cum counterinsurgency officer hoisted the conductor through the skylight window of the 'gents' and lowered him into a police car waiting on the street outside.

This incident, which had some ingredients of a college prank, was recalled by Strauss with gleeful undergraduate bravado, complete with heavy winks and hearty chuckles. 'This was my personal revenge on the Ruskis,' said the prime minister of Bavaria.

* * *

There was a large Pakistani community in the Federal Republic of Germany, many of whom were legal residents, while most were illegal immigrants. The liberal asylum policies of the Bonn government were an incentive that had been fully exploited over the years, so, apart from those fleeing religious persecution, we had Pakistanis who claimed to have fled from political persecution by the Bhutto regime, and later by others who claimed to have fled from persecution by the Zia regime. Finally there were some who were fleeing the Soviet occupation in Afghanistan. Frequent instances of transit passengers seeking German asylum, as soon as they set foot on German soil in the transit lounge, compelled the immigration authorities to prohibit the use of sky bridges to the PIA, and insist that its aircraft be parked on the tarmac, and only those passengers holding valid documents could be brought in by bus.

There had always been a considerable Muslim population in the Federal Republic of Germany, most of whom were of Turkish origin, and it was rumoured that there were as many Turks in West Berlin as there were in Istanbul. One result of the increase in the Muslim influx was the establishment of numerous mosques all over the country, and one day Counsellor Cheema informed me that there had been an invitation for the ambassador to inaugurate a mosque which had been newly built by a congregation comprising both Pakistani and German origin Muslims. A cursory review of the modest theological knowledge that I possess in the case of my own religion indicated no barriers to performing such a function. I accordingly went to Frankfurt and inaugurated the mosque, speaking in Urdu and German, after which the designated Maulvi led the prayers. Arnaz happened to be in Pakistan at the time and was paying a courtesy call on Begum Zia when the president entered the room and informed her with some delight, 'Mrs Marker, I believe your husband has inaugurated a mosque in Germany!' When I mentioned this part of my activity to Roedad Khan during one of our regular telephone conversations, his reaction was, as usual, accurate, and perfunctory: 'Jimmy, this is unprecedented.'

MEANWHILE IN PAKISTAN

The flow of refugees from Afghanistan had by now become a flood, which would eventually extend to over three million people, most of whom were located in refugee camps in the North West Frontier Province and Balochistan. The problems posed to Pakistan by this huge influx were massive and multifarious. Firstly, there was the humanitarian aspect of having to provide shelter, food, clothing, and medical facilities for such a large group of displaced persons. Although foreign donors eventually made a considerable contribution, the major burden fell upon Pakistan. But as time went on, the camps became the recruiting grounds for the resistance movement, the storage area for their arms, and more ominously a centre for the production of drugs. The deplorable link between arms, drugs, and terrorism had just begun, and what later came to be known as the Kalashnikov culture had commenced in Pakistan.

In his cool, calculated and methodical manner, Ziaul Haq had embarked upon his two-track strategy of consolidating his own domestic position, whilst at the same time garnering support from abroad for his opposition to the Soviets. He was determined to give clout to Pakistan's newfound designation as 'a front line state'. In this connection his first act was to bring the ISI, which had hitherto been hovering tentatively on the sidelines of power, firmly onto centre stage. Its formidable Director General, Lt.-Gen. Akhtar Abdur Rehman, was made the point man for the entire Afghanistan operation, working directly with Zia. Shortly after the Soviet troops had moved into Kabul, Zia made a telephone call to the King of Saudi Arabia, the result of which was the establishment of a direct personal link between General Akhtar and Prince Turki bin Faisal, the head of Saudi intelligence. A short while later, immediately following the commencement of the Reagan administration, Zia was instrumental in establishing another high powered personal link, this time between General Akhtar and William Casey, the hawkish and fiercely anti-communist Director of the US Central Intelligence Agency. An agreement signed in 1981 provided the framework and outline for a package of arms supplies worth $3.2 billion over the following five years. Zia also made sure in the agreement that the distribution and supplies would be handled exclusively by the ISI, a condition that enabled the Agency not only to hold sway over the disparate Mujahideen groups but also to direct their activities. It was in this period of the Zia administration that the status of the ISI moved from lukewarm to red hot, and as a consequence it became the powerful agency it now is.

In the Foreign Ministry also, there was a significant change, with the retirement of Foreign Minister Agha Shahi. His successor was Sahibzada Yaqub Khan, a scholarly and sophisticated soldier-diplomat, who was a fluent linguist and had served as ambassador in Paris, Washington and Moscow. His removal as the martial law administrator in East Pakistan, because of his opposition to Yahya Khan's policies, brought to an end a distinguished military career during which, as Lieutenant General, he had been Ziaul Haq's superior officer in the Armoured Corps. When we first heard of this change of foreign ministers my good friend, the late Ambassador Aziz Khan, in reference to a bygone age of cricket which only a dedicated and ancient fan could understand, made the wry and apposite observation, 'I see that the Players are out, and the Gentlemen are now in.'

It was obvious that because Afghanistan was a crisis of international dimensions, it was absorbing most of Zia's time and attention. But this did not prevent him from dealing with a domestic situation that was by no means settled and required constant supervision. Although prepared to use ruthless methods, Zia mainly exercised power through his superb organizational capability. Of all the presidents with whom I have had the privilege to work, none had his hands more firmly on the administration. Also, coming from a pious and industrious middle class background, he seemed to have had a quite uncanny sense of the thoughts and feelings of the common man during the early years of his rule. His personal piety remains unquestioned, but observations during my repeated visits to Pakistan gradually convinced me that his emphasis on religion was a political tool that he was manipulating with some cynicism and much skill. Whilst this enabled him to attain his immediate objective of retaining power, its long-term consequences on the country were profoundly and disastrously reactionary.

Despite his external and internal preoccupations, Zia did not let his sight waver from his other major objective. It became obvious to me that, with the close collaboration of able patriots like Ghulam Ishaq Khan, Zia was pursuing the nuclear programme with stealth and determination. His policy towards India was also a most interesting study. Like all good generals, he did not believe in fighting on several fronts at the same time. Without being in any way effusive, he kept relations with New Delhi on an even keel, eschewed provocative pronouncements, and thus discreetly shifted Kashmir to the back-burner. As a sideline, he refurbished the Sikh shrines in Pakistan and encouraged pilgrimages, leading me to the suspicious thought that Zia had a secret soft spot for the Sikhs.

My visits to Islamabad had increased in frequency, involving not only conferences and meetings with visiting delegations, but also occasional restricted consultations with the president and foreign minister. These meetings were mostly late night sessions at the Army House, and provided me with a close exposure to Zia's methods of work. Always cool and composed, he was both a good listener and a quick learner, and never seemed to take offence, regardless of the outrageous nature of the provocation. The meetings were conducted in a civilized manner, and a frank and candid expression of views was encouraged, with Zia smoothly intervening to cool things down if the discussion became heated. Also, with Ghulam Ishaq as a frequent participant, one could be sure that the talks remained focused. Very often at the end of these meetings, I was unsure of what decisions, if any, had been taken, but I always left that drawing room with the certainty that there were sound hands at the helm of affairs. And always there was President Ziaul Haq to walk you to the door, shake hands warmly, see you into the car, and give you his farewell smile and bow, as you drove away.

CHAPTER TWENTY

France

We arrived in Paris in late July 1982 and moved straight into the embassy residence. This was a beautiful classical building, appropriately called an *hotel particulaire* in Paris, with a splendid interior of marble floors and columns, oak panelled and mirrored walls and doors, and a magnificent wide, marbled staircase at the top of which was an enormous and very valuable Gobelin tapestry. The living accommodation was also very ornate, but extremely comfortable. It was as good as any other embassy in Paris, and is probably the most beautiful of all our embassy buildings. It was purchased for the government by Sami Dehlavi when as Counsellor he opened our mission in Paris, and is one of the many monuments to the initiative and sagacity of this distinguished officer in his dedicated service to the country. It is situated in the most elegant part of Paris on the Rue du General Appert, a street so quiet that it remains as unknown to its citizens as the General after whom it was named. The chancery was another beautiful building, thanks again to Sami Dehlavi, with a large reception hall and elegant rooms for the officials, and was very centrally located on Rue Lord Byron, just off the Arc de Triomphe. It used to be one of my great pleasures, whenever I had the time and the weather permitted, to walk between the Residence and the chancery, along Hausmann's splendid broad boulevards, and past the beautiful stately buildings that he had constructed. Shortly after our arrival, whilst working in the office one afternoon, I received an alarming report that there had been an explosion outside our residence and that the building was being evacuated under threat of fire. I rushed back home to a scene of carnage and devastation, with flames coming out of the Iraqi embassy, which was situated adjacent to our residence, and the street filled with fire-fighters, ambulances, and security vehicles. The road had been blocked off and I had difficulty getting past the police cordon. I was immensely relieved to find that Arnaz and Feroza, as well as our domestic staff, were all well, and that although all the doors and windows had been completely shattered, the flames had not yet reached our beautiful building. In due course the efficient French fire-fighters extinguished the blaze and we were able to move back into the residence so that we could clear the rubble and repair some of the damage caused by the explosion. It seems that a vehicle loaded with explosives had been parked outside the Iraqi embassy and set to go off just when it was crowded with people who had come to pick up their visas. This was at the time when the Iran–Iraq war was at its height, and there was obviously no lack of well-wishers for our resident neighbours. However, the really chilling aspect of the incident was that Arnaz and Feroza were on their way home, and had walked past the bomb-laden vehicle and entered our residence a bare five minutes before the explosion. Truly, God had placed His beneficent hand over their beautiful heads.

The officers in our Paris embassy were, as to be expected, of the highest quality. The Deputy Chief of Mission was Mir Abad Hussain, a retired Brigadier who had done a spell at the Foreign Office, and brought to bear his considerable organizational skills and calm, measured assessment to our work. The other diplomatic officers were Counsellor Mustafa Kamal Kazi and First Secretary Shahid Kamal, both of whom were intelligent and dedicated officers, and each of whom went on to hold ambassadorial appointments later in their careers. Our Commercial Counsellor was Mirza Qamar Beg, a CSP officer with a brilliant mind, a depth of knowledge, wide-ranging interests and a subdued but very sharp sense of humour. We had an ample assortment of commercial relations with France, ranging from textiles to telecommunications, automobiles and power generation, and Qamar attended to the multifarious requirements, including the inevitable and vexatious trade disputes, with quiet efficiency, whilst also vigorously pursuing avenues for our exports. His office was situated some distance from the main chancery, but our working relations were so close and smooth that I never really noticed it. More importantly, Qamar ran such an efficient and effective operation that there was neither the desire nor the necessity for any supervision on my part. My role, with which I was quite content, was limited to hosting receptions for visiting commercial delegations, or opening the Pakistani pavilions that Qamar had skilfully organized at exhibitions. Qamar's lovely wife, Majo, comes from a leading Quetta family, and as Qamar has also served as Chief Secretary, Balochistan, we have a parochial as well as family friendship.

Our military relations with France were very important, particularly with the air force and the navy, and we had some outstanding air and naval attaches. Captain Khalid Mir, PN, and his successor Captain Zahir Shah, PN, were two of my colleagues who have become lifelong family friends. Both officers did a splendid job during their tenure in Paris, spoke fluent French, and previously had brilliant careers as submariners. Each went on to become an admiral in the Pakistan navy, and I must admit that my long-distant association with the service made me particularly partial to these two colleagues. Also, as a former lowly lieutenant it was reassuring, at last, to be able to look not one, but two, admirals in the eye and not quaver.

I presented credentials to President François Mitterrand at the Elysée Palace on 18 June 1982 in a simple ceremony abbreviated to the extent that written texts of our brief speeches were exchanged in advance and not delivered on the occasion. This provided more time for the informal conversation, between Mitterrand, Foreign Minister Claude Cheysson, and myself, that followed the ceremony. Naturally the Afghanistan issue figured prominently in the discussions, and Mitterrand said that 'in its refusal of accepting a *fait accompli*, and in lending a generous and helping hand to the victims of this situation, and indeed to a whole people, Pakistan may count on France's active support (and also) in the search for a political settlement'. Mitterrand did all the talking while the dour Cheysson occasionally grunted assent. This was my first encounter with a fascinating personality, whom I got to know quite well during my subsequent four years in France. Although we reached a reasonably good intellectual understanding, it never extended to emotional warmth. My initial impression of François Mitterrand was that of a person with obviously profound intelligence, which was reflected in a composure of great serenity and assurance. Kindly in expression and courteous in gesture and demeanour, he received me at a time when he was under pressure from some very difficult domestic issues, but nothing in his manner betrayed any suggestion that he was preoccupied with the most serious crisis that his government had faced since he had assumed office. In a phenomenon somewhat reminiscent of De Gaulle, François Mitterrand appeared to have acquired a Napoleonic aura of serene hauteur, characteristic of other great French leaders. This impression was somewhat paradoxically juxtaposed with that of a dedicated socialist, vigorously, and perhaps even injudiciously, committed to a crash programme of socio-economic egalitarianism in a basically conservative and individualistic society. François Mitterrand has been the subject of many studies and books, written both during and after his lifetime, and this eminent but enigmatic political leader will continue to attract the attention of historians and biographers for many years. His method of rule was almost universally viewed as being Byzantine: '*Il ne fai jamais ce qu'il dit, et il ne di jamais ce qu'il fait*' ('He never does anything that he says, and never says anything that he does') was the observation of Franz-Olivier Giesbert, a political columnist.

Mitterrand's wife, Danielle, was a doctrinaire socialist, far more committed to the ideology than her pragmatic husband, and was a lively and prominent political activist. In their personal lives there was both affection and understanding, and she accepted the fact that he had a mistress, by whom he had a daughter, both of whom lived in government-owned apartments on the exclusive Quai Branly. In accordance with sophisticated French social customs, the arrangements were accepted, everybody knew about it but nobody talked about it. At Mitterrand's state funeral, his wife, mistress, and her daughter were all in prominent attendance. One of Mitterrand's brothers, General Jacques Mitterrand and his wife Giselle became very good friends of ours. A graduate of St. Cyr, the elite French military academy, General Mitterrand followed a distinguished military career with his appointment as Director General of the General Delegation d' Armament (DGA), a state organization which supervised the entire French armament industry, including aircraft manufacture, shipyards, and arms production. In addition to these heavy responsibilities, General Mitterrand often served as a troubleshooter and undertook delicate and sensitive political missions abroad on behalf of his brother. Arnaz and I used to dine with the Mitterrands frequently, pleasurable occasions for stimulating conversation amidst smoke from the excellent cigars to which he and I were addicted, and which we used to exchange with enthusiasm. This social friendship was, of course, a tremendous asset in my diplomatic activity, but in addition it helped in promoting our specific objectives, since General Mitterrand headed an organization that was of considerable importance to our national armed forces. Pakistan had close ties with the French defence industry, having acquired sophisticated items such as Mirage aircraft, Agosta submarines, and Crotale anti-aircraft missiles. Since French sales were not subject to political constraints, either at the time of transaction or thereafter, the process possessed an obvious attraction. The disincentive was that the French knew this and had no compunctions about inflating their charges. The bottom line was, of course, that we each got what we wanted.

One of the interesting items revealed to me by General Mitterrand was the extent to which the French government was implementing its decision to support Iraq in its ongoing and bloody conflict with Iran. Following a visit by Deputy Prime Minister Tariq Aziz, the French agreed to supply Iraq with sixty Mirage fighter bombers, helicopters, and missiles. President Mitterrand had acceded to the Iraqi request for the ostensible reason that it was in the interest of Western Europe to maintain an equilibrium between Iran and Iraq, and that a power vacuum in Iraq following Saddam's defeat, coupled with a victorious and militant Iran, would constitute a grave threat to world peace. I considered that whilst this political assessment contained some merit, the basic factors which motivated Mitterrand's decision were somewhat more venal, and certainly much more fundamental. France had approximately $7 billion worth of investments tied up in export credit guarantees in Iraq and a further $3 billion in outstanding projects. Moreover, there was a crucial Saudi intervention on behalf of Saddam, since Iraq and Saudi Arabia accounted at that time for about 70 per cent of French arms exports. Just a month earlier, the Saudis had deposited $2 billion in French banks, with a public assurance of a further $6 billion, a gesture which had served to stabilize the French franc in a dramatic fashion. Under the circumstances it was difficult for Mitterrand to even demur at the Saudi suggestion that sophisticated aircraft be made available for Iraqi defence. This was the beginning of a major and sustained campaign of political support for Iraq, and one which was endorsed by most political leaders, including Jacques

Chirac. As I observed these developments, I thought to myself that not too long ago Ayatollah Khomeini had been the beneficiary of political asylum in France, from where he had flown to Tehran, and then had launched the revolution that brought down the Shah, establishing a regime which France now considered as a threat to the West. To my mild amusement I detected, in this scenario, something of the Lady Pettigrew syndrome.[1]

François Mitterrand's assumption of office in 1980 ended a spell of forty years spent in the political wilderness, and the prospect of confrontation with the legacy of rule under a constitution framed by General De Gaulle in 1966. Immediately after taking power, Mitterrand set in motion the most radical and wide-ranging transformation of France's socio-economic institutions since the Liberation. Key industries and nearly all private banks were nationalized, measures were taken for a genuine devolution of political and administrative power from Paris to the provinces, and large sums were invested in the increase of social security benefits. The results were not a complete success, because although these measures succeeded in creating a more egalitarian society, the economic consequences of attacking unemployment rather than inflation were nothing short of disastrous. Three devaluations of the French franc and an imposed period of austerity had brought the Mitterrand administration to its lowest point of popularity at the time that I arrived in Paris. However, confident in his assured term of seven years of office, a system imposed upon the Fifth Republic by De Gaulle over Mitterrand's bitter opposition back in 1966, Mitterrand and his socialists had by now continued their exercise of the vast administrative powers available to them under the constitution of the Fifth Republic, bequeathed to them by General De Gaulle. As I made my calls among the politicians and journalists, the differences between *les anciens* and *les nouveaux* were clearly noticeable, as was the acrimony that existed between them. The prime minister was Laurent Fabius, a bright, young, and dedicated socialist, whose family background as leading antique dealers did not prevent him from vigorously implementing the government's policies. However, as far as French foreign and defence policies were concerned, Mitterrand maintained the position of his predecessors. In Claude Cheysson as the Foreign Minister, whose tank had been amongst the first of the Free French armoured formations under General De Gaulle to enter Paris during the Liberation, and Charles Hernu as the Defence Minister, a distinguished expert on military affairs, President Mitterrand had two competent officials who supported him in maintaining a policy that had been initiated by De Gaulle. These concepts, which have remained largely unchanged over the years, are a defence force consistent with French political objectives and economic capability; an independent nuclear deterrent; a token military presence in NATO; and an independent Rapid Action Force (*Force de Frappe*) for emergency deployment in French overseas territories.

Quite soon after my arrival in Paris, I made a courtesy call on François de Grossouvre, Special Adviser to President Mitterrand. It was the beginning of a close and warm personal friendship that enriched our stay in France and provided Pakistan with an important and stalwart supporter for many years. De Grossouvre, who was a medical doctor, had been a close personal friend of Mitterrand for many years. As *Chargé de Mission*, de Grossouvre had his office in the Elysée Palace, in order to maintain constant contact with the president. Also, he and his girlfriend, the sweet and lovely Nicole Alheinc, lived in an apartment in the same exclusive residence as Mitterrand's mistress on the Quai Branly, an arrangement that enabled both couples to spend quiet evenings together, free from care and public scrutiny. De Grossouvre was an avid hunter, and as president of the Society of Hunters and Fishermen, used to organize the most lavish shoots at different chateaux in the beautiful French countryside. As far as I knew, president of this society was the only official position that he held, but from his small spartan office situated in the Elysée Palace a few metres from Mitterrand's own, ornate *cabinet*, de Grossouvre carried out the most delicate and sensitive missions, both domestic and foreign, assigned to him by the president. Perhaps his most important function was to supervise and coordinate the work of the different French intelligence agencies, and one of his most frequent interlocutors was the famous and formidable Comte Alexandre de Marenches, known in the world's shadowy intelligence fraternity by his code name Porthos. Arnaz and I escorted de Grossouvre and Nicole when they spent a week in Pakistan on an official visit. Apart from Islamabad, we went to Peshawar, Lahore and Karachi, and de Grossouvre had very productive meetings with the president, the foreign minister, the director general ISI, and the governors and chief ministers of the NWFP, Punjab, and Sindh. The discussions centred on the usual topics, and de Grossouvre backed up his verbal assurances of support with a satisfactory economic and military commitment. The arrangements made by the Foreign Ministry were excellent, and with a boar shoot in the Punjab and a partridge shoot in Sindh under his belt, he went home a happy man. For Arnaz and me, the week provided an opportunity to further our happy friendship with François and Nicole.

François de Grossouvre was a fit and compact little man, with a face that carried a trim goatee beard and a perpetually thoughtful expression. Always immaculately dressed, he was fastidious about clothes and manners, and had the true bearing of the French aristocrat that he was. Needless to say, the only language that he spoke was impeccable French. His high intelligence and decisiveness made him a formidable administrator, and he never suffered fools gladly, and his criticism could be quite scathing. Needless to say, these characteristics, coupled with his closeness to Mitterrand, made him a number of enemies, and he frequently anguished with me over their intrigues. But he was a man of intense loyalty and his fondness for Pakistan, and commitment to its cause, were absolutely sterling. Some years later, I was horrified to receive a telephone call from Said Dehlavi, our ambassador in Paris, informing me that de Grossouvre had committed suicide by shooting himself while seated in his office. There were rumours about possible murder, but all I could think about was the travails of my highly emotional friend, within the confines of Mitterrand's court, which had so often been described as Byzantine.

The Afghanistan crisis was being very closely followed at the Quai d'Orsay, and there was much interest in the diplomatic activity that it generated, particularly the 'proximity talks' under the auspices of the United Nations, and I was sometimes called to Geneva for consultations with Foreign Minister Yaqub Khan. At the same time in Paris, I used to discuss the issue with an old friend, Soviet Ambassador Yuli Vorontsov, one of the most able of Soviet diplomats and one of the sincerest and most humane persons that I have ever met. Vorontsov was too experienced a diplomat to say so, but he knew that the Soviet military intervention was a blunder, and his desire for a political solution through diplomatic methods was very evident. We, therefore, eagerly followed the twists and turns of the tortuous negotiations conducted in Geneva under UN auspices, by the Undersecretary General, Diego Cordovez, an adroit and resourceful Ecuadorean diplomat.

The cultural opportunities that were available in such profusion in Paris were a constant and unending delight, and one that Arnaz and I enjoyed to the fullest extent. We spent many happy hours together, as well as in the company of the many friends who visited and stayed with us in Paris, at the Louvre, and the many other museums and monuments which glorify the city. But my real delight was my personal exposure to the world of music, which has been a lifelong passion. The famous conductor Zubin Mehta, whose parents Mehli and Tehmina had been our old friends, came to Paris for a series of concerts, and spent quite a lot of time with us. Zubin introduced us to Daniel Barenboim, the Director of the Orchestre de Paris and one of the world's greatest pianists, who subsequently became as close a friend as Zubin. The months that followed were amongst the most magical of my life, and our friendship with these two artistic geniuses and their wives, Nancy and Elena, grew from those days into a lifetime of affection and understanding. On that early occasion of my association with them, Zubin and Daniel were preparing a formidable concert that comprised the First and Second Piano Concertos of Johannes Brahms, and were kind enough to permit me to sit in on their rehearsals. I had no compunction whatsoever in disappearing from my office and sitting spellbound for hours in the Salle Playel, watching and hearing these two superb musicians bring to life the glorious melodies of Brahms. I told them later that it was like sitting on the floor of the Sistine Chapel and watching Michelangelo at work on the ceiling. Later, we thanked the Orchestre de Paris by inviting the entire orchestra to dinner at the embassy residence for a rousing party laced with Pakistani food and music. I am told it is still remembered with pleasure.

Ustad Nusrat Fateh Ali Khan visited Paris with his troupe and was, quite literally, a roaring success. He was at that time almost unknown in the West, and came to France, under the auspices of our cultural agreement, for a brief tour. Among the limited attendance at his first concert were some representatives of Radio France, and seizing the opportunity offered by their enthusiasm, I persuaded them to broadcast a repeat performance of the concert on the radio. The large and positive listener response led to more public concerts as well as a recording contract. Nusrat's masterful artistry had now spread from his native land and had begun to take the world by storm. Years later, when we met at one of his large concerts in New York, the Ustad fondly recalled our earlier meetings in Paris. Now that he is no longer with us, I listen to his recordings, which continue to provide inspiration and joy, and in some magical fashion also project the humanism that radiated from this musical genius.

Events in South Asia were closely followed by the French during 1983–84, and whilst political issues were given due importance there was particular emphasis on economic collaboration, particularly in the case of India. There were a number of projects for profitable Franco–Indian collaboration, but above all the French, in their attempts to break the Soviet monopoly on arms supplies to India, achieved some success in the sale of Mirage aircraft and their subsequent assembly in India. An espionage-related scandal caused a temporary setback, but this was corrected through the efforts of General Jacques Mitterrand, who flew to New Delhi and smoothed ruffled feathers. The assassination of Indira Gandhi came as a particular shock since her Francophile attitude had constituted one of the pillars of the Franco–Indian collaboration. Consequently, when Rajiv Gandhi came on a state visit, shortly after assuming the office of the prime minister, he was given a rousing and extremely warm reception. But I was informed by officials at the Quai d'Orsay, even at that time, about their deep concern over the Indian military intervention in Sri Lanka. Subsequent events, such as the ignominious withdrawal of Indian forces and the assassination of Rajiv Gandhi, were proof that these reservations were well founded.

One morning I received an urgent summons from de Grossouvre, and was told on meeting him that his officials had just informed him that Shahnawaz Bhutto had died in Nice under mysterious circumstances. I immediately informed Islamabad and was told that Mohsin Manzour, an official from our High Commission in London, would proceed to the area in order to help the French authorities in their investigations. In the meantime, I followed developments through de Grossouvre and his intelligence team, which was clearly the most effective course to follow. The final report, conveyed to me verbally by de Grossouvre after about six weeks, was that the incident had commenced in a restaurant in Nice, where the immediate Bhutto family, comprising Begum Nusrat, Benazir, Sanam, Murtaza, and Shahnawaz, together with their wives, had gathered for dinner. There was a heated conversation, reportedly over money matters, and the brothers came to blows. The party then broke up, and Shahnawaz and his wife, after returning to their hotel room, were followed by Murtaza, and another altercation took place between the brothers. The French police, when they arrived at the scene a little later found that Shahnawaz was dead and accordingly arrested his wife and Murtaza. The latter was released on production of a Syrian diplomatic passport and immediately fled the country. Shahnawaz's wife was charged under a French law that imposes culpability on any person that fails to assist, or call for assistance, in aid of a victim in distress. I was told that she had obtained a lawyer and was prepared to defend herself in court, but was dissuaded from doing so by the family, and eventually both wives left the country. Although no autopsy was carried out, the French thought that a drug overdose was the cause of death. De Grossouvre told me that the French Law Minister Robert Badinter, who was a friend of the Bhutto family, had helped in bringing the unsavoury affair to a close. The French intelligence authorities, having ascertained that the case had no terrorist connections or implications, and also taking into consideration the fact that no French nationals were involved in the matter, had decided to take no further action. After all, de Grossouvre informed me cynically, a *crime de passion* was neither unusual nor infrequent amongst the locals and foreigners who inhabited and intermingled in the glitzy world of the south of France.

The Pakistan ambassador in Paris was also accredited as Representative to the UNESCO, and I duly presented credentials to its Director General Amadou-Mahtar M'Bow. An intelligent and forceful Senegalese diplomat, he ran the organization with a combination of arrogant authority and manipulative skill that made him more feared than admired as an administrator. We had two representatives who were regular and very welcome visitors from Pakistan. The first of these was Dr Atiya Inayatullah who attended the regular sessions of UNESCO and later became a member of the executive board, and the other was Justice Abdul Kader Sheikh, whose sterling work on

Mohenjo Daro brought him to Paris regularly. Atiya's lively enthusiasm, tireless efforts, and networking skills, made her a very effective delegate and a worthy representative of Pakistan. Justice Sheikh was the point man on Mohenjo Daro, which had been declared a World Heritage Site by the United Nations, and the preservation of which was the responsibility of UNESCO. It was thanks to the efforts of Justice Sheikh, and the trust and confidence in his ability reposed by states members of UNESCO that we were able to secure the funds and the technical expertise for the preservation of this famous prehistoric site.

As for UNESCO, the high-handed conduct of the director general, and his often whimsical decisions, had created considerable dissatisfaction among the delegations, particularly the United States and other Western nations. Added to this was his adroit use of delegates, particularly from Africa, whose support he obtained through offers of jobs and perks, a modus operandi that added to the anger of his opponents. Like all bureaucratic empire builders, he indulged in and tolerated unethical practices, so that a sense of corruption began to emerge from UNESCO headquarters. The last straw that broke the camel's back was his overambitious plan to set up, within UNESCO, an international news agency organization. The United States strongly resisted this move and put teeth into its opposition by withdrawing from the organization, a Republican administration move that was both radical and unprecedented. This action was immediately followed by Singapore, while other Western nations greatly reduced their contributions, leaving the organization to operate under severe financial constraints. At the time that I left Paris, UNESCO was limping in a somewhat forlorn fashion, and the situation was only restored after M'Bow had retired from office. When the time came to elect his successor Pakistan suffered a setback, because although Dr Abdus Salam, the distinguished Nobel Laureate, had expressed an interest in the post, the government's official choice was Foreign Minister Sahibzada Yaqub Khan. This was a mistake, because all of his sterling qualities could not overcome the incongruity, in international eyes, of a former general heading a United Nations organization dedicated to education and culture. After taking preliminary soundings we wisely withdrew the nomination, but I am quite certain that Professor Salam could have won the post in a canter.

The World Bank Consortium on Aid to Pakistan, which held its annual meetings in Paris, was attended by senior officials from the ministries of finance and economic affairs in Islamabad. These were important negotiations, chaired by a World Bank vice-president, and during my tenure the Pakistani delegations, which were led in succession by Finance Minister Mahbub ul Haq, Finance Secretary A.G.N. Kazi, and Ejaz Naik, Secretary Economic Affairs, achieved significant results. This was due not only to the satisfactory state of the country's financial and economic situation, but also to the thorough professionalism and negotiating skills of our representatives. As the Pakistan ambassador in Paris was also included in the delegation, I had the good fortune to follow the proceedings in some detail. Our delegations came with briefs that were meticulously prepared and they made their presentations with confidence, but above all, I was impressed by their thorough knowledge and understanding of World Bank procedures and methods of work. It all made for smooth negotiations leading to satisfactory results.

The Aga Khan had located his Jamatkhana at Aiglemont, in the beautiful countryside north of Paris, with a splendid chateau as his residence and a modern building as his office. From this elegant location the Aga Khan, assisted by his brother Prince Amyn, directed with great success an organization that is unique in history. His Highness Karim Aga Khan displayed admirable sagacity from the very young age at which he became the Imam of the Ismaili community, and over the years he humbly fulfilled his religious obligations to his disciplined adherents worldwide, in the impeccable style and manner that maintained their devotion and unity. At the same time the Aga Khan conceived and built a prosperous modern enterprise, with global economic and commercial impact, and included banking, hotels and resorts, transport and communications, and other varied activities. Most important of all was the Aga Khan Foundation, whose activities ranged over Africa, South Asia, and Central Asia, and which established modern, well-run hospitals, universities and centres of excellence, as well as a host of development projects. Last but not the least was the emphasis that the Aga Khan placed on Islamic architecture, art and history, through the establishment of a number of foundations and prizes. Being an essentially modest person, His Highness carried out these high profile duties in almost complete anonymity, and abhorred publicity of any kind. His considerable experience and global presence gave him access to several heads of state and government who sought his counsel on a variety of issues, knowing that it would always be motivated by a desire for good governance and the betterment of peoples. Notwithstanding his low public profile, which he maintains with great deliberation, there is no doubt that the Aga Khan is one of the great personalities of the century, with an influence that is as wide-ranging as it is beneficial. We got to know him and his family very well in Paris, and worked on a number of issues that were of importance to Pakistan, both in terms of his own organization and in his intersession on our behalf with world leaders. Dinners at Aiglemont were always splendid affairs, with guests from the highest strata of French and international political, financial, and literary circles. Although himself a teetotaller and non-smoker, the Aga Khan's wine cellar at Aiglemont was reputed to be among the best in France.

During the latter part of my stay in Paris there was a considerable increase in my peripheral involvement in the negotiations over Afghanistan. This included frequent discussions with Yuli Vorontsov in Paris, as he continued to exercise considerable influence on the issue in Moscow. It also involved visits to Geneva, Rome, and London at the times when Yaqub had meetings in these capitals. The UN-sponsored negotiations had not so far produced any substantive results but were, thanks to Diego Cordovez's lively and sometimes erratic negotiating techniques, capable of producing the occasional surprise. It was against this tense but confused background that I received a visit from Walter Zimmermann, an American citizen resident in Paris. What follows is an intriguing tale of a shadow chase being woven in Paris, and played out at the highest levels in Islamabad and Moscow. In retrospect, the net result appeared to me to have been some shadow boxing in Islamabad, Moscow, New York, and Paris, with political consequences that were equally shadowy. It also led to the creation of a very good friendship between Wally Zimmermann and myself.

On 16 September 1985, Walter Zimmermann called at my residence, introduced himself as an American businessman residing in Paris, and recalled his earlier business activities in Pakistan, where he had met

Arnaz during his stay at the Metropole Hotel in Karachi. He said that he was currently engaged on a wide range of projects in the Soviet Union, and that he had extensive contacts with high levels of the leadership in Moscow. Zimmermann said that three days earlier, in Moscow, he had been pulled out of a meeting with the vice-president of Gosplan (the USSR Planning Commission), and summoned to a meeting with Soviet Deputy Prime Minister G. Marchuk, who was responsible for Science and Technology, and Major General G.L. Kotov, of the KGB. They told Zimmermann that the Soviet Union was dissatisfied with the situation in Afghanistan and that Mikhail Gorbachev wanted to enter into direct negotiations with Pakistan, as he felt that the UN process was too slow. For this purpose the Soviets wished to use Zimmermann to contact the Pakistani authorities in order to commence negotiations at a reasonably high level, and left the arrangements to Zimmermann's discretion, stressing only the complete secrecy of the undertaking. When the latter expressed reservations on the grounds that he was essentially a businessman, Kotov said that eighteen years of business relations had convinced the KGB of Zimmermann's reliability and hinted that his response would obviously affect the course of his future business.

Zimmermann replied that he could do no more than report this conversation to the Pakistan ambassador in Paris. Zimmermann added to me that from his conversation he had gathered the impression that the Soviets were willing to withdraw their forces from Afghanistan according to a schedule, if the Pakistanis prevented border infiltration. I expressed surprise and scepticism to Zimmermann. When there were competent ambassadors present in Moscow, Islamabad, and New York, who would obviously respect the Soviet desire for secrecy, this clandestine approach, through the indirect contact of the Ministry of Science and Technology, appeared to be highly dubious. Zimmermann agreed, and said that he could only repeat to me what he had promised to his Soviet interlocutors. He thought that the offer was a serious one and that the Soviets were expecting an early response. I immediately reported this development to government, and in the meantime did a background check on Zimmermann through the help of François de Grossouvre and his intelligence agencies. I learned that Zimmermann was born in north-eastern China of missionary parents and received his early education there. He spoke Russian, Chinese, French, and

German fluently, and had worked in the Office of Strategic Services of the USA (OSS) in the China–Burma–India theatre in the Second World War. He later told me that he was 'a trained intelligence officer'. He had built up a very successful business and had residences in Paris, Geneva, Nice, and Monte Carlo. French intelligence confirmed his extensive Soviet business activities, and gave him a clean bill of health in terms of his political and business ethics. After due consideration, we decided to go with Zimmermann on a Track II[2] basis of negotiations and, taking into account his nationality, informally conveyed this to the Americans. He made several trips to Moscow, and also met the president and prime minister in Islamabad, and for a while it appeared that the various verbal messages, drafts and non-papers exchanged between the parties might lead to something substantial, especially when Kutov asked for reassurance that General Arif was in the picture—'It is important that the army on both sides should be informed,' he said. However, when the last feeler that was sent from our side met with no response, we decided to let Track II disappear. While later discussing the reasons for this, Wally Zimmermann felt that the Soviet decision was probably prompted by the unexpected recent progress in the Geneva negotiations. A further factor could have been Gorbachev's apprehension that Viktor Grishin, his rival in the Politburo, might make use of the forthcoming Communist Party Congress to accuse Gorbachev of commencing secret negotiations with Pakistan whilst Soviet soldiers were being killed in Afghanistan. Whatever the reason, while Track II died a peaceful death, my personal friendship with Wally Zimmermann bloomed, until his own peaceful death some years later.

The supply of a nuclear reprocessing plant was perhaps the one contentious issue in our relations with France, and was never really resolved. The Pakistan Atomic Energy Commission had signed an agreement for the supply of this plant and had already made a substantial down payment, when the French government, under intensive United States pressure, intervened, and prevented the sale and export of the equipment. Despite diplomatic efforts at the highest levels of our president, the prime minister, and the foreign minister, successive French administrations maintained their position, and had no compunction about having reneged upon an international political, as well as a commercial, agreement. Our forlorn efforts at the level of the International Chamber of Commerce obtained some token repayments, but the reprocessing plant was never obtained.

The legislative elections of March 1986 brought about a dramatic and significant change in French domestic politics. The Constitution of the Fifth Republic, which had been framed by General De Gaulle, made this in no sense a straightforward election, conducted in order to designate the transfer of political power, through the simple expression of popular will. The elections pertained only to the legislature, and left the president untouched in the exercise of his formidable powers for a further two-year period. This system worked perfectly so long as the president and prime minister were of the same political persuasion, but the legislative elections of March 1986 were won by a rightist coalition led by the charismatic Jacques Chirac and his Gaullist Rassemblement pour la République (RPR) party. This compelled Mitterrand, the Socialist President, to work with Chirac, the Gaullist Prime Minister, under a system that was immediately named 'cohabitation', which unleashed a whole host of problems.

Under the French Constitution the president's powers included the appointment of the prime minister and other ministers who subsequently have to obtain parliamentary approval; the right to preside over all cabinet meetings; as commander-in-chief of the armed forces, the right to preside over meetings of the National Defence Committee; responsibility for negotiating and ratifying all treaties and international agreements; refusal to sign new laws and return legislation for reconsideration by the National Assembly; and refusal to accept the prime minister's recommendations for senior civil and military posts. Finally, and most important of all, the president was empowered to 'take exceptional measures', if he considers that the institutions or the security of the country are in danger. On the other hand, the major curb on the presidential powers was contained in Article 20 of the constitution, which stipulates that while the president is responsible for the overall requirement of 'the regular functioning' of the government, it is for the prime minister 'to determine and conduct the policy of the nation'. In addition to this, the prime minister also possesses significant additional executive powers, for he is 'responsible for national defence', and appointment of all senior military and civil officers. His countersignature is required on ratification of all treaties and the appointment of ambassadors. On legislative issues the prime minister's powers are even more substantive, for he cannot be removed from office unless he tenders his government's resignation, and he must be consulted before the assembly is dissolved. Finally, the prime minister exercises a tight control over the budget of the president. Under the constitution, the budget of the Elysée is strictly limited to the salaries of the domestic staff and a modicum of entertainment offered by the president. All other allocations, including travel expenses at home and abroad, appointment of presidential counsellors etc. had to be obtained through the office of the prime minister and the ministries concerned. Given this glaring potential for conflict, it came as no surprise to me that problems in 'cohabitation' became increasingly manifest during the last few months of my tenure in France. I discerned at that time some ominous similarities with the situation in Pakistan: the 'cohabitation' between President Ziaul Haq and Prime Minister Mohammad Khan Junejo was turning into a tussle.

In France, as in most other countries in Western Europe, there were a large number of Pakistani nationals, most of whom were illegal immigrants, and lived in considerable hardship. My instructions to our consular staff was to give them every form of assistance, and above all not to be concerned about their illegal immigrant status, which I regarded as the responsibility of the French authorities. Possession of a Pakistani driving licence was helpful in securing employment, but it needed certification by our embassy. In the past we would refer the case to the issuing authority in Pakistan for confirmation of authenticity, and it could take months for a reply, if one ever came. I changed the procedure and instructed our consular staff to certify the licence two weeks after application, unless we received a rejection from Pakistan during that period. Also, there was a square in the city, which came to be known as Pakistan Chowk, where Pakistani immigrants used to gather in the mornings and be recruited for casual manual labour on a daily basis by French employers, mostly in the textile business. I made it a point to visit Pakistan Chowk at least two mornings in a month to meet these people and ascertain if we could help them in any way. We would then gather in a humble, nearby bistro for a chat and a cup of coffee, and I found these sessions with my deprived countrymen, to be quite as enjoyable as any meal in an elegant Parisian restaurant.

In mid-March 1986 I was instructed to join the prime minister's delegation in Stockholm, where he and the foreign minister had gone to attend the funeral of the Swedish prime minister. Whilst there, I was informed by Prime Minister Junejo that I had been selected as the next Pakistani ambassador to Washington, and that I was expected to take up my new assignment in the summer.

In July 1986 Prime Minister Junejo made a brief working visit to Paris, and met both President Mitterrand and Prime Minister Chirac. We reviewed the satisfactory nature of Franco–Pakistan relations, and concluded some economic cooperation agreements, as well as the upgrading of military equipment. Since the Government had accepted my suggestion to exclude from our agenda the reprocessing plant issue, for I saw no point in flogging the carcass of a horse that was already long dead, the talks went quite smoothly. An interesting development was Chirac's request to Junejo for Pakistan's good offices in French attempts 'to improve relations with Iran'. As a consequence Foreign Minister Yaqub Khan took up the matter with Iranian Foreign Minister Dr Ali Akbar Velayati during a meeting in Islamabad the following month, and the text of the Iranian proposals was conveyed by me to Chirac. Following further communications between the two sides, which were conveyed by Velayati to Yaqub and Chirac to me, an agreement was reached, whereby the Iranians released some French hostages and the French released $350 million in frozen funds. Diplomatic relations were then established between Paris and Tehran, and Chirac expressed to me his profuse gratitude for Pakistan's efforts.

Two pleasant events of a personal nature figured in my very happy, and I think productive, tenure in Paris, which ended in the summer of 1986. The first was a farewell lunch at the Elysèe Palace given in honour of Arnaz and myself by President François Mitterrand, a gesture which was somewhat unusual. It was an intimate and informal affair, attended by about fifteen close friends. Since Mme Mitterrand was out of the country, the president was kind enough to suggest that Arnaz should substitute for his wife at the head of the table. The honour of a luncheon with the President could not have been compounded in a more gracious fashion. The other honour was the decision of the French government to confer upon me the award of

Grand Officier de L 'Ordre National du Mérite, in recognition of my contribution to Franco–Pakistan relations.

Goethe once said that Paris was the centre of the world. Victor Hugo was more modest, and declared Paris as the centre of Europe. As we said a fond farewell to the lovely city, and boarded an Air France jet for Washington, I decided that I was on the side of the German.

CHIAROSCURO

The famous Egyptian actor, Omar Sharif, was naturally the cynosure of all eyes at a dinner at our embassy. Like all our other guests, Arnaz and I thought that he was even more good-looking in real life than he appeared on the screen, and his polite modesty added to the considerable charm of his conversation. In addition to being a movie superstar, he was also a bridge player of international repute, and I knew that his regular columns on the game had been syndicated in newspapers worldwide. What I did not know, until that evening at my residence, was that he was a great cricket enthusiast, having played the game as a schoolboy in Alexandria. His eyes lit up when told about my past connection with the sport as a test match commentator in Pakistan, and from the lively conversation that followed it was clear that he had a very sound knowledge of cricket. This led to his suggestion that we organize a friendly fixture in Paris, collecting players from the various Commonwealth embassies and foreign business houses in the city. 'Let's have a match,' he said with a wink and a wicked grin, 'Whites vs. Wogs!'

* * *

When we visited Monaco, illness prevented Prince Rainier from meeting us on our scheduled official call, and we were received instead by Her Serene Highness Princess Caroline, whom we found to be beautiful, charming, and gracious. At the time of our departure I extended to her, as was customary, an invitation to a dinner in her honour at the embassy the next time that she was in Paris. Some weeks later I received a call from the Palace in Monte Carlo, and was pleasantly surprised to find that what I thought had been a pro forma invitation had in fact been accepted, and that Princess Caroline had even suggested a date and time. In confirming this, I requested a guest list and an indication of any security measures that might be required. With the guest list came the reply that whilst special security was not necessary, it was requested that representatives from the press and TV that accompanied the princess would be admitted into the embassy and allowed to cover the proceedings.

The dinner went off very well. Princess Caroline, who was accompanied by her husband, looked lovely, was as charming and gracious as ever, and appeared to have enjoyed herself very much. But camera crews of all description covered the event, from the princess's arrival at the embassy door, through cocktails and dinner, until the farewells exchanged on the Rue du Général Appert. It is doubtful if so many klieg lights had ever decked the walls of our embassy premises. I concluded that the evening was, in fact, a part of the function of the duties of Monaco royalty, which was to project the image of the glamour and sophistication that epitomizes the unique nature of Monte Carlo, and is so essential to its viability.

* * *

We had arranged a partridge shoot in Sindh for François de Grossouvre during his visit to Pakistan. Our host was the genial and ever hospitable Pir Mahfouz, whose arrangements were splendid as always. As de Grossouvre was an excellent shot he accumulated a substantial bag. He also evoked the admiration of the beaters, who had seen, over time, a great many VIP hunters. In accordance with their customary instructions, they followed the sycophantic tradition of slipping a few extra birds into the collection of the VIP guest. De Grossouvre noticed this and deliberately rejected all attempts to add to his bag any bird that he had not shot. This added to the *haris*' (farmers') admiration of him, and I overheard one of them say to another that the visitor was 'a real *shikari* (hunter), not like a Pakistani general'.

* * *

In October 1985, President Ziaul Haq stopped for a day in Paris on his way home from the USA, and had a very successful meeting with President Mitterrand. The Pakistani delegation was lodged on the third floor of the famous Hotel Crillon. The prime minister of Israel, who was then on an official visit to France, was also lodged with his delegation on the second floor of the same hotel. As a result, the elegant public rooms of the Hotel Crillon were filled with Pakistani and Israeli diplomats and staff members simultaneously trying to avoid and yet bumping into each other. Ambassador Mark Sofer of Israel, an ardent Likud man, was intelligent, sharp, and aggressive— qualities to be expected in an Israeli representative in a high profile post like Paris.

At the conclusion of his visit, President Zia, escorted by the French chief of protocol, walked through the foyer of the Crillon on his way to enter the motorcade parked at its entrance, on the Place de la Concorde. I was walking a few paces behind them, accompanied by Ambassador Michel Combal, the Chief of the Asia Division at the Quai d'Orsay. Just then Ambassador Sofer, who happened to be standing in the lobby at the time, made a quick dash across the room and greeted President Zia with a warm handshake. Camera flashbulbs gave me the sinking feeling that the Israelis had recorded the incident, and the gesture was all the more irritating because it had taken me by surprise. Zia was his usual courteous self and responded to Sofer's handshake with equal warmth. Immediately afterwards I revealed to the president the identity of the man who had just greeted him, and apologized for my inability to forestall the encounter. Zia was completely unfazed, 'Marker Sahib, if someone has the courtesy to come over and shake my hand, of course I will also shake him by the hand.'

MEANWHILE IN PAKISTAN

The Afghanistan problem had by now become a major political issue within Pakistan, with ramifications that extended over the entire spectrum of national life. The Reagan administration's support for General Ziaul Haq was manifest in the $3.2 billion aid package that was put into motion, some of which was delivered in covert fashion through the CIA–ISI channel, with General Akhtar Abdul Rehman in charge of the distribution process. Whilst stoking the fires of resistance within Afghanistan, Zia maintained, in typical fashion, the facade of negotiations with the Soviets for a peaceful settlement. A meeting with the CPSU General Secretary Yuri Andropov in November 1982 produced only a Soviet declaration of disbelief in Pakistan's profession of good intentions. A subsequent meeting between Zia and an emergent Gorbachev in March 1985 was little short of disastrous, with the Soviet leader abruptly terminating the proceedings. 'In general, it [Zia's presentation] was pure demagoguery, with a perversion of facts' was Gorbachev's scathing report to the Central Committee of the Soviet Communist Party.

At the same time, and as Pakistan entered into negotiations under the UN auspices, Zia's appointment of Sahibzada Yaqub Khan as the Foreign Minister completed the trio of Presidency, ISI, and the Foreign Ministry that would henceforth exercise a co-ordinated control over Afghan policy, with Zia remaining, as always, *primus inter pares*.

The KGB, in co-ordination with the Afghan intelligence agency Khadamat-e Etela'at-e Dawlati (KHAD), had not been idle, and found a useful surrogate in the Al Zulfikar Organization (AZO) led by Murtaza Bhutto, the son of Zulfikar Ali Bhutto, who was receiving funds from Muammar Qaddafi. They directed operations first from Kabul and then from Damascus. The AZO failed in two attempted missile attacks on President Zia's special aircraft, but succeeded in taking a hijacked PIA plane to Kabul, where, on orders from Murtaza, they shot one of the passengers, a Pakistan foreign service officer, and released the aircraft and remaining hostages in exchange for PPP activists imprisoned by Zia. Increasingly efficient and ruthless measures adopted by the Pakistani intelligence and security agencies prevented further incidents of a spectacular nature, but bomb blasts in urban centres continued.

Ziaul Haq, meanwhile, proceeded to consolidate his grip on power. Initially this was done by draconian application of martial law punishments, but later, as the country subsided into acquiescence, he methodically brought the administration into line, first by exploiting the bureaucracy's instinctive willingness to co-operate with authority, and then by refurbishing it with a substantive influx of military personnel. In due course, Zia imposed his authority on every aspect of civilian administration, and conducted the affairs of state in the same deft and implacable fashion till the end of his regime. Of all the presidents with whom I have worked, the grip that Ziaul Haq exercised on the conduct of government was without doubt the most firm. In his heyday, not only did he seem to have his hands on all the levers of power, but also appeared to have an uncanny finger on the public pulse. Thus, the creeping Islamization that he wrought into the body politic of the nation was achieved with the stealth and force of a strong and deep undersea current. In the army he was the first commander-in-chief who was not from the Sandhurst–Indian Military Academy elite, and his humble middle class origins, which he acknowledged with pride, gave him a thorough feel for the moods and sentiments prevalent in the myriad components of the powerful organization that he led. Although it is a matter of no great consequence, I noticed, with much personal regret, the evolution in ceremonial that came about in regimental officers' messes, the slow disappearance of traditional dinner nights, with gleaming silver on the tables and the circulation of port after the meal. But I knew and accepted that times had changed.

On the economic front there had been a noticeable resurgence, thanks to prudent management by a disciplined bureaucracy under Ghulam Ishaq Khan, and the timely infusion of US and foreign assistance. This factor, coupled with the prevalence of public order that had been imposed by military rule, had combined to lull the country into a state of perceived stability. But the presence of a glaring political vacuum could not be disguised for long, and it was this issue that next attracted the attention of General Ziaul Haq. Conscious of the need for political legitimacy, he established a nominated assembly of advisers, appropriately named Majlis-e-Shura, but soon realized that it was at best a temporary answer to the problem. He then resorted to holding a referendum, the standard formula applied by all authoritarian regimes seeking legitimacy. And, as is normal on such occasions, the person who calls the referendum also defines the rules of procedure— not unlike selecting the style and colour when picking a suit. In this case, instead of lifting the garment off the readymade shelf, Zia, who was never less than himself, decided to go in for a bit of bespoke tailoring. The referendum was framed as a 'yes or no' answer to support for the President's policies to 'bring the laws of Pakistan in conjunction with the injunctions of Islam as laid down in the Holy Quran and Sunnah'. An affirmative vote would automatically be regarded as confirmation of Zia's election as president for a five-year term. The not unforeseen result of the referendum was announced by the Election Commission, which also reported a 60 per cent turnout of voters. Opposition leaders and some impartial observers reported substantial rigging.

Zia's next move was to hold party-less elections to the National Assembly, a process which was duly completed in 1985, with the party affiliations of members clearly known though not pronounced. Immediately thereafter, Zia appointed as Prime Minister Mohammad Khan Junejo, a long-standing member of the Pakistan Muslim League, and a lesser known but very upright and honest politician from Sindh. It was a fateful choice that was to have unforeseen and uncomfortable consequences for both men. The constitution that Zia thought he had so carefully framed contained the fatal flaw, from his standpoint, of vesting executive authority in the prime minister, who was responsible for the daily working of the government. The president only retained the right to dismiss the prime minister and his government, followed by fresh elections. In the rivalry that almost immediately ensued between Zia and Junejo, it became clear that whilst the president retained the 'nuclear' option, the prime minister possessed the 'conventional' weapons, which Junejo was using with increasing assertiveness in the conduct of national affairs. The relationship got off to a disastrous start when, according to reliable accounts, Junejo asked Zia at their first meeting, 'When are you going to lift the martial law, Mr President?' My visits to Pakistan on consultations took place during the time of this uncomfortable transition period, and to me it was a bit like Mitterrand, Chirac, and 'Cohabitation' all over again. At that time I had exercised considerable tact and caution in my dealings with the two most powerful men in France. Now I was again required to exercise the same due diligence, only this time it was my president, my prime minister, and my country.

In the summer of 1986, whilst still in Paris, I was included in the delegation of Prime Minister Junejo on his official visit to Washington. As the ambassador-designate, I joined Ambassador Ejaz Azim, my soon-to-be predecessor, in the talks that Junejo had with the US leadership. The talks went off very well, as the events in Afghanistan had generated a great deal of goodwill and support for us, and above all because of the enthusiastic endorsement of President Ronald Reagan himself. The formal session between the two delegations provided me with the first opportunity to meet the charismatic

American president, and I was instantly impressed by his kind and humane attitude. I had heard and read unkind, and obviously uninformed, tales about Reagan's vagueness and lapses of concentration, slanderous innuendos that had frequently emanated from vicious and frustrated elements in the left wing media. This first encounter with President Reagan convinced me that nothing could be further from the truth. He was in complete command of the session, fully aware of all the issues, focused in his approach and decisive in his manner. At the formal session Reagan was assisted by Vice-President George Bush; Secretaries of State, Treasury, and Defence (George Schultz, Jim Baker, and Caspar Weinberger, respectively); Chief of Staff Don Regan; Admiral John Poindexter, the Chairman of the National Security Council; and Undersecretary of State Michael Armacost. This was a group of officials of formidable power and talent, but there was no doubt about their complete acceptance and deep respect for the leadership of the president. Reagan was at all times sharp and focused, but was never overbearing and did not hesitate to seek advice and opinions from his colleagues whenever necessary. Above all, he conducted proceedings with an easy informality and a great sense of humour.

Participation in Prime Minister Junejo's delegation to Washington also provided me with an opportunity for early interaction with the new political and bureaucratic association that was emerging in Islamabad. Sahibzada Yaqub Khan continued as the Foreign Minister, but Zain Noorani was inducted as the Minister of State for Foreign Affairs, and played an active part both in the Foreign Ministry and the National Assembly. Zain, who was an old family friend, was an ardent and loyal Muslim Leaguer of long-standing. His background was in journalism and public relations, blended with the 'street smart' political activity of Karachi. It was difficult to resist the impression that he had been brought in by his patron Junejo to keep an eye on Yaqub, who had been Zia's nominee. Noorani later became Foreign Minister for a brief period, the crowning glory of his tenure being his presence in Geneva and his signature on the accords that were signed there. But he ended up as a casualty in the fallout of the 'nuclear' option eventually exercised by Zia.

Perhaps the most significant development in the politics of Pakistan during this period was the removal of martial law in December 1985.

This was followed, in April 1986, by the return of Benazir Bhutto from exile in Europe. She was accorded a tremendous reception in Lahore and Karachi, followed by equally enthusiastic responses in her countrywide tour. Other political parties also began to reorganize and commenced their activities. The country had become weary after eight years of Zia's stifling Puritanism, and the politicians who sensed this only too well were beginning to sharpen their knives, as they cast their longing eyes on the ballot boxes. It occurred to me at this time that military rulers have only a fixed shelf life; politicians, on the other hand, are a recyclable commodity. As my friend Abu Kureishi said, 'Do not believe that any Pakistani politician is finished until you actually attend his *chelum*'.[3]

NOTES

1.   'The Devil, having nothing else to do
     Went off to tempt my Lady Pettigrew.
     My lady, tempted by a private whim,
     To his extreme annoyance, tempted him.'
     – Hillaire Belloc
2.   Track II diplomacy is a specific kind of diplomacy in which non-officials (academic scholars, retired civil and military officers, social activists, public figures, etc.) engage in dialogue, with the aim of conflict-resolution or confidence-building.
3.   Religious rites performed for the deceased forty days after the funeral.

CHAPTER TWENTY-ONE

Ireland

'I know that I shall meet my fate
Somewhere among the clouds above;
Those that I fight I do not hate,
Those that I guard I do not love;
My country is Kiltartan Cross,
My countrymen Kiltartan's poor;
No likely end could bring them loss
Or leave them happier than before.'

– William Butler Yeats
From 'An Irish Airman Foresees his Death'

The concurrent accreditation to Ireland assigned to the Pakistan ambassador to France was a bit like putting delicious icing on a very rich cake, and was an act of benign generosity which is usually noticeably absent in the administration department of our Foreign Office. The only drawback was that heavy commitments in Paris prevented me from visiting Ireland as frequently as I would have wished, and spending longer periods of time in that beautiful country.

I presented credentials to Dr Patrick Hillery, the President of the Republic of Ireland, in Dublin, on a misty morning in November 1982. The simple ceremony comprised a review of a guard of honour, followed by short speeches as the credentials were presented, and an informal conversation with the president thereafter. I briefly reported on the current regional situation, mentioned the Afghan problem, and gave a short account of President Ziaul Haq's ongoing peace initiatives with India. Dr Hillery was a slim man of medium height and immaculate bearing. Soft spoken, intelligent, and kindly, he had the scholarly look and manner of his academic background, and it left me to wonder how he had managed to cope with the rambunctious politics of Ireland. Clearly there must have been a steel frame under that velvet exterior. In a typically modest response to my report, he said that Ireland was a small country, far remote from South Asia, but that whatever moral and political resources his country possessed would be firmly and completely devoted to supporting Pakistan in ensuring regional stability. I had a half-hour meeting with Foreign Minister Gerard Collins, in his office in the parliament building, where he took time off from urgent politicking in order to receive me. Our discussions were similar to the talk that I had with the president and other senior Irish officials. The government of Prime Minister Charles Haughey fell a couple of hours after my meeting with the Foreign Minister, and the political atmosphere in the Dáil was, not surprisingly, somewhat volatile.

Fresh elections were held later in the month and the opposition Fine Gael party was returned to power. Since this was the third general election held in Ireland over the past eighteen months, it was clear that election fatigue had replaced election fever in the country. Irish politics at that time tended to devolve a great deal around personalities, and the Fianna Fail party, which had hitherto ruled with a coalition, was led by the charismatic Charles Haughey, a dynamic, blunt, self-made millionaire, with a reputation for being a pugnacious political fighter, and a political survivor of great tenacity. The high expectations of firm economic management that had brought him to office had remained largely unfulfilled, and Ireland's economic situation was in difficulties. In addition, Haughey's government was plagued by scandals, including one involving the prime minister's close friend Patrick Connolly, who was forced to resign as Attorney General, following the arrest in Connolly's Dublin home of a man wanted for two murders. Prime Minister Haughey had also taken a tough line against the British and opposed the recent Whitehall Constitution Proposals for Northern Ireland. His departure was, therefore, regarded with some glee in London. Dr Garret Fitzgerald, the leader of the Fine Gael party, was a much less flamboyant personality, but his popularity remained high, and in due course he revived the British–Irish Council which he had set up with Margaret Thatcher, an interim measure that had reduced tensions and in some ways laid the groundwork for the eventual settlement of the vexatious Irish problem.

In retrospect it seemed to me that the period of my tenure in Ireland was at a moment of slack water in the country's political and economic life. The tide had begun to turn from ebb to flow, and Ireland had just commenced its dramatic change from being one of the poorest countries in Western Europe into one of its more stable and prosperous components. In the Foreign Ministry there was great excitement and anticipation about its forthcoming presidency of the European Union, which it had recently joined, and there was an air of optimism, which was amply justified by the events of the forthcoming years.

The only Pakistanis in Ireland at the time were a few students under training in the medical and agricultural professions. Since Ireland itself had been a land of emigrants there were no possibilities for immigration. All this changed over the next few years, and we now have not only a thriving community of Pakistani doctors and other professionals, but have also opened a resident embassy in Dublin. The diplomatic corps at my time was not very large, but as so often happens in this occupation, one meets old colleagues from former posts. The Swiss Ambassador, Dr Hans Miesch, had been a close friend in East Berlin and told me how much he relished the change. Another close friend was Ambassador Alexei Nesterenko, whom I had known in Karachi since 1964, when he was the Soviet ambassador to Pakistan, and then later in Moscow when he was Chief of the Department of International Relations in the Foreign Ministry. Reunions of this kind, with former colleagues, are not only a very pleasant form of camaraderie, but can be of great professional benefit from the advice and counsel willingly rendered by old friends.

The lively informality of the Irish made it easy to get to know people from all walks of life, ranging from the sophisticated members of Irish aristocracy and officials in the government and the civil and diplomatic services, and businessmen and lawyers, to the small shopkeepers, and the casual acquaintance that one could make in the delightful pubs that dotted the countryside. The lushness of the colour green, when first seen from the air as one descends through the clouds, makes an impression that is both unique and indelible. I developed a great fondness for the city of Dublin, with its splendid architecture, its historical and literary associations, its spacious parks and the ready accessibility to the rural beauty of its outskirts. But above all, for me, Dublin was associated with James Joyce's *Ulysses*, a work that had captivated me forty years before I first saw the city. On each occasion that I visited Dublin I used to wander the streets taking in the sights, and at the same time visualizing in my mind the scenes and sounds of that one day in the life of Leopold Bloom.

PART IX

THE UNITED STATES OF AMERICA AND JAMAICA

CHAPTER TWENTY-TWO

The United States of America and Jamaica
1986–1987

'Interwoven as is the love of liberty with every ligament of your hearts...'

– George Washington

'*Le grand avantage des Americains est d'etre arrivès à la democratie sans avoir sufrier des revolutions democratiques et d'etre nèe egaux au lieu de le devenier.*'
('The great advantage of the Americans is to have obtained democracy without having to suffer democratic revolutions, and to have been born equal without having to attain it.')

– Le Comte Alexis de Tocqueville

We arrived in Washington, D.C., on the afternoon of 17 September 1986 and took rooms at the Madison Hotel, where we spent a week pending the completion of repairs at the residence. The proprietor of the Madison was the legendary Marshall B. Coyne, sometimes called 'Innkeeper to the World' because of the international dignitaries, including heads of state and government, who stayed at the Madison during their visits to Washington. Marshall was a pillar of society and a true 'insider' of the capital's establishment, with wide access and friendships that covered the entire range of Washington's power elite, from the White House and Congress to financiers, diplomats, and the media. Although known for his tough business methods, he was a kind and generous friend and we developed a warm and happy relationship that lasted until his death. Marshall was also a great supporter of Pakistan, never hesitated to use his considerable influence on our behalf, and richly deserved the high civil award that was bestowed upon him by our government.

The chancery was situated on Massachusetts Avenue, with the residence located in close proximity. Both were in the prestigious Embassy Row area in an ideal location, with the chancery designated as a landmark building. Time and inadequate maintenance had combined to cause considerable deterioration in the property, added to which there was the inconvenience of an increasing inability to accommodate our growing staff. Later in my tenure in Washington, I got to know that the State Department had just established a diplomatic enclave, not far from our present location, where plots were very much in demand. I pulled out all the stops and used every resource to obtain one for Pakistan, and was fortunate enough to arrange a stone-laying ceremony at the site by Prime Minister Benazir Bhutto when she came on an official visit to Washington at the end of my tenure. We now have a fine modern chancery building and have also retained the old property on Embassy Row.

The day after our arrival in Washington, I called on Deputy Secretary John Whitehead at the State Department and presented to him a copy of my letters of credence. This simple and practical arrangement provided ambassadors-designate with the official status that enabled them to immediately assume their functions. Suave, soft spoken, and impeccable in appearance and bearing, John Whitehead was a successful and wealthy financier from Wall Street. He typified what I regarded as the revolving door of the American political system, whereby persons of talent, capability, and wealth move into public office, often at personal financial cost, and place their skills and experience, at the service of the nation. At a given point they make an honourable return to their private occupations, ceding their place to others like them. That first meeting with John Whitehead was as pleasant and productive as one could have wished, and although for administrative reasons my subsequent official dealings with him in the State Department were comparatively limited, our personal friendship flourished over the years. Secretary of State George Schultz, who was amongst the most talented officers in Ronald Reagan's high-powered cabinet, directed the State Department with the benign firmness of a self-assured leader. He knew that he was in charge of a stable filled with thoroughbreds. A burly, taciturn figure, who could at first appearance be a trifle forbidding, he possessed a wry sense of humour and could be acerbic in conversation, but the kindly smile in his eyes was testimony to an essentially gentle person. Much to my regret I was not able to see as much of Schultz as I would have wished, but on the occasions that we did meet the outcome was always positive, and I knew that he had been fully posted about my activities. Schultz was, above all, a man of great principle and courage, qualities that he demonstrated to the full at the time of the Iran–Contra affair.

The State Department, where ambassadors necessarily spend a great deal of their time in Washington, is the massive organization that is needed by a superpower as the instrument for the projection and implementation of its policies worldwide. It is staffed by a collection of the most competent and professional diplomats that I have ever worked with, although presumably, in an establishment of such size, there probably were some dimwits, but I never found any. The officials with whom I worked in the South Asia Department were led by Undersecretary Michael Armacost, and included Richard Murphy, Robert Peck, Howard and Teresita Schaffer, Edward Djeridjan, James Hagerty and a number of other equally talented people, working with whom was always a stimulating experience. My closest association was with Mike Armacost. Arnaz and I developed a special and enduring friendship with Mike and his wife Bonnie. A big muscular man, he exuded quiet confidence without being overbearing in manner or speech. His high intelligence was wrapped in a cloak of modesty, understatement, and a subtle sense of humour. Calm and even-tempered, he was always in complete command of his facts and his brief, qualities which, combined with his innate diplomatic skills, made him a masterful negotiator. In the highs and lows that characterized our political relations with the Americans, the steadfast attitude that he maintained kept things on an even keel. Mike always had his eye on the major essentials, and was never distracted by the emotions generated by setbacks. Likewise, he took success in his stride and, in the manner of the true professional, moved on to the next issue. Our shared love of western classical music added a bonus to the pleasure and stimulation of working with one another.

For obvious reasons the Pakistan embassy in Washington was one of our largest missions, with a number of departments—political, financial and economic, defence, information, commercial, agricultural, and education and community affairs. In addition, we had two fully-staffed general consulates in New York and Los Angeles, and honorary consuls general in Boston, Chicago, and Houston who performed sterling work. The officers and staff of the embassy were of the highest calibre, and included Tariq Fatemi and Mueen Afzal as Political and Economic Ministers, respectively, Counsellors Shaheed Malik and Babar Malik, and First Secretaries Ayesha Riaz and Amir Zeb. All of them went on to become ambassadors, except Mueen who became Secretary General, Finance. Our Defence Attaché Col. Hamid Javed was later Chief of Staff to President Pervez Musharraf, and his deputy, Lt.-Col. Farrakh Alam Shah, became a dynamic member of the Peacekeeping Department in the United Nations. Our Consul General in New York was Hadi Reza Ali, a real live wire whose premature death was not only a deep personal bereavement, but also deprived the Foreign Service of one of its ablest officers. Tariq and Hadi had joined my mission in Moscow as Third Secretaries and Russian language students.

The day after my meeting with John Whitehead I began making my calls. The list was wide and seemingly never-ending, but the encounters were always interesting and stimulating. On taking stock of the situation upon my arrival in Washington I had concluded that for our specific purposes there were a number of centres of power and influence in the American system, each important and independent, and yet interlinked. These were the White House and the National Security Council, the Congress, comprising the Senate and the House of Representatives, the State Department, the Department of Defence, the print and electronic media, the think tanks and the universities, and the major banking and industrial houses. Two other very important institutions for our work were the international financial institutions, the World Bank and the International Monetary Fund, and the growing Pakistani community. As a backdrop to this vast stage, was the fabric of a free society which encouraged innovation and initiatives, devoid of all restriction save that of public accountability. While discussing my mission with President Ziaul Haq prior to my departure for Washington, he made the astute observation that being friends with America was like living on the banks of a great river. Every four years it changes course and one is left either inundated or high and dry. It was a remark that always drew applause whenever I repeated it during my many lectures all over the country. Another feature, unique to the American political system, was the accessibility of legislators, provided that one knew how to go about it correctly. There were many occasions when my bright officers, fully cognizant of the working system in Congress, collaborated with the staff members of a congressman or senator, in providing inputs into draft legislation. I was once asked, during a speaking engagement, whether I found any differences between working in Washington and in other posts where I had served. I replied that if I did the things that I was doing in Washington in any other capital in the world, including my own, I would immediately be declared *persona non grata* for interfering in the internal affairs of the country. However, in Washington, if I did not act as I did, either out of timidity, laziness or ignorance, I should be sacked for not doing my job.

Shortly after my arrival in Washington, and after giving the matter due consideration, I obtained government sanction for the appointment of a professional lobbyist. Hitherto there had been considerable resistance in the ministry to this proposal, in the justified belief that if the embassy did its work properly there was no need for a lobbyist. However, I felt that the special circumstances that prevailed in Washington made the services of a Congress registered lobbyist as an essential ancillary to the activities of the embassy, with the caveat that the lobbyist remained firmly under the direction and control of the ambassador. This was an essential requirement because lobbyists, by nature, possess considerable influence in the convoluted inner recesses of Washington politics, and it was important for us to ensure that at no time did the tail wag the dog. There was a wide and extensive choice in making a selection, with some large firms carrying some high profile Washington insiders on their boards and staff, such as former senators and cabinet officers, with corporate budgets that matched the national budgets of many developing countries. I consulted Charlie Wilson, a colourful and vibrant Democrat Congressman from Texas, who was one of the closest friends and strongest supporters that Pakistan has ever had, and on his advice appointed Neill & Company, a mid-level firm with a good reputation. Neill's other government client, Egypt, was a country whose size, political orientation and relations with the Americans were somewhat similar to ours at the time, and whose ambassador expressed his satisfaction at their performance to me. Denis M. Neill gave us very good service during the course of my tenure and was helpful in exactly the manner that was required. Subsequently, when Benazir Bhutto became the Prime Minister, she appointed her old friend, Mark Siegel, as our lobbyist, a change that was inevitable, though not to my liking, but at least it retained the concept of maintaining a registered lobbyist.

I presented credentials to President Ronald Reagan at the White House on the afternoon of 24 November 1986. The protocol, which was devoid of all fanfare, had the delightful and uniquely American touch, of including ambassador's family at the ceremony. Accordingly, Arnaz and Feroza, looking beautiful in Pakistani attire, accompanied me as Ambassador Gosen of the State Department protocol took us in two limousines from the residence to the White House. After a short wait in an anteroom, we were ushered into the reception hall to meet the president. The moment we entered, Reagan walked up to me beaming his broad and famous smile, and shaking me warmly by the hand, said, 'Happy birthday, Mr Ambassador! Many happy returns of the day!' This unexpected greeting, clearly a case of good staff work, came as a very pleasant surprise, and through my somewhat startled pleasure I could clearly discern a twinkle in Reagan's eyes, and felt his sense of fun at the joyful surprise evoked by his gesture. There were no speeches, Reagan simply welcomed me to the United States as he accepted my letters of credence, and we posed for a photograph that included Arnaz and Feroza with the president. Reagan and I then had a short conversation during which I conveyed to him the greetings of President Ziaul Haq, and gave him a quick briefing on conditions prevalent in Pakistan and on the Afghan border. He seemed to be fully aware of the matter, and I felt that nothing I said was in any way new to him. He told me that he was following the situation very closely, and assured me of US support—'We will stand by you, Mr Ambassador'—and wished me success in my mission. As we took our leave, Reagan's farewell greeting to the three of us was as warm and friendly as before, combining a firm handshake with a light hug. Although I thought that they came pretty close to it, neither Arnaz nor Feroza swooned.

Shortly after our return to the embassy we took off for New York, where we attended a dinner in our honour, hosted at their residence, by Zubin and Nancy Mehta. He was at that time the Musical Director of the New York Philharmonic Orchestra and has remained a close and dear friend for many years. The guests were a fascinating combination of musicians, artists, financiers, doctors, and business tycoons. Among them were James and Elaine Wolfensohn with whom Arnaz and I were to become good friends. Jim was at that time a leading Wall Street financier, and later went on to serve two very successful and memorable terms as president of the World Bank. Zubin's elegant party, comprising as it did the elite of New York's intellectual and cultural society, provided conversation which was as wide-ranging as it was stimulating. For me it was, indeed, a memorable ending to a very happy birthday.

Arnaz had lived in New York as a 'Bachelor Girl' for ten years before I had the supreme good fortune to meet her there, and she owned an apartment in Lincoln Towers, which we retained, and to which we returned after Zubin Mehta's dinner. There, as I contemplated that eventful day in my life, my thoughts inevitably turned to my meeting with Ronald Reagan, and I considered his extraordinary personality. So much has been said and written about him that it is necessary to eschew biographical details and merely express random thoughts engendered by my limited personal exposure to the president and his administration. In the first place, I thought that he had a good, practical mind, totally devoid of any sharp nuances of a Byzantine or Machiavellian nature. He exercised the tremendous powers of the president of the United States in a largely benign manner, maintaining a consistent focus on major issues of principle, and pursuing them with a consistency and determination which were frequently disguised by his thespian charm. He was essentially a kind person, a quality that emerged in both his personal and public conduct, sometimes with disastrous consequences in political situations. He also possessed an uncanny ability to feel the pulse of the American people, to sense their mood, and most important of all, to communicate with them—the media's description of him as 'The Great Communicator' could not have been more apt. This was confirmed to me during my meetings with various senators and congressmen, some of whom told me with a sense of alarm, that at times when they opposed the president's initiatives, Reagan had a tendency to go over their heads and appeal directly to their constituents, after which 'our mail boxes and telephone exchanges are jammed with protests from our districts'.

I was twice a witness to Reagan's innate charm and gentility. The first was when Foreign Minister Sahibzada Yaqub Khan delivered a letter from President Zia to Reagan. The meeting took place in the Oval Office of the White House where, as we entered, Reagan walked up to greet us, with Schultz, Weinberger, and Don Regan standing in a group nearby. Yaqub commenced by conveying Zia's greetings and expressions of admiration of Reagan's role as the leader of the free world. Just as Yaqub got into his stride with further praises of Reagan's leadership successes, the president put his arm around Yaqub in a friendly fashion, gently took the letter from his hands, and turning to the group of the cabinet officers standing close by, said 'Hey guys! Let's get him on our campaign trail!' That charming gesture ended superfluous formalities and set the tone for a very productive meeting. The second occasion was in New York when Prime Minister Junejo met Reagan, who was accompanied this time by Schultz, Jim Baker, Mike Armacost, and other officials. The first part of the meeting was devoted to Afghanistan and went reasonably well, but on the other agenda item, the nuclear issue, the American advisers took a very tough line and implied that with Afghanistan now almost out of the way, US tolerance of our nuclear activities was also almost at an end. Just as I thought that the atmosphere of the meeting was about to heat up from the uncomfortable to the acrimonious, Reagan intervened to say to Junejo, with a smile and in the gentlest of tones, 'Mr Prime Minister, you know that I have to certify to your activities. Please help me and make it easier for me to do so.' No bluster, no threats, no intimidation from the leader of a superpower, just a meaningful suggestion couched in a modest fashion.

It is my personal view that after Franklin Roosevelt, the two greatest American presidents of the twentieth century were Harry Truman and Ronald Reagan, and in defending that opinion I am prepared to take on all comers. This is because of an evaluation of the diverse qualities of their leadership, and the manner in which they were exercised, to meet the requirements of the circumstances and the era in which they functioned. The fact that the actions of one drew the parameters that started the Cold War and the actions of the other the parameters that hastened the end of the Cold War, may be symbolic but is coincidental. To the Soviet ambassador's protest that he had never been spoken to in such a harsh manner before, Truman's response was to advise him to fulfil his treaty obligations. Reagan stood at the Berlin Wall and said, 'Mr Gorbachev, pull down that wall!' It may be remembered that Truman was a Democrat and a failed haberdasher from Missouri, and that Reagan was a Republican and a B-movie actor from Hollywood. The fabric of a society, and a system that provides such fundamental egalitarianism, and opportunity for transformation of this magnitude, is truly unique and worthy of both contemplation and admiration. In this context it would be appropriate to recall the observation of the famous historian, Arnold Toynbee, expressed after the announcement of the Marshall Plan in 1947:

> It was not the discovery of atomic energy, but the solicitude of the world's most privileged people for its less privileged that will be remembered as the signal achievement of our age.

One of the most fascinating aspects of an ambassador's function in Washington is not only to observe the workings of the American political system, but also to participate in its myriad processes, and to flit between the Congress and the administration. President Lyndon B. Johnson once said to Abba Eban, the legendary Israeli diplomat, 'I am fully aware of what three past presidents have said, but that is not worth five cents if the people and the Congress do not support the President.' Lyndon Johnson, who had spent a lifetime in Congress, certainly knew what he was talking about. However, his respect for the power and sanctity of the institution was tempered by a realistic, earthy, and profane approach to handling any of its recalcitrant occupants: 'If you get them by the balls, their hearts and minds will follow.' I stressed to my officers that while, in our dealings at Capitol Hill, Johnson's ideological concept was worthy of emulation, his methods of implementation were well outside our pay grade.

Our associations with the administration and the judiciary were based on an impeccable code, with appointments scheduled, and conducted with due decorum. In the case of the Congress, however, it was entirely different, with ambassadors often being involved by legislators in the informality and cheerful backslapping prevalent in their environment. Appointments were difficult to obtain, and were frequently subject to delays resulting from the more urgent demands of the legislative business. Quite often a senator or a congressman, after keeping me waiting in his office, would bustle in from a caucus meeting and rush off for a vote on the floor of the House. We would then have to travel from his office to the legislative chamber by the underground shuttle service, and conduct our business whilst en route. I quite enjoyed this, but many of my colleagues, particularly from some Latin American and Arab countries, found it difficult to cope with such assaults on their ambassadorial *amour propre*. A very important component of the congressional system is the institution of the 'staffers' in the office of the legislator. These are not clerks, but highly intelligent persons with a well-informed and fine-tuned political sense, who are inquisitive, hard working and, of course, well versed in the minute details of the legislative process. They come in all ages, from the enthusiastic and bright young college graduate to the sober, grizzled veteran, whose judgments are tempered by experience and a touch of cynicism. My officers and I paid particular attention to this group, for it was their research and advice that influenced the thinking of their boss, the senator or the congressman.

When dealing with the members of the US Congress another important consideration was the element of parochialism in their thinking. Their concerns were almost completely confined to the axis between Washington and their constituency. I was astonished to find that during my time in Washington over 60 per cent of the members of the congress did not even care to possess a passport. On the other hand, those legislators who did have an interest in foreign affairs were extremely difficult to reach in Washington. This was not surprising, considering that there were over 150 ambassadors resident in the capital. I, therefore, used a bit of the subterfuge that is possible under the system. Every legislator in Washington reads two newspapers, *The Washington Post,* and the leading daily paper from his or her hometown. I accordingly instructed our lobbyist Denis Neill, to set up an appointment with my targeted legislator when he was in his district over a weekend; failing that, he should arrange for my interview with the local TV station and the editorial board of the local journal. This provided me with an opportunity to say nice things about the legislator, and also convey Pakistan's message. Usually, this tactic worked, and I was able to obtain a meeting the next time that I requested it in Washington.

Having said this, there were a number of members of Congress who were key players in the Pakistan–US relations, who became good friends and whose kindness made them readily accessible. First among these was Charlie Wilson, a Democrat congressman from Texas, a colourful, hard living and swashbuckling personality whose devotion to the cause of Pakistan and the Afghan resistance became the stuff of legend. His achievements were recorded, first in a television show, *Charlie Did It*—Ziaul Haq's words—and later in a book, *Charlie Wilson's War*, by George Crile, which was subsequently made into a film. Beneath the swagger and braggadocio was a quick, thoughtful, and intelligent mind, with a profound knowledge of history and military affairs, and a sharp and lively skill in the conduct of legislative procedures. He used these talents with considerable success on our behalf in the complicated balancing act that we were constantly maintaining at the Hill. Above all, Charlie was a man of great understanding and compassion, and the truest of friends. His relations with Zia got off to a rocky start, but soon developed into a very strong attachment. When he heard of Zia's death, this tough Texan locked himself into his office for the day and wept copiously. Charlie's legislative rival, and also ours, for that matter, was Stephen J. Solarz, a Democrat from New York, and an important and influential member of the House Foreign Affairs Committee. A sharp and clever legislator, Steve, with the help of a large war chest, had acquired considerable support in the House, and had a deep knowledge and insight into the affairs of the South Asian subcontinent. In fact, it was largely through his legislative efforts that a South Asia bureau was created in the State Department. Solarz was an unabashed supporter of India, and was appointed as a lobbyist for India after his retirement. Circumstances made constant interaction between Solarz and myself inevitable, and in due course we got to be quite good friends despite our wide political divide. Later on, following a realignment of precincts in New York which excluded his solid Jewish base of support, Solarz lost his seat. A contributory factor was the assistance rendered to his opponent by dedicated members of the Pakistani community who provided everything from taxis to restaurant food. In the Senate our support came from members of both parties, Republicans Warner, Humphrey and Helms, and Democrats Dodd, Pell—who was sometimes difficult—and Sarbanes.

The Pakistani community in the USA was well established by the time I arrived in Washington, and consisted of two distinct groups.

One was the prosperous element, consisting of professionals such as the doctors, lawyers, bankers, academics, and businessmen, whilst the other group comprised the workers such as the taxi drivers, and those employed in factories and the catering business. But regardless of their social standing their patriotism was outstanding and I could always count on their support whenever necessary. Some of them had just begun to form friendship groups and associations, and though this was a commendable development in itself, it also led to much *inter se* rivalry and feuding. The worst of our national traits began to manifest themselves, and since the presence of the ambassador was much sought at the functions of each association, I had to assess all invitations with care. Eventually I let it be known that I would attend any function, provided the organizers would obtain, as my co-chairman, an American political figure from either party. By this means I hoped to channel their activity into the mainstream of American politics, but I did not stay long enough to know whether my idea worked at all.

In addition to the two groups of Pakistanis mentioned above there was a third group of Pakistanis in America at that time, which constituted a minuscule elite of brilliance, talent and achievement, and whom I regarded as my mentors. First and foremost amongst them was Moeen Qureshi, Senior Vice-President at the World Bank, a brilliant economist with administrative talents to match, and a soft spoken, low profile disposition. I first met Moeen and his lovely wife Lelo, in Ghana, when he was posted as the World Bank representative. Here he did a superb job in reviving the country's economy after the depredations of Nkrumah. Our friendship grew over the years until he became my boss as the Prime Minister of Pakistan at the time when I was the country's Permanent Representative at the United Nations in New York. The short spell of his leadership was remarkable for the measures taken by him to restructure the economic and administrative framework of the country. In terms of quantum of achievement within limitations of tenure, it remains a feat unsurpassed in Pakistan's history. Lee Kuan Yew (Prime Minister of Singapore, 1959–1990) told me, when I met him in Singapore during my negotiations over East Timor, that in his congratulatory message to Prime Minister Nawaz Sharif he had advised the latter to implement and follow the policies of Moeen Qureshi. Another of our great friends and companion in

Washington was Dr Ayub Ommaya, a neurosurgeon of world repute and a gifted patriot and humanitarian, who worked silently for Pakistan and the Pakistanis. Ayub was the Oriental version of the Renaissance man. In addition to his scientific and surgical skills, he was an athlete who had swum the English Channel, and was an operatic tenor. He told me that at one time he had to decide whether to be a singer or a doctor, and had chosen the latter profession when told by his Italian voice teacher that as a singer he would be good but not great. So he became a great neurosurgeon, and indulged his passion for song by vocalizing in the cafes of Georgetown in the evenings. His death through cancer was a great loss to humanity and a devastating personal blow to me. Others in this elite group of our Pakistani friends were Shahid Javed Burki and Shahid Hussain, both of the World Bank, and their wives. Their warm friendship, and frank and mature counsel, were of tremendous support to us.

Relations with the two major International Financial Institutions (IFIs), the World Bank and the International Monetary Fund (IMF), constituted one of the major responsibilities of the Pakistan ambassador in Washington during the period of my tenure. The importance of this charge needs no elaboration, given the long standing and vital role played by these two institutions in the financial and economic development of our nation. By the same token, Pakistan had over the years developed an expertise in its working relationship with the IFIs, partly due in equal measure to the sheer competence and professionalism of our officials in the finance and economic affairs ministries and the State Bank in Pakistan, and augmented by the presence of officials of equal calibre in our mission in Washington. Furthermore, in the World Bank and IMF there were a number of distinguished Pakistanis who occupied senior and mid-level positions, who had acquired a most felicitous amalgam of international obligation and patriotic inclination. Moeen Qureshi, as Senior Vice-President at the World Bank was, of course, the most important of them. But there were also Shahid Hussain and Shahid Javed Burki as Vice-Presidents, and Aziz Ali Mahomed at the IMF. Consequently, I found on my arrival in Washington, that as far as the important IFIs were concerned, I had been gifted with a situation that I felt was of munificence.

It was also my good fortune to find in Washington my old friend Michel Camdessus, the Managing Director of the IMF, with whom I had previously worked when he was governor of the Bank of France in Paris, and before that as members of the 'debt set' at UNCTAD in Geneva.

It was clear to me that if we were to derive the full benefit of this large and powerful latent resource at our disposal in the IFIs we would need to have a competent and effective component in the embassy. Here again, fortune smiled on us, and in Mueen Afzal we had a Minister, Economic Affairs, who was of the highest calibre. He combined, in the most admirable fashion, an excellent professional knowledge with outstanding diplomatic skill, and was regarded with great respect and much affection in the halls, offices and corridors of the Bank and the Fund. Thanks to Mueen, we had no problems at these institutions, and work was always pleasant and productive. Mueen Afzal subsequently became secretary general, finance, and guided the economic policies of the country to one of the few rare periods of successes that it has known.

The year 1987, which was to evolve in an eventful fashion, commenced on a happy note. I attended a meeting of the Council of the Organization of American States (OAS) which had its headquarters in Washington. The Chairman of the Council for that year was Ambassador Llanes, the Permanent Representative of Paraguay to the OAS who, in a brief ceremony, inducted Pakistan into the OAS with the status of permanent observer. Subsequently I made an occasional appearance at some of the council's meetings, which enabled me to keep abreast of the politics in Latin America. The continent has had more than its share of drug wars, but it had been virtually free of war between its states over the past half century, and that owed much to the OAS for its role in the peaceful settlement of disputes. Also, my wanderings in the corridors of the Council of OAS provided the opportunity to strike up a few friendships which were continued during the ambassadors' subsequent postings as permanent representatives in New York.

In July, Arnaz and I made a quick trip to Jamaica for the purpose of presenting credentials. Unfortunately, there had been some violent riots in Kingston the day before our arrival and most of the town was under a curfew. My activity was, therefore, confined to a short visit to the Government House for the purpose of presenting my letters of credence to the governor general. For reasons of security we remained confined to our hotel and left Jamaica a day later. Clearly, the unfavourable circumstance of our visit was unfortunate, and my commitments in Washington kept me so occupied that I could make only one further trip to Kingston, and had to rely on my officers to maintain our largely symbolic diplomatic links with Jamaica. This was the one accreditation in my career where I wished I could have done more, and it will always remain a cause for deep personal regret.

My tenure in the United States was dominated by the issue of the war in Afghanistan. It was accorded the highest priority in the daily staff meetings of the embassy officials, and took me to all the centres of power in Washington, from the National Security offices in the White House, to the State Department, the Pentagon, and the CIA headquarters in Langley. My officers and I were at Capitol Hill much of the time, working with legislators and staffers on issues that involved everything from the supply of mules, to the eventual acquisition of Stinger missiles. This activity has since been depicted, in a somewhat dramatic fashion, in George Crile's book and there is no doubt about the key role of this colourful and dynamic Congressman from Texas. Charlie and I were in constant contact with each other as we rode this roller coaster of exhilaration and frustration, and I was filled with admiration for his mental brilliance and his sheer personal dynamism. My activities often necessitated visits to the Central Command Headquarters (CENTCOM) in Tampa, Florida, from where the Afghan operations were conducted, and there I had a glimpse of the structural organization of the US military.

It was quite clear to me that we were in the midst of a momentous historical development. Hitherto the rivalry between the two superpowers had been conducted on the basis of a standoff between NATO and the Warsaw Pact in Europe, with a series of proxy wars being conducted elsewhere, in Angola, Mozambique, the Congo, the Horn of Africa, in South East Asia, and in Latin America. However, there had also been a substantive move in the direction of peaceful co-existence, resulting in the Helsinki Accords and considerable progress in the SALT negotiations. Détente had replaced confrontation, and there was a tacit understanding that frontiers established at the end of the Second World War would remain undisturbed. Brezhnev's brash invasion of Afghanistan had blatantly destroyed this delicate fabric of detente, and Reagan's robust response had set the stage for a direct confrontation with the USSR, quite removed from the surrogate conflicts that had hitherto occurred, and were in fact still continuing. In Washington I had the feeling that we were at an historical moment of tectonic change in the existing international order. An article in *The New York Times* described it as 'one of the great geopolitical battles of the 1980s', and I had the exciting sensation of being involved, even as a very small cog, in the rolling wheel of history.

In Washington our basic objective in 1987, as far as the Congress was concerned, was to obtain approval for an aid package of $4.2 billion for disbursement over a six-year period under renewal of a presidential waiver of the Symington Amendment, which was due to expire in September. The exercise was conducted in circumstances where a hitherto dynamic and powerful president, ever helpful to our cause, had just been dealt a series of body blows, through the so-called 'Iran–Contra affair', that had crippled his administration. The presidency was already handicapped under the lame duck status of the final year of a second term incumbency. The Republicans' loss of the Senate majority, despite Reagan's personal intervention, followed by the Iran–Contra scandal, not only seriously weakened the administration, but rendered it an attractive target for Democratic opposition on every possible issue, including its firm support for Pakistan. For us, the year began inauspiciously with a series of disconcerting attacks on our nuclear policy, the most significant of which were Ambassador Deane Hinton's speech at Islamabad, and the publication of a report by Leonard Specter, a respected authority on nuclear issues, of the Carnegie Endowment. This was followed by Kuldip Nayyar's interview with A.Q. Khan, published in papers all over the world, the devastating effect of which remained unrelieved despite our denials. The nuclear issue thus became a major subject of contention, and the anti-Pakistan lobby, led by powerful legislators like Glenn, Pell, and Solarz, immediately decided to get tough with Pakistan and obtain maximum concessions on the aid package. We countered with a vigorous campaign at the Hill, as well as the media, stressing the peaceful nature of our nuclear programme and the need for a regional approach to the issue. We also emphasized the geostrategic importance of the US–Pakistan friendship, especially in the context of Afghanistan.

We closely monitored the Congressional hearings on the Foreign Assistance Authorization Bill, which commenced in early March. Thanks to the sterling support of our friends including Charlie Wilson, Gordon Humphrey, Chris Dodd, David Drier, John Warner and others, and of the efforts of our officers as well as our lobbyist, we obtained approval of the aid package in the Foreign Relations Committees of both houses, as well as a waiver of the Symington Amendment for a period of two years beyond September 1987. Our success in the two committees was so overwhelming that it discouraged our opponents from taking the matter to the floor of both the houses. In addition, we went a step further, and taking advantage of the sympathy and goodwill generated in America by reports of increasing cross-border raids by Soviet aircraft, we commenced negotiations for further military assistance in the form of early warning systems. Foreign Minister Yaqub Khan came to Washington in May, and the discussions that he held with Schultz, National Security Council Chief Frank Carlucci, and Howard Baker, Reagan's Chief of Staff, revealed that notwithstanding our recent success in Congress we were by no means out of the nuclear woods. They all expressed serious concern over clandestine purchases of nuclear equipment both in the USA and Europe, and gave dark warnings of the consequences of what they described as continuing acts of transgression. Unfortunately, their concerns proved to be only too true.

Just as I had begun to relax in the wake of our success in Congress, suddenly, out of a bright blue July sky, there came a thunderstorm of biblical proportions. I read in the newspapers that Arshad Pervez, a Canadian citizen, had been arrested for illegally attempting to export maraging steel to Pakistan. This was a highly sensitive item used in the nuclear industry, and although the circumstances of his arrest bore all the imprints of a scam operation, there was no doubt in my mind as to the seriousness of the charge and of its consequences. I said this to President Zia who called me as soon as the news broke, and told him that this would most certainly trigger the Solarz Amendment and probably lead to the immediate stoppage of all forms of assistance to Pakistan. Zia responded, somewhat lamely, that there was no official involvement in this transaction, that it was a purely commercial affair, and that I should convey this to the US authorities. What we left unsaid on the telephone was that he knew, and I knew, that we had been caught with our hand in the cookie jar. The public outrage that followed was predictable both in ferocity and volume, and I found it difficult to know who was frothing at the mouth more, the politicians or the press. Solarz called it 'an outrageous violation of American laws and an arrogant disdain for the promises given by Pakistan regarding its nuclear programme' and an editorial in *The New York Times* was entitled 'Punish Pakistan's Perfidy on the Bomb'.

Before this incident, Solarz had accepted my invitation to a dinner in his honour at the embassy. He now called me to say that he was about to issue a very strong statement following the arrest of Pervez, and that he would quite understand it if we were to cancel the dinner. I replied that I expected him to issue a statement, and that I also expected him to attend the dinner. We had invited some important guests that night, including Zbigniew Brzezinski, whose many accomplishments included being Solarz's university professor, and I thought that the evening would be an interesting one. Accompanied by his wife Nina, Solarz arrived wearing a cream coloured raw silk *achkan*, made for him, he informed me, by President Zia's tailor. I thought Steve's sartorial gesture was a trifle theatrical, but nevertheless very kindly. Conversation at dinner was very animated and obviously centred on the topic of Pervez's arrest. Brzezinski, who was at his brilliant best, started off by telling me, 'You have done the stupidest thing possible.' He then turned his heavy guns on Solarz, and asked him if he had fully considered the consequences of the legislative action that he was contemplating, 'If you cut off all assistance to Pakistan then it will mean the end of the Afghan resistance. It will also possibly mean the fall of the present Pakistan government. You would then have the Soviet Union on the border of a weak, destabilized Pakistan in possession of the bomb anyway.' Discussion continued on the enigma that we had placed before the Americans. They had to consider whether or not to enforce their laws and punish us, even at the cost of their vital international interests, including possibly their security. I terminated this inconclusive debate by raising a toast to Solarz, and saying that there was a rumour at Capitol Hill that morning that our guest of honour was going to bring his food taster with him to the dinner. I was glad and grateful that his presence at our table testified to his determination to bring relations between our two countries back to an even keel despite temporary setbacks. I urged our American friends to take a wider perspective, as Dr Brzezinski had just done with his usual incisive brilliance and clarity, and recognize the key role that Pakistan was now playing, at great cost to itself, in defence of the free world and its cherished values. Pointing out that Pakistan was now host to over three million Afghan refugees, I asked our guests to cast their minds back to recent history and said, 'If during the 1930s powerful and affluent countries like the USA and Western Europe had done what an impoverished and embattled Pakistan was now doing, the horrors of the holocaust could have been largely mitigated.' The dinner ended in a pleasant fashion, but to my surprise I discovered that the gist of my remarks had somehow attracted public attention. The very next morning, and over the subsequent few days, I received phone calls and messages of appreciation and support for Pakistan, many of them from Jewish groups and associations, some of whom even called at my office. Whilst this was a matter for personal satisfaction, it also brought a sobering reminder of the vigilance, unity, initiative, and power of the Jewish community in the United States.

I continued with my normal duties in Washington, meeting members of the Congress, the administration, the World Bank, the IMF, and the media; giving lectures all over the vast country, in cities as far apart as San Francisco, San Diego, St. Louis, and Chicago; and also attended to the numerous delegations and visitors from Pakistan. But my main focus was on the ongoing legislative process, and to repair the serious damage done to our interests by the Arshad Pervez affair. In a closed door Senate Foreign Relations Committee meeting, its Chairman Senator Claiborne Pell told Mike Armacost that Pakistan was treating the United States with contempt; the US meant business and would not accept any more lies. He also dismissed our offer to set up a committee of enquiry into the Pervez affair by remarking that 'it was like asking the fox to take care of the chickens'. Similarly, Dante Fascell, Chairman of the House Foreign Affairs Committee, addressed a letter to President Reagan urging temporary suspension of all aid to Pakistan pending an enquiry into the Arshad Pervez case. Testifying before a joint hearing of the sub-committees led by Congressmen Solarz and Bonker, Assistant Secretary Richard Murphy made a balanced and moderate statement in which he said that despite the Administration's best efforts 'Pakistan proceeded to the threshold of nuclear weapons possession. India seems similarly poised on the brink.... (however) whatever their nuclear capabilities, neither has moved irrevocably across the nuclear threshold'. Murphy referred to the administration's dilemma: 'How to ensure that our laws are upheld; protect our non-proliferation interest; prevent the outbreak of a nuclear arms race in South Asia and continue our support to Pakistan in its opposition to the Soviet occupation of Afghanistan. The outcome depends to a very large extent on Pakistan's response. We wish to believe the assurances of a good and deserving friend such as Pakistan. But under present circumstances these assurances must be matched by their actions.' At the end of July the House Appropriations Committee proposed a draft bill that approved the 'earmarks' for our civilian and military requirements as requested by the administration, but subjected it to crippling caveats such as requiring presidential reports on our uranium enrichment levels and our actions on the prosecution of Arshad Pervez. The Senate passed a similar 'Sense of the Senate' resolution, but in this case our efforts met with some success in that it also referred to Pakistan's proposal for a regional approach to the nuclear issue.

At this stage I decided to review our strategy and held some intensive consultations with my officers and our lobbyists. It seemed to me that the defensive role that we had been playing thus far was inadequate, and that the legal niceties being advanced by us in terms of the Pervez case were becoming counterproductive. We, therefore, decided to change our strategy completely and to adopt a new position. We would present the Pervez case as an aberration which the Government of Pakistan deplored, since we held the US laws in the highest regard. We also decided to vigorously present the nuclear issue in the regional context, stressing that if the US was serious about non-proliferation then it should address the whole issue in the South Asian context and not simply by assaults on the sovereignty of Pakistan alone. We would stress that the usual excuse that the US had 'no leverage over India' was not tenable, in view of the fact that in 1987 alone India would walk away with credits worth $8 billion from the World Bank and the IMF. We would then emphasize that the situation in Afghanistan was reaching a critical stage, and any reduction of US support for Pakistan would harden the Soviet position, with consequences which could be disastrous for both Pakistan and the West.

On 30 September Congress passed a Continuing Resolution to permit day to day government disbursements, whilst we concentrated our energies working on Senators Inouye and Kasten, who had been forcefully briefed by Schultz on the necessity of continuing aid to Pakistan and the provision of a six-year waiver. We also managed to convince the two senators, as well as Senators Lugar and Dodd, to adopt a regional approach to non-proliferation. It was at this stage that we and our lobbyists were able to influence the drafting of the proposals contained in the Inouye–Kasten resolution which was adopted by the Senate Appropriations Committee on 3 December 1987. The main elements of the resolution were inter alia (a) no country in South Asia which the president determines is producing weapons grade enriched uranium or separated plutonium in unsafeguarded facilities may receive any US assistance; (b) during the time that assistance is cut off, the President shall instruct US representatives to the multilateral development banks to oppose loans to that country; (c) in order to waive these provisions, the president must certify that a second country in South Asia is producing weapons grade uranium or separated plutonium in unsafeguarded facilities, and that the failure of the second country to agree to cease production of such materials is a factor in the continued production of such materials by the first country. This Senate Appropriations Committee resolution represented the first formal acceptance by a committee of the Congress of our plea that Pakistan's nuclear programme should not be viewed solely as a US–Pakistan bilateral issue and that true non-proliferation in South Asia cannot be achieved without taking into account the Indian nuclear programme as well. The Indian reaction was predictably strong and violent, and there were hysterical outbursts in the Indian parliament and the press.

The effect in Washington was also predictable, and the Administration went to work on smoothing ruffled Indian feathers by trying to dilute some of the Inouye–Kasten proposals during the Senate and House conference stage. The Final Continuing Resolution, as pertaining to Pakistan, incorporated the following: a two-and-half-year waiver of the Symington Amendment; $260 million in Foreign Military Sales, with $30 million of this as 'forgiven' loans; $220 million in Economic Support Funds; $50 million in Development Assistance; $80 million in PL-480; no reports on Pakistan's nuclear programme or the Pervez case; and no new conditions or restrictions on Pakistan's nuclear programme. Also important was the fact that we had achieved, through Inouye–Kasten, a committee resolution that included India in an entirely new approach to the US non-proliferation policy. We had of course expected violent opposition from our adversaries, but in their efforts to remove restrictions on India, they became more amenable to lifting restrictions on Pakistan, which was the original objective of our exercise. It had been a long and bruising battle, and as I thought back on it I recalled the words of the Duke of Wellington's famous observation after Waterloo, 'It has been a damned nice thing— the nearest run thing you ever saw in your life.'

CHIAROSCURO

Dr Henry Kissinger was kind enough to receive me from time to time, and since, like so many others, I regarded him as a mentor, these encounters were always fascinating. His association with Pakistan was deep, long-standing, and almost emotional, and there was no doubt about his appreciation of our key role in his epic first journey to Beijing. Kissinger had a particular regard for Yaqub Khan and always mentioned him in affectionate terms in all our conversations. He also had an admiration for Z.A. Bhutto, whom he regarded as a man of considerable but fatally-flawed talent, and said to me that Bhutto's execution was a cruel and inexcusable blunder.

Kissinger was my guest at a tête-à-tête luncheon at an elegant New York restaurant. After taking his seat at the table, he looked around with appreciation and said, 'I like this restaurant. Some of the prettiest girls come here.' Just then, one of those 'prettiest girls' sitting at a nearby table, greeted Kissinger with a friendly smile and a cheerful wave, which he acknowledged with equal charm. Henry then turned to me and whispered sotto voce, 'I don't recognize her. Maybe I am getting Alzheimer's.' I reassured him by saying 'Dr Kissinger, I don't think you need to worry too much about not recognizing her. The time to worry would be if she doesn't recognize you.' Turning to me and nodding his head, Kissinger said to me in his deep, heavily-accented style, 'You've got a point.'

Among Kissinger's many admirable qualities is his fondness for dogs. At a dinner at our residence in New York, he suddenly disappeared from the salon and one of the several guests who were seeking him out for his words of wisdom discovered him in the library. The formidable Dr Henry Kissinger was sitting on the carpet, crouched over Lady, our clumber spaniel, patting her head and mumbling sweet baby talk to her in German.

* * *

'Outside of the killings, Washington has one of the lowest crime rates.'
– Marion Barry, Mayor of Washington, later indicted on charges of corruption.

* * *

'If guns are outlawed, how can we shoot liberals?'
– Mike Gunn, Mississippi State Senator.

* * *

In the basement of the New York Athletic Club, there sat an old black man whose job was to shine shoes, but whose wit and wisdom far exceeded the requirements of his calling. After seating me in his box with a courteous greeting, he asked whether I was a Democrat or a Republican. Anticipating his political inclination by the colour of his skin and the menial nature of his occupation, I solicited his approval by declaring myself a Democrat. 'That's good, that's good,' he said in a satisfied mumble. 'What would you have said if I told you that I was a Republican?' I asked. His judicious response was as truthful as it was pragmatic. 'Ah don' care,' he said with a shake of his grizzled head. 'Ah jes wanna know how to fraame mah conwo sayshun.'

* * *

'If you want a friend in Washington, buy a dog.'
– President Harry S. Truman

* * *

I attended an exhibition hockey match in Washington, following which the organizers awarded a certificate to each member of the Pakistani team. During the ceremony I overheard one of the players say to another, '*Yeh vapas kar. Keh mujhay green card deh.*' ('Return this and ask for a green card instead.') The Pakistani sense of humour remains as irrepressible as ever.

* * *

The Pakistani community had arranged a celebration on Independence Day at the Lincoln Memorial in Washington. It was a happy event, with the participation of families and children, music and games, and Pakistani food stalls. During the course of the evening, Arnaz tripped on the steps of the memorial and took a nasty fall. Luckily, she was saved from serious injury when her head struck my foot instead of the marble step. It seems that this misadventure was mentioned in a story of the festive celebration that appeared in one of the Urdu newspapers in Pakistan. This was a period when I used to be in almost daily telephone communication on official business with President Zia, so I got out my pad and pencil and put on my reading glasses as soon as I was told that the president was on the line. There was no official business; it seems that Begum Zia had read the story in the Urdu papers, and Zia was calling on both their behalf to enquire about Arnaz's welfare, and also whether she needed any particular medical treatment. Both Arnaz and I were touched by this spontaneous gesture so characteristic of Zia. In expressing thanks to the president for his consideration I was also able to inform him that the only injury sustained by Arnaz was to her sense of dignity and decorum.

* * *

Professor Daniel Boorstin, the eminent historian, was also Librarian of Congress at the time that I was in Washington, and the few occasions when I was able to meet him were to be cherished. Like all persons of intelligence and great knowledge, Boorstin was modest in disposition and soft spoken, but his brilliance was unmistakable and his presentations fascinating. During one of our talks, I pointed out that there was a period in history, while Europe was still in the grip of the Dark Ages, when there existed in Baghdad a marvellous civilization which made it the epicentre of the world. It flourished in mathematics, astronomy, navigation, chemistry, architecture, and a host of other creative endeavours. Then what went wrong? What caused it to cease and wither? Boorstin's response was that he too had often thought about this phenomenon, but could not come to any definite conclusion. He had some tentative ideas, but like all genuine scholars he was unwilling to advance them with assurance. He said to me that perhaps the printing press played a role in this conundrum. The Muslim religious clerics, fearing the spread of knowledge among the people, had insisted on handwritten copies of the Holy Quran and banned its printing, thus restricting general literacy. In Europe, on the other hand, the first book printed by the inventor of printing, John Gutenberg, was the Bible, through which there was a spread of literacy and the subsequent printing of literature. Boorstin insisted to me that this was only a tentative thought, and that it needed a vigorous and thorough research in terms of both logic and history. Unfortunately neither of us had the time to discuss this topic any further, and with Boorstin's death the issue has become for me only a fleeting, vague, and inconclusive matter of speculation.

MEANWHILE IN PAKISTAN

During the year, I was obliged to make a number of visits to Pakistan on consultations. These were fleeting two-or three-day visits, charged with calls on the president and the prime minister, and meetings at the Foreign Ministry. Each of these trips increased my concerns about the relations between the power elite of the country. Differences between the president and the prime minister appeared to increase with the passage of time, with attitudes moving from suspicion to acrimony and finally to downright hostility. Much of this was reflected in the Foreign Ministry, with Yaqub and Noorani engaged in a surrogate role of cautious sparring. It was not a comfortable situation, and was by no means conducive to the unity and understanding so essential to meet the three major foreign policy issues that confronted us. These were, as I saw them at the time, our relations with Washington, where we were simultaneously dealing with the aid package and the nuclear issue; the negotiations in Geneva, which were in their penultimate stage; and the unexpected threat from India posed by Operation Brass Tacks, an ominous and massive military exercise unleashed by its hawkish army commander, General Sunderjee.

Initiated in the early winter of 1986, Operation Brass Tacks proceeded through to the spring of 1987, and employed large elements of all three armed forces, with heavy formations concentrated in the Rajasthan area. Pakistan responded by moving formations to its border with India in the southern Punjab, and tensions began to escalate. In Washington my urgent enquiries about Indian intentions were initially met with soothing responses, but they became less reassuring as Operation Brass Tacks evolved. It was at this stage that Zia defused the situation in masterful fashion. He flew to Ajmer where he first performed a religious pilgrimage, and followed it up by a secular pilgrimage as he watched a cricket match between India and Pakistan.

But in the case of the Geneva negotiations, serious differences began to emerge amongst the Pakistan leadership, differences that would grow out of all proportion in the coming year. In the process of exercising his legitimate authority as Prime Minister Junejo had aimed a series of pinpricks at Zia. These ranged from petty matters, like removing Zia's nominees from lists of delegations proceeding to conferences abroad, to taking decisions on important issues either without consulting Zia or else deliberately discarding his recommendations. As this process continued, and the pinpricks changed into darts, Zia's frustration was steadily turning into an anger which even he could not always conceal. On my increasingly frequent visits to Islamabad, I observed that these tensions were reflected in the atmosphere that had begun to prevail in the drawing room of the Army House.

Within Pakistan also, there was the hint of a breeze of change. It had not yet become a wind, but the leaves on the trees of political consciousness had begun to stir, and their rustle could be heard all over the country. I sensed, also, that the 'cohabitation' had loosened Zia's grip on the administration of the country, and that his touch was no longer as sure as it had been over the past eight years. Not only had Junejo achieved considerable success in shaking off his shackles, but other politicians and political parties, notably the PPP, were beginning to feel their oats, and were galvanizing themselves to meet the challenges and opportunities that they correctly sensed were coming their way. In December 1987 I was once again on brief consultations in Islamabad, and at the end of the visit, as I looked out of the window of the aircraft at the fast disappearing landscape below, I sensed that the New Year was likely to repeat its cyclical pattern and again unleash a turbulent change in the politics of this troubled land.

CHAPTER TWENTY-THREE

The United States of America 1988

'Of all forms of national community, a federal system is the most complicated. It demands the greatest flexibility and imagination to harmonize national interests. The Constitution of the United States is thus not a historic parchment in a glass case. It is a continuous process of delicate government adjustments. And its judicial application is not a mechanical exercise, but a profound task of statecraft, exercised by judges set apart from the turbulence of politics.'

– Justice Felix Frankfurter

'The best government is a benevolent despotism, tempered by an occasional assassination.'

– Voltaire

'We are told, "We should not protect those who do not have full democracy." This is the most remarkable argument of the lot. This is the leitmotif I hear in your newspapers and in the speeches of some of your political leaders. Who in the world, ever, on the frontline of defence against totalitarianism, has been able to sustain full democracy?'

– Alexander Solzhenitsyn, address to the American Federation of Labor and Congress of Industrial Organizations (AFL-CIO), 1975.

The year 1988, which was to prove tumultuous even by Pakistani standards, commenced in Washington in a sanguine manner. On 15 January, President Ronald Reagan signed a determination that waived the restrictions of the Solarz and Glenn–Symington Amendments affecting aid to Pakistan. While determining that there had been a violation of Section 670 of the Solarz Amendment, the determination also invoked the waiver contained in Section 670(a)(2), which states that withholding aid from Pakistan 'would be seriously prejudicial to the achievement of United States non-proliferation objectives and otherwise jeopardize the common defence and security.' The president further determined that 'the provision to Pakistan under the Foreign Assistance Act through 1 April 1990, is in the national interest of the United States', and he, therefore, waived the provisions contained in Section 669 of the Act for that period. This enabled us to get moving on approvals and funding for a number of projects. The $50 million in development and $80 million in PL-480 Funds were obtained with relative ease, but military requirements proved to be more difficult.

The nuclear issue continued to dominate thinking in the Congress. The greatest impediment to the regional approach to non-proliferation as proposed by Pakistan, and the most powerful weapon in the hands of our opponents, was the ongoing disagreement over uranium enrichment. The US intelligence agencies routinely informed the congressional committees that Pakistan was enriching at a level somewhere between 85 and 95 per cent. The Congress believed that Pakistan had committed itself not to enrich beyond 5 per cent, as the 'threshold' proclaimed by our officials. This discrepancy generated the impression that Pakistan was 'lying', whereas India was not. Ambassador Triloki Nath Kaul of India had written a letter attacking Pakistan's nuclear non-proliferation stance, and succeeded in having it inserted in the Congressional Record. My letter in response was also inducted into the record, but apart from pairing the two positions in equal form and style in the record, it did little to alleviate the prevailing suspicion. In 1979 all US economic and military aid to Pakistan was terminated by the Symington Amendment, based upon allegations that Pakistan was trying to acquire enrichment technology. However, the Soviet invasion of Afghanistan, and Zia's skilful exploitation of the situation, resulted in the addition of a new Section 620(e) to the law, which permitted the president to waive Section 669 'if he determines that to do so is in the interests of the United States'. This secured the way for a six-year $3.2 billion assistance package. But as further evidence of Pakistan's clandestine nuclear activities began to surface, particularly after a foiled attempt to export nuclear components from Texas, Senator John Glenn moved for stronger measures. The administration, rightly anticipating that these would inhibit its efforts in Afghanistan, drafted a resolution with looser language which would provide it with more flexibility. The administration also drafted in the services of Larry Pressler, a comparably unknown senator from South Dakota, to move the amendment in Congress. Until that time, Pressler probably knew a great deal more about edible oil than he did about uranium enrichment. The charge, now voiced with much indignation in Pakistan, that the Pressler Amendment was Pakistan-specific, is true in letter but not in spirit. The amendment, drafted entirely by the administration, was designed to help Pakistan, not punish it. Once again we were caught with our hand in the cookie jar, and the administration, in pursuit of their own international priorities, was compelled to make compromises. Of course the Pressler Amendment was Pakistan-specific, but then so were the Glenn–Symington and Solarz Amendments, thus providing us with the dubious record of being the subject of three Pakistan-specific Congressional Amendments. But despite the enormous difficulties created by these three amendments, in the final analysis it was the skill, determination, dedication, and patriotism of men like Ziaul Haq, Ghulam Ishaq Khan, Abdul Qadeer Khan et al. that prevailed.

President Reagan signed the latest certification as required under the Pressler Amendment on 18 November 1988. However, this was done after intense debate among the various branches of the administration. In previous years there had been some difference of opinion between the intelligence agencies on the current state of Pakistan's nuclear capability, and the president had signed the certification on the basis of this doubt. In 1988, however, the intelligence agencies were unanimous in their view that Pakistan had, during the previous year, taken major strides in its pursuit of a nuclear weapon. The White House, therefore, found itself in an awkward situation and had difficulty finding suitable language that would enable the president to issue the certification despite these intelligence reports which, as required by law, had also been brought to the attention of select members of Congress. Yet President Reagan took a bold initiative, overrode the negative findings of the intelligence community, and issued the requisite certificate. I was informed, by an impeccable source, that Reagan took this decision for reasons that were as much personal as they were political, out of a desire to avoid any controversy that would mar the completion of a major foreign policy commitment. Nevertheless, it was a decision that could only have been taken in the president's last year (so much for the 'lame duck' theory!), and was announced, with due circumspection, only after the presidential campaign was over and George Bush had been duly elected.

To return to the activities of the spring of 1988, we successfully negotiated two major arms sales packages through Congress. The first included eleven F-16 jet fighters as well as several types of missiles, and the second involved three P-3C Orion maritime surveillance aircraft. In pursuance of this package I visited the aircraft manufacturing facilities at Fort Worth, Texas, and Burbank, California, and met the CEOs as well as senior staff and test pilots of the General Dynamics and Lockheed Corporations. Jim Wright, the Speaker of the House of Representatives in Washington, had his home base in Fort Worth, so we flew there with him in his chartered 'Speaker Jim Wright's Cow Town Special', and I got a glimpse of the power play between the American plutocrat and the American politician. On this particular occasion it was a phenomenon that helped in our quest for our F-16s and Orions. Another productive outcome, in terms of defence equipment, was the acquisition of three frigates and a supply vessel for the Pakistan navy. This was entirely due to the understanding and co-operation of Richard Armitage, who was an influential Assistant Secretary at the Pentagon, and one of Pakistan's best friends in the administration. These vessels were due to be decommissioned from the US navy, and Armitage had the brilliant idea of transferring them to Pakistan. We discussed the matter, and since there were no funds available for a direct purchase, it was agreed that the frigates be leased to the Pakistan navy on a no-cost basis. Moreover, Armitage arranged the funds for the cost of the refit of the ships, amounting to about $1 million per unit. Accompanied by our Naval Attaché Captain G.Z. Malik, we took ceremonial delivery of two frigates at Charleston, South Carolina, and one at San Diego, California. For me it was a nostalgic moment to once again board a warship and salute the quarterdeck. Unfortunately, these leased vessels had to be returned to the USA two years later, when Congress once again terminated assistance to Pakistan, following the Bush administration's refusal to issue a certification.

Our busy diplomatic life continued in Washington, and we relished the opportunity of cultivating friendships with interesting personalities from all walks of life. My friendship with Moeen Qureshi flourished, aided by the similarity of our background, our thoughts and ideas, and the fact that we could exchange them in bilingual fashion. We also made great friends with Chief Justice William Rehnquist and his lovely wife Nan. Normally reserved and somewhat reclusive, Bill was a fascinating authority on American history and the constitution. It was he who called my attention to the Frankfurter observation quoted at the commencement of this chapter, and displayed moving personal stoicism later at Nan's death from cancer. Katharine Graham, the formidable owner of the iconic *Washington Post*, graced us with her presence (there is no other way to put it) at dinners at our embassy, and also invited us to her magnificent residence. Here we met politicians, financiers, diplomats, artists, writers, and all the power brokers of the capital. We also met the famed journalists on her staff, Ben Bradlee, Bob Woodward, and Robert Kaiser. At one of Katharine Graham's parties, humorist Art Buchwald said to a group of us guests, in his own irreverent manner, 'There is only one thing that brings all these people here—FEAR!' Notwithstanding Buchwald's comment, Katharine Graham was the gentlest and most gracious of persons, and was the epitome of the American 'gentle lady'. Soft spoken and reserved, she had an easy informality that was captivating, and it came as no surprise to me that she and Arnaz became such good friends. Her daughter, the lively and vivacious Lally Weymouth, was also close to us, and was grateful for the facilities that we arranged for her on her frequent visits to Pakistan. In return, she regaled us with stories of her travels and encounters, especially with Zia who seemed to have fascinated her. Another media icon whom we got to know very well was Arnaud de Borchgrave, the editor of *The Washington Times*, whose journalistic career and successes could fill volumes. A determined martinet, with a mind like a steel trap, Arnaud was an intellectual rather than emotional conservative, and discussions with him were always a rewarding experience. He was a great supporter of Pakistan, and had an undisguised fondness for Ziaul Haq. Ambassador Dan Tera was a wealthy Chicago financier whose Republican affiliations brought him to the State Department as head of the cultural section. Dan and his wife Judy had established a museum in Chicago which had a superb collection of American art. They were in the process of establishing a facility for American painters on the grounds of Monet's home in Giverny, France. The Teras were a delightful couple and we spent some happy and interesting times together, sharing so many common interests, including a love of painting and of France. Zbigniew Brzezinski was a friend and mentor whose counsel was of immense value and was always freely given to me. We used to meet, sometimes at my home but mostly in his office, and his sharp intellectual clarity emerged as vividly in his conversation, as it did in his books. On looking through my old engagement diaries, I find that on 2 June 1988 we gave a dinner at the embassy in honour of Mr George Bush, Jr. and Mrs Laura Bush. Jeb and his wife were also there, together with some other friends. I do not recall very much about the evening, apart from it being a friendly and pleasant occasion, and whilst Arnaz and I were aware that we were entertaining members of a powerful political family, we certainly had no idea that we had in our home that evening, a future two-term President of the United States, and a future two-term Governor of Florida.

Overshadowing the interesting and pleasant aspects of our diplomatic life in Washington were the momentous events unfolding on the international scene and notably in Pakistan. In February, Gorbachev had announced his intention to withdraw Soviet troops from Afghanistan, and he commenced the process in May. The Geneva negotiations, following a hectic climax, had been concluded with the formal signature of the accords on 10 April 1988. Thus, all the affected parties were now manoeuvring for position in a post-Soviet Afghanistan. Back in Islamabad, the friction between Zia and Junejo had been exacerbated by the tensions that led up to the signature of the Geneva Accords. A leading element in the disruption was the curious intervention at an earlier point in time by Armand Hammer, the American millionaire who had lifelong interests in Russia. His involvement in the Afghanistan issue was a much more high profile version than that of Wally Zimmerman in the previous year. But whereas I had taken great care to keep Junejo fully informed of all our dealings with Zimmerman, in the case of Armand Hammer the negotiations were restricted to Zia, Yaqub, and the Director General, ISI. The plan was to replace Mohammad Najibullah, the current President of Afghanistan, with King Zahir Shah, the former ruler now in exile in Rome. The plan itself was not even given serious consideration, but when Junejo heard about it he was furious about his exclusion, and reacted by dismissing Yaqub and replacing him with

Zain Noorani as the Foreign Minister. Thus, the Geneva Accords were signed on behalf of Pakistan by Zain Noorani, who proudly retained the pen with which he did it, and then went on to do a massive victory lap in his constituency, Karachi. The persistent, main concern of all the parties to the accords, was the nature of the regime that would be established in Kabul after the Soviets withdrew. A corollary to this was the quantum of arms that would be available in Afghanistan to the contending parties. Thus, with a view to maintaining some semblance of equilibrium, the Geneva Accords stipulated the concept of 'Negative Symmetry', whereby, once the accords were signed, neither Pakistan nor the Soviet Union would send further arms into Afghanistan. True to his style, Zia made a last-ditch effort to delay the signing of the accords so that he could maximize the flow of military hardware to the Mujahideen. He telephoned me to try and persuade the Americans to delay matters, on the grounds that we first needed to carefully assess the nature and structure of the future Kabul government.

When I met Schultz at the State Department and conveyed this rather lame argument as a reason for delaying the signature of the accords, the secretary expressed an understandably astonished disbelief. He rightly observed that for all these years we had been jointly working for a withdrawal of Soviet forces and now, just as it was about to happen, we wanted a delay. He added that, in any case, his reports from Moscow indicated that the Soviet decision was very delicately poised and that if we did not act immediately, 'we might miss the train'. My next appeal was to the much respected Senator Robert Byrd, who had always mistrusted the Soviets and was much more responsive to the call of caution. He reacted immediately by making a forceful statement on the floor of the Senate that same evening, mentioning his discussion with me and urging the administration not to rush into any hasty action. Needless to say, this development did not endear me to my friends in the State Department, but nor did it deter them from their course. I duly sent a report on these proceedings, including my meetings with Schultz and Byrd, in a cipher telegram to our government.

This routine action on my part led to some unforeseen and not very pleasant consequences. Zia had been arguing for a delay in signing the Geneva Accords, whilst Junejo was anxious to expedite the procedure. This was, in my view, a genuine difference on policy issues, and not on personalities. It was, therefore, an entirely proper subject for a dispassionate debate. When Junejo told Zia that the Americans were also pressing for an early signature, Zia responded by saying that this was not entirely true, and quoted the cipher telegram that reported my discussion with Senator Byrd. Junejo had apparently not seen this telegram. It is difficult to say whether this was due to administrative oversight or to Junejo's customary preference for aural rather than written reports. In any case, as I was later told by officials in the Foreign Ministry, the prime minister apparently directed that all future cipher messages be passed to him for clearance before being submitted to the president. This was an extraordinary administrative action, and I have seen no documentary evidence of any such order emanating from the office of the prime minister. Even though the frigid atmosphere that existed at the time gives it an air of probability, I obviously cannot vouch for the complete authenticity of this account. On the other hand, I have great trust in the sincerity of my colleagues in the Foreign Ministry who gave me a verbal account of these developments. A big question mark hangs over this issue, as it does over so much else in Pakistan, and one is left to wonder if, assuming that this was true, it contributed in any way to Zia's final exasperated action in dismissing the Junejo government just after the prime minister returned from a foreign tour on 19 May 1988.

This action proved to be a watershed for the Zia regime. Having endured two years of provocation by Junejo's 'conventional' weapons, Zia had used the 'nuclear' option. On hearing the news of the dismissal of the Junejo government, my sense of foreboding was further darkened by the informally conveyed information that the ensuing elections would be conducted on a non-party basis. I recalled the perceptive observation of A.J.P. Taylor, the British historian,

> The deterrent failed to deter. This was expected sooner or later. A deterrent may work ninety-nine times out of a hundred. On the hundredth occasion it produces a catastrophe. There is a contemporary moral here for those who like to find one.

Ironically, within a week of the signing of the Geneva Accords in early April, and just a month prior to the political explosion of Junejo's ousting, there occurred a massive explosion at Ojhri Camp, a military facility located between Islamabad and Rawalpindi. This had been a storage depot for military supplies to the Mujahideen in Afghanistan, and had obviously been overfilled with ordnance in the attempt to rush supplies into that country before the 'Negative Symmetry' of the Geneva Accords could go into effect. The explosion that occurred at Ojhri was truly massive, it reportedly measured over 3.5 on the Richter scale, with considerable loss of life and damage to property caused by the bombs and missiles that descended over the twin cities. Although sabotage could not be ruled out, the probable cause was the kind of careless accident that often results while working under pressure. Shortly after hearing about the accident, I received the expected call from the Pakistani president. Anticipating an urgent request for fire-fighting and rescue equipment, I was surprised that although the sense of urgency was very much there, the request was for ammunition and rockets to replace the ones lost in the explosion. Zia was still hell-bent upon getting arms into Afghanistan, and I was quite sure that rockets were still exploding around Islamabad while he was asking for more over the telephone. He instructed me to make a personal appeal on his behalf to Judge Webster, the Director of the CIA, stressing the necessity and urgency for the replacement of ordnance. Webster received me immediately upon my arrival at Langley, and had already assembled some of his assistants in his office. Expressing his distress and concern about the Ojhri Camp explosion, he offered the CIA assistance in any rescue or recovery operations that we might need. Judge Webster had a calm and imperturbable personality, but I could see that the audacity of Zia's request had caused him some astonishment. Although the director kept his cool and did not make an immediate response, I overheard one of his surprised collaborators whisper, 'The guy's got balls.' After a moment, Judge Webster said that immediate deliveries could probably be effected from stockpiles in Egypt, but they might not be much. The major quantities were with NATO reserves in Germany, and he was not allowed to touch those. I respectfully suggested that the best deployment of weapons was where they were being actively used in engaging the Russians, and that replenishments of NATO stocks could take place in due course. Judge Webster assured me that he would do his best, and I conveyed this assurance to a highly satisfied Zia.

There is an amusing addendum to the previous narrative. At about the time that the Geneva Accords were being concluded, Richard Armitage and Richard Murphy, the important Assistant Secretaries from the Defence Department and the State Department respectively, met President Ziaul Haq in Islamabad. At the first session, which was devoted to the nuclear issue, the Americans conveyed their grave concerns with regard to Pakistan's activities. Zia gave solemn assurances about its peaceful activity, but they knew that he had lied to them. The second session was related to the post-Geneva scenario in Afghanistan, and here Zia made his usual strong pitch for the supply of arms. When it was pointed out to him that the Geneva Accords prohibited the further induction of arms into Afghanistan, Zia's response was that the Americans should send the arms and leave the rest to him, asserting that Islam permitted him to lie for a good cause. The American officials are reported to have concluded that on both occasions Zia 'lied to us for a good cause'.

On 11 July 1988, I left for Pakistan for consultations in connection with a proposed visit to Washington by President Zia. The dismissal of the Junejo government had created a very adverse reaction in the United States, and the view, especially in the Congress, was that of a rampant military dictatorship that could not tolerate even the façade of a democracy that had been its own creation. Furthermore, the promise to hold party-less elections was seen as waving a very large red flag to a very enraged bull. With the withdrawal of Soviet forces from Afghanistan well under way, and due for completion by February, our hitherto heroic status as a frontline state in the international battle for freedom had become, in the German idiom, yesterday's snow (*Schnee von gestern*). Meanwhile, pressure on our nuclear programme was growing, and my discreet enquiries had revealed that the different US intelligence agencies were in complete accord that Pakistan had crossed the enrichment threshold and that the next presidential certification was not only improbable but impossible. Bearing these grim tidings, I arrived in an Islamabad reeking with political uncertainty and an administration that seemed to have lost its touch. My meetings with senior officials, particularly Ghulam Ishaq Khan, Yaqub Khan, and Roedad Khan, who have always been pillars of strength, were reassuring in as much as they were fully cognizant of the difficulties, seemed determined to deal with them, and were not in the state of euphoric denial that has characterized so much of our political life. In the country itself, I sensed that a mood of uncertainty was being mixed with a desire for change, and that the political parties were beginning to assert themselves in a meaningful fashion. The return of Benazir Bhutto, and the massive ovations that she had received all over the country were proof of these newly emerging realities. She had metaphorically blazed in from the skies, but other politicians, seasoned, gnarled and grizzled, were also beginning to emerge from the woodwork.

My tight schedule permitted me only one day's transit in Karachi and two days in Islamabad. My first day in the capital was filled with meetings with the officials, and in the afternoon of the second day I was to call on the president at the Aiwan-e-Sadar in Islamabad, drive with him to the Army House in the evening and catch a plane for New York that night. I found Zia looking tired and haggard, and watching him from the waiting room of his office as he received and held discussions with various political and religious personalities (mostly the latter), my mind went back to the days, almost a decade earlier, when Zulfikar Ali Bhutto was engaged in the same exercise, with the same sort of people, in the same atmosphere and location. When his talks were finished and he came over to me, smiling, courteous and gentle as ever in his manner, he was the same Ziaul Haq whom I knew, respected, and whom I had grown so fond of. As we drove to the Army House in his car, a Toyota Corolla, I seem to recollect, there were only the driver and an orderly in the front seats, and only a pilot jeep ahead of us. I told Zia about the situation in the United States and warned him that things would be very different from his past visits. President Reagan and Arnaz were likely to be the only pleasant faces that he would see in Washington, and he should anticipate a moderate reception from the administration, a rough one from the Congress, and an even rougher one from the media. Zia took in all of this in his usual cool manner, and we went on to discuss the options and courses that were open to us. I could see that Zia was looking forward to his visit to Washington, but was doing so in a combative spirit and not one of pleasurable anticipation. There was also a touch of anxiety in his questions, and his body language lacked its earlier cast of a coiled spring in a crisp *achkan* or uniform. His mind was as sharp as ever, and he exuded his usual calm courage as we war-gamed the pattern of his forthcoming Washington visit. As I took leave of him, Zia was as gracious as ever and asked me to convey his warmest greetings to Arnaz. He thanked me for my services to Pakistan, said that we would remain in touch with each other on the telephone, and looked forward to our meeting in Washington. Fate decreed that this would be my last meeting with this great, admirable, and courageous patriot.

On the morning of 17 August 1988, as we were packed and ready to fly to New Orleans to attend the convention of the Republican Party, I made a quick visit to the chancery to check out any messages before we left for the airport. Whilst there, I received an urgent telephone call from Mike Armacost seeking confirmation of an alarming report that he had just received about a plane crash in which both President Zia and US Ambassador Arnold Raphel had been killed. I immediately called Islamabad and got through to Foreign Secretary Humayun Khan, who confirmed the worst. There followed a flurry of telephone calls to Islamabad, the State Department and Ambassador Robert Oakley at the National Security Council. I conveyed the horrible news to Arnaz, who forthwith rang her twin sister Aban Jamall in Karachi with instructions to immediately go to Nancy Raphel and be by her side at this time of devastating personal tragedy. The following days were filled with sadness as we followed the events in the media as well as through conversations with Islamabad and the State Department. A particularly poignant moment was the funeral at Arlington Cemetery. Secretary of State George Schultz had returned from Pakistan in a special plane, bringing with him the bodies of Arnie and the US Military Attaché Brigadier General Herb Wassom, who had also been on that ill-fated presidential aircraft. It was a simple, moving ceremony, during the course of which I ended my short eulogy to Arnie with a quotation from Shakespeare that was later inscribed on his tombstone:

'His life was gentle; and the elm'nts
So mix'd in him, that Nature might stand up,
And say to all the world, *This was a man!*'

Much has been speculated on and written about the cause of this fateful crash, but there have been no definitive conclusions. From the little evidence that I could gather, the possibility of some form of sophisticated sabotage cannot be excluded. I pondered over the quirks of fate that affect the lives of us all. Did death save Zia from a political humiliation that he certainly did not deserve, but might well have suffered in the coming months? There may be cause for speculation, but obviously there are no answers. So far as my other friend, Arnie Raphel, is concerned, it was surely the most malign of fates that caused him to leave his own plane, in order to perish in that ill-fated C-130. The tragedy was both profound and unmitigated. Not only was he one of the finest diplomats that I have ever known, intelligent and professional to the core, but he was also the kindest and gentlest of human beings, always cheerful and always ready to help. He had served in Pakistan as a junior officer and loved the country and its people. Fluent in spoken and written Urdu, he had a wide range of friends who reciprocated his warm and hospitable nature. Above all, he had in Nancy a wife who was the perfect partner, a career diplomat who specialized in legal and human rights issues, and who, after Arnie's death, returned to the State Department and served as the first US Ambassador to Slovenia. She remains one of our closest friends largely because we have so much in common, including above all a love for Arnie. Nancy once told us that their posting in Islamabad was the happiest moment in Arnie's diplomatic career, and that he relished every moment of his time spent in Pakistan. For us, whom he left behind, there is some consolation that his last days in our homeland were so joyful.

Very shortly after Arnie's funeral, I got a call from Mike Armacost informing me that the State Department had nominated Robert Oakley as Ambassador to Pakistan, and requested an early clearance of his agreement. This was recognition both of the importance of Pakistan and of the necessity for continuation of a high-level representation. Oakley, who was working in the National Security Office at the White House, was thoroughly familiar with the situation and was in no need of any orientation. A real live wire, with a sharp mind and exuding determination, he made an immediate impact in Pakistan, and handled with firmness and tact a number of the delicate issues that emerged in the immediate, post-Zia period. Bob Oakley, together with his wife Phyllis, who was also a career diplomat and one time spokesperson for the State Department, made an admirable contribution to the development of Pakistan–US relations, albeit in a style and fashion somewhat different from that of his predecessor. His sharp wit and outspoken manner, especially during his frequent contacts with the media, resulted in one weekly publication naming him as the 'Viceroy'. I think Bob rather enjoyed that. The Oakleys managed to acquire a real feel for Pakistan, and their fondness for the country and its people was unmistakable. They carried and projected this comprehension in their many activities since retirement, and Arnaz and I continue our warm friendship with Bob and Phyllis.

In September 1988, I signed a lease agreement for our new chancery building in the diplomatic enclave in Washington. These plots, as already indicated, were very difficult to obtain, and we were lucky to get almost the last one that was available. The spooks from our government raised an objection on the plea that there was a 'security risk' on account of its proximity to the Israeli embassy. I countered with the contention that we would be the indirect beneficiaries of the Israelis' own formidably efficient and effective security measures. We decided to take no chances on losing the site, and at Tariq Fatemi's suggestion, we arranged for a foundation stone laying ceremony during the forthcoming visit of Prime Minister Benazir Bhutto. She performed this with her customary grace and charm, and we now have a modern chancery building in a prime location and which combines architectural appeal with all the functional requisites.

During the last quarter of 1988, there were a number of important visitors from Pakistan, including General Mirza Aslam Beg, the Chief of Army Staff; Admiral Iftikhar Ahmed Sirohey, the Chief of Naval Staff; and Foreign Minister Yaqub Khan. Their meetings and talks with US officials were both timely and useful, and provided a measure of reassurance in the atmosphere of uncertainty that prevailed after Ziaul Haq's death.

The US presidential election, which commenced in the autumn, was the obvious object of interest and attention, with results that were of great interest to us. With the election of Vice-President George Bush as President, the Republicans retained the White House, and the message seemed to be that the electorate opted for stability and continuity, rather than switching to the uncertain economic and defence policies of Governor Michael Dukakis. For the Democrats, the national mood translated into continued control over both Houses of Congress. While the Democrats mourned their inability to capture the administration, they were obviously relieved at Reagan's departure. Bush was a realist and pragmatist, not burdened by Reagan's ideological fervour, and was, therefore, expected to be better at working with Congress. Bush's cabinet appointments also had track records as competent and skilful managers, rather than being ideological standard bearers. James Baker as Secretary of State, John Tower as Secretary of Defence, and Brent Scowcroft as the National Security Adviser, were all veteran defence and foreign policy experts with unblemished records of honesty and integrity.

Meanwhile the elections in Pakistan, and the re-instatement of democracy that brought Benazir Bhutto to power, had a profound impact in the United States. The administration, Congress and the media reacted in a positive manner, and there was a fund of goodwill for Pakistan in general and for Benazir Bhutto in particular. It was a source of considerable satisfaction for me to find that, while our friends continued to remain steadfast, our previous critics were becoming our enthusiastic supporters. Stephen J. Solarz even went to the extent of telling me that henceforth he would be 'The Voice of Pakistan on the Hill'. It seemed to me that, all things being equal, the asset of democracy would provide an effective counterweight to the inevitable diminishing of priority resulting from the Afghanistan settlement. The only sticking point was the nuclear issue. Knowing as I did the evaluation of the US intelligence agencies that we had crossed 'the nuclear threshold', in December 1988, I could not visualize how we would get around this problem. The only straw that I could cling to was to pursue the regional approach, and in this I saw a faint hope in a statement that Bush had made to a group of editors on 15 April 1988. He had stated,

The stability of the Subcontinent is threatened by nuclear competition between these two nations. India has exploded a nuclear device and Pakistan is not far behind. I believe that it is in the interest of neither country to move forward in this direction. Because regional tensions underlie each country's desire for weapons, as the President I will do all I can to move Islamabad and New Delhi towards a bilateral agreement that would verifiably constrain any further development of nuclear weapons there.

These were brave words, and although they sounded almost like music to my ears, I feared that they were considerably distant from the political ground realities.

CHIAROSCURO

Professor Stanley Wolpert, the distinguished scholar and historian at the University of California at Los Angeles (UCLA), had written a book on Jinnah which remains, in my view, the definitive biography of the Founder of Pakistan. Wolpert has also written a number of other books on the history of South Asia, and on its prominent political leaders such as Bal Gangadhar Tilak, Gopal Krishna Gokhale, and Jawaharlal Nehru, as well as a devastating account of Mountbatten's viceroyalty. Wolpert's scholarly works must surely rank him as one of the foremost authorities on South Asian history.

At the time of publication of Wolpert's *Jinnah of Pakistan*, our Ministry of Information, in a familiar display of its zeal for censorship, demanded that the author excise certain passages from the text adding, again in its customary fashion, that failure to do so would result in a ban on the sale of the book in Pakistan. Wolpert, true to his commitment as a historian, quite properly refused to comply, and our Ministry, equally true to its bureaucratic tradition of bully and bluster, promptly banned the book. Meanwhile, President Ziaul Haq had read *Jinnah of Pakistan* and appreciated it so much that he kept a stockpile in his office and distributed copies as a gift to the many foreign dignitaries who called on him. Such incongruities are by no means rare in Pakistan.

When I called on the president prior to my departure for Washington, he instructed me to extend an invitation to Wolpert to visit Pakistan as his personal guest. Accordingly, on my first trip to Los Angeles I called on Professor Wolpert and extended to him the president's invitation. This was very politely but firmly refused. Wolpert asked me to convey his thanks to the president, but said that he could not possibly visit a country where one of his books had been banned. I pointed out to Wolpert, somewhat lamely, that Zia had appreciated his book so much that he used to distribute it as a gift to his friends. Wolpert replied that he was aware of that, and gently added, with a touch of irony, that he was also aware of the fact that the sale of freely available pirated copies of *Jinnah of Pakistan* in shops all over the country had not led to any protests, riots or arson.

On my next visit to Islamabad I repeated to the president exactly what Professor Wolpert had said to me. Zia's reaction was an immediate understanding and appreciation of Wolpert's feelings, 'He's quite right. We made a big mistake'. He then telephoned Prime Minister Junejo, recounted to him my exchange with Wolpert, and suggested that the government lift the ban on *Jinnah of Pakistan*. Junejo's reply was a flat refusal, telling Zia, 'You imposed the ban on the book, and now you want to expose me to public anger by lifting the ban.' This incident was a sad reflection of the suspicion and distrust that existed between the president and the prime minister.

Two days after the dismissal of the Junejo government I received a call from Zia informing me that he had rescinded the ban on *Jinnah of Pakistan*, and instructing me to renew his invitation to Wolpert for a visit to Pakistan. I did so with alacrity and he accepted in his usual gracious fashion. Since then Professor Wolpert has visited Pakistan many times, given lectures all over the country, and has very deservedly been awarded a high civil decoration.

* * *

Following my return to Washington after consultations in Islamabad in mid-July, there was an increase in the number of telephone calls from the president, mostly in connection with arrangements for his forthcoming visit to Washington.

These calls usually came at about two o' clock in the afternoon. I could visualize him in the drawing room of the Army House taking up this matter after he had concluded all his other business late at night. Accordingly, I made it a point not to accept luncheon invitations, and to stay at home in order to be readily available to take a call from Islamabad. On Friday, 19 August, the telephone rang just as Arnaz and I had finished lunch, and I instinctively moved from the table to the telephone stand. After taking a couple of steps I checked myself and let the telephone continue to ring. The person at the other end of the wire was no longer Ziaul Haq.

MEANWHILE IN PAKISTAN

Many of the events that occurred in Pakistan in 1988 had a direct bearing on my work in Washington and have already been related in the foregoing account. Briefly, the first-half of the year was characterized by the increasing tension between Zia and Junejo, leading to the dismissal of the latter, and followed by the even more traumatic death of Zia. In the second-half of the year the country was engaged in making the political readjustments necessitated by the sudden end of the decade of Ziaul Haq's firm and dominant rule.

Following a hurriedly convened meeting, General Aslam Beg, now the Chief of Army Staff, wisely refrained from proclaiming the martial law and allowed events to take their course as envisioned in the constitution that Zia had imposed upon the country. As Chairman of the Senate, the formidable and durable Ghulam Ishaq Khan, assumed office as the Acting President, armed with the extensive powers available to him under Zia's tailor-made Eighth Amendment to the constitution. This arrangement by no means excluded the army's role in the exercise of power and, in fact, gave a new lease of life to the army–bureaucracy configuration that was the mainstay of the Zia regime. It was also decided to hold general elections on 16 November 1988, the date originally fixed by Ziaul Haq, but this time with the participation of all political parties. Benazir Bhutto's return to the country had galvanized the PPP, and this, in turn, aroused concern among the conservative and religious elements. The death of General Akhtar Abdul Rehman in the Bahawalpur air crash had led to the eventual appointment of Lt.-Gen. Hamid Gul as the Director General ISI. Assertive and outspoken, Hamid Gul was deeply conservative, and played an active role in bringing together the Muslim League and other like-minded parties into a coalition called the Islami Jamhoori Ittehad (IJI), as a counter to the PPP. Allegations of interference by the ISI, including charges of bribery, began to surface at the time and have never since disappeared.

Ziaul Haq's sudden and unexpected departure had obviously left a vast void in Pakistan, and the area in which this was most noticeable was that of the administration. Zia's domination over the army, the legislature, and the civil administration had been complete. Now that he was gone, succession in the army proceeded smoothly through the process of seniority, but in the other two departments there was a scramble for authority and positions. From my distant perch in the USA, I followed the machinations that led to the understanding which brought Benazir to power. Whilst backroom wheeling and dealing is a normal part of the democratic process, it is normally restricted to the political parties concerned. On this occasion, the feedback in Washington revealed to me the nature and extent of the American involvement in this exercise. The astute and energetic Bob Oakley was clearly very active, not only conveying messages between the army chief and Benazir, but also providing advice, to the latter in particular. This was in pursuit of an American policy decision to support Benazir, and she in turn made no secret of her reliance on their support.

The elections went off smoothly, and out of a total of 207 seats in the National Assembly the PPP obtained 93, the IJI came in second with 55, and although the Muttahida Qaumi Movement (MQM) obtained only 13, they had control of Karachi and Hyderabad. Following intensive and highly complicated negotiations between the army, Ghulam Ishaq Khan, and Benazir Bhutto, with significant inputs from the Americans Bob Oakley, Richard Armitage, and Richard Murphy, an arrangement was cobbled together whereby Benazir Bhutto became Prime Minister, but was subject to a number of conditions. These included no interference in the defence, nuclear, and Afghanistan policies, no interference in the administration of the army, and the acceptance of Sahibzada Yaqub Khan as the Foreign Minister. Despite these constraints, it was with clearly evident euphoria that Benazir Bhutto took the oath of office as Prime Minister on 2 December 1988. There was considerable justification for this elation, because Benazir had created history by being the first female Prime Minister of an Islamic country. But in Pakistan, ultimate authority remained vested in President Ghulam Ishaq Khan and the COAS, Mirza Aslam Beg.

CHAPTER TWENTY-FOUR

❧

The United States of America 1989

'*Perché! sempre una mutazione laschiae lo addentellato per la edificazione dell altra.*'
('For one change always leaves an indent for the edification of the next.')
– Niccolo Machiavelli, *The Prince.*

'Being friends with America is like living on the banks of a great river. Every four years it changes course, and leaves you either flooded or high and dry.'
– President Ziaul Haq, in a conversation with the author.

W e began 1989 with new administrations in both Pakistan and the United States, and with our international relations facing both challenges as well as opportunities. One piece of evidence demonstrating Pakistan's importance to the United States was the fact that we were the fourth largest recipient of American economic assistance and military sales programmes.

While the Democrats mourned their inability to capture the White House, they were relieved at the departure of Reagan, and their control of both Houses in Congress gave them assurance in the prospect of dealing with President Bush, who was a great deal more pragmatic and less ideological than his predecessor.

In Washington there was no shortage of goodwill for Pakistan and the new regime of Benazir Bhutto, and on Capitol Hill this was effectively spearheaded by Peter Galbraith, a brilliant and articulate staffer in the office of Senator Claiborne Pell, the Chairman of the Senate's Foreign Relations Committee. Peter was the son of John Kenneth Galbraith, the famous economist and one-time US Ambassador to India, and was a dyed-in-the-wool Democrat. He was a contemporary of Benazir Bhutto at Harvard, where they became good friends, and subsequently Peter used his considerable influence to put pressure on Ziaul Haq to release Benazir from internment. Galbraith later went as US Ambassador to Croatia during the Yugoslav crisis, after which he was in Iraq working closely with the Kurds. He had unique success in both assignments and filed some very perceptive dispatches. We had a very pleasant meeting many years later in Dili when he worked with Sérgio Vieira de Mello at the United Nations Mission in East Timor. Peter and I used to spar with each other during the earlier period of my tenure in Washington, and even though there was never any rancour, it was nice to have him fully on our side.

One of our priorities was to arrange for a visit by Prime Minister Benazir Bhutto to Washington. Since both governments understood the necessity for this, it was simply a question of finding a mutually convenient date and then working out the details. This was fixed for early June, and preparations commenced for what I anticipated would be a very productive visit. Shortly after Benazir Bhutto assumed office as Prime Minister in December 1988, I had submitted my resignation as Ambassador of Pakistan to the USA. I did this, in the first place, on the principle that I had followed throughout my diplomatic career, of resigning office when there is a change of government. In this instance, there were two other factors that motivated my decision. One was my reservations with regard to Benazir's style and management, not to mention the choice of her collaborators as there was a whiff of incompetence and corruption. The other was my conviction that any Pakistani ambassador in Washington must have direct access to, and must possess, the confidence of the head of government. In my case this was clearly not so. Accordingly, I submitted my resignation and in my letter offered to remain at my post until the conclusion of the prime minister's visit. I also suggested that she include my successor in her delegation. Benazir was kind enough to accept my resignation and also my two suggestions, retaining me in Washington for her visit, and bringing with her the excellent choice of Air Chief Marshal Zulfikar Ali Khan. In her letter to me she was gracious enough to state, 'I should like to place on record the Government's appreciation of the valuable services you have rendered to your country during a record spell as Ambassador. You have served with distinction in some of the most important countries and often at difficult times.'

The preparatory work for the prime minister's visit commenced with familiarization trips by a number of officials from Pakistan, including Happy Minwalla, Arnaz's brother, who had now been appointed Ambassador at Large. His earlier affiliation with the PPP was subsequently reinforced by a personal friendship with Benazir, as he had stood by her during the years of her exile. Happy was a close and trusted adviser during the early months of the Benazir administration, and functioned out of an office in the prime minister's secretariat in Islamabad. His association with the administration ended when President Ghulam Ishaq Khan dismissed the Benazir government for inefficiency and corruption in August 1990. It was a curious episode in which Happy, who was involved in the negotiations for the survival of the PPP government, was sent as Benazir's emissary to Ghulam Ishaq Khan, and reported to the prime minister the president's assurance that he would act strictly under the constitution. The latter did exactly as he said he would, with implications that had clearly not been envisioned by either the prime minister or the adviser. Subsequently, Happy wisely withdrew from active politics, and concentrated his attention on his various business interests. But in the spring of 1989 he was deeply involved in the arrangements for the prime minister's forthcoming visit and came to my office accompanied by Mark Siegel, who had replaced Denis Neill as our official lobbyist. Siegel had been a long time friend of Benazir Bhutto, was intensely loyal to her, and had very effectively projected her image in Washington during the period of her long exile. His appointment as the lobbyist was inevitable, but I had too many reservations to build up any meaningful working relationship with him.

There was now a plethora of visitors from Washington in Islamabad, all expressing goodwill and support for the Benazir government. These included everyone from influential senators like Daniel Patrick Moynihan, to sturdy workhorses such as Peter Galbraith. And always there was Mark Siegel. On one of these occasions I was astounded to note the accessibility accorded to the Americans as they attended meetings in the prime minister's office and participated in the preparation of briefs for the visit. Even matters as sensitive as the nuclear issue were raised in the discussions, but it was clear that on this subject the prime minister was not fully aware of the situation as it existed. Ghulam Ishaq Khan had kept it under close lock and key, and was guarding the box like a ferocious watchdog. American intelligence on our nuclear programme was only selectively revealed to Benazir, with a feeling of deep concern, by Brent Scowcroft and Judge Webster, when she got to Washington a month later.

Benazir Bhutto's official visit to Washington was a *succès fou*. She arrived at Andrews Air Force Base on a sunny June morning and looked spectacular as she emerged from the PIA Boeing 747. A large crowd, consisting of Pakistanis, Pakistani-Americans, and Americans, gave her an ecstatic greeting as she walked past them waving cheerfully. Benazir was accompanied by her husband Asif Ali Zardari, and a very large delegation which included a provincial chief minister, the chief justice, ministers, advisers, senior officials, and a plethora of media representatives and security staff. There could not have been too many empty seats on that aircraft. The United States government protocol for official visits was uniformly applied to all states and strictly observed. Eleven persons, including the leader of the delegation, were treated as state guests and provided with all facilities during the three-day duration of the official visit. Everything above and beyond that, in terms of numbers and time, was the responsibility of the visitors. Calculating the cost to the Pakistani taxpayer of this particular junket seemed to me to be an act of futility, because I had seen many similar expeditions that were far less productive.

The prime minister was flown from Andrews to downtown Washington by helicopter and was accompanied by her husband, Foreign Minister Yaqub Khan, myself, and some US officials. Senior-most amongst these was Judge Webster, the Director of the CIA, who spent almost the entire half-hour of the flight providing the prime minister with a brief that revealed the CIA detailed knowledge of our nuclear programme, and a serious warning about the consequences of its continuation. Benazir appeared to have reacted to this presentation with equanimity, and as events would soon reveal, this heavily concealed warning was the only point of contention in an otherwise very successful visit.

The first afternoon's proceedings included a welcome by President Bush at a colourful arrival ceremony on the South Lawn of the White House, complete with a guard of honour. This was followed by a one-to-one meeting between the president and the prime minister, after which there was a formal meeting between the two delegations. The

Americans were reassuring in their expressions of support for the prime minister, and she achieved a major success when the US authorities sanctioned our purchase of the F-16 aircraft. When the formal meeting was over, Brent Scowcroft, the National Security Adviser, spoke to Benazir and a few others. In contrast to the goodwill and understanding that had hitherto prevailed, Scowcroft expressed an undisguised concern. His soft tone and gentle manner could not conceal his serious apprehension over our nuclear programme, and he pointed out that, according to his information, we had already exceeded the threshold on uranium enrichment. He suggested a freeze on these activities, if not a rollback, and warned that a continuation would have the most serious implications for both our countries. The Ancient Mariner, with the albatross around his neck, had made his presence felt at the glittering wedding party.

President Bush was host at a banquet in the White House that night and the cordiality was enhanced by the warm speeches that followed. Benazir concluded hers with the delightful observation that speaking as a Harvard alumnus, the friendly manner in which the president had conducted the day's negotiations had persuaded her to overlook Bush's past associations with Yale. It was a touch of sophisticated humour that went down very well with the American audience. The next day the Benazir cavalcade continued at full strength with a visit to Capitol Hill, where she met the members of the Senate and House Committees on Foreign Relations and then addressed a joint session of the Congress, where again she received an enthusiastic ovation. That evening, the prime minister hosted a return banquet for the Americans represented, as is customary, by the vice-president. Dan Quayle had been the subject of many snide jokes that did the rounds in Washington, one of which was that he went through a journey of Latin America under the impression that Latin was the official language of the continent. In her banquet speech Benazir extended an invitation to Quayle to visit Pakistan, adding that he would not need to know Latin for the purpose. It was a sick joke, entirely inappropriate to the occasion, and although I saw the vice-president's face flush in anger, his response was generously moderate. This remark had not been in the draft when we went over Benazir's speech the previous day, so I was taken by surprise and could only conclude that one of her American advisers had made a last-minute insertion. It was the kind of tasteless joke that could sometimes be found in domestic American politics, but was entirely unsuitable for this occasion. It ended a highly successful visit on an unnecessarily sour little note.

The prime minister's schedule next took her to Boston, where she was presented with an honorary degree by her alma mater. Since this was a private function, she was accompanied only by her husband and a few close friends. The rest of the delegation moved on to New York for the last part of the visit. For the period of her stay in Boston, Benazir had left her infant son Bilawal, together with his nurse, in our care, and they duly accompanied us to New York. He joined his parents when they arrived at their suite at the Waldorf Astoria Hotel. The next two days were confined to meetings between the prime minister and a number of important American personalities including President Richard Nixon.

The prime minister and her large delegation took off from New York at the end of what had clearly been a very successful visit. As she said goodbye, she was kind enough to give Arnaz a kiss and to thank me for the work done by my staff and myself to make a success of the visit.

As I stood on the tarmac of JFK airport in New York, I thought back to the time twenty-four years earlier when I had stepped down onto the tarmac at Accra airport. It had been a long journey, both in time and in space.

CHAPTER TWENTY-FIVE

❦

Interregnum 1989–1990

W e left Washington on 1 July 1989, and moved into a house that we had purchased in St. Petersburg, Florida. My frequent visits to CENTCOM in Tampa had made me familiar with the region, and we loved the climate, and the easy, laidback style of the residents. We were not too far from New York, where both our daughters, and Arnaz's sister Mitzie and her husband Khurshed lived, and there were also good communications with Pakistan. Arnaz and I thought that in many ways St. Petersburg reminded us of Karachi during the halcyon days of the 1950s, and we looked forward to a pleasant existence dividing our time between Karachi and Florida. An important factor that influenced our decision to live in St. Petersburg was the presence of our very good friends Dr Robert Good and his wife Dr Noorbibi Day. He was an eminent oncologist who had performed the world's first bone marrow transplant, and she was a leading immunologist. Bob Good's death through cancer, a few years later, was the ultimate ironical tragedy and a devastating personal blow to us.

When I told Mike Armacost at the State Department about my intention to move to St. Petersburg, he suggested that I meet his brother Dr Peter Armacost who was President of Eckerd College, a small and very innovative liberal arts college which was part of the United Presbyterian group. I was happy and honoured, therefore, when he appointed me to the faculty as Diplomat in Residence. It was agreed that I would teach a course in Diplomacy and International Relations, and thus began a new career. It is one that I enjoyed tremendously, and count the years that I spent at Eckerd among the happiest in my life. There is nothing more joyful and stimulating than to find oneself among bright young minds, eager to learn and expressing themselves with vigour and originality. Everything went smoothly after I had recovered my equanimity from the initial cultural shock. I was not prepared for the presence, in the front-row desks, of long-limbed Florida girls, clad in shorts, some munching apples, as I dwelt on the implications and intricacies of *notes verbales*, demarches, protests, and ultimatums. Some years later, Dr Peter Armacost retired from Eckerd College and became President of my alma mater, Forman Christian College in Lahore, when it was privatized by President Pervez Musharraf and restored to the United Presbyterian mission. Peter did a superb job and restored the college, from the depredations suffered after Bhutto's nationalization, to its former prestigious status.

The serenity of my pleasant life in Florida was interrupted from time to time by the news emanating from Pakistan. The glow of Benazir's triumphal visit to Washington had disappeared soon after her departure from the US, and had been replaced by the familiar pattern of differences between the president, the prime minister and the army chief. Added to this was the mounting evidence of incompetence and corruption within the Bhutto government, and an increase in recriminations between the army and the civilian administration, particularly over the former's refusal to use force against the PPP's political opponents. The result of a combination of these elements was the dismissal of Benazir Bhutto's government by President Ghulam Ishaq Khan in August 1990, and the appointment of a caretaker government with Ghulam Mustafa Jatoi, a senior political leader and former PPP elder, as the Prime Minister. The army leadership had also changed, with the retirement of General Aslam Beg and the appointment of General Asif Nawaz as his successor. The latter was a brilliant officer, a thorough professional with an outstanding service record and an impeccable reputation. His death, of a mysterious, and never quite explained heart attack, a year and a half later, was a devastating blow to Pakistan and to the army. Devoid of all political ambition, and known universally as a soldier's soldier, Asif Nawaz had become, during the short period of his tenure, a symbol of strength and stability in the whirlwind of the Pakistani political scene. His untimely death was indeed a bitter loss for Pakistan.

I was in Karachi during the summer of 1990, when I received a call from Islamabad summoning me to a meeting with President Ghulam

Ishaq Khan. He told me that he wished to appoint me as Pakistan's Permanent Representative to the United Nations in New York. The post was vacant as Nasim Ahmed, its previous incumbent, had died of a sudden heart attack in July. I had known Nasim for many years as a journalist and senior correspondent for the newspaper *Dawn*, and his appointment to New York by Benazir Bhutto was the culmination of his close association with the PPP.

I was naturally delighted and honoured to accept the honour offered by President Ghulam Ishaq Khan, and started preparations to take up my post in New York in time for the commencement of the General Assembly session in September. This included, of course, the matter of my association with Eckerd College in Florida. Peter Armacost was kind enough to realize my compulsions, and arranged it so that I could return to Eckerd on the conclusion of my tenure at the United Nations.

Accordingly, Arnaz and I left for New York in August 1990. It had been an eventful interregnum while it lasted, but now it was at its end.

PART X

THE UNITED NATIONS, NEW YORK

CHAPTER TWENTY-SIX

The United Nations, New York 1990–1992

'Where there is discord, may we bring harmony. Where there is error, may we bring truth. Where there is doubt, may we bring faith. And where there is despair, may we bring hope.'

– St. Francis of Assisi

'This organization (the United Nations) was created in order to save you from going to hell. It was not created to take you to heaven.'

– Dag Hammarskjöld

We arrived in New York in August 1990 and moved into the very comfortable residence on East 92 Street, which had been acquired, through his usual foresight, by Ambassador Amjad Ali. The chancery situated on East 65 Street had been in our possession since 1948, and was another splendid building with an imposing interior. However, its distance from the United Nations building occasionally caused logistical difficulties, particularly during the busy UN General Assembly sessions. Our officers' residences were located all over Manhattan, whilst our staff lived in the neighbouring borough of Queens. Although our government owned some of the officers' apartments in Manhattan, we were still paying high rents for the rest. Accordingly, during my tenure I proposed that we obtain a loan from the National Bank of Pakistan for the purchase of five more apartments as there was a comparative slump in property values in Manhattan at the time, and paying interest instead of rent. At the conclusion of the deal we would not only be in possession of valuable property, but its financing would only involve the transfer of funds from one of the government's pockets into another. By submitting the proposal to Nawaz Sharif, when he was the Prime Minister, I had correctly counted on his decisive business acumen. His immediate sanction eliminated all red tape, and after ensuring due transparency in the purchase procedures, we were in possession of permanent accommodations for our officers. This might also mean that, simultaneously with accommodation, we had provided our officers with one of the most difficult landlords in the world, the Government of Pakistan. But that was a different matter.

Shortly after our arrival in New York I presented credentials to Javier Pérez de Cuellar, the Secretary General of the United Nations. A distinguished Peruvian diplomat, whose gentle manners, smooth demeanour, and soft spoken approach were testimony to a personality that was both intelligent and civilized. Javier was an old colleague who had served in Moscow as the Peruvian ambassador at the same time as I did. We became good friends, but neither of us could back then have foreseen the circumstances of our current encounter. We often stood next to each other (Pakistan, Peru) in the line-up at diplomatic receptions at the Kremlin, and whiled away the boredom of waiting to shake hands with the visiting VIP by exchanging either the latest Kremlin gossip or else sheer inanities. He told me that when he left Lima for Moscow, his government said he could take with him either the best secretary in the ministry or the best cook in Peru. He wisely chose the latter. Our first meeting in New York was as pleasant as I had expected it to be, and we went over the likely issues that would be of concern to us, the most important one being the end run of the Afghanistan problem. Javier was assisted by Virendra Dayal, his *chef de cabinet*, an accomplished, urbane, and always immaculately dressed Indian diplomat, who had been in the UN for many years. He was the nephew of Rajeshwar Dayal, who had been the Indian High Commissioner to Pakistan, and had later worked for UN Secretary General Dag Hammarskjöld in the Congo. The subsequently published correspondence between Hammarskjöld and Dayal, provides a fascinating insight into the manner in which these two highly civilized and competent international civil servants dealt with the problems in the early days of United Nations peacekeeping. Shortly after leaving the office of the secretary general, I went to the delegates' lounge where, to my great delight I ran into Soviet Ambassador Vorontsov, my dear and old friend from Moscow and Paris. We went into a bear hug, after which he declared, 'Neither you nor I will leave New York until Afghanistan is solved!' I left the UN building that evening with the feeling that the first day of my assignment at the United Nations had gone off reasonably well.

The professional excellence of the staff of our mission in New York was only to be expected, and remained high throughout my tenure, all newcomers being as good as the ones they replaced. Apart from the excellent standard of professional diplomatic skills, most of our staff was also masters at multilateral diplomacy having a familiarity with the intricacies of UN procedures. Our language proficiency in the mission included French, Spanish, Russian and Arabic speakers, and since we were later joined by a Chinese speaker, we covered all the working languages of the UN system. During the course of a little over fifteen years, Pakistan has three times been elected to the Security Council. When one considers that theoretically there are over 180 member states in contention for five Security Council seats each year, the mathematical odds against Pakistan getting a seat even once are pretty heavy. However, diplomacy is not based on simple arithmetic, and it is a tribute to the skill and professionalism of our diplomats that Pakistan has always played an active role in multilateral diplomacy, and has been held in high esteem at the United Nations. Pakistan does not have the clout of a major military or economic power, nor does it possess strategic commodities such as oil, and yet its voice is sought and heard in all the important international fora. Apart from its repeated membership of the Security Council, Pakistan has been regularly elected to all the other major United Nations bodies such as the Economic and Social Council (ECOSOC), human rights committees, and the financial and administrative bodies that regulate all UN operations. In addition to that, Pakistan is one of the major troop contributors to UN peacekeeping operations that are conducted on a daily basis worldwide. I always had the impression that Pakistan was fighting way above its weight in the United Nations, and the reason that it was doing it with so much success was due entirely to the skill, professionalism, and dedication of its diplomats. In the demanding and hard school that exists in the corridors of the United Nations, Pakistan's skill in the deployment of its human resources is an asset that is viewed with admiration, and is regarded as on a par with the guns or oil that manipulate the diplomacy of some of the other more powerful member states.

Since I had previously attended a number of sessions of the UN General Assembly as a member of the Pakistan delegation, I was reasonably familiar with its procedures and process. However, this time my responsibilities as the Permanent Representative were considerably more diverse. Foreign Minister Sahibzada Yaqub Khan was the leader of our delegation and discharged his responsibilities with his usual aplomb, accompanied by his associate dynamos Shaharyar Khan, Najmuddin Sheikh and the duo of Tariq Fatemi and Rafat Mehdi ('the Fatemites and Mahdis' as Yaqub called them). The General Assembly session had been preceded by a very high-level conference of heads of state and government under the aegis of the UNICEF, and jointly chaired by the president of Mali and the prime minister of Canada. It was intended that the third co-chairperson would be Benazir Bhutto of Pakistan, but the fall of her government, and the absence of a successor prime minister at that time, left Pakistan in a state of limbo, with Yaqub valiantly attempting participation in an associate capacity.

The conference was initiated by James Grant, the dedicated and indefatigable Director General of UNICEF, with the objective of obtaining firm public commitment, at the highest levels of governments, for programmes of health care and education of children, particularly in the developing countries. Because of Benazir's support of the conference, Pakistan had been an active participant in its preparatory work, and I found myself involved in the negotiations as soon as I arrived at the UN. It was my first meeting with Jim Grant, whose commitment to the cause of UNICEF was almost religious, and who worked for the success of the conference with messianic zeal. As we were to realize shortly thereafter, this inspiring and dedicated humanitarian was fighting a losing battle with cancer even as he was fighting to save the lives of under privileged and malnourished children all over the world. Whilst drafting the rules of procedure, during our preparatory work for the conference, it was decided to impose a strict time limit on each statement, since there were so many participants and so little time. I thought that it would take considerable temerity to impose a time limit on the speech of even one head of state, let alone about a hundred. But in the end it worked out quite well, and most of the captains and the kings stayed within reasonable limits of their allotted time. The only exceptions, not surprisingly, were Fidel Castro and Margaret Thatcher.

This exposure to UNICEF, and in particular to Jim Grant, early in our tenure, inspired Arnaz into active participation in the work of this splendid agency, and she carried out many activities as a UNICEF representative, both in New York and elsewhere. In due course, and in recognition of her effective contribution to other aspects of the work in the UN, she was elected as President of the Association of UN Ambassadors' Wives, and was re-elected to the position until our departure from New York. This was a busy organization that not only actively supported all kinds of UN-related activities, but it also obtained interesting speakers at their monthly luncheons. Sometimes these were complaisant husbands drafted to this duty by their wives. When it came to my turn I felt a bit like Daniel in the lionesses' den.

The first three weeks of the General Assembly session were devoted to policy statements delivered in a plenary session by presidents, prime ministers, and foreign ministers. These monologues, almost always long and repetitive, were framed essentially for domestic political consumption. Most of these cliché ridden documents required only a change of name and date to differentiate them from the previous year's paper. But the real benefit of this procedure, during the first three weeks of the session, was the opportunity that it provided for the important world leaders to meet each other in almost total privacy, not only for a frank exchange of views, but sometimes even to initiate policy exchanges. These bilaterals were sometimes held in the missions of the countries involved, but most took place in the neutral territory of the United Nations building, in rooms or enclaves especially set up for the purpose. I greatly looked forward to these meetings because I always found them to be interesting, important, and worthwhile. But they also involved a charade which triggered some irreverence. The administrative complexities of requirements and schedules necessitated diversity in the venues and timings of the bilaterals. As a result there was a constant movement of groups of diplomats, either dressed in impeccable dark suits or colourful national costumes, carrying their files and documents as they guided and fluttered around their formidable chief, whose distant look bore clear testimony to the burdens of the world which he was obliged to carry on his shoulders, and which he was about to exchange at the next meeting with a similarly burdened and equally exalted colleague. These groups were like a convoy composed of a majestic battleship, surrounded by fussy little destroyers and sloops, proceeding along the spacious corridors of the UN building. As one convoy passed another, one of two things could happen. If the two countries involved were friendly, there would be a temporary disruption, with the battleships engaged in a hearty, friendly hug, and the lesser elements exchanging polite handshakes. The two convoys would then resume their formations and their respective courses. If the two countries were not friendly, the formations would tighten up and the two convoys, passing each other without apparently seeing one another, would purposefully stay on course, spreading waves of cold animosity in their wake.

Prime Minister Ghulam Mustafa Jatoi visited New York for a few days and held meetings with the secretary general, the presidents of the General Assembly and the Security Council, as well as with a number of ambassadors. It was basically a goodwill visit which enabled the prime minister to review the work of our UN mission and more importantly to provide the secretary general and other personalities with news of the ongoing political situation in Pakistan.

During the early part of the General Assembly session there was a minor suspension of the general debate in order to enable delegations to express condolence over the death of my predecessor, Ambassador Nasim Ahmed. This gesture, which symbolized the humanitarian aspect of the United Nations protocol, was all the more touching for that reason. There were some laudatory eulogies, for which I expressed appropriate thanks, and then sent a copy of the record of the General Assembly proceedings to Nasim's widow.

With the conclusion of the general debate in the General Assembly, work began in the various committees, and with the arrival from Pakistan of members of our delegation, we settled into the daily routine of our duties. I met with my officers in staff meetings at the mission every morning, and held meetings of the full delegation three mornings in the week. Our ambassador from Geneva joined us and took charge of work in the First Committee with his usual competence, and the members of our delegation followed proceedings in their respective committees, supported by officers from the mission. It was customary for all statements to be drafted by a diplomatic officer who would, after clearance by me, present it to the delegate for his intervention in the committee. As far as Pakistan was concerned there were no major contentious issues in the forty-fifth session of the UN General Assembly, apart from the hardy perennial of Kashmir, reference to which was made in the formal statement of the foreign minister to the General Assembly, and by our delegation in the Third Committee. To the best of my recollection the Indians did not even exercise their right of reply. This was in line with their policy decision to try and bury the issue by keeping things cool.

Pakistan has always been a major troop contributor to the United Nations, and Pakistani military contingents have participated in peacekeeping operations all over the world. Their discipline and professionalism have justified the admiration of the United Nations officials and have made a major contribution to the success of its various missions. The Undersecretary General for Peacekeeping Operations was Marrack Goulding, a purposeful British diplomat with a longstanding UN association, and Pakistan's vital role in UN peacekeeping obviously made it necessary for me to remain in close touch with his department. The Assistant Secretary General was Kofi Annan, a soft spoken, gentle Ghanaian, with a razor sharp mind, whose service with the UN throughout his working life had familiarized him with the intricacies of every aspect of the functions of the organization. The Director in the department was S. Iqbal Riza, a former Pakistan Foreign Service officer. Brilliant, industrious and highly idealistic, Iqbal epitomized the best in both national and international diplomacy. After attaining considerable seniority, his promising career in the Foreign Service was abruptly terminated by his resignation in protest against the excesses committed by Bhutto's internal repression. He then joined the United Nations in a lowly position, but through sheer brilliance, industry, and proven capability to take initiatives, he had attained a position of considerable responsibility. The trite expression that Pakistan's loss was the UN's gain did not quite apply in this case, partly because Iqbal's presence in the organization was a very favourable reflection of the image of Pakistan, and also because he kept a watchful eye on the interests of Pakistan, without letting it in any way impinge on his impeccable conduct as an international civil servant. Both Kofi and Iqbal were to go far in the coming years, and working with them in the Department of Peacekeeping Operations (DPKO) was as instructive as it was professionally rewarding. Our main preoccupation at that time was the situation in Somalia, where Pakistan had a major presence in the peacekeeping force, and we followed, with mounting concern, the turbulent reports that emanated from Mogadishu at that time.

The other issue I followed closely from the time of my arrival at the United Nations was that of Afghanistan. Vorontsov had rightly called attention to it when he met me shortly after I had presented my credentials, and I was looking forward very much to working with him on this problem. Meanwhile, the United Nations had appointed a special representative for Afghanistan, and he had already set up his office in Islamabad. Benon Sevan was back in New York for consultations, and I decided to take advantage of the occasion to get to know him. We met for lunch at one of the restaurants that dot the neighbourhood of the UN building, which provided reasonably good food in a reasonably comfortable working environment. Benon was a dynamic Cypriot of Armenian descent, who had graduated from New York, and had worked in the United Nations for many years. A burly figure, exuding good cheer and self-confidence, Benon proved to be the ideal choice for a difficult and demanding assignment. Based in Islamabad, Benon was constantly on the move in Afghanistan, shuttling between Najibullah and his ministers in Kabul and the Mujahideen leaders in Kandahar and the countryside. At the same time he established the most cordial relations with the ministers and officials in Pakistan, and he and his lovely wife Michelle were one of the most popular couples amongst the diplomats in Islamabad. Benon was equally at home sipping sweet, milk-laden tea and exhorting the bearded Mujahideen leaders in their camps in the barren mountains of Afghanistan as he was sipping a cocktail and conducting negotiations with sophisticated officials and diplomats in the drawing rooms in Islamabad. There is no doubt about the extent of Benon's contribution towards the peace process, but I do know that his bitterest disappointment was the UN's failure to protect Najibullah from a brutal death whilst in asylum on its premises. Over the years Arnaz and I developed a close friendship with Benon and Michelle, which continues during our retirement. After his assignment in Afghanistan, Benon returned to New York and later worked with me when I was on the Security Council. He then went on to head the Iraq Oil for Food programme, an enormous and complicated assignment, with considerable success. However, he fell victim to an unfortunate series of circumstances that almost shook the foundations of the UN system, and leaving Benon Sevan as the fall guy, ended the long and productive career of a dedicated international civil servant.

Two other issues dominated the forty-fifth session of the UN General Assembly. The first of these was the election of the next Secretary General. Pérez de Cuellar's second term was due to expire on 31 December. The election of the UN secretary general has always been conducted in a Byzantine process in which charter requirements are compounded with conventions and political realities. The role of the Security Council is supreme. Whilst citizens of any of the five permanent member states are ineligible, the contender must first obtain a majority of votes in the Security Council. In the previous election, China had adopted a position of principle that the secretary general must be a citizen of a developing country, and accordingly had five times vetoed the re-election effort of the stubborn and controversial Kurt Waldheim. This resulted in the election, after much diplomatic flurry, of a candidate from Latin America, Peru's Pérez de Cuellar, who was at that time an Undersecretary General at the UN. According to the convention that had just been established, and in accordance with a general understanding it was Africa's turn to assume the post. After some intensive and occasionally acrimonious negotiations, the Organization of African Unity nominated Boutros Boutros-Ghali of Egypt. The formality of his election was completed in December, and on 1 January 1991 he took office as the sixth Secretary General of the United Nations.

Boutros Boutros-Ghali was the scion of a noble Egyptian family of Coptic Christians who had long been active in Egyptian political life. I first met Dr Boutros Boutros-Ghali at the Non-Aligned Conference in Havana where, as leader of the Egyptian delegation, he made a spirited defence of the Camp David Accords and utilized his considerable diplomatic skill and resources in resisting an organized and well-orchestrated campaign for the expulsion of Egypt from the Non-Aligned Movement. Combining considerable political and diplomatic experience with an impressive academic background, Boutros-Ghali made an immediate impact upon assuming his office. In contrast to the somewhat laissez-faire style of his predecessor and the considerable devolution of authority, Boutros-Ghali immediately took measures to centralize authority, and gradually concentrated the decision-making processes, including those related to comparatively routine administrative matters, in the office of the secretary general. In Ambassadors Chinmaya Gharekhan of India and Jean Claude Aimee of Haiti he had two competent and capable advisers, but the increasingly autocratic tendencies in Boutros-Ghali's management style provoked a corresponding resentment both amongst the permanent representatives as well as senior officials in the secretariat. Boutros-Ghali was a highly intelligent, somewhat reclusive individual who did not make friends easily and certainly did not suffer fools gladly. His acerbic sarcasms might cause his subordinates to cringe, but could have been more counterproductive with the permanent representatives. As his term proceeded, and one crisis followed another, Boutros-Ghali's secretive and Byzantine management style provoked a perceptible sense of resentment. My own relations with Boutros-Ghali were very good and I always enjoyed my meetings with him, both in our official as well as social encounters. He had neither the desire nor the ability to make small talk, but after making due allowance for his natural reserve, a serious conversation with Boutros-Ghali could be the most fascinating of experiences. He and his elegant wife Leah came to a number of our dinner parties, and reciprocated by inviting us to their official residence. I understood that the secretary general was quite selective in his social activities, which were restricted to a comparatively few heads of missions, so I was very touched by the gesture. Of the many world leaders whom I have met, Boutros-Ghali was one of the few who was averse to maintaining eye contact, and I found that he only did so when a discussion became serious and the issue was a matter of particular concern to him. On such occasions his brown eyes would flash with a fierce and convincing intensity. Boutros-Ghali was not only an essentially reserved person, but was also steeped in the tradition of Arab nobility, a combination which induced a dignified reserve in his relations with women. Arnaz, with her forthright, vivacious charm, managed to break through this reserve, after which I noticed that Boutros-Ghali always gave her a gentle friendly smile whenever they met.

The other major issue before the forty-fifth session of the UN General Assembly in 1990 was the Iraqi invasion of Kuwait. There was widespread outrage over the military occupation of one member state by another, and the UN was locked in a series of intensive negotiations, with Tariq Aziz, the Iraqi Foreign Minister whom I was to get to know quite well later on, making frequent appearances before the Security Council. I observed, with much interest, the deliberate manner in which President Bush, together with Jim Baker, his able Secretary of State, was articulating the US response to the Iraqi invasion, and to the adroit diplomacy that was exercised in the process. There was a methodical process of consultations and negotiations, and a scrupulous adherence to the norms of international law—the latter even provoking Margaret Thatcher's impatience with her famous exhortation to Bush, 'Now George, this is no time to go wobbly!' At the same time there were negotiations with Saudi Arabia and other Arab states which led to the build up of military forces in the area. As the General Assembly session ended, and we moved into the new year, the United Nations continued its preoccupation with the problem, and we followed the almost continuous proceedings in the Security Council with close attention. The lessons of this entire and valuable exercise were obviously quite lost on the president's son George Bush, Jr., several years later, when he embarked upon his disastrous and almost unilateral invasion of Iraq. I paid a brief visit to Pakistan and was frankly appalled at the thinking that prevailed among our senior military leadership at that time. They seemed to be out of all touch with reality.

In 1990, however, as the US-led coalition's Operation Desert Storm got under way, Pakistan agreed to send a force in support, on the condition that it would be deployed solely for the defence of Saudi Arabia and not used for offensive action in Iraq. Considering the anti-American sentiments prevalent in the country at the time, the decision was understandable, but what surprised me was the extraordinary error of judgement in our military's forecast of the conflict in Iraq. Foreign Secretary Shaharyar Khan told me that he had specifically sounded out the ambassadors in the region, and the unanimous forecast was that Saddam was headed for a major defeat. This assessment was contemptuously rejected by the army leadership, and General Aslam Beg predicted a campaign that would continue into the summer months, with the US forces bogged down by the strength of the Iraqi forces, and suffering the same fate as the Soviets in Afghanistan. It is believed that the Director General ISI General

Hamid Gul, and his predecessor General Javed Nasir, had provided considerable input into an appreciation, wherein ideological wishful thinking appears to have overtaken the reality of military force deployments. Shortly after Beg's speech in January 1991, the coalition forces entered Kuwait and expelled the Iraqi occupiers.

In the summer of 1991 the Iraqi war was over, and work began in the United Nations for a sanctions resolution that was designed to curb Saddam's military power, particularly in respect of his possession of weapons of mass destruction, and in extracting compensation in cash and kind for the destruction caused by the invasion and occupation of Kuwait. There was some criticism of Bush's decision to halt the campaign when he did, instead of going on to Baghdad, toppling Saddam, and destroying the Guards Divisions which were still relatively unscathed. There was also the dark implication that the Guards Divisions had been left intact as a future counterweight to Iran. Whilst there may be an element of truth to the second assumption, I have no doubt that on the main issue Bush's decision was both wise and correct. The Security Council resolution specifically called for the vacation of Iraqi occupation of Kuwait. It did not authorize the occupation of Iraq, nor did it call for the removal of the Iraqi government. The occupation of Baghdad would not have been permissible under international law, and would have been a strategic blunder of the highest magnitude, as the wildly intemperate actions of George Bush, Jr., would later prove.

The United Nations landmark resolution on Iraq had two basic components. In the first instance it established a commission which, in co-operation with the International Atomic Energy Agency (IAEA) in Vienna would monitor the progress in the elimination of stockpiles and delivery systems of the weapons of mass destruction, and report about its progress on a regular basis to the Security Council. This Commission (UNSCOM) was initially chaired by the distinguished Swedish diplomat, Ambassador Rolf Ekéus, and did a superb job. The second body, designated as the United Nations Oil for Food Programme, was designed to monitor the sale of Iraqi oil, and disburse the proceeds for reparations and the purchase of food and other essentials for consumption by the Iraqi people. This was headed by Benon Sevan who did a superb job against all odds. These included blatant sanctions busting and illegal trading in oil by Saddam and his coterie. Sanctions are one of the few instruments available to the Security Council for implementation of its resolutions, particularly those under Chapter VII of the UN Charter, but they are a blunt instrument, and almost always penalize the more vulnerable sections of society, such as the poor, the elderly, and the children. Saddam and his colleagues continued to obtain their whiskey and other luxuries, but for the people of Iraq the long torment of life under the UN sanctions had just begun.

Pakistan chaired the group of the OIC at the UN in New York, and we continued our active participation in the discussions, meetings and resolutions on Palestine. However, our attention was now being directed towards the disintegration that commenced in Yugoslavia, where the Muslims in Bosnia were increasingly been victimized through the barbarous process of ethnic cleaning. This issue provided the mission with considerable activity and occupied a fair amount of our time and attention. Meanwhile, my informal contacts revealed that there was a possibility of obtaining the chairmanship of the Group of 77 for the coming year. Although this was an additional commitment which we were by no means obliged to assume, I felt that we possessed a cadre of capable and dedicated diplomats in the mission who were quite capable of taking on this arduous responsibility and making a success of it. After discussion with our nimble-minded and perceptive Deputy Chief of Mission Shaukat Omer and other colleagues, we embarked on a campaign which resulted, without too much difficulty, in Pakistan's election as Chairman of the Group of 77 for 1992.

The forty-sixth session of the UN General Assembly session commenced in September 1991, and was attended by a Pakistan delegation that reflected the changed political climate in the country. It was led by Siddique Kanju, a stalwart Muslim League politician from the Punjab, who had now become Foreign Minister. Gentle, kind and humble, with a perpetually benign smile on his face, Kanju's leadership style emphasized consultation and co-operation, and completely eschewed assertion. It is one more of the ironies of fate that Siddique Kanju, one of the kindest and gentlest of persons, was later gunned down whilst on a political campaign in his home district. The delegation also included Akram Zaki, who was now Secretary General in the Foreign Ministry, and whose pugnacious personality was in direct contrast to that of his benign foreign minister. Bright, well read, well informed and energetic, Zaki's career in the Foreign Service had been somewhat tempestuous, and I suspect that his abrasive style had not only found victims but also accounted for his own occasional victimization. His subsequent forays into politics produced mixed results.

The Pakistani delegation made its useful contribution to the work of the forty-sixth General Assembly session, where the Middle East situation and the growing crisis in Yugoslavia dominated the debates. The Kashmir issue remained on the table, but there was no progress, and Pakistan and India continued to express their differing viewpoints. The rest of the delegations had heard it all before.

CHIAROSCURO

President Richard Nixon never wavered in his affection for Pakistan, and never hesitated to express it, both in private and in public. Despite the many other demands on his time, he used to occasionally receive me in his office for a short discussion. His assessments of the American political scene were incisive and revealing, and had me completely enthralled. But it was in his *tour d'horizon* of international affairs that his presentations were at their masterful best and revealed his genius as a statesman and practitioner of the art of diplomacy. In 1989 he invited me to dinner at his home in Hackensack, New Jersey, where the other eight guests were the Swiss ambassador in Washington and the presidents or CEOs of some major American corporations. The excellent dinner was complemented by superb wines from Nixon's cellar, the qualities of each being described with the pride and knowledge of a true connoisseur. He conducted the conversation during dinner with the precision and firmness that he probably employed in his cabinet meetings. The Tiananmen Square incident had just occurred in Beijing, and Nixon asked each one of his guests whether he should accept the Chinese government's invitation to visit the country. When it came to my turn, I said I thought it very important that Nixon go to Beijing. His relations with China were not only special and personal, but were of historic importance. The circumstances that moved the Chinese leadership to take this brutal action had a compulsion that few outside the country could understand, and had obviously been taken after anguished consideration. Nixon should project his visit as an occasion for counsel amongst friends. I found that in expressing this view I was in the minority among the guests at the table. When Nixon had done the rounds he told us that he had already accepted the invitation, because he felt very much as Ambassador Marker did, but made it clear that he 'did not want to be seen drinking toasts in the Great Hall of the People's Republic'. He added that when he telephoned his acceptance to the Chinese ambassador in Washington, 'I could hear the guy almost sobbing with relief'.

On another occasion President Nixon came to dinner at the embassy. When I introduced Arnaz to him he said, quick as a flash, 'Then who was that blonde you brought to my office the other day?'

* * *

The rivalry between Pakistan and India was perpetually present in the corridors of the United Nations, and was subject to the swings of mood that reflected the situations prevalent in New Delhi and Islamabad at the time. They varied from the extremely heated debate in the Security Council in December 1971 to an extremely cordial joint session in commemoration of Allama Iqbal, which was hosted by the Indian and Pakistani delegations, and held in the Trusteeship Council Chamber in the mid-1980s. Nevertheless, Indo–Pakistan relations were viewed in the corridors of the United Nations as a prickly affair, and one which delegates either avoided completely or else approached with considerable caution. The general feeling was that no matter what was said, it was bound to offend either one side or the other. An exasperated European delegate once said to Zulfikar Ali Bhutto, 'We are tired of you Indians and Pakistanis constantly snapping at our heels'. The vintage ZAB response was 'Be careful. Next time we may aim higher'.

* * *

During the General Assembly sessions Yaqub and I usually tried to get together for one tête-à-tête meeting for an exchange of views and ideas. On one such occasion I was informed that Yaqub would receive me in his hotel room in the late evening, followed by dinner in the ground floor dining room at the hotel. The staff work for this event was undertaken by the always efficient Tariq Fatemi and Rafat Mehdi, who departed from the hotel as soon as they had seen me safely ensconced in the Foreign Minister's hotel suite. After our meeting was over we descended to the foyer of the hotel, and instead of turning left and proceeding into the dining room Yaqub turned right and gently led me to the hotel exit. There he bade me a fond and courteous goodbye, and without any demur I found myself on East 65 Street. Meanwhile Yaqub proceeded to his table in the dining room and awaited his guest. As I was walking home, I encountered our two brilliant staff officers, and in reply to their astonished enquiry I mumbled something about a change in plans. Meanwhile Yaqub dined alone, after waiting for a while and fuming at the inefficiency of Tariq and Riffat. He discovered the faux pas after he had returned to his suite and looked at his engagement schedule. The spectacle of Pakistan's foreign minister and one of its senior-most ambassadors, exuding reticence and politeness as they fumbled out of a carefully scheduled dinner engagement, sent a wave of mirth through the corridors of the Foreign Ministry.

MEANWHILE IN PAKISTAN

Elections held in November 1990, following the dismissal of the Benazir Bhutto government, brought into power the IJI (Islami Jamhoori Ittehad), an alliance of rightist parties under the prime ministership of Nawaz Sharif. Subsequent evidence has revealed the key role played by the ISI in the manipulation of the electoral process, but there can be little doubt that ineptitude and corruption were the basic causes of Bhutto's downfall. Another major change was the reluctant retirement of General Aslam Beg as Chief of the Army Staff on the expiry of his term in August 1991. Beg had been playing an increasingly active political role, a tendency that probably irked both President Ghulam Ishaq Khan and Prime Minister Nawaz Sharif. His replacement was the very popular General Asif Nawaz, an excellent officer and a gentleman, who was determined to maintain and improve the professional standards of the Pakistan army. In his first Order of the Day, General Asif Nawaz proclaimed, 'I would like it to be understood that the Army must have nothing to do with politics. Let the elected representatives do their job while we concentrate on acquiring ever greater professional excellence.'

When I read a copy of this Order of the Day at my office in New York I was considerably moved, and thought it was an excellent start to the new relationship between the army and the civil administration, and between an incoming prime minister and an incoming chief of army staff. However, my optimism proved to be short-lived and there were disturbing reports about increasing differences between the two. Not surprisingly, these were attributed to the prime minister's covert attempts to influence senior army officers, through crude tactics such as offering them incentives and perks. It thus became a case not of the army entering into politics but of politics entering into the army.

The relations between the political parties in Pakistan remained as acrimonious as ever, and during my visits home I noticed that Ghulam Ishaq Khan, who as president had been an outstanding rock of stability between the different factions, was gradually being drawn into a conflict with Nawaz Sharif. I took off for New York with the feelings that the blessings of democracy were proving to be very mixed one indeed. The only comfort was the reassuring presence of General Asif Nawaz and his determination to keep the army out of the politics of the country.

During the year 1992, the work of the Pakistan mission was largely devoted to discharging its responsibilities as Chairman of the Group of 77. The normal requirements of coordinating the Group's position concerning the ongoing issues with regards to economic and financial subjects, and the implementation of resolutions adopted during the current and previous General Assembly sessions, were carried out in a series of meetings which were usually held three or four times a week. The Group of 77 was a heterogeneous collection of so-called developing nations, set up to co-ordinate policies and positions for negotiations with the developed countries. Its original membership of seventy seven had by now expanded to 129, but it still retained its original designation of the Group of 77. Unlike the Non-Aligned Movement (NAM), which was a political organization, the Group of 77 was essentially concerned with economic issues, and included many states that were not members of NAM. The Group of 77 comprised states of every political orientation, from monarchies to Marxists, and from democracies to dictatorships. It also included high income countries like Saudi Arabia, Kuwait, and Singapore, and impoverished nations like Somalia and Guinea-Bissau. I anticipated that my role as chairman, coordinating policies in a group with such multifarious interests and priorities, was not going to be an easy one, and in this, at least, I was right. Obviously, every issue was subject to two phases of negotiations, first within the Group of 77 and then with the industrialized countries in the G-8. The contrast in the numbers, though suggestive, does not reflect the totality of the considerations that confront the chairman of the Group of 77.

As we proceeded through the year in a series of multifarious negotiations, I observed a noticeable similarity in the positions of the Group of 77 and China, and pondered on the possibility of establishing a formal link between us. For obvious reasons it would not be possible to make China a member of Group of 77, but I could see that some form of formal association could bring widespread benefits for us both. I put the idea to my friend and colleague, the permanent representative of China, who was not only receptive but enthusiastic, and immediately sought his government's approval. After some discussion we thought that our association should be formalized in the United Nations by the designation 'The Group of 77 and China'. Once we got the clearance from Beijing, I commenced work on the members of my group. Most were supportive, but there were a few diehard opponents. These included some Arab oil-rich states with an instinctive tendency to keep their distance from the People's Republic of China, and some African states that maintained diplomatic relations with Taiwan. But a combination of pleading, backslapping and arm twisting during the course a few lunches persuaded these reluctant delegations to either support or abstain on the proposal to incorporate China with our group. Eventually I convened a formal session of the Group of 77, attended also by the Chinese delegation, during the course of which we passed a resolution establishing official links with China, and assumed the official designation within the United Nations as 'The Group of 77 and China'. This was a result that brought me considerable personal satisfaction.

The United Nations Conference on Environment and Development (UNCED) was scheduled to take place in Rio de Janeiro, Brazil, in June 1992, and would be attended by more than 130 heads of state and government. The Swedes had, as usual, been among the earliest to sound alarm bells over the issue of global environmental depredation, and had called attention to this in a UN conference in Stockholm in the early 1960s. Since then there had been a massive deterioration in the situation, but one that was matched, fortunately, by an increased awareness of the problem. The UNCED conference was, therefore, convened in order to address these issues at the highest international level, and was preceded by a series of Preparatory Committees (PrepComs) in New York and elsewhere. The Secretary General of UNCED was a dynamic and dedicated Canadian, Maurice Strong, who was not only a very wealthy and successful businessman, but also had a record of distinguished public service both in his own country and with the United Nations. His able deputy was Nitin Desai, a senior official in the Indian Finance Ministry, who had been seconded to the UN as Undersecretary General. Strong and Desai not only provided the administrative facilities for UNCED, but actively guided the work of the conference by providing working papers and participating in the negotiating process. The Chairman of the Executive Committee was Ambassador Tommy Koh of Singapore, formerly his country's ambassador to the United States and also Permanent Representative at the United Nations. Tommy was one of the brightest, ablest, and most skilful diplomats that I have ever known. A highly intelligent, cool, low key and soft spoken little man, Tommy was a consummate negotiator, who could never be provoked and always retained his composure, coupled with a subtle sense of humour, in every situation of stress and crisis. And there was no shortage of these either in the PrepComs or at the summit in Rio.

As chairman of the Group of 77, Pakistan played a key role in UNCED, and during the two PrepComs in New York my excellent staff, especially Alamgir Babar and Tehmina Janjua, received support from the Ministry of Foreign Affairs and the Environmental Department in Islamabad. This was a bit of a curate's egg—some were sound, but others were free riders and a major debilitation on the already strained resources of the mission. My obligations and duties as Chairman of Group of 77 kept me fully occupied with negotiations within the Group, where the Chinese delegation was most helpful, and also with the G-8 delegations. Here we ran into difficulties with the Americans from the very start, and their rigid positions, especially on the issue of emissions, formed a major and formidable obstacle. I could also foresee this as an issue that would cause fissures in the Group of 77, as it was bound to find support from delegations such as Saudi Arabia and Kuwait. Nevertheless, it was an absorbing experience to work at close quarters with thorough professionals like Tommy Koh, Maurice Strong, and Nitin Desai, and after the second PrepCom, I thought that we were in good shape for the Rio summit.

The Pakistan delegation to the Rio Conference was led by Prime Minister Nawaz Sharif, who came with a large entourage, including the Environment Minister Anwar Saifullah, Presidential Adviser Roedad Khan (whose long, single-handed dedication to the preservation of the Margalla Hills qualifies him as an all-time environmental Sherpa), Foreign Secretary Shaharyar Khan, and several politicians and officials. Rio de Janeiro must be one of the most beautiful cities in the world. Like Istanbul, San Francisco, and Sydney, its surroundings are a felicitous combination of ocean, azure skies and lush green hills, each seemingly fashioned by the Creator when in a beneficent mood. But the natural beauty of Rio is blighted by the scourge of human poverty and deprivation, and its concomitant of insecurity and crime. The Brazilian government had taken precautionary measures, and there was a noticeable presence of armoured cars and security patrols along the broad boulevards of the Copacabana. Even so, I was advised by the hotel staff to leave my wristwatch in the room safe when I went for a walk along the beach. I had one day of sightseeing before being plunged into the work of the conference, after which my time was spent in meetings that often lasted up to two or three o' clock in the morning.

Apart from the official delegations, there were a large number of NGOs and media representatives, with the Americans of course being the most numerous. They formed a curiously contradictory group, with the official delegates vigorously pursuing the hard line approach of the Republican administration, and the non-governmental participants, with Al Gore leading the charge, equally vigorously campaigning for liberal, broad-based environmental legislation. The negotiations on almost every issue were tough and hard fought, and I did my best to emulate the calm and sophisticated style of Tommy Koh. There was one occasion, however, when my patience was stretched to its limit. After a great deal of difficulty, we had arrived at an understanding over a certain formulation in a particular draft resolution, but when it came up for the vote one delegation changed its position and demanded a review. This request came at about two in the morning, and in responding to it I recalled something that I had read many years earlier in a tract by my friend Bobby Kooka. I said that the official stand of my delegation was to acknowledge the sovereign right of any delegation to review its position before the vote, and we, therefore, acceded to the request. But if the chairman would permit an observation in my personal capacity, I had to confess that I had no time for the man who beats his wife, or plays a weak 'no trump', or overtakes on the right, but he is my buddy compared to anyone who reopens an agreed understanding. If that happens, strong men weep when they see the look in my eyes. The ever patient Tommy Koh, who had also been through this tortuous process, gave me a smile and a wink as he conveyed the customary chairman's thanks for the statement of the Pakistan delegation. I cannot, at this moment, recollect either the text or the fate of that draft resolution.

The Rio conference marked a watershed in terms of global environment issues, and its conclusions not only established important new international institutions such as the Global Environment Facility (GEF), but also established the definitive link between environment and development, through the concept of Sustainable Development, i.e. if you cut down a tree, you plant a tree to replace it. The conference also initiated numerous measures connected with topics as diverse as marine biology and the transfer of technology. But most important of all, it addressed the issue of global pollution and climate change, and although the results were disappointing from the point of view of the Group of 77, it did initiate negotiations that led to the Kyoto protocols. Pakistan played a key role in the negotiations and the staff of our mission, as well as those supporting us from the headquarters, remained fully involved in the arduous and often acrimonious mechanics of the process. The prime minister's stay in Rio was comparatively short and, as expected, he devoted his attention to bilateral meetings with other heads of government, some of which I attended when I was free from UNCED occupations. Most of the rest of the delegation took the opportunity offered by the standard benefits of a junket and had a good time in Rio. Some of them even managed to look important as they did so.

On return to New York we immediately commenced lobbying efforts for membership of the Security Council. The two major contenders for the Asian seat were Pakistan and Indonesia, and as the forty-seventh session of the General Assembly commenced in September 1992 we intensified our efforts by meeting the various foreign ministers as they arrived in New York. Obviously we would need to concentrate on the Asian Group, whose endorsement would be both a prerequisite as well as an assurance of success. I had very good personal relations with Nana Sutresna, the Indonesian Permanent Representative in New York, and also with Ali Alatas the Indonesian Foreign Minister, who had been my friend and colleague at the UN in Geneva. When the latter arrived in New York, Nana and I worked out with him an understanding that Indonesia would withdraw its candidature in favour of Pakistan and that we would support Indonesia's candidature at the conclusion of our term on the Security Council. This understanding was conveyed to the Asian Group, and having secured the group's endorsement, our path to membership of the Security Council for 1993–1994 seemed to have been cleared. Even so, we needed to continue our lobbying efforts among all the delegations until the elections were concluded in late November. I thanked Alatas and Sutresna for their co-operation and understanding, and above all for their friendship. None of us realized at that time how much closer this friendship would grow in the coming years when I became involved in the negotiations over East Timor.

CHAPTER TWENTY-SEVEN

The United Nations, New York 1993–1994

'I would count everywhere on the individual hostility of the Great Powers but would endeavour so to arrange that they were not united against me.'

– Lord Curzon

'Ideals are like stars. You will not succeed in touching them with your hands. But like the seafaring man on the desert of waters, you use them as your guide, and following them you reach your destination.'

– Carl Schurz

'To realize the relative validity of one's convictions and yet stand for them unflinchingly is what distinguishes a civilized man from a barbarian.'

– Isaiah Berlin, *Four Essays on Liberty*

'*Paciencia y barajar.*' ('Have patience and keep shuffling the cards.')

– Cervantes

The United Nations Security Council is the epitome of the concept of the organization itself, and is an institution which, though essentially guided by ideals, yet attempts to reconcile them with the compunctions of political reality. The basic mechanism for achieving this objective is the clause in the charter that provides for five designated permanent members in the council, each equipped with the power to veto any issue that comes before the council. Despite the revulsion provoked by this obviously undemocratic arrangement, I take the iconoclastic view that without it the United Nations would, soon after its inception, have repeated the disastrous disappearance of its predecessor, the League of Nations. The veto provided to the superpowers the assurance that their vital interests would always be secure. Whilst this frequently froze the activities of the Security

Council, it permitted the other vital subsidiary organizations of the United Nations (FAO, WHO, UNHCR, etc.), to take root and to flourish. Thus, the impression that remained most firmly imbedded in my mind during the two years that I served on the Security Council was that of working with colleagues who were always motivated by the ideals of the United Nations, notwithstanding their frequent, vigorous, and often cynical, pursuit of national interests.

In January 1993, Pakistan assumed its membership of the UN Security Council, and over the next two years provided me with a unique and fascinating experience. In terms of the profession it could not have been more stimulating and absorbing, replete with challenges, and involving a constant interaction with fourteen of the world's top diplomats. The problems and situations that we encountered during my tenure were neither greater nor less than those that have come before the Security Council over the years, and the procedures and methods employed to deal with them have been well tried and tested. The UN secretarial staff that attend to the work of the Security Council are among the most able that the organization possesses; expert professionals with admirable institutional memories and a thorough knowledge of the workings of the UN system. Much the same can be said about the simultaneous interpreters allocated to Security Council duties, who not only possessed a sound political background and knowledge, but provided a remarkably accurate and constant rendering of the proceedings. In fact, I thought that quite often the interpretation sounded better than the original expression.

The formal meetings of the council took place in the elaborate Security Council Chamber, made famous throughout the world through photographs and films. The members of the Security Council are seated, in alphabetical order of their respective countries, at a large horseshoe table, with seats for the secretary general of the UN and the assistant secretary general (ASG) for Security Council affairs being placed to the right and left, respectively, of the current president of the Security Council. Since this high office is rotated every month, the delegations' seating follows a counter clockwise rotation, but the secretary general and the ASG remain firmly fixed in their positions, rather like the Pole Star and its satellite. The seats at the ends of the horseshoe table are allocated, when necessary, to representatives of the two contesting parties in the dispute before the Security Council. The substantial space that separates the two ends of the horseshoe table provides passage for the secretarial staff who occupy tables in the centre of the room. It also provides distance between the representatives of the contending parties, who could glower at each other if they wished, but were at least spared the discomfort of being seated in close proximity. Finally, there is provision in the chamber for the accommodation of the permanent representatives of each of the member states, who can follow the Security Council debates and participate in them when permitted to do so by the president of the council. In the early years of the UN these debates used to be lively affairs, with resolutions and amendments being discussed and voted on in full view of the UN membership and the press. Over time, the practice of 'informal consultations' entered into the work of the Security Council, so that basic decisions were first taken during these informal consultations, and the resulting draft resolutions were subsequently passed in the formal sessions of the Security Council. This practice had its advantages, since the closed doors provided delegations with considerable flexibility in the process of negotiations, but this exclusivity also provoked a natural resentment amongst a number of delegations.

As the presidency of the Security Council rotated on a monthly basis, in the alphabetical order of the country's seat at the council table, the congruence of elements in the Roman alphabet and the Gregorian calendar decreed that Pakistan assumed the presidency of the Security Council twice during my tenure, in April 1993 and July 1994, and both sessions proved to be eventful. Just beside the large Security Council Chamber there was a room reserved for the informal consultations process, fully equipped with desks, microphones, and facilities for simultaneous interpretation. Access to this room was restricted to members of the Security Council, the UN secretariat staff, and any guests especially invited, if the president considered their presence necessary at the time when the council was discussing a specific issue. Thus, when I was president and the council was discussing the situation in Bosnia, we invited Cyrus Vance and David Owen for their advice and participation in the consultations. Some years later, I again found myself in the same room, this time reporting to the members of the council in my capacity as the Special Representative of the Secretary General for East Timor. Next to the consultations room there was an office for the secretary general and another for the president of the Security Council. These rooms were simply furnished, with sofas and tables on the side where visitors could be received, and were situated so as to provide a delightful view of the East River and its constantly flowing traffic. At the time of Pakistan's presidency of the Security Council we decorated the office with our own national emblems, the Pakistani flag and a portrait of the Quaid-i-Azam. It was customary for the incoming president to have a meeting with the secretary general and discuss with him the work programme for the coming month, as well as an agenda of the items that the president proposed to place before the council. After that the president would receive in his office, individually, the permanent representative of each of the members of the council, present them with the agenda, obtain their approval, and discuss with them any issues that were of particular importance to them.

Just as the Security Council was settling into its work on the basis of the agreed agenda we encountered an unforeseen crisis. I received a letter from Dr Hans Blix, the Director of the International Atomic Energy Agency (IAEA) in Vienna, informing me that the North Korean government had declared its withdrawal from the Nuclear Non-Proliferation Treaty (NPT) and had banned the IAEA inspection teams from carrying out their work. The normal procedure in such a situation required the president of the Security Council to bring the IAEA communication to the notice of all members, and convene a meeting of the council to consider a course of action. It seemed to me that whilst immediate action was clearly necessary, a full-scale Security Council meeting might prove counterproductive, and accordingly decided to defer convening one. I felt that there were occasions when a Security Council president should exercise his authority and assume an initiative rather than adhering closely to the conventions. I proposed to the members that we meet in the Council, issue an anodyne presidential statement urging the North Koreans to adhere to the NPT, and then commence informal consultations. In deciding on this course of action I was guided by Benjamin Disraeli's wise counsel, 'Next to knowing when to seize an opportunity, the most important thing in politics is to know when to forego an advantage'. The council met, and I issued a presidential statement expressing the Council's concern and urging Pyongyang and the IAEA to 'resolve their dispute over weapons verification'. I then met the ambassadors of the P-5 (the five permanent members) individually, as well as the ambassador of Japan (who was already on the Security Council), and the ambassadors of North and South Korea. Except for the North Koreans, the others' responses were encouraging. The North Koreans took a very rigid position, and maintained that their government was invoking a clause in the NPT which permitted withdrawal. He was silent when I countered that the same clause also stipulated one year's notice, but he did add that his foreign minister was due in New York shortly, and would be available for further discussions. This was encouraging, because the North Koreans had obviously not turned their backs on us, as became evident in my discussions with the minister when I met him. The South Korean foreign minister also displayed considerable understanding and flexibility, and provided a fund of valuable information about the prevailing conditions in the Democratic Republic of Korea. Following intensive discussions, and taking particular account of the views of the Chinese, Japanese, and the South Korean representatives, who were the most affected by, and most knowledgeable about the situation, I concluded that Pyongyang had three major concerns. The first was a looming humanitarian crisis caused by severe food shortages, the second was a perceived threat invoked by the forthcoming joint US–South Korean military exercises (Pyongyang's foreign minister told me that his government's action was meant 'to show the world that we are strong'), and the third was the necessity for nuclear power to meet their growing energy requirements. Once we had ascertained their motivation, it became possible to address the North Korean concerns.

In response to the North Korean complaints the US came forward with generous food aid, and thereby prevented what might have been a devastating famine, the Americans and South Koreans were persuaded to call off their joint war games, and negotiations were commenced for a nuclear power plant under the IAEA safeguards, with western technology and Japanese finance. In return, Pyongyang withdrew its notice to abrogate the NPT, and opened the doors to the IAEA inspectors. Thus the crisis was defused without need for further formal recourse to the UN Security Council. This was an interesting instance of how the council maintained its efficacy through the judicious application of self-effacing methods. In later years, after the beloved leader Kim Jong Il had succeeded the great leader Kim Il Sung, the North Koreans commenced a serious reactivation of their nuclear programme, which in turn triggered a series of high level negotiations conducted in Beijing under Chinese auspices. Although we had fulfilled our first two understandings with Pyongyang, and commenced implementation of the third, my information was that the nuclear power plant project ran into snags and was not completed. So perhaps the North Korean's suspicions were not altogether unfounded.

The issue of sanctions is constantly in the forefront of the Security Council's consideration. It is one of the very few measures available to the United Nations for the imposition of its authority, and its invocation, under Chapter VII of the UN Charter, is the subject of profound thought and debate. This is as it should be, for sanctions are a blunt instrument, and often have a devastating effect upon the more vulnerable members of the society on which the sanctions have been imposed. However, once the Security Council passes a sanctions resolution, it also creates a Sanctions Committee, composed of the members serving on the council, to enforce the resolution by monitoring and supervising its implementation. Apart from the sanctions dealing with Yugoslavia and Bosnia, which occupied a considerable amount of the council's time and attention, there were two other sanctions resolutions that I was required to address during my tenure both as the president and member of the Security Council. The first of these was Security Council Resolutions 731 and 748, passed in April 1992, calling on Libya to co-operate with the international community, particularly the USA, Britain, and France, in connection with the trial and punishment of the perpetrators of the bombings of the Pan American and UTA airliners. The implementation of sanctions came up for review after every 120 days, and although there had been some progress in the matter there had still not been full compliance. The council accordingly renewed the sanctions on Libya, which essentially consisted of an air and weapons embargo. The Europeans' heavy dependence upon Libya's oil and gas exports had excluded these items from the gambit of the sanctions.

The sanctions imposed against Iraq under Security Council Resolution 687 (1991) presented us with a much more complicated problem, with humanitarian consequences of a heart-wrenching nature. The resolution, which was passed after the Iraqi withdrawal from Kuwait in 1991, demanded that Baghdad co-operate with the UN mission charged with the dismantling of Iraqi weapons of mass destruction, return all Kuwaiti assets, accept a UN-imposed demarcation of the boundary with Kuwait, and pay compensation for the expenditure of the process. In my meetings with Iraqi Ambassador Nizar Hamdoon, a seasoned and sophisticated diplomat; the wily Tariq Aziz, Iraqi Deputy Prime Minister and Foreign Minister; and General Amar, who headed the Iraqi arms programme, I conveyed my anguish at the sufferings of the Iraqi people and urged an early and complete compliance with the terms of the sanctions by the Iraqi government. In my address to a closed session of the Security Council I said that the sanctions 'had adversely affected the well-being of the more vulnerable sections of the Iraqi population who bear no responsibility for their government's actions'.

It was abundantly clear that Saddam Hussain was evading and delaying the implementation of the sanctions as much as he could. Rolf Ekéus's regular reports to the Security Council revealed that the UN commission was making definite progress in dismantling Iraq's 'weapons of mass destruction', but this was due more to the tenacity of the inspectors than it was to the co-operation of Iraqi officials. General Amar, confessing to me his personal anguish said, 'Mr Ambassador, I built these facilities for my country with my own hard work, and now I am obliged to destroy them with my own hands. You cannot imagine how painful this is for me. And yet now, when I return to Baghdad with the sanctions still remaining, my young son will say to me "Father, what is the use of all this?"' I told him that I fully sympathized with the plight of the Iraqi people living under sanctions, and would do all I could to help a brother Muslim country, but my task would be considerably helped if his president could display some flexibility and sincerely extend his co-operation to the UN. During my regular meetings with Tariq Aziz we went over much the same issues, and I got to admire his sharp mind and quick comprehension. I noticed also that in moments of tension a slight but distinctive twitch would appear just below his right eye. At one time during the course of our discussions, when I suggested that it would be very helpful if Saddam made a statement acknowledging the sovereignty of Kuwait, that twitch under the right eye turned into a positive quiver. The fear of Saddam's fury had transcended continents and oceans.

The break-up of Yugoslavia brought in its wake a series of geopolitical and ethnic conflicts, the most serious and long standing being the war in Bosnia. But this disintegration also produced another offshoot in the case of the Macedonian problem, which had already been on the boil when I assumed the presidency of the council. For almost a year, Greece had delayed Macedonia's admission to the United Nations. Macedonia was a new republic which had splintered from the former Yugoslavia. The population of Macedonia was about 70 per cent Slavic and 20 per cent Albanian, but the name of the nation, as well as its flag, had the strongest Greek connotations, with Ancient Macedonia being regarded as the home and kingdom of Philip II, father of Alexander the Great. This two-thousand-year-old connection, though entirely devoid of relevance in the current political and ethnic realities, was nevertheless a deeply emotive issue in the volatile Balkans, and threatened a new conflict in an already war-torn region. The Greeks objected not only to Slavs living in a country named Macedonia, but also to the Macedonian flag, which had first been flown by King Philip II. Added to this was Athens's apprehension that Skopje might use these symbols to extend territorial claims over the northern Greek province of Macedonia.

Our discussions with the Greeks and the Macedonians were conducted for the most part on the basis of 'proximity talks', as I deemed it prudent to keep the contending parties apart in the initial stages. After much shuttling between the two delegations we arrived at a rather convoluted arrangement whereby Macedonia would be admitted as the 181st member of the United Nations under the awkward sounding name of 'the Former Yugoslav Republic of Macedonia', the same name under which it was admitted to the membership of the World Bank and the IMF. This did not prevent Macedonia from using that name for itself or in its relations with the other countries. The issue of the flag was even more complicated, and whilst it was agreed that it could be flown in Skopje and at its embassies abroad, its use in the United Nations would be held in abeyance until the issue was finally settled. Thus, for the first and only time in UN history, the flag hoisting procedure was omitted from the ceremonies of admission of a new member state. It took a great deal of effort on my part to persuade the Macedonians to agree to these arrangements, but I think their eminently practical foreign minister finally accepted my suggestion that further delay might well derail the process. The important thing was for Macedonia to take its seat in the UN General Assembly chamber. Once this was done, the flag was bound to follow. After 'The Former Yugoslav Republic of Macedonia' had been formally admitted to the United Nations, Secretary General Boutros-Ghali described the mediation as 'preventive diplomacy'—an effort to defuse a crisis before it flares up. In my statement to the press I said, 'The importance of having this resolved is that one can be sure of peace in an area which is so obviously volatile.' The Macedonian foreign minister issued me with a gratefully accepted, but not yet utilized, invitation to visit Skopje.

The issue that absorbed most of my time, attention and energy, both as the president and member of the Security Council was the crisis in Bosnia. It involved the most intensive aspects of diplomacy, including long and protracted negotiations, the clash of wills and temperaments, and many moments of despair, frustration and sadness. There was a negotiating process well under way at the time when Pakistan assumed its seat on the Security Council, and we received a briefing on this, at a meeting in early January 1993, by Cyrus Vance, a former US Secretary of State, and David Owen, a former British Foreign Secretary. The United Nations could not have found a more eminent pair of negotiators, and their presentations to the Security Council were vintage diplomacy. Both were experienced statesmen of the highest intellectual calibre, but after some interaction with them in the council, I came to the conclusion that whilst Vance was driven by idealism, Owen was essentially pragmatic. In many ways this was an ideal combination. Their different temperaments were also clearly manifest, for whilst Vance was warm, friendly, and easy to talk to, Owen was aloof, with a perceptible intellectual arrogance, and considerable reserve. Informal talks with American and British diplomats confirmed my impression that whilst Vance was a kindly and understanding minister to work for, Owen was prickly and difficult. Over time Arnaz and I became good friends with the Vances whose apartment was not far from our residence in New York, but I never really got to know Owen.

The Vance–Owen Plan, which envisaged a reasonable method of dealing with the complicated ethnic patchwork of the Balkan quilt, was being rapidly overtaken by events, the most alarming of which were the increase in fighting and the spread of 'ethnic cleansing'—an ominous new concept in the field of human rights and repression. At the time the conflict first began in Yugoslavia, the government in Belgrade obtained, from a willing Security Council, a resolution imposing a ban on the supply of weapons to Yugoslavia. This 'original sin', as I called it in one of my statements to the council, resulted in the breakaway states such as Croatia, Bosnia, and Slovenia, being born under a Security Council sanctions resolution (SC 713) and thus denied the right of self-defence as guaranteed by Article 51 of the UN Charter. This incongruity was dangerously exacerbated by the fact that most of the heavy weapons were in the possession of the Serb-dominated Yugoslav Peoples Army (JNA). There was no shortage of weapons in the region, it was just that they were in the hands of one, the wrong, party. This debate, between the right to self-defence, guaranteed under Article 51 of the UN Charter, and the implementation of sanctions imposed under Security Council Resolution 713, was the leitmotif of the negotiations carried out both in the General Assembly and the Security Council.

Until the time Pakistan joined the Security Council, support for the Bosnian cause had been rather ragged and disjointed. The Russians had maintained a firm and unwavering support for Belgrade, partly out of ethnic Slav solidarity but largely because Boris Yeltsin's precarious domestic situation rendered him a hostage to Serb nationalist passions. The early United States position, to which Boutros-Ghali provided tacit UN compliance, was to regard the Balkans as an essentially European problem to be addressed by the Europeans only. Britain and France thus augmented their role as the key players by providing the bulk of the peacekeeping forces. But as the atrocities committed against the Bosnian Muslims increased in an alarming fashion, and as the United Nations Protection Force (UNPROFOR) seemed unable to contain them, concern in the OIC was made manifest at a ministerial meeting in New York, when the Malaysian Foreign Minister Abdullah Badawi urged the hitherto dormant OIC Contact Group on Bosnia, to take urgent measures 'to address the problem in its entirety'. Following Badawi's speech the OIC commenced active lobbying both in the General Assembly and in the Security Council. These were not particularly productive, but at least it was a start, so that we had something to work on when Pakistan became a member of the council in January 1993. By a happy coincidence Djibouti also joined the council at the same time as us, and with Morocco already a member, we had not only the nucleus for initiating action in the Security Council, but also the skill, dedication and talent of the extremely capable diplomats who headed their respective delegations. Ambassador Ahmed Snoussi of Morocco was a dynamic and forceful character, heavily built and imposing in appearance, with a loud, hearty, laugh that reflected an impish sense of humour, and a fund of stories, most of them at his own expense. But together with this effusive bonhomie there was a mind like a steel trap and a determination forged in iron. His powerful interventions in the Security Council debates, delivered in impeccable French redolent with the classical oratory of the language, were as masterful as they were effective. Djibouti's ambassador Roble Olhaye was exactly the opposite of Snoussi, except in the similarity of considerable intelligence. Tall, slim, and soft spoken, Roble worked with the noiseless determination and intensity of a beaver, and maintained his calm composure regardless of crises or provocations. He was also accredited as his country's ambassador to the United States, and commuted between New York and Washington in execution of what must be the world's highest diplomatic charge, and an obvious tribute to his standing within his government.

My position as president of the OIC group at the UN in New York, presented me with an opportunity to project the positions of the Islamic Conference, provided that it was exercised with discretion. This was particularly important when I assumed the presidency of the Security Council. Here I had to balance my obligations as president of the council with those of the president of OIC, and those of the permanent representative of Pakistan. Whilst contemplating my dual role, I recalled Henry Kissinger's observation that relations between the US State Department and the National Security Council (NSC) had never been as amicable as they were during the period when he simultaneously held the portfolios of the Secretary of State and the Chairman of the NSC. In my case, I followed a few basic guidelines. I made sure that the council received a copy of every resolution, declaration or letter emanating from the OIC, and at the same time kept the OIC contact group informed of proceedings in the Security Council. Also, in my statements to the Security Council I would always make references to the OIC's decisions, and suggest that the views expressed were not simply those of one Islamic member state but those of an organization that represented almost a third of the total membership of the United Nations. I also worked with my brilliant and innovative friend, Ambassador Diego Arria of Venezuela, in co-opting Ambassador José Luis Jesus of Cape Verde into our group, which now consisted of Cape Verde, Djibouti, Morocco, Pakistan, and Venezuela. Through a subtle hijacking of nomenclature, we designated ourselves as the Non-Aligned caucus in the Security Council. Our other colleagues in the Council had a more disdainful, but perhaps more accurate name for us. They called us the 'Peasants' Group', doubtless a reflection of our Third World status. By the same token, our vigorous struggle on behalf of Bosnia in the Security Council was sometimes called 'The Peasants' Revolt'. For the two years that we worked together, the Non-Aligned caucus played an effective role in the negotiating process, and its contribution formed an important element in the final settlement. But as far as the Security Council was concerned, the efflux of time and the resultant changes in the composition of its membership, brought the 'Peasants' Revolt' to a quiet end.

The personalities seated at the horseshoe table in the Security Council chamber have always constituted a galaxy of diplomatic stars. It was so in my time, and is no different today. The description 'Fifteen Men on a Powder Keg' is indeed an apt one, rendered only slightly inaccurate in its omission of such distinguished women as Jean Kirkpatrick and Madeleine Albright. I had the honour and the unforgettable experience of working with giants such as Tom Pickering and Madeleine Albright of the United States, David Hannay of the United Kingdom (Winchester, New College Oxford, and a brilliant career in the Foreign Office), Lin Biao of China, Jean-Bernard Merimee of France, Yuli Vorontsov and Sergei Lavrov of the USSR/ Russia, Juan Antonio Yanez-Barnuevo of Spain, together with many other equally distinguished diplomats. The differences in our political views and positions, whilst always acknowledged, were never allowed to detract from the essentially collegial atmosphere of the members of the council and their staff, it being understood that our purpose was to find solutions to often intractable problems, and not to exacerbate them. Our primary responsibility to the international community that had elected us to the Security Council was to work for peace.

On the issue of Bosnia there were, quite naturally, differences in the positions of the members of the Security Council. The Russians remained firmly in support of the Serbs, and the Chinese equally firmly followed their stated policy of neutrality and non-interference. The British and the French, whose diplomatic as well as military interests were deeply involved, were the most difficult and complicated to deal with, and often carried with them the 'neutrals' such as Spain and Japan. Their insistent view that the conflict was a civil war and not, as we maintained, a case of international aggression, was a major point of difference. The US's position was the closest to the Non-Aligned group, as both felt that it was primarily a case of Serbian aggression against Bosnia, and both supported the concept of a multi-ethnic Bosnian state and opposed 'ethnic cleansing', and both supported the lifting of the arms embargo. In my discussions with Madeleine Albright we also agreed to propose UN military intervention, the so called 'lift and strike' option. But despite Albright's often emotionally expressed commitment, the Clinton administration basically stood aside and left the Balkans to the Europeans.

Our only success, which was by no means insignificant, was the establishment of an International War Crimes Tribunal for Yugoslavia, an achievement which could not have been possible without active and forceful US diplomacy. At a later stage, we were also able to obtain a Security Council resolution establishing a 'No Fly Zone' over Bosnia, but its effectiveness was limited by the numerous conditions imposed on its operation. However, our main thrust remained the issue of the lifting of the arms embargo and of ensuring the Bosnians the right of self-defence. The British and the French, who had provided the major components of the United Nations Protection Force (UNPROFOR), were using this as a lever in the negotiating process, thereby increasing Bosnia's vulnerability to Serbian aggression. I was so indignant at this development that I made an offer of a substantial contribution of Pakistani troops to UNPROFOR, and did so without either instructions or clearance from my government, confident that Islamabad would support my action. But even as I made my offer I knew that it would be rejected by the Security Council. The infusion of a substantial Muslim force into a European conflict was obviously anathema to most of its members. In June 1993, we presented another draft resolution to the Security Council, as part of our ongoing attempts to exempt Bosnia from the restrictions of Resolution 713.

Introducing the draft resolution Ambassador Jesus of Cape Verde said, after deploring the lack of political will on the part of the five permanent members of the council, 'If the United Nations is unable to take action to halt the armed conflict and to defend the Bosnian Muslims, the minimum that can be done by the Council is to allow them to defend themselves.' In my statement I warned of the impact on the Islamic world,

> Those in the Muslim world who believe that the West has acquiesced in the defeat of the Bosnian Muslims will be strengthened in their convictions. Those who believe that the United Nations will use force only against Muslims but not in their defence will feel fortified in their belief. If aggression is allowed in Bosnia the forces of moderation will lose. The forces of extremism will be strengthened.

At the end of a passionate and bitter debate, in which about twenty-five delegations participated, the Security Council proceeded to the vote. The five members of the Non-Aligned Group, together with the United States, voted in favour of the draft resolution, the rest of the members of the council abstained. Since it lacked the minimum of eight votes needed for its acceptance, the resolution failed. There was no need for a veto. Our Pyrrhic victory lay in our success in isolating the United States from its traditional allies, one of the few occasions that this has occurred. After the president of the Council had announced the result of the vote, a friendly hug with Madeleine, in the full glare of the Security Council chamber, was the only consolation derived at the end of a dismal day.

It was a source of constant anguish to me that as we were holding debates by the East River in New York, men, women, and children were being brutally massacred in Bosnia. President Alija Izetbegovic of Bosnia visited New York at the time when I was president of the Security Council, and I was particularly keen that he address the council in an open session. Since the Russians strongly opposed the idea, I was obliged to abandon the Security Council proposal, and instead arranged to hold the meeting in one of the other chambers in the United Nations building. Furthermore, invitations had to be extended in my capacity as permanent representative of Pakistan, and not as president of the Security Council. Izetbegovic was a gentle, kindly, old man with smiling blue eyes and a courteous disposition. A devout, practicing Muslim, without a trace of fanaticism of either religious or political ideology, his career had been a lifelong struggle on behalf of Bosnians, regardless of their religion or ethnicity, and he had endured many years of imprisonment for his cause. He made a most eloquent presentation of his ideals and his objective in creating a multi-religious, multi-ethnic democracy in Bosnia. He described the horrors that were taking place in his country, and expressed his determination to resist aggression, but at no stage did this noble and proud old warrior ask for aid or assistance. I believe he left that to our consciences.

The deteriorating situation in Bosnia had reached alarming proportions when I assumed presidency of the Security Council in April 1993, particularly in Srebrenica where over 60,000 Bosnian refugees were being attacked by Serb forces. As there was obviously no countervailing military force to meet the Serbian threat, I thought that the only option available to us was to declare the area as a 'Safety Zone' under UN protection, for which the NAM Group moved a draft resolution. The compulsions of realpolitik then intervened, and consideration of the draft resolution was delayed until 16 April. The reason given was the delicate domestic situation prevalent in Russia, and the necessity to ensure against a Serbian backlash that would adversely effect Yeltsin's re-election. Four of the five permanent members of the Security Council, as well as some of its other members, seemed to consider the argument powerful enough to justify restraining any meaningful response to the killings that continued around Srebrenica. This delay continued until a tense and dramatic session of the Security Council, when Resolution 819 was passed just before midnight on 16 April 1993.[1] The resolution called for 'the immediate cessation of armed attacks against Srebrenica', and declared 'Srebrenica and its surroundings as a safe area which should be free from armed attack or any other hostile act'. After the council meeting, I told reporters at a press conference, 'We have stopped the fall of the town, and what could have been a bloodbath has been halted.' These words, spoken after prolonged tension, and in the first flush of relief and optimism, will haunt me for the rest of my life.

Notwithstanding my brave words in public, I continued to be concerned about the way things were going, and accordingly addressed a letter the very next day to the Security Council on behalf of the NAM Group, calling for an urgent meeting of the council because 'the conditions that justified the adoption of Resolution 819 had not been met'. In a discussion with the sharp, nimble-minded, and indefatigable Diego Arria, I pointed out to him that this request too would be subject to the usual delay, and, therefore, wished to take some immediate and tangible action in the matter. I proposed exercising my presidential initiative and obtain the council's authorisation for a Security Council Fact Finding Mission, under the leadership of Ambassador Arria, to visit the region and report back to the council with its observations and recommendations. Diego jumped at the idea and executed the mission with his usual verve, enthusiasm and brilliance. Participation in the mission was available to all member states of the Security Council, but those that participated were France, Hungary, New Zealand, Russia, and Pakistan (Deputy Permanent Representative Sher Afgan Khan). Diego's report to the council on his return confirmed our worst fears. Although the ceasefire was holding, the Serb forces were literally in control of Srebrenica, had cut off water and electricity to the town and were preventing the delivery of relief supplies. He described the town as 'an open jail'. The Arria Mission recommended the establishment of 'safe areas' which, once established, would be defended by UNPROFOR. Based on these recommendations, the Security Council passed Resolution 824 on 6 May 1993, declaring Sebrenica, Sarajevo, Gorazde, Zepa, Tuzla, and Bihac as safe areas, 'free from armed attacks and from any other hostile acts which endanger the well being and the safety of the inhabitants'. We had established a geographic demarcation of the safe areas, but had neither defined the nature of these enclaves nor indicated how they could be defended. In June, Russia, France, and the UK presented a draft resolution to the Council, which Diego and I considered to be a travesty of the letter and spirit of our resolution and which, if implemented, would perpetuate the existence of these open air ghettos, or besieged refugee camps. I indicated in my statement that 'The Serbs will have full control over the movement of people and goods', and that the resolution in its present form endorsed the 'preservation of the status quo which was to the benefit of the aggressor'. I went on to reiterate

Pakistan's offer of troops to safeguard these areas, an offer that was rebuffed with a deafening silence. Consequently, Pakistan and Venezuela were the only members of the Security Council to register their abstention on SC Resolution 836 (1993).

The changes in the membership of the Security Council on 1 January 1994 effectively broke up our band of happy hunters in the NAM Group. Cape Verde, Morocco, and Venezuela had been replaced by Nigeria, Oman, and Rwanda, and it was with a sense of some foreboding that I took my seat at the council table in the New Year. Of the new members, Rwanda was the only non-member of the OIC, and was in the throes of its own incipient civil war, and while one could count on the support of Oman, the position of Nigeria, which had twice voted against a resolution in the General Assembly calling for the lifting of the arms ban on Bosnia, could at best be regarded as dubious. An attack on an open market in Sarajevo, which had killed many people and caused extensive damage, spurred the Security Council into action, but it was one that I deplored intensely. The previous September the Czech Republic, Russia, Britain, France, and Germany had introduced a draft resolution easing some of the sanctions imposed on Yugoslavia under Resolution 820. This was as a reward for Belgrade's acceptance of the International Contact Group's Peace Plan. We had hitherto fiercely and successfully opposed this move, but the composition of the council's new membership was also a new reality of life. I found, to my consternation, that Pakistan and Djibouti were a minority in our own group in opposing to the easing of sanctions on Belgrade. Resolution 943 was passed by a majority of eleven votes, Djibouti and Pakistan voted against it, and Nigeria and Rwanda abstained. After this disaster I recalled Cervantes' advice and tried to shuffle the cards again. In a desperate attempt to redress the damage done by Resolution 943, we proposed a draft resolution that would cut off Belgrade's support to the Bosnian Serbs, and obtained for this the co-sponsorship of the NAM group together with Egypt, Turkey, Croatia, and Bosnia. We tabled the Draft Resolution on 2 December 1994, and it was supported by thirteen members of the Security Council. China abstained, as expected, but Russia vetoed it without giving any explanation. This was the only time that it used its veto on the matter of Yugoslavia. This ended my direct involvement with the issue of Bosnia because the last day of the month also brought with it the end of Pakistan's term on the Security Council. If there was any satisfaction to be obtained from this final episode it was that by engineering a split, we had somehow brought into perspective a clear indication of the political positions of the five permanent members of the Security Council.

Concurrent with Bosnia was another major conflict, a bloody civil war in the small African republic of Rwanda. Like most other wars in that strife-torn continent, its origins were an amalgam of ethnic rivalry and post-colonial legacy, but the ferocity and scale of the carnage far exceeded the one in Yugoslavia. Yet the Security Council seemed powerless to do anything about it, a passivity which provoked Secretary General Boutros-Ghali into making a statement charging the council with devoting more time and attention to a lesser conflict in Europe than it did to a far greater war in Africa. The norms of morality and humanity fully justified the righteous outrage of the secretary general, but the compulsions of realpolitik prevailed, as always, in international affairs. Rwanda was a tiny country deep in the heart of Africa, whose very isolation contained the fall-out of the conflict. The disintegration of Yugoslavia, on the other hand, affected the balance of power in Europe and beyond. These harsh realities were reflected, as always, in the chambers of the United Nations in New York. One of the first acts of the Security Council was to pass an arms embargo resolution, a routine document that was necessary for the record, but was utterly worthless in terms of ground realities. The atrocities were being perpetrated through the use of locally made knives and machetes, and by arson. Nobody was trying to bring tanks or howitzers into the country. The only way in which the massacres could have been stopped was by a rapid deployment of substantial UN forces, but the political will for such action was entirely absent. After the conflict had run its bloody course, the Security Council created a War Crimes Court, similar to the one established for Yugoslavia, which now functions in Arusha, administering justice in accordance with international law.

During the conflict I recall receiving a late night call from the secretary general requesting urgent assistance for Rwanda. His requirement was for the mobilisation of bulldozers needed for the grisly task of mass disposal of human bodies, in order to prevent epidemics. My only other direct involvement with the Rwanda situation was a somewhat delicate diplomatic assignment. Rwanda was then a member of the Security Council, and the permanent representative was a nominee of the ruling Hutu regime, which was committing atrocities against the Tutsis in Rwanda even as its ambassador, seated in the council chamber, was collecting the council's reprimands for the actions of his government. The incongruity of the situation threatened to become much worse, with the certainty that the rotation system would entitle Rwanda to become the president of the Security Council the next month. Faced with this very uncomfortable but clearly looming possibility, my colleagues in the council assigned to me the task of persuading the Rwandan permanent representative to voluntarily defer his assumption of office for three months, by which time the crisis in his country would hopefully have abated, thus providing him with flexibility in the exercise of his functions as president of the Council. Ambassador Jean-Damascène Bizimana accepted an invitation to a tête-à-tête luncheon at my residence (I expect that at the time the poor fellow did not receive too many), where I augmented my gentle persuasion with considerable quantities of liquid refreshment. His initial reluctance slowly turned to uneasy assent, as I agreed to his suggestion of a three-month postponement instead of the six months that had been my original bargaining position. When this decision was conveyed to the Security Council secretariat very late in the afternoon, there was a palpable sense of relief shared also, I think, by Ambassador Bizimana. The end of the tale is, however, a sad one from Bizimana's point of view. The Hutu government was overthrown in Rwanda, and it was his Tutsi successor who assumed the council's presidency.

Events in Pakistan had a direct effect on my activities in New York during this period. An evolving political crisis between President Ghulam Ishaq Khan and Prime Minister Nawaz Sharif, that also involved the Supreme Court, resulted in a move by General Abdul Waheed, the successor to the late General Asif Nawaz as Chief of Army Staff, which forced the resignations of both the president and the prime minister. An interim government was hastily set up, charged with toning up the administration and preparing for general elections after a period of three months. The organizers of what was essentially a well-camouflaged army coup selected Moeen Qureshi as the interim prime minister. Moeen had just retired after a spectacular career in the World Bank, and had recently established his own investment firm in Washington. His sterling performance at the World Bank had evoked the admiration and respect of leading international financiers and his was a well known name in the corridors of power all over the world. His modesty and quiet demeanour had kept him out of the public eye, and he was clearly an independent figure in terms of Pakistan politics. His acceptance, after some reluctance, of the office of the prime minister was one of the best things to have happened to the country. During his limited tenure Moeen did more to restructure the administration and the economy of Pakistan than other prime ministers who were in office for much longer periods.

Moeen Qureshi's ministerial cabinet consisted entirely of apolitical figures, and included professionals, businessmen, and retired bureaucrats. Amongst them was Syed Babar Ali, an old personal friend, one of Pakistan's leading entrepreneurs and philanthropists, who was appointed as the Finance Minister. Also inducted into the Cabinet, as Minister for Water and Power, was my younger brother Khursheed, a Cambridge graduate with a degree in biology, who had headed the family pharmaceutical manufacturing business in Quetta, and then gone on to serve on the boards of a number of banks in Karachi, leading to a long stint as Chairman of the Pakistan Industrial Credit and Investment Corporation (PICIC). Khursheed is perhaps the most reticent of us three brothers, but was by far the best sportsman, excelling at cricket, swimming, and track athletics. A cruel fate early in his marriage struck his lovely wife Roshan with polio, leaving her in his tender care until her death. God compensated them with three talented children, Aban, Meher, and Ardeshir, who are now grown up and flourishing. Although he has always been an industrious person, Khursheed told me that he never had to work as hard as he did when he was in Moeen Qureshi's cabinet. My long association with ministers in the Pakistan government would suggest that this eventuality was very much an exception. It could also be because Khursheed is by nature a serious person with a deep sense of public duty.

Moeen came to New York on a working visit, and instructed me to accompany him to Washington. The ambassador's post had been vacant for a while, and I had been carrying out a holding operation to counter some very vigorous lobbying by Indian diplomats in their attempts to have Pakistan labelled as a terrorist state. As Moeen did the rounds of the power elite in Washington, all of whom were either his personal friends or knew of his capabilities, I was quite convinced that not only was the once dangerous bogey of being labelled a terrorist state laid to rest, but that support in full measure from the United States government was assured.

At the United Nations the major issue emerging, as the General Assembly commenced its forty-ninth session in the autumn of 1994 was the election of the secretary general. Boutros-Ghali, who had just completed his first term of office, was eligible for a second term, hoping to follow a tradition that had made it a customary practice. He had secured the endorsement of the African Group, as well as a number of other member states, but it soon became clear that he was encountering a substantial obstacle. During his term there had been differences between him and Madeleine Albright, the powerful and dynamic US Permanent Representative. Initially they were matters of style rather than substance, but over time they escalated from mutual dislike to almost mutual hostility. Both have expressed in their memoirs their respective perceptions of these events, and judgement is best left to those who read them. But, as one who worked fairly closely with both of these highly intelligent and dynamic personalities, there were a number of observations which are inescapable. The first was the contrast in their outward style and demeanour. Madeleine was cheerful and outgoing; Boutros-Ghali was introspective and reclusive. Madeleine was vigorous, purposeful, and almost flamboyant, in her pursuit of US interests, which frequently ran counter to those of other countries, particularly in the Third World. Boutros-Ghali, following his conscience, not only opposed them but was scathing in his criticisms.

Most American ambassadors that I have encountered at the United Nations tend to regard themselves as *sui generis* or unique, and can only be met by their colleagues when 'walking on water' with forbidding preoccupied looks, between the US mission and the Security Council chamber. The outstanding exceptions were Tom Pickering and Madeleine Albright, who would break out of the clutch of their aides with an effusive greeting, and stop for a chat. Boutros-Ghali's relations with most of the permanent representatives were aloof and distant. Happily, I did not feel this in my personal case, because he was always friendly and communicative, speaking in either English or French as the mood took him, and conducting meetings in his office with the utmost courtesy and understanding. But I knew that this was somewhat exceptional, and several colleagues, even from Arab and African countries, expressed their resentment towards his general attitude. They took particular exception to Boutros-Ghali's tendency to go over their heads and communicate directly with their presidents or foreign ministers in their capitals. Madeleine Albright once told me, with much relish, that Boutros-Ghali was slapped down when he tried the same tactic with her and attempted to communicate directly with Washington. It was suggested to him that he deal with the permanent representative at the UN who was also a cabinet officer. I have often wondered about the impact of this episode on the exacerbation of their personal relations. On the two occasions that Madeleine and Boutros-Ghali were both present at a dinner at my residence it was evident that, beneath the façade of polite good manners, there was palpable static in the atmosphere.

However, as the informal negotiations became prolonged and increasingly acrimonious, it was clear that the US would indeed maintain its veto on Boutros-Ghali. The latter, in an uncharacteristic emotional fashion, withdrew his candidature, and the path was cleared for the election of Kofi Annan. Notwithstanding the unpleasantness that preceded it, the selection could not have been more felicitous. In this quiet, soft spoken, intelligent Ghanaian, the United Nations had acquired its greatest secretary general. Kofi had grown in the system, worked his way up through talent and sheer professionalism, and was familiar with every aspect of the organisation. But above all he was enthused by the ideals of the United Nations. Every secretary general of the United Nations had been skilful in diplomacy, and most had been competent administrators. Kofi possessed all of these attributes, but in addition he had the streak of idealism that is, in my view, the most important requirement for a secretary general of the United Nations. This was something that was not very discernible in any of his predecessors, with the exception of Dag Hammarskjöld. On 1 January 1995 Kofi Annan moved from the thirty-seventh floor to the thirty-eighth floor of the United Nations building, and took with him a number of his colleagues from the Department of Peacekeeping

Operations to make up his secretariat. These included three dynamos, Iqbal Riza, Shashi Tharoor, and Elizabeth Lindenmeyer.

The forty-ninth session of the United Nations General Assembly, which commenced in September 1994, was attended by a large and unwieldy delegation from Pakistan. Benazir Bhutto had once again become the prime minister and the composition of the delegation reflected the compromises and favours incumbent in a rambunctious democratic environment. There were some outstanding delegates such as Shafqat Mahmud, Raza Rabbani, and Aitzaz Ahsan, with Hamid Nasir Chattha making a brief appearance. But most of the rest of the delegation were on a taxpayer-funded joyride, whose extra-curricular occupations at least had the benefit of keeping them out of our hair. Foreign Minister Sardar Asef Ahmed Ali's statement to the General Assembly was amongst the longest on record, with elaborate references to Kashmir, and I am not sure whether the modest applause that it evoked at the end was motivated by appreciation or relief. My previous understanding with the government was that our brief on Kashmir was to restrict it to speeches and debates in the General Assembly and the concerned committees, where our exchanges with the Indians would follow the usual verbal pyrotechnics. However, all this changed with the arrival of Nawabzada Nasrullah Khan, who seemed determined to obtain a new United Nations resolution on Kashmir.

Nawabzada Nasrullah Khan had started from Pakistan with the fiery endorsements of his supporters ringing in his ears, and visited a couple of European capitals, where his meetings with the local Pakistani communities appeared to have convinced him of support from the governments where they resided as immigrants. After he arrived in New York I presented him with a realistic appreciation of the situation, and said that under the prevailing circumstances there would be very little support for a draft resolution on Kashmir. A heavily defeated resolution would wipe out our claims under the previous Security Council Resolution, which had been the bedrock of our position on Kashmir over the past three decades. As my arguments were angrily brushed aside, I realised that once again we were dealing with the damaging issue of national self-denial. I convened an emergency meeting of the OIC and set Bosnia as the first item on the agenda, knowing that it would elicit universal support, and hoping that this spirit of unity would carry through in our discussions on the draft resolution on Kashmir, which was the second item on the agenda. I was right in the first aspect of my assessment, but was both surprised and shocked at the response on Kashmir. Turkey and Bosnia gave it their unqualified support, but most others, including Saudi Arabia, reserved their position. Ambassador Snoussi of Morocco, a good and true friend, made a passionate appeal that we make a cool reappraisal of the prevailing realities and reconsider our position. The Indonesian representative, not Ambassador Nana Sutresna this time, strongly denounced our move and said that not only would he vote against the resolution but also warned against any attempts to table it under OIC auspices. Malaysia also supported Indonesia, though in less stringent terms. The remaining delegations remained silent.

I reported the proceedings of the OIC meeting to Prime Minister Bhutto on the telephone and urged her not to insist on tabling the draft resolution, again pointing out the likelihood and consequences of its rejection. An obviously unsure Benazir then dispatched Ambassador Iqbal Akhund to review the situation, and after he had concurred with my assessment, she called me with instructions not to table the resolution. Nawabzada Nasrullah remained in New York while we awaited the government's decision, and departed in a surly and irascible mood thereafter. Later, in a friendly chat with Nana Sutresna, he gave me the two main reasons for Indonesia's acerbic reaction to the Kashmir issue, one of which was political and the other personal. The political issue involved Jakarta's own problem in East Timor, whose accession through military intervention was similar to that which had occurred in Kashmir. The other aspect was President Suharto's personal animosity towards Zulfikar Ali Bhutto, who had not only officially condemned the overthrow of Sukarno, but had made a public show of his support and friendship for Sukarno's wife Devi. The personal animosities between captains and kings can have implications in international relations that can indeed be both far-reaching and of long standing.

As this disagreeable episode came to its end, I too came to the conclusion that the government in Islamabad was becoming dysfunctional, and although during one of our occasional telephone conversations, Benazir had graciously indicated that she wished me to remain in New York, I was having serious doubts about my ability to continue at my post. This was despite the fact that I had just been elected as president of ECOSOC for the calendar year 1995. I had no regrets, therefore, when Foreign Secretary Najmuddin Sheikh informed me that the prime minister wished to appoint Ahmed Kamal as the Permanent Representative to New York. I used the rest of my time and effort to ensure that, notwithstanding the fact that I had been elected in a personal capacity, Pakistan would assume the Presidency of ECOSOC in the New Year.

I then took off for Karachi, where I spent some time before proceeding to Florida and resuming my academic activities at Eckerd College. In less than a year I was back at the United Nations in New York, as the Secretary General's Personal Representative for East Timor, with the rank of the Undersecretary General. This reincarnation of my diplomatic life, which involved the exhilarating experience of working with and for Kofi Annan, has been recorded in a separate memoir.

CHIAROSCURO

The President of Haiti, the quixotic Jean-Bertrand Aristide, who had been deposed in a military coup and sought asylum in Washington, was awaiting a return to his country. Intensive negotiations had been conducted by the UN as well as the USA. A high-powered delegation, that included General Colin Powell, had persuaded a group of colonels, through a combination of threats and incentives, to leave the island and hand back authority to the democratically elected president. The colonels had been flown out of Haiti, and the negotiators were impatiently awaiting Aristide's arrival in Port au Prince. Aristide, for reasons best known to himself, was reluctant to return and had gone into hiding, but was located by the Americans and was now lodged in a safe house on Second Avenue in New York City. I took a late night call from Madeleine Albright requesting me, in my capacity as president of the Security Council, to go to Aristide and persuade him to return to his country and assure him of his safety on behalf of the UN. I was aware of Aristide's enigmatic and quirky reputation, but was quite unprepared for what I encountered that night. The building was surrounded by security agents, and after going through the checkpoints, I entered the apartment, which was dimly lit, smoky with some peculiar incense, and filled with all manner of masks and juju dolls. Some of Aristide's sinister bodyguards were lurking in attendance, and in my lurid imagination I fully expected one of them to sacrifice a squawking chicken in my presence before allowing me to meet their president. A soft recording of throbbing drums added to the eeriness of the silence in which we all waited. In due course Aristide arrived, tall and emaciated with a wild, distant look in his eyes. He extended a limp hand in welcome. I told him that the international community was waiting for him to resume his functions as president. More importantly, his own people were anxious to welcome him back. All security precautions had been taken. As soon as I started talking and explaining to him the arrangements that had been made for his return to Haiti, he came down to earth with a thump. The distant look disappeared from his eyes, to be replaced by a sharp, almost piercing scrutiny, and I sensed gradual reassurance in his mind. He then asked to be excused while he went into the next room and talked to God. The divine conversation concluded after a while, and Aristide returned to tell me that he was now ready to leave for Haiti. We discussed his departure arrangements, and he gave me a faint smile as I left that voodoo den. I returned home, telephoned Madeleine, and poured myself a double Scotch.

* * *

In a talk to one of the francophone societies in New York, Secretary General Boutros Boutros-Ghali once said that when relations between him and his wife were normal they spoke to each other in Arabic, and when they were good they spoke in French. When relations between them were bad they spoke to each other in English.

* * *

Amongst Madeleine Albright's many sterling attributes is her sense of humour. Above all, she possesses the ability to laugh at herself, a quality which I hold to be the hallmark of gentility, and the characteristic of a truly civilized person.

She told me that she once went to Saks Fifth Avenue to return a newly purchased Ferragamo shoe that had some defect. The little shop assistant serving her immediately took back the shoe and offered Madeleine the choice of a full refund, an exchange, or a store credit. After some hesitation, Madeleine said to the girl, 'I don't know. What do you think I should do?' The cute little shop assistant answered Madeleine's question with a question of her own, 'You are Madeleine Albright. Aren't you the one who decides whether we have war or peace?'

* * *

As chairman at a UN seminar on water resources, I was seated next to Secretary General Boutros-Ghali, on the dais. A francophone African delegate who, combining the oratorical volubility common to so many of his brothers, with the redolence inherent in the French language, swept into a lyrical panegyric on the importance of water, commencing each sentence with 'Without water there would be no...' After he had completed a long list of the vital necessities of life which would be unavailable without water, Boutros-Ghali whispered impishly in my ear, 'And without water there would be no whisky.'

MEANWHILE IN PAKISTAN

The last two years of my tenure in New York were constantly influenced, and frequently overshadowed, by the turn of events in the internal politics of Pakistan. President Ghulam Ishaq Khan had dismissed the Benazir Bhutto government for incompetence and corruption in August 1990. In the general elections that followed, the IJI, a coalition of rightist parties, obtained a majority, but there were dark reports of intensive ISI interference. The new government under Prime Minister Nawaz Sharif took over from the caretaker administration of Ghulam Mustafa Jatoi, and immediately began to assert itself. Differences between the president and the prime minister over a number of issues manifested themselves, with Nawaz Sharif constantly emphasizing the 'mandate' he had received from the people in the elections. At the same time Nawaz Sharif also had his differences with General Aslam Beg, the Chief of Army Staff, with the result that the triumvirate that had ruled Pakistan since the death of Ziaul

Haq—president, prime minister, chief of army staff—was coming apart at the seams.

Within the army, also, there were major changes. Following General Beg's somewhat reluctant retirement, the new COAS was General Asif Nawaz, who had brought with him a much needed change of air. He visibly moved the army out of politics and equally visibly concentrated on improving its professionalism. But his untimely death, after an all too brief period of command, dealt a devastating blow to the leadership structure of Pakistan. There is some malign fate that makes a habit of depriving Pakistan, in the most cruel premature fashion, of its most inspiring and effective leaders. The president appointed General Abdul Waheed as Nawaz's successor, a nomination which aroused some resentment in the prime minister.

On the political front, the deterioration of relations between the president and prime minister had now become public, with talk of the prime minister using his 'mandate' to remove the Eighth Amendment and the president using the amendment to remove the prime minister. A hard-hitting public speech by Nawaz Sharif, in which he accused Ghulam Ishaq Khan of all kinds of machinations, finally tipped the scales. The president dismissed the Nawaz Sharif government, on charges of incompetence and corruption, and appointed a caretaker government under Balkh Sher Mazari pending fresh elections. However, Nawaz Sharif challenged the presidential order of dismissal in the Supreme Court of Pakistan which, to the surprise of many including myself, accepted the plea of the petitioner, and restored the Nawaz Sharif government. This political pickle was tackled in a series of tense negotiations between Ghulam Ishaq Khan, Nawaz Sharif and General Abdul Waheed, as a result of which both the president and the prime minister were persuaded to resign. A caretaker government under Moeen Qureshi was set up, with army backing, and charged with the responsibility of revitalizing the economy and the administration, and arranging free elections at the end of a three-month period. Moeen, as already indicated, completed these tasks to perfection.

After the elections that followed in 1993, the PPP under Benazir Bhutto once again came into office and elected, as President of Pakistan, Sardar Farooq Ahmed Khan Leghari, a senior member of the PPP with a distinguished record of public service. The course of politics prevalent in Pakistan at the time went on to follow its Byzantine pattern, so that in 1996 Leghari used his presidential powers to dismiss the Bhutto government on the familiar charges, regrettably all too true, of mismanagement and corruption.

At the end of my four years' assignment in New York on 1 January 1995, I checked the batting order on the scorecard of my masters in Pakistan. It read: two presidents, seven prime ministers, three chiefs of army staff, and three foreign ministers.

NOTE

1. A vivid account of the evening is contained in a dispatch by Masood Haider, the veteran correspondent of the Karachi *Dawn* whose expertise on the UN and reporting on its affairs are of the highest standards, and among the best that emanate from the International Correspondents' Office at the UN Headquarters in New York. Appendix II.

EPILOGUE

Herodotus of Halicarnassus has said, 'It is my duty to report what people say, but I am not required to believe it.' This cautionary observation, admirable in detachment and equanimity, frequently came to my mind as I lived through the events recollected in this memoir. Knowing also that there exists a clear contrast between the spontaneity of the diarist and the clinical objectivity of the historian, my consequent endeavour has been to record not only the events, but also my personal thoughts and reactions at the time that they occurred. I did not keep a detailed diary during the course of my diplomatic career, and the narration of events is, therefore, quite literally a memoir. My daily calendars, containing dates and times of my appointments, have served to fix events in time and space, but reports of the events are based entirely on memory. The major exceptions are in respect of some important meetings and conversations in Moscow, Washington, and New York, which I recorded for my personal reference at the time. I have also made use of some public documents available in the records of the US Congress and in publications issued by the United Nations.

Winston Churchill is reported to have said, in his usual frank and outright manner, that history would be kind to him because he intended to write it himself. For giants like Churchill who created history, the record of a personal account is in itself a further historic achievement. But for the rest of us mortals, who are at best peripheral bystanders at the unfolding of history, a memoir of this kind, if it is to be at all worthwhile, must vigorously eschew all forms of self-justification. Although I have tried to adhere to this maxim, it is an insidious component of the subconscious, and I am not at all sure that it has been excoriated.

Through the years I have had the good fortune to meet and know a number of prominent people, not only in the realm of politics, but also academics, artists, musicians, and scientists. I have become friends with many of them and learned much from all of them. The one common attribute among the greatest of them, whether political leaders, diplomats, artists, scientists, or philosophers, is the element of idealism and intellectual humility. This is the spark that drives the creative urge in them and is clearly discernable in their attitudes and actions. I have also met a great many leaders, particularly in the field of politics, whose exercise of power might evoke apprehension but not admiration. All political leaders possess self-assurance, which is an essential component of leadership, but all too often this degenerates into vanity, with the disastrous results that I have frequently witnessed. Otto von Bismarck, whose own exercise of authority was as formidable as any, said, 'When I estimate the danger that is likely to accrue from any adversary, I first of all subtract the man's vanity from his other qualities.' It is this element of vanity in political leadership that provoked many of the downfalls and changes of fortune that I have witnessed all over the world.

Diplomatic careers are studded with successes and failures, and one that has been as long and as replete as mine has had a fair share of both. All that can be said in conclusion is that my efforts have been conditioned by two guidelines. The first has been to try and do whatever is good for Pakistan, no matter how small or insignificant, and ensure that no harm comes to the country, no matter how small or insignificant. The second is a personal credo, to follow the immortal exhortation of Parmenides: 'Heed not the blind eye, the echoing ear, nor yet the tongue, but bring to this great debate the test of reason.'

APPENDIX A

Working Profile: Jamsheed K.A. Marker

Linchpin of U.S.-Pakistan Alliance
by Robert Pear
Special to *The New York Times*

Washington, Aug. 31—Take a strategically situated country that receives large amounts of economic and military aid from the United States, that is developing the ingredients for a nuclear bomb and that is next door to a country torn by civil war for the last eight years.

What kind of envoy does such a country, in this case, Pakistan, send to Washington?

Jamsheed K.A. Marker, the Ambassador of Pakistan, is described as tough, shrewd and cultivated by State Department officials and members of Congress.

Off all the diplomats in Washington, few work so intimately with the Reagan Administration as Mr Marker. He has helped forge a joint strategy with the United States in one of the great geopolitical battles of the 1980's, the effort to expel the Soviet Army from Afghanistan. In the process, he has dramatically strengthened relations between Pakistan and the United States, American officials say.

In 23 years of diplomatic service, Mr Marker has served as ambassador to 15 countries, including Ghana, Rumania, the Soviet Union, Canada, East Germany, West Germany, Japan and France.

'He has been everywhere and knows everybody, not just Helmut Schmidt and Francois Mitterrand and senior Soviet officials, but literary and cultural figures as well,' said Robert A. Peck, a State Department official with 20 years' experience in South Asian affairs.

Mr Marker said he talks to State Department officials 'almost every working day' and meets at least twice a week with officials from the State Department, the Pentagon, the National Security Council or the Central Intelligence Agency. 'Our relationship has never been closer,' he said.

A Minority in His Homeland

The relationship, never a romance, was born of mutual need and strategic necessity. Tensions between Washington and Islamabad appeared to increase in the last few months. American officials expressed concern about Pakistan's nuclear program and also asserted that the country was not making enough progress toward democracy. Mr Marker sought to allay such concerns.

Unlike most Pakistanis, Mr Marker is not a Moslem, but a Parsee, a member of a Zoroastrian sect descended from refugees who fled Persia centuries ago. His family, like many Parsees, was active in business and commerce, and before he became Ambassador, Mr Marker worked in family-owned shipping and pharmaceutical companies in Baluchistan. He was also a radio commentator on cricket matches and is a keen fan of the opera, often attending festivals in Bayreuth, West Germany, and Salzburg, Austria. He speaks English, French, German, Russian, Urdu and Gujarati.

His appointment as Ambassador to the United States in 1986 stirred a bit of controversy in Pakistan. People asked how President Mohammad Zia ul-Haq could name a non-Moslem to represent an Islamic country that was striving to bring its own laws into conformity with the tenets of Islam.

Mr Marker said his selection 'shows the tolerance that exists in Islam, as practiced in the Islamic Republic of Pakistan.'

Amid the continual rivalry between India and Pakistan, Mr Marker has won many friends here for his country. Representative Charles Wilson, Democrat of Texas, said, 'I have bottomless admiration for the intrepidness with which the Pakistani people have endured Soviet pressure and intimidation, and made it possible for us to prevail over the Soviet invasion of Afghanistan.'

Senator Gordon J. Humphrey, Republican of New Hampshire, said Mr Marker was 'a superbly effective, very smooth and self-assured diplomat, a real heavyweight.' He said the Ambassador 'played a major role in smoothing out the bumps in U.S.-Pakistani relations,' especially disputes over Pakistan's nuclear program.

Conduit for Weapons

Pakistan has been the main conduit for American weapons delivered to the Afghan guerrillas, and it has provided a temporary home for more than 3 million Afghan refugees.

'What we did in Afghanistan had a motivation of self-preservation, no doubt,' Mr Marker said. 'We saw the danger to Pakistan immediately following the Soviet invasion of Afghanistan in 1979. We could have tackled the problem diplomatically, tried to negotiate an agreement with the Soviet

Union. That would have been the easy solution, and in the short term it would have bought us temporary security.

'But that was never a serious option for Pakistan. There was an instinctive feeling of revulsion at the Soviet action, a spontaneous sense of abhorrence that manifested itself in Pakistan's public policy.'

Mr Marker said that Pakistan's refugee policy was a model for other nations. 'If the affluent countries and democracies of Western Europe and the United States had shown even half the compassion that impoverished, embattled Pakistan has shown now, much of the damage of the Holocaust might have been avoided,' he said.

Nuclear Bomb and Refugees

Born 65 years ago in Hyderabad, in south central India, he was educated at the Doon School, in Dehra Dun, an elite boarding school attended by many of India's future leaders, including Rajiv Gandhi, who is now Prime Minister. Mr Marker also graduated from Forman Christian College in Lahore, where he studied economics.

Mr Marker recalled that 'we were in the doghouse with the United States in 1979–80,' mainly because of American concerns that Pakistan was trying to develop nuclear weapons. He resents the suggestion that Pakistan stood up to the Soviet Union to secure more American aid.

'In fact,' he said, 'we stood up to the Soviets as a matter of principle before the first aid from the United States for the mujahedeen (Afghan guerrillas). We did what we did as a matter of principle, to prevent a superpower from behaving in such a manner—and, even more important, as a matter of Islamic brotherhood.'

Two Views of India

Pakistani officials deny that Pakistan was or is trying to build a nuclear bomb. American officials say, however, there is strong evidence that Pakistan has all the components needed to assemble such a weapon. Some members of Congress, alarmed at the evidence, have tried to reduce American aid to Islamabad. Mr Marker, working with State Department officials, has helped thwart those efforts through a combination of gentle persuasion and aggressive lobbying.

The Pakistani envoy said he had 'good personal relations' with India's Ambassador to the United States, P.K. Kaul, whom he described as 'a very pleasant gentleman.' But he combined this compliment with a verbal thrust, saying that India, because of its economic and political ties to the Soviet Union, had taken 'a pusillanimous position' on the Soviet invasion of

Afghanistan, abstaining on United Nations resolutions to condemn the invasion and welcoming the Afghan President in May with a 21-gun salute.

Mr Marker met his wife, Arnaz Minwalla, in New York, where she was in the hotel business. Her family owns what is, in effect, the grand hotel of Karachi. 'She is his equal as a diplomat,' said a family friend. 'They are a real team.'

After President Zia was killed in a plane crash two weeks ago, the Pakistani Embassy received hundreds of letters of condolence from Americans who admired the Pakistani leader. Mr Marker answered them all, sending handwritten notes in response to many. He also attended a condolence ceremony held at the mosque here by Afghans grateful for President Zia's support in their struggle.

APPENDIX B

Passage of 'Mother of All Resolutions'
From Masood Haider. *Dawn*, May 1993.

United Nations, 2 May: Pakistan assumed the presidency of the 15-member United Nations Security Council, at one of the most crucial and eventful juncture, in the history of the world body.

The Vance-Owen peace process was all but dead, since the Serbs had refused to sign on, the genocide of the Bosnian Muslims had taken the turn for worst, the Council was hamstrung in assuming any decisive position as the Russians and the Americans voicing concern over the fate of President Boris Yeltsin stalled for time.

The Armenians invaded Azerbaijan and Turkey positioned itself to enter the war, the North Koreans withdrew from the Nuclear Non-Proliferation Treaty, the question of imposing tougher sanctions against Libya was brought up, there was crisis in South Africa following the death of ANC leader Chris Hani.

Through all this, Pakistan's Ambassador Jamsheed Marker, remained calm and cool and emerged as a consumate negotiator and mediator.

Mr Marker, got high marks from his colleagues, for skillfully handling the crisis which emerged in the Security Council, as the news reports poured in of the mass scale genocide of the virtually unarmed Bosnian Muslims, and the reluctance of the permanent members specially Russia and America to go for tougher sanctions against Serbia.

The Non-aligned caucus in the Security Council consisting of Venezuela, Cape Verde, Djibouti, Morroco and Pakistan was restless with the inertia afflicting the Council as the tragedy in Bosnia and Herzegovina unfolded.

Mr Marker, found himself in an unviable position as he was not only the leader of the Non-Alligned caucus but also the President of the Security Council. He had to listen to both opposing points of view and then bring about a consensus.

At one time most of the members of the Council pushed for early vote of the sanctions resolution, its two most powerful members, namely Russia and the United States stalled for time. Russia at one time even threatened to veto the sanctions resolution, if it was considered before April 26th, the day after the Russian referendum.

On April 16th, as the situation worsened in Srebrenica, and in fact there were reports that it's fall was imminent, the Council passed resolution declaring Srebrenica a "safe area," asking the United Nations forces to protect the besieged population, although they had no specific mandate to do it. The sanctions resolution, it was said could only be considered after April 25th.

But then things changed. On April 17th, the French government representative at the United Nations, Jean Bernard Merimee, called Ambassador Marker at home saying that according to his government's information the conditions is Srebrenica were worst than those presented by the United Nations Secretariat and that it had actually surrendered to the advancing Serba.

He had in fact felt that the population in Srebrenica faced annihilation, if no action was taken immediately.

An emergency meeting of Security Council was then called to consider the sanctions resolution. The Serbs had tested the patience of the members to the hilt. The French ambassador and the Non-Aligned caucus reportedly criticised the UN Secretariat for not providing the Security Council with the accurate and correct picture on the ground. They proceeded to press for the resolution.

In the meantime, Russian Ambassador Yuli Voronstov, (incidentally Mr Voronstov was deputy foreign minister during the Afghan war), kept low profile as the members got ready to call a formal meeting to pass the resolution.

However, as reported by sources, when one ambassador asked Mr Voronstov as how he would vote when the resolution was tabled, he shot back "I will veto it."

This assertion by the Russian threw the Council in quandary. The emotions ran high, as the Third World caucas, insisted that the Council proceed and let the Russians veto it. As one diplomat said "the emotions and tensions were so high that you could cut it with a knife."

But then, it is said that the three permanent members of the Council—United States, France and Britain—prevailed upon the Council to delay the vote, and asked Mr Voronstov to get instructions from Moscow.

They had also suggested a compromise wherein the sanctions resolution against Serbia would come into effect after April 26th, but they all agreed that no time should be lost in sending a strong and decisive message of indignation to the Serbs.

However, no one wanted to risk a Russian veto and set a precedence since the end of cold war. Russians had not vetoed a resolution since 1990. They wanted to preserve unity and an unblemished track record.

The meeting which was called at 5 pm on April 17, was then delayed until the Russian ambassador got his instructions.

Around 11 pm Mr Voronstov came back, saying he was unable to get anyone in Moscow to get instructions as it was 4 am in the morning there and it was also orthodox Eastern Sunday. He said he would go back to the Russian mission and try again.

Many members of the Security Council became irate, started to question whether the resolution would see the light of the day. Moreover, the delay was cutting into their weekend activities. One ambassador, of a Non-Aligned western country came up to the correspondents and quipped 'after 28 billion dollars from us, they have the nerve to threaten the Security Council with veto.'

Then around 11.45 pm Mr Voronstov, was seen coming back to the Security Council chambers.

One correspondent caught him on his way in and asked him, 'Mr Ambassador, are we going to see a vote tonight?' to which obviously exasperated and beleagued Russian envoy said 'I think so, I think so—.'

The obvious indication in his tone was that some sort of compromise was perhaps in the offing.

The Security Council met again, that night in anticipation that the Russians will abstain and not veto the resolution.

Diplomats here say that it was because of Pakistan's Ambassador's powers of persuasion he was able to prevail upon the Russians to seek a compromise, while dissuading the Non-Aligned caucus to push for meeting when the Russians had threatened to veto.

Through the intense diplomatic drama and activity, Ambassador Marker kept a positive posture and co-ordinated consultations between various members and was able to work through to see the passage of the most debated resolution.

And as he emerged out of the Security Council chambers, after the adoption of the resolution, Mr Marker, announced with great sense of relief and accomplishment, "the mother of all resolution was passed tonight."

The Russians had blinked.

INDEX